EUL VERLAG

QUANTITATIVE ÖKONOMIE

Herausgegeben von Prof. Dr. Eckart Bomsdorf, Köln, Prof. Dr. Wim Kösters, Bochum, Prof. Dr. Winfried Matthes †, Wuppertal, Prof. Dr. Mark Trede, Münster, Prof. Dr. Ansgar Belke, Essen, und Prof. Dr. Markus Pütz, Lahr

Band 162
Philippe Wittmann
Das Testen der Martingaleigenschaft
Lohmar – Köln 2010 • 140 S. • € 43,- (D) • ISBN 978-3-89936-956-4

Band 163
Stephan Scholze
Kurzfristige Prognose von Tageszeitreihen mit Kalendereffekten
Lohmar – Köln 2010 • 196 S. • € 49,- (D) • ISBN 978-3-8441-0000-6

Band 164
Sue Man Fan
Multiple Tests für die Evaluation von Prognosemodellen – Eine Analyse am Beispiel der Prognose von Vermögenspreisen
Lohmar – Köln 2010 • 192 S. • € 49,- (D) • ISBN 978-3-8441-0001-3

Band 165
Martin Meermeyer
Prognose von betriebswirtschaftlichen Zeitreihen auf Basis von Splineregressionsmodellen – Mit einem empirischen Anwendungsbeispiel aus der Warenwirtschaft
Lohmar – Köln 2011 • 168 S. • € 47,- (D) • ISBN 978-3-8441-0036-5

Band 166
Valentin Braun
Dynamic Copulas for Finance – An Application to Portfolio Risk Calculation
Lohmar – Köln 2011 • 176 S. • € 48,- (D) • ISBN 978-3-8441-0040-2

Band 167
Andreas Rees
Money as a Global Phenomenon – An Empirical Analysis of Global Excess Liquidity and its Impact on the Global Economy, National Economies and Central Banks
Lohmar – Köln 2011 • 308 S. • € 59,- (D) • ISBN 978-3-8441-0076-1

JOSEF EUL VERLAG

MONEY AS A GLOBAL PHENOMENON

AN EMPIRICAL ANALYSIS OF GLOBAL EXCESS LIQUIDITY AND ITS IMPACT ON THE GLOBAL ECONOMY, NATIONAL ECONOMIES AND CENTRAL BANKS

Dissertation

zur Erlangung des akademischen Grades eines

Doktors der Wirtschaftswissenschaften

(Dr. rer. pol.)

durch die Fakultät für Wirtschaftswissenschaften der

Universität Duisburg-Essen

Campus Essen

vorgelegt von

Name: Diplom-Volkswirt Andreas Rees

Geburtsort: Herbolzheim

Essen 2011

Tag der mündlichen Prüfung: 22. Juni 2011

Erstgutachter: Professor Dr. Ansgar Belke

Zweitgutachter: Professor Dr. Gerhard Wagenhals

Reihe: Quantitative Ökonomie · Band 167

Herausgegeben von Prof. Dr. Eckart Bomsdorf, Köln, Prof. Dr. Wim Kösters, Bochum, Prof. Dr. Winfried Matthes †, Wuppertal, Prof. Dr. Mark Trede, Münster, Prof. Dr. Ansgar Belke, Essen, und Prof. Dr. Markus Pütz, Lahr

Andreas Rees

Money as a Global Phenomenon

An Empirical Analysis of Global Excess Liquidity and its Impact on the Global Economy, National Economies and Central Banks

With a Foreword by Prof. Dr. Ansgar Belke,
Universität Duisburg-Essen

EUL VERLAG

Bibliografische Information der Deutschen Nationalbibliothek

Die Deutsche Nationalbibliothek verzeichnet diese Publikation in der Deutschen Nationalbibliografie; detaillierte bibliografische Daten sind im Internet über <http://dnb.d-nb.de> abrufbar.

Dissertation, Universität Duisburg-Essen, 2011

ISBN 978-3-8441-0076-1
1. Auflage September 2011

JOSEF EUL VERLAG GmbH
Brandsberg 6
53797 Lohmar
Tel.: 0 22 05 / 90 10 6-6
Fax: 0 22 05 / 90 10 6-88
E-Mail: info@eul-verlag.de
http://www.eul-verlag.de

FOREWORD

Andreas Rees addresses in his doctoral thesis an interdisciplinary topic from the areas of international macroeconomics and time series econometrics. He also takes into account various specifics related to financial markets. Although much broader in its fundamental import, the topic assumes unimagined new topicality within the context of the 2008 financial crisis and the unconventional monetary policies in the US and the UK. Within the framework of the current EU debt crisis, the European Central Bank is taking a leaf out of the book of the Fed and the Bank of England and is investing massively in sovereign bonds of overindebted eurozone countries. In the process, it is accepting an unrestricted monetization of sovereign debt, a money overhang, and over the medium term even inflation.

What is the motivation of the dissertation? Despite rapid globalization of financial markets, most empirical analysis of monetary policy – in contrast to the doctoral thesis submitted by Mr. Rees – continue to adopt a primarily national perspective. Where external influences are addressed, most studies discuss as a rule the exchange rate or above all the synchronization of national business cycles. Because of increasing foreign trade and a stronger division of labor in the global economy, formerly segmented goods markets are growing together. This can trigger changes in domestic variables such as the output gap and the Phillips curve. In recent years, however, cross-border capital flows have increased substantially more strongly than the exchange of goods and services.

This is the starting point of Mr. Rees' doctoral thesis. Shifts in the portfolios of international investors are possibly resulting in increasing synchronization of money markets. Whether this is the case can be tested econometrically and is examined empirically in this dissertation using sophisticated tools – among others a Factor Augmented Vector Autoregression (FAVAR). If this hypothesis can be confirmed, Mr. Rees believes the consequences are a synchronicity of national money supplies and the emergence of a global monetary liquidity factor. The exchange rate is not a perfect cushion in this event to protect the domestic economy from cross-border liquidity shocks. As an example, Mr. Rees cites carry trades. They are based on a lack of efficiency in FX markets and trigger a monetary liquidity transfer between countries with a high and a low yielding currency.

If this hypothesis is correct, the environment for central banks could change substantially. The classic trilemma of open economies would no longer be valid: Despite the existence of flexible exchange rates, open capital markets limit monetary policy autonomy. It is not national interest rates and money supplies that primarily influence domestic macroeconomic variables but the global monetary liquidity factor. This is the most important finding of this dissertation. Central banks lose room to maneuver and are compelled to factor developments on international financial markets more strongly into their deliberations. In addition, the transmission mechanisms of monetary policy change. If, for example, a central bank raises its key interest rate or shortens its balance sheet, international capital is attracted from abroad. The domestic money supply increases as a result, thereby counteracting the originally restrictive monetary policy.

As a result, globalization entails not only advantages but also drawbacks for central banks. The need for central banks to coordinate their actions at the international level increases dramatically. The principal achievement of this doctoral dissertation is that it bases this view that is often expressed in politics and in the media on solid research using sophisticated econometric methods.

Essen and Berlin, 13 August 2011 Ansgar Belke

ACKNOWLEDGEMENTS

Many people contributed to this dissertation in innumerable ways. I am grateful to all of them. First and foremost, I would like to thank my primary advisor Professor Dr. Ansgar Belke. His mentorship was paramount in providing valuable guidance and insights, thereby broadening and deepening my understanding of the topic. Without his support, this dissertation would not have been possible. I would further like to express my sincere gratitude to Professor Dr. Gerhard Wagenhals for serving as secondary advisor.

I wish to extend special thanks to Thorsten Weinelt. He brought the subject of global liquidity to my attention and encouraged me to write this thesis. Furthermore, Thorsten provided me with the necessary leeway at my employer UniCredit.

This dissertation also benefited enormously from comments and suggestions of the following people: Professor Dr. Jörg Clostermann, Christian Gokus, Dr. Thomas Hueck, Cornelia Klaila, Dr. Julian von Landesberger and Professor Dr. Franz Seitz. I am heartily thankful to Dr. Harm Bandholz and Alexander Koch. Despite being pressed for time, Harm scrutinized the thesis and improved it substantially. Besides making valuable comments, Alexander did a lot of extra work at UniCredit due to my absences. I would also like to thank seminar participants of the following conferences for helpful suggestions: the ROME workshop in October 2009 in Frankfurt, the Midwest Finance Association in February 2010 in Las Vegas and the Verein für Socialpolitik in September 2010 in Kiel. All remaining errors are, of course, mine.

Last, but certainly not least I would like to thank my father and my girlfriend Stefanie for their unwavering love, support and encouragement. This dissertation is dedicated to them.

Munich, August 2011 Andreas Rees

TABLE OF CONTENTS

LIST OF FIGURES

LIST OF TABLES

LIST OF APPENDICES

LIST OF ABBREVIATIONS

AIC	Akaike Information Criterion
AR	Autoregressive
ARCH	Autoregressive conditional heteroskedasticity
BCBS	Basel Committee of Banking Supervision
BPG	Breusch-Pagan-Godfrey
CPI	Consumer price index
CRB	Commodity Research Bureau
CVAR	Cointegrated VAR
DSGE	Dynamic Stochastic General Equilibrium
EMU	European Monetary Union
EViews	Econometric Views
FAVAR	Factor Augmented Vector Autoregression
FAVEC	Factor Augmented Vector Error Correction
FDI	Foreign direct investment
FX	Foreign exchange
G7	Group of seven industrialized countries
GARCH	Generalized autoregressive conditional heteroskedasticity
GARCH-M	Generalized autoregressive conditional heteroskedasticity in mean
GDP	Gross domestic product
GVAR	Global VAR
HP	Hodrick-Prescott
HWWI	Hamburgisches Weltwirtschaftsinstitut
IFS	International Financial Statistics

IMF	International Monetary Fund
IRF	Impulse response function
KPBG	Kydland, Prescott, Barro, Gordon
LCP	Local currency pricing
LM	Lagrange Multiplier
LR	Likelihood Ratio
LTCM	Long Term Capital Management
MF	Mundell-Fleming
MFD	Mundell-Fleming-Dornbusch
MFI	Monetary and financial institution
MSCI	Morgan Stanley Capital International
NAIRU	Non-Accelerating Inflation Rate of Unemployment
NOEM	New Open Economy Macroeconomics
OECD	Organisation for Economic Co-operation and Development
OLS	Ordinary Least Squares
PC1	First principal component
PCA	Principal Component Analysis
PCP	Producer currency pricing
PPP	Purchasing Power Parity
PTM	Pricing to market
RBC	Real business cycle
S.D.	Standard deviation
SFAVAR	Structural Factor Augmented Vector Autoregression
SVAR	Structural Vector Autoregression
TFP	Total factor productivity

TRAMO SEATS	Time series Regression with ARIMA noise, Missing values and Outliers; Signal Extraction in ARIMA Time Series
UK	United Kingdom
US	United States
VAR	Vector Autoregression
VECM	Vector error correction model
3M	Three-month
10Y	Ten-year

LIST OF SYMBOLS

α	Coefficient
β	Coefficient
$\delta_{ij}(L)$	Lag polynomial for testing exclusion restrictions (FAVAR)
$\delta_{N,N}(L)$	Idiosyncratic lag polynomial (FAVAR)
ε_t	N-variate vector of residuals (structual shocks) in VAR at time t
ε_A	Idiosyncratic shock in country A
ε_{Ft}	r-variate vector of global reduced-form shocks at time t (FAVAR)
ε_{Xt}	N-variate vector of the sum of global and idiosyncratic reduced-form shocks hitting a country at time t (FAVAR)
ε_t^M	Residual, i.e. shock in autoregressive persistent deviations of actual money supply (M_t) from equilibrium money supply (M^*) at time t
ε_t^m	Global non-technology innovation at time t (Galí model)
ε_t^z	Global technology innovation at time t (Galí model)
ϕ_s	Autoregressive coefficient of $PC1_{t-s}$
$\phi_{r,r}(L)$	Global lag polynomial (FAVAR)
π_t	Inflation at time t
π^*	Central bank target level of inflation
η_t	r-variate vector of global reduced-form shocks at time t
η_{ft}	Global liquidity shock at time t
η_t^{PC1}	First principal component shock at time t

$1-\iota$	Forecasting ability of central bank
κ	Break date of the global factor dynamics
κ^{PC1}	Break date of the first principal component
o	Break date of the conditional variance of the country-specific shocks
μ	Intercept
μ_1	Zero mean of e_1
μ_2	Zero mean of e_2
θ	Autoregressive coefficient of persistent deviations of actual money supply (M_t) from equilibrium money supply (M^*)
ϑ_t	Residual (shock) at time t
ρ	Persistence parameter of $PC1_{t-1}$
ρ^d	Persistence parameter of $PC1_{t-1}$ in dummy approach
σ_1, σ_2	Standard deviations of e_1, e_2 (Cukierman approach)
$\sigma_{e,t}^2$	Variance of foreign money supply disturbance at time t
$\sigma_{t\ u^M}^2$	Variance of u_t^M
$\sigma_{t\ \varepsilon^M}^2$	Variance of ε_t^M
$\sigma_{w,t}^2$	Variance of foreign inflation disturbance and domestic share price shock, respectively, at time t
$\sigma_{\eta,t}^2$	Variance of global FAVAR shock at time t
$\sigma_{v,t}^2$	Variance of idiosyncratic FAVAR shock at time t
ς	Difference between the first principal component shock before and after the break
τ	Break date of the conditional variance of the global shocks

τ^{PC1}	Break date of the conditional variance of the first principal component shocks
υ	Break date of the factor loading matrix Λ
υ^{PC1}	Break date of the factor loading matrix Λ^{PC1}
ω_t	r-variate structural global shock vector (FAVAR) at time t
ξ_t	m-variate vector of structural country-specific shocks (FAVAR) at time t
ψ_t	Residual at time t in interest rate equation (2.2.8)
ψ_{Xt}	Residual at time t in FAVAR interest rate equation (7.3.1)

Δ	First difference
$\Phi(L)$	$r \times r$ matrix lag polynomial
$\Phi_a(L)$	$r \times r$ matrix lag polynomial in sub-sample a (counterfactual)
$\Phi^d(L)$	$r \times r$ matrix lag polynomial in dummy approach
Λ	$N \times r$ factor loading matrix
Λ_a	$N \times r$ factor loading matrix in sub-sample a (counterfactual)
Λ^{PC1}	N-variate factor loading vector of first principal component
Θ	Diagonal matrix with the diagonal elements as variances of the structural shocks ε_t (VAR)
$\Psi(L)$	r-variate lag polynomial (FAVAR)
Σ_a	Variance of ε_{Xt} in sub-sample a (counterfactual)

a	Coefficients in the A_0, H and Q matrix
$A(L)$	Lag polynomial (VAR)

A_0	$N \times N$ matrix describing the contemporaneous relation among variables collected in vector X_t (VAR)
b	Coefficient
b_1, b_2	Coefficients
$B^1(L)$	Moving average polynomial of structural country-specific shocks (FAVAR)
$B^2(L)$	Moving average polynomial of structural global shocks (FAVAR)
c	Constant
c_{1P}	Constant (first period shock)
$c_0, c_1, c_2, etc.$	Coefficients in Wald test
c_A	Coefficient measuring impact of common liquidity disturbance
$corr$	Correlation coefficient for contemporaneous relation between reduced-form VAR innovations
$C(L)$	Lag polynomials (Galí model)
d	Coefficient measuring effect of foreign money supply shock on π
d_t	Dummy variable at time t
$D(L)$	$N \times N$ matrix lag polynomial
$D_a(L)$	$N \times N$ matrix lag polynomial in sub-sample a (counterfactual)
e, e_1, e_2	Shocks (Cukierman approach)
er	Intertemporal elasticity of substitution
f_t	Global factor
F_t	r-variate vector of global factors at time t
$F(e_2)$	Distribution function of e_2

g_t	Pseudo-disturbance (wild bootstrapping approach) at time t
$G(e_1)$	Distribution function of e_1
$G(L)$	$N \times N$ matrix lag polynomial
h_t	Persistent deviation of actual money supply (M_t) from equilibrium money supply (M^*) at time t
h_{rr}	Coefficient in the H matrix (FAVAR)
$hours_t$	Log hours at time t (Galí model)
H	$r \times r$ matrix (FAVAR)
i_t	Interest rate at time t
i_A	Interest rate in country A
k	Number of lags in VAR and FAVAR
$k_o(L)$	m-variate lag polynomial vector in national VARs (FAVAR)
K	Number of lags in autoregressive approaches
$K(L)$	Restricted and diagonal $o \times o$ matrix lag polynomial (FAVAR)
L	Central bank loss function
L_A, L_B	Money demand in country A and B
l_t	Dummy variable for factor loading Λ^{PC1} at time t
m_{CB}	Rate of inflation envisaged by central bank
m	Number of elements in lag polynomial $k_o(L)$
M_A, M_B	Money supply in country A and B
M_t	Money supply at time t
M^*	Equilibrium money supply
n	Number of lags (ARCH)

N	Number of variables
p	Number of lags (FAVAR)
p -value	Probability value
P_A, P_B	Price level in country A and B
$PC1_t$	First principal component at time t
$prod_t$	Log productivity at time t (Galí model)
Q	$N \times N$ matrix (FAVAR)
r	Number of static factors
$r_{A/B}$	Ratio in which investors hold currencies A and B
ra	Intratemporal elasticity of substitution
R	Spot exchange rate
R_i^f	Forward exchange rate
R^{PC1}-squared	R -squared of first principal component
T	Number of observations per variable
u_t	N -variate vector of reduced-form residuals (shocks) in VAR at time t
u_t^M	Residual (transitory deviations of actual money supply M_t from equilibrium money supply M^*) at time t
up_t	Unemployment at time t
up^*	Central bank target level of unemployment
v_t	N -variate vector of idiosyncratic reduced-form shocks at time t
v_t^{PC1}	N -variate idiosyncratic disturbance vector of first principal component approach at time t
$v_{A,t}$	Idiosyncratic shock hitting country A at time t

w_t	Foreign inflation disturbance and domestic share price shock at time t, respectively
W	Number of newly generated time series in the wild bootstrapping approach
X_t	N -variate vector of observable national variables at time t
$X_{A,t}$	National excess money in country A at time t
Y_A, Y_B	GDP in country A and B
Y_P	Potential output

CP	Commodity prices
CPIexEMU	Global CPI excluding the EMU
ER	Real effective exchange rate
GELexEMU	Global excess liquidity excluding the EMU
HP	House prices
M3	Broad monetary aggregate
PI	Consumer prices
SR	Short-term interest rate
SP	Share prices
YR	Real GDP

"In a world where capital is increasingly mobile [...], it is important to consider the extent to which changes in monetary conditions in one major country may be associated with changes in monetary and financial conditions elsewhere."

(Baks, Kramer 1999, p. 3)

1 INTRODUCTION

The large increase in international financial integration has been one of the most striking aspects of the global economy over past decades. In recent years, the rise of capital flows between countries has been particularly dramatic. One frequently used measure of financial globalization is the sum of stocks of foreign assets and liabilities in percent of nominal GDP. According to Lane and Milesi-Ferretti (2007, p. 234), this ratio had been 45% for industrialized countries at the start of the 1970s. In 1987, cross-border holdings equaled 100% of nominal GDP. From the mid-1990s onwards, the process of financial globalization has accelerated markedly, reaching 200% in 1998 and 300% in 2004. As a result, even modest shifts in cross-border portfolio allocation might lead to huge international capital flows.

There have been various drivers of financial globalization which are well known (Rajan 2005, p. 5f.). Capital account liberalization has removed barriers between countries, thereby leading to greater integration of financial markets. Deregulation has enhanced the competition between products and jurisdictions. The process of institutional change and disintermediation has created new entities which operate on an international level. Examples are hedge funds, private equity companies and pension funds. Furthermore, the rapid pace of financial innovation has fostered cross-border integration.

With pools of capital available from all over the world, economies may no longer solely depend on national capital as suggested by the Feldstein-Horioka puzzle (Feldstein, Horioka 1980). In their study, the two authors find that OECD countries with high saving rates also have high investment activities and vice versa. Feldstein and Horioka conclude that savings tend to remain in the country in which they originate. Capital markets are still segmented and apart from the exchange rate, monetary policy works primarily through domestic channels. For instance, if the central bank raises the short-term interest rate, arbitrage causes the real long-term interest rate to increase as well. The result is a temporary dampening of economic activity and a reduction of price pressure.[1] However, this traditional view of monetary policy transmission may crack open in the light of financial globalization. For instance, the hike in the domestic short-term interest rate could also trigger cross-border portfolio shifts, thereby attracting capital inflows from abroad. If one realistically assumes that money is endogenous in the short run, the availability of money in the economy increases despite a tightening of monetary policy.[2]

Hence, the question I am asking here is as follows. Has money become a global phenomenon due to financial globalization? Excessive money growth in one country may spill over to other economies, thereby resulting in synchronously rising monetary aggregates across a variety of countries. As a result, a common and therefore global liquidity force would exist which significantly affects domestic macroeconomic and financial variables.[3] Since international capital flows may occur swiftly, a global money variable internalizes liquidity spillover effects and cross-country movements in monetary aggregates. The consequences could be severe, as the ability of central banks to influence domestic monetary conditions is curtailed. A change in the national money supply or the key interest rate would now have a smaller impact on the domestic economy than it used to in the pre-globalization age. In an extreme scenario, with pools of capital from all over the world becoming available, economic and financial transactions in one country no longer depend on national but solely on global monetary liquidity. Structural change in the form of rising financial globalization undermines the effectiveness of domestic policies. A thorough understanding of these effects on national economies could therefore become an important issue for today's policymakers. The ability to gauge the timing and the magnitude of liquidity spillovers contributes to a better assessment of developments in the domestic economy. The process of financial globalization may even have repercussions on the choice of optimal monetary policy. Central banks could have to adjust their strategies in order to cope with the new challenges. Since isolated policy measures designed to counteract global

[1] Of course, such a chain of events is highly stylized and only used for illustrative purpose here. For instance, if the central bank hikes the short-term interest rate after inflation expectations have risen, the real long-term interest rate may remain unchanged or even decline.

[2] This transmission process is explained in more detail in the following theory section in chapter 2.

[3] In the following, money and (monetary) liquidity will be used synonymously for reasons of notational simplicity. In section 5, different types of liquidity and their relation to each other will be presented.

developments prove to be ineffective, coordinated central bank action may be necessary.

Paradoxically, despite the dramatic rise in international financial integration over the last two decades, comparatively little research has been done to examine the impact of global money until recently.[4] Instead, in the field of globalization and monetary policy, the focus has rather been on the real economy and topics like the Phillips curve. The majority of studies shows that the output-inflation trade-off has flattened due to the rise in international trade and production specialization across counries. Examples are the work by Galí and Monacelli (2005), Batini, Jackson, Nickell (2005) and Benati (2007). In contrast, Rogoff (2006) emphasizes that increased competition in goods and factor markets weakens the power of domestic companies and labor unions. The result is higher price and wage flexibility, a lower natural rate of unemployment and a steepening of the Phillips curve. Borio and Filiardo (2007) extend the traditional Phillips curve specification by including various measures of global economic slack. They find that domestic inflation has become sensitive to variations in the international business cycle. Central banks shall therefore increasingly pay attention to developments in global rather than domestic output gaps.

One major reason for neglecting the issue of global money might be the classic trilemma view. Accordingly, a country can choose no more than two of the following three features of its policy regime (Bernanke 2005b, p. 1f.): 1. free international capital mobility, 2. a fixed exchange rate, and 3. independent monetary policy. In this view, major industrialized countries gave up fixed exchange rates in favor of the other two elements. A flexible exchange rate regime provides enough insulation against nominal shocks in the form of monetary spillover effects and surprising changes in foreign central bank behavior.

While the traditional trilemma perspective is still standard in economic textbooks, it has recently come under attack by empirical research. For instance, Rüffer and Stracca (2006) find that common money disturbances across countries are a driving

[4] One may argue that the currency-substitution debate in the 1970s and 1980s is an early example of analyzing global money and its implications for national variables. However, at that time, authors discussed the general question whether flexible exchange rates insulate economies from foreign monetary spillover effects. One classic example is the work of McKinnon (1982). Financial globalization, steadily rising cross-border capital flows and their consequences for central banks did not play a role back then and were not considered. In section 2.1.2, the idea of currency substitution is explained in more detail.

force of macroeconomic variables in the EMU. Belke, Orth and Setzer (2010) emphasize the role of global monetary liquidity shocks for the world economy. Both consumer and house prices in OECD countries are influenced by developments of international money. As indicated by the divergence from fundamentals for lengthy periods, exchange rates cannot completely ward off monetary impulses from abroad. A second string in the literature concentrates on the question whether global money is a suitable leading indicator for identifying asset price booms and busts. According to Alessi and Detken (2009), the global M1 gap and the global private credit gap contain useful information for detecting such cycles across countries.[5]

The purpose of the following thesis is to investigate empirically the existence of a global money market and its relevance for macroeconomic and financial variables, both on a domestic and international level. Such an approach does not necessarily imply that the national perspective of monetary transmission is irrelevant. Instead, taking a global view may deliver additional insights which cannot be gathered by concentrating solely on the domestic level (Belke, Orth 2007, p. 9). If changes in monetary aggregates across countries are partly driven by a common cause, i.e. financial globalization, the importance of national idiosyncracies for central banks diminishes. Differences in country-specific economic structures, institutions and policies become less relevant.

The thesis is structured as follows. In chapter 2, theoretical aspects on cross-border monetary spillover effects are briefly presented. Section 3 deals with previous econometric research on global monetary liquidity and its major results. In chapter 4, hypotheses are formulated for empirical testing. Section 5 describes issues concerning data and variables. Chapters 6 to 8 include the results obtained from the implementation of various econometric approaches. One major contribution of this work is the estimate of a global Structural Factor Augmented VAR model (SFAVAR). In section 9, policy implications are discussed. Chapter 10 concludes.

[5] This approach will be presented in more detail in chapter 3.

"Exchange rate flexibility produces a decentralized world monetary system where each country faces the consequences of its own monetary responsibility or irresponsibility rather than having to live with each others' mistakes."

(Frankel, Schmukler, Servén 2004, p. 706)

2 THEORETICAL ASPECTS

In this chapter, two different strands of theories will be presented and discussed. In section 2.1, it will be illustrated how various macroeconomic concepts deal with monetary spillover effects and their transmission between open economies. In chapter 2.2, the focus will be on asymmetric behavior of central banks and a resulting inflation bias. In each section, the purpose is to concentrate on major aspects in the context of international capital flows.

2.1 INTERNATIONAL MONETARY SPILLOVER EFFECTS

2.1.1 MONETARIST VIEW

In monetarism, there is a clear-cut distinction between monetary spillover effects in a fixed and a flexible exchange rate system. Under a fixed exchange rate regime, the central bank has the obligation to maintain the national currency's foreign exchange rate value. Monetary independence on a national level is therefore impossible. Consider a once-and-for-all increase in money supply by the central bank in country A, thereby exceeding money demand. As a result, money flows out through the balance of payments to country B with the balance-of-payments deficit in country A equaling the balance-of-payments surplus in country B (Miles 1978, p. 428). The exchange value of A's currency therefore falls relative to B's. When the central bank in B intervenes, it purchases currency A in exchange for currency B. Consequently, B's money supply increases as well. As the original monetary shock has been transmitted from one country to another, a common rate of inflation in A and B can be observed. By pegging exchange rates, central banks make domestic and foreign money perfect substitutes. Equilibrium on money markets across countries can be described by a single equation which states that the world demand for money equals the global money supply. The international distribution of the given world money supply is determined endogenously in line with demand for money (Frenkel, Razin 1987, p. 5).

Flexible exchange rates eliminate this source of monetary interdependence, thereby insulating national money supplies from monetary developments abroad. Central banks are not obliged to intervene on foreign exchange markets in order to guarantee the value of their currencies. This in turn makes currencies perfect non-substitutes on the supply side and prevents net money flows between countries, with the balance of payments always to be zero (Miles 1978, p. 428). National money becomes a "non-tradable" asset whose relative price, i.e. the exchange rate, is determined freely on foreign exchange markets (Frenkel, Razin 1987, p. 34). In contrast to the system of fixed exchange rates, the money supply in each country can be controlled exogenously by national central banks. Money demand is assumed to be stable and not dependent on external factors. Thus, a country's inflation rate lies solely in the responsibility of its own monetary policy. The exchange rate fluctuates freely in response to relative movements in money supplies, thereby ensuring external balance. This "mechanism" can be illustrated by three equations which form the basic building block of the monetarist open economy model McKinnon 1981, p. 546ff.):

(2.1.1.1) $P_A = R \times P_B$

with P_A as domestic price level (country A), P_B as foreign price level (country B) and R as spot exchange rate expressed in units of domestic currency per unit of foreign currency

(2.1.1.2) $\frac{M_A}{P_A} = L_A(i_A, Y_A)$ and $\frac{M_B}{P_B} = L_B(i_B, Y_B)$

where M_A (M_B) is the domestic (foreign) money supply, L_A (L_B) is the domestic (foreign) money demand, i_A (i_B) is the domestic (foreign) interest rate and Y_A (Y_B) equals domestic (foreign) GDP[6]

[6] Typically, in monetarist theory, the transaction motive of holding money in form of national GDP or income dominates, whereas the interest elasticity of money demand is assumed to be rather low.

(2.1.1.3) $$i_A - i_B = E\left[\frac{dR_t}{dt}\right] \text{ and } E[R_{t+1}] = R_t^f$$

with R_t as spot exchange rate and R_t^f as forward exchange rate, each at time t

Equation (2.1.1.1) shows the goods market in equilibrium. According to the Purchasing Power Parity (PPP) theory, the exchange rate R equals the relative price level of countries A and B. The exchange value of A's currency falls relative to B's, if the price level in A increases. Equation (2.1.1.2) shows the domestic and foreign money market in equilibrium. In contrast to a fixed exchange rate system, there are two national equilibria on money markets instead of a single global equilibrium. By combining equation (2.1.1.1) with expression (2.1.1.2), one gets the equilibrium exchange rate $R = \frac{M_A \cdot L_B(i_B, Y_B)}{M_B \cdot L_A(i_A, Y_A)}$. The exchange rate R is determined by the relative demand and supply of the two currencies. Since each national money demand is assumed to be stable, turbulence on foreign exchange markets is typically associated with erratic changes in the national money supply and hence the monetary policy stance. Equation (2.1.1.3) is labeled Fisher Open and shows the asset market equilibrium by assuming uncovered interest parity to hold. The interest rate differential $i_A - i_B$ is equal to the expected rate of change in the exchange rate. Moreover, the current forward exchange rate R_t^f is an unbiased predictor of the future spot exchange rate. The Fisher Open links expected changes in the monetary policy stance with variations in the current exchange rate (McKinnon 1981, p. 548). For example, an increase in country A's money supply will lead to higher domestic inflation expectations and hence to a rising interest rate. This in turn triggers the anticipation of a depreciating currency A and an appreciating currency B. Thus, a higher domestic money supply does not affect foreign inflation in B. The real exchange rate is kept unchanged, as PPP holds with goods prices being completely flexible. As a result, there are also no real spillover effects stemming from differences in national monetary policies.

It is important to note that the monetarist theory framework only allows the international transmission of monetary imbalances to occur "indirectly". Money supply shocks trigger variations in the interest rate differential and in the nominal exchange rate. "Direct" spillover effects from foreign into domestic monetary aggregates are ruled out. The freely fluctuating nominal exchange rate acts as a buffer and perfectly insulates countries from foreign nominal shocks. Despite international capital flows, domestic monetary policy is independent (trilemma view). There is no need for central banks across countries to coordinate their behavior. Instead, monetary policy is inward-looking. Domestic money supplies shall be kept stable in order to avoid volatile exchange rates.

With respect to international monetary spillover effects, there are especially five aspects in the monetarist approach which seem to be critical both from a theoretical and an empirical viewpoint.[7] First, money supply may not be completely exogenous and perfectly controlled by central banks. Second, money demand could not only depend on domestic influences but also on external factors (currency substitution). Third, the Fisher Open may not hold empirically as indicated by the forward premium puzzle. Fourth, goods prices are not always completely flexible, since menu costs for companies and downward wage rigidities exist. If goods prices change more slowly than do exchange rates, monetary disturbances in country A may lead to changes of real variables in country B. This is true even if the exchange rate is fully flexible. Fifth, the concise type of monetary shock can play an important role for the international transmission process. If information is imperfect, the private sector may not be able to distinguish between disturbances to money supply levels and innovations to the money growth target of the central bank. The five points are discussed in more detail in the following theory sections and in chapter 4 where the hypotheses for empirical testing are presented.

2.1.2 CURRENCY SUBSTITUTION

Given the lack of intervention on foreign exchange markets by central banks and the corresponding elimination of currency substitution on the supply side, the monetarist theory framework derives complete monetary independence. However, this argument implicitly assumes that currencies are non-substitutes on the demand side as well (Miles 1978, p. 428; McKinnon 1982, p. 320). It is conceivable that domestic residents also

[7] In general, one can put the monetarist open economy model further into question. For instance, domestic money demand may not always be stable, even if foreign influences do not exist. PPP does not hold, since there are non-traded goods, etc.

hold foreign currencies for transaction purposes or speculative motives.[8] As a result, changes in monetary policy lead to variations in the relative costs of holding currencies and hence to portfolio adjustments. Monetary shocks can therefore spill over from one economy to another even under flexible exchange rates.

For the purpose of illustration, consider a simple and stylized extension of the monetarist open economy model presented in the previous chapter in form of the following two equations:

(2.1.2.1) $$r_{A/B} = (L_A / L_B)$$

(2.1.2.2) $$L_A(i_A, Y_A, R) = \frac{M_A}{P_A} \text{ and } L_B(i_B, Y_B, R) = \frac{M_B}{P_B}$$

There are two differences to the monetarist framework. First, investors hold two currencies of countries A and B simultaneously according to the ratio $r_{A/B}$ (Miles 1978, p. 429). Second, money demand does not only depend on interest rates (i_A and i_B) and GDP levels (Y_A and Y_B) but also on the exchange rate (R). Now assume an unexpected once-and-for-all increase of the money supply in country A (M_A). B's money supply (M_B) remains unchanged in the beginning. After the central bank increases M_A, the price level in A (P_A) rises and currency A depreciates as suggested by PPP. This in turn increases investors' opportunity costs of holding currency A relative to currency B. As a result, $r_{A/B}$ declines, since both foreign and domestic investors reduce their A holdings and increase their B share. The rising demand for currency B leads to a declining price level in country B. If B's central bank wants to offset this effect, the additional money supply in A can trigger a similar behavior in B: The central bank in B increases the money supply as well (Batten, Haffer 1984, p. 7).

However, synchronous changes in money across the two countries are also conceivable without any central bank action in B. This is the case if one realistically assumes that monetary aggregates cannot be controlled perfectly by monetary policy. Instead, they are at least in the short run endogenously determined by money demand. In the example described above, investors shift out of money holdings in currency A

8 Recent literature on currency substitution emphasizes domestic high inflation rates and inflation uncertainty as major reasons for holding foreign currencies in emerging markets. Examples are the work of Neanidis, Savva (2006) and Seater (2008).

and increase their B share. The additional B money units do not stem from the central bank in B but from private banks in country B by creating new money (endogenous money and credit creation process). As a result, the rising money demand of investors for currency B leads to an increase of the monetary aggregate in B.[9] Inflation can then be transmitted between countries without any central bank intervention on foreign exchange markets. The degree of monetary and inflationary spillover effects is proportional to the extent of substitution between currencies. In the limiting case where M_A and M_B are perfect substitutes, domestic money demand functions are highly unstable. Investors swiftly shift their money holdings from one country to another due to (expected) variations in exchange rates. One world currency exists, thereby preventing the independence of national monetary policy (Miles 1978, p. 432).

Critically, one can argue that currency substitution is not a necessary condition for generating international monetary spillover effects. For instance, assume the following two attributes of the open economies A and B. First, currency substitution does not take place. Second, money is not completely exogenous. Now consider again an unexpected once-and-for-all increase of the money supply in country A. If the monetary excess liquidity is not completely used for purchasing goods in A, parts of the additional money flow into B. Since the demand for currency B rises, an endogenous money and credit creation process in country B sets in. As a result, monetary aggregates in B also rise.

A further critical point of currency substitution is that the transmission process after a monetary shock is ambiguous. Arango and Nadiri (1981) show that the net effect of exchange rate depreciations on money demand is a priori indeterminate. This ambiguity arises from two different – and opposing – adjustment processes. The first one is the so-called asset-substitution effect. Assume once again a sudden increase in money supply by central bank A and a corresponding depreciation of currency A. If investors evaluate their portfolios in terms of domestic currency (A), a weaker currency A means that the value of securities held in currency B increases. B assets are therefore sold with the received funds used to buy A assets to maintain the desired proportion of

[9] In contrast, if the quantity of money is completely exogenous, domestic monetary aggregates cannot be affected by definition. Belke and Polleit (2009, p. 79f.) provide such an example by illustrating an international payment transaction between the US and the EMU. Solely an exchange of currencies takes place assuming a given money stock. Hence, only variations in the exchange rate could – if not statistically corrected for – affect domestic monetary aggregates in the US and the EMU.

the portfolio assets. This portfolio-adjustment effect can lead to a rising demand for money denominated in currency A after the decline in demand for currency A immediately after the positive money supply shock. The second adjustment process is called expectations or currency-substitution effect. If currency A initially depreciates, investors may expect a further weakening of currency A in the future. Consequently, they will additionally reduce their money holdings L_A and increase L_B in exchange. Whether this expectations effect will materialize or not, depends on the exact kind of expectations building. For example, investors with adaptive expectations will substitute M_A for M_B, since devaluation prompts expectations of further currency weakness. In contrast, in the case of rational expectations, participants on foreign exchange markets do not see any automatism between changes in the exchange rate today and tomorrow (white noise process due to random-walk behavior of the exchange rate).

The currency substitution view implies the need for international policy coordination among central banks. Monetary policy should also be outward-looking and not solely concentrate on domestic variables.

2.1.3 MUNDELL-FLEMING-DORNBUSCH MODEL

The Mundell-Fleming (MF) model is an open economy version of the IS-LM approach with the inclusion of capital flows as an important driver. The MF approach is designed for the analysis of macroeconomic policy in an open economy and concentrates on short-run effects. Since its introduction in the 1960s, it had been the workhorse of both theorists and policymakers for many years (Borondo 2000, p. 2).

Assume an unexpected rise in money supply in country A which leads to a reduction of the domestic interest rate. Consequently, currency A depreciates through capital outflows, making producers in A more competitive. An expenditure-switching effect from foreign to domestic goods takes place with global spending directed from country B to A. The result is an increasing output and an improvement of the trade balance in A, whereas adverse effects occur in B (beggar-thy-neighbor).

Since the MF model assumes nominal rigidities, wage and price changes cannot take place in order to reach new equilibria in the two economies as postulated in the monetarist setting. Instead, the necessary adjustments are accomplished via real exchange rate variations and corresponding changes in quantities like output and exports. The international transmission of monetary shocks solely occurs indirectly via the trade balance and not through monetary aggregates (Borondo 2000, p. 2). However, one can extend the MF model by assuming an endogenous reaction of foreign monetary policy in country B. The assumed asymmetric shock is then transformed into a symmetric one. Since B's central bank tries to undo the expenditure-switching effect, the B money supply is increased as well.[10] The counter-reaction creates a positive co-movement between national monetary aggregates across the two countries. However, it is important to note that even in this case no direct money spillovers occur.

The MF model forms the background of the Dornbusch approach. In the MF model, money and the nominal exchange rate increase by the same amount in response to money supply shocks. In contrast, in Dornbusch's overshooting analysis, a positive money supply disturbance generates a larger instantaneous depreciation of the nominal exchange rate, followed by a subsequent appreciation (Dornbusch 1976, p. 240f.). The reason for this overshooting is the different speed of adjustment to equilibrium. Financial markets adjust instantaneously to an exogenous shock with the effects of monetary expansion dominated by capital mobility and asset markets in the short run. In contrast, goods markets react rather sluggishly. Only in the long run, the money supply determines the domestic price level and PPP holds.

Consider again an unexpected increase in the national money supply of country A. Non-traded goods prices change only slowly toward their new equilibrium after the disturbance, whereas traded goods prices swiftly increase proportionally to the money supply due to the depreciation of currency A. Hence, the overall price level is comparatively sticky and rises less than the money supply in A, leaving domestic demand for money lower than supply. This excess money causes domestic interest rates to fall and the nominal exchange rate to overshoot its new equilibrium before returning to it. A temporary beggar-thy-neighbor effect takes place through the trade balance, whereas foreign monetary aggregates are not directly affected. Eventually, the excess money supply leads to rising spending in country A and hence increasing non-traded goods prices. The real money supply declines and interest rate increases cause the domestic currency to appreciate toward its long-run purchasing power level.

---

[10] More precisely, national monetary policy directly reacts to the appreciating currency. In the previous chapter, the central bank in B responds to a lower price level, as currency substitution leads to a rising demand for currency B and hence to declining prices.

The Mundell-Fleming-Dornbusch (MFD) model revolves around two major critical assumptions. First, the MFD analysis is carried out in a completely deterministic framework, thereby leading to an oversimplified or even contradictory nature of monetary shocks. The assumption made is that a higher money supply is ex ante not anticipated (static expectations). However, the increase in the money supply is ex post expected to be permanent. Investors have therefore complete information regarding the future intention of central banks. In a more realistic stochastic framework, market participants cannot easily distinguish transitory from persistent disturbances (Andersen, Beier 2005, p. 493f.). Accordingly, changes in the money-supply process in one country ($M_t - M^*$) may include transitory and persistent elements:

(2.1.3.1) $$M_t - M^* = h_t + u_t^M$$

with M_t as actual money supply, M^* as equilibrium money supply, h_t as persistent changes and u_t^M as transitory variations in which the money supply is only affected in one period

(2.1.3.2) $$h_t = \theta h_{t-1} + \varepsilon_t^M \text{ with } 0 < \theta < 1$$

The disturbances u_t^M and ε_t^M are independently and normally distributed mean-zero shocks with variances $\sigma_{t\,u^M}^2$ and $\sigma_{t\,\varepsilon^M}^2$. Since u_t^M reflects pure noise, it does not contain useful information about the future behavior of central banks. However, it may take substantial time before investors will learn the "true" transitory nature of the change. Such a learning process can therefore imply systematic errors in expectations' building. Anticipating the change in the future money supply is a question of forecasting its persistent component: $E(M_{t+1} - M^*) = E(h_{t+1})$. If investors cannot readily separate noise shocks from fundamental changes in central bank behavior, they may react too strongly to the former and too little to the latter. For example, a transitory increase in the money supply could trigger an even more pronounced overshooting of the exchange rate than derived in the Dornbusch setting.

A second string of critique focuses on assumptions made with regard to the expenditure switching effect. For example, in the MFD model, international trade implicitly involves only highly substitutable consumption goods. If there is also trade in complementary intermediate (capital) goods, a deprecation of the exchange rate may lift the domestic cost of production (Dellas 2006, p. 1472). Hence, in a globalized world with strong production interdependencies across countries, a beggar-thy-neighbor policy could be less successful in stimulating domestic growth. Even if the assumption of international trade exclusively in consumption goods is sustained, an expenditure switching effect may not set in after a positive monetary shock. In the case of a limited degree of substitution between home and foreign consumer goods, a significant positive impact on production in the home country is missing. A weaker currency primarily reduces domestic aggregate purchasing power in international markets.

Perfect substitutability is not only assumed with regard to consumer goods but also for money and financial assets. Only if the degree of substitution between money and bonds is high, a sudden monetary expansion will lead to declining (long-term) interest rates and trigger the chain of events described in the MFD framework. In contrast, asset market models like the portfolio balance approach stresses the complementary nature of money and financial assets due to the risk assessment of investors. Risk premia could at least partly hamper the transmission of monetary policy shocks between economies.

Moreover, there may be two additional channels which dampen the beggar-thy-neighbor effect. The first one is the so-called "locomotive effect": The demand for foreign goods also rises as part of the increase in aggregate demand in country A (Corden, Turnovsky 1983, p. 289). However, these second round effects will only materialize if monetary expansion takes place in big – and not in small – economies. The second channel deals with the appreciation of the foreign currency B. As a result, B's price level falls, thereby raising foreign real balances and providing a stimulus to demand for goods produced in B.

Finally, another implicit assumption in the MFD setting is that exports (imports) are denominated in domestic (foreign) currency, i.e. producer currency pricing (PCP) dominates. After a sudden increase in the domestic money supply and the corresponding currency depreciation, import prices exhibit a complete exchange-rate pass-through. Domestic products become more competitive, thereby causing the expenditure-switching effect. However, local currency pricing (LCP) is conceivable as well. A more detailed explanation of PCP and LCP and their implications will follow in the next sub-section with a short description of the New Open Economy Macroeconomics.

2.1.4 NEW OPEN ECONOMY MACROECONOMICS

The New Open Economy Macroeconomics (NOEM) started in the 1990s with the objective to provide a new theoretical framework for the analysis of open economies. These models are characterized by a higher standard of analytical rigour than the MFD approach, thereby overcoming some limitations (Neri, Nobili 2006, p. 7). One key feature of the NOEM is the explicit microfoundation of households' and companies' decisions by specifying underlying preferences and the introduction of budget constraints. Hence, the equations are not ad-hoc as is the case in the MFD setting but the result of an optimizing behavior (Borondo 2000, p. 2). The NOEM also incorporates stochastic shocks and imperfect competition on goods and labor markets into the analysis. For example, monopolistic companies set the prices of imperfectly substitutable goods. As a result, equilibrium production falls below the social optimium. Small variations in demand do not trigger price changes due to the existence of menu costs or other frictions in the price adjustment process.

A further major difference to the traditional Keynesian approach such as MFD becomes evident when the transmission of international monetary spillover effects is analyzed. The MFD model focuses on *intratemporal* decisions of companies and households. The depreciating home currency after a domestic monetary expansion leads to a demand shift away from foreign goods. This is a purely static effect, since the substitution of goods takes place within one period. The NOEM, in contrast, is a dynamic analysis which adds a second transmission channel based on *intertemporal* behavior. Consider once again a sudden change in the domestic money supply (country A). Prices will initially remain unchanged but are expected to rise in the following period. Current period goods become therefore cheaper in comparison to future goods, i.e. the real interest rate as the intertemporal relative price decreases (Svensson, van Wijnbergen 1989, p. 795). Since a global capital market exists, the foreign real interest rate declines as well. The consequence is that demand both at home and abroad is shifted towards the present. In the MFD setting, such intertemporal considerations are missing, as consumer expenditures and saving decisions are assumed to be independent of the real interest rate.

Whether the intertemporal or the intratemporal effect dominates is depending on the intertemporal elasticity of substitution in consumption (er) relative to the intratemporal elasticity of substitution (ra). er equals the willingness to substitute consumption across periods, while ra is the degree of substitution between domestic and foreign goods at one point in time (Svensson, van Wijnbergen 1989, p. 793ff.). If $er > ra$, as typically assumed in the NOEM, then the beggar-thy-neighbor result will be transformed into a prosper-thy-neighbor outcome. A domestic monetary expansion in country A raises output both at home and abroad, thereby contributing to a synchronized business cycle pattern in A and B. If one assumes that money is at least partly endogenous, the upswing will cause the monetary aggregate in B to rise as well. Consequently, monetary aggregates in both countries will show a positive co-movement. Again, the synchronization is not caused by direct monetary spillover effects via capital flows but only indirectly through business cycle linkages. However, in contrast to the MFD model, which focuses on the trade balance, the NOEM highlights another transmission channel of international monetary shocks: real interest rates and a global capital market.

The reason why the trade balance does not play a decisive role in the NOEM also stems from the assumption of imperfect goods markets. Firms may have market power and are able to segment markets internationally by charging different prices for the same good at home and abroad. Examples are automobiles and some electronic goods for which international arbitrage is difficult or perhaps even impossible. The result is that prices are set in local currencies at levels differing from a competitive world price (VanHoose 2004, p. 199). Such a price discrimination behavior is called local currency pricing (LCP) or equivalently pricing to market (PTM). In conjunction with sticky prices, LCP breaks the linkage between domestic and foreign price levels as assumed in the PPP theory, allowing for endogenous adjustments of the real exchange rate. For example, assume for the purpose of illustration full LCP and a positive money supply shock in country A. In this case, there is no pass-through from the exchange rate deprecation of currency A (relative to B) to import prices. The price level in A is completely unaffected by exchange rate movements and the expenditure switching effect fails to materialize. In such a setting, the exchange rate cannot play the stabilizing role of adjusting relative prices and equilibrating demand in response to monetary disturbances (Bowman, Doyle 2003, p. 8). Instead, considerable volatility of the real exchange rate is generated without having any allocative effect on international demand as described in the MFD model. The elimination of the expenditure switching effects enhances the probability of output co-movement across countries further.

Critically, it remains doubtful whether LCP can really explain persistent fluctuations in the macroeconomy and on financial markets. Usually, trade invoicing applies to contracts of 90 days or even less. Price and wage stickiness may therefore be more important for generating persistent variations (Sarno 2001, p. 31). For example, rigid *real* wages may increase the likelihood of transmitting negative shocks from one country to another. The analysis conducted by opponents of the NOEM shows further weak spots. For example, changes in the domestic real interest rate will only cause variations in its foreign counterpart, if the domestic economy is sufficiently large. Otherwise, it is hardly conceivable that significant spillover effects on a global capital market can occur. In addition, central bank behavior is only analyzed rudimentarily. On the one hand, strong emphasis is placed in the NOEM on the microfoundations of decisions made by private households and companies. On the other hand, central banks are often modeled as selfless entities only caring about the welfare of the private sector. Such an approach completely neglects principal-agent issues in discretionary monetary-policy making and the closely related time inconsistency problem. Finally, the derived international transmission effects after monetary shocks can be quite sensitive to the precise specifications (Lane 2001, p. 261f.). Slight changes in additional structural parameters like the elasticitity of substitution between goods in each country or in the degree of home bias in consumption may alter the results significantly.

2.1.5 ALTERNATIVE APPROACHES

Besides the above-presented – and well-established – theories, there are other, sometimes rather fragmentary, explanations which also shed light on international monetary spillover effects. In the following, these approaches are subsumed under the buzzwords "common shocks", "fears of floating" and "common beliefs".

In the *"common shock"* approach, non-monetary disturbances affect many countries simultaneously, thereby leading to a positive co-movement of national monetary aggregates across countries. The importance of technology shocks in driving business and money fluctuations is stressed in the real business cycle (RBC) theory. Technological innovations may not only occur in specific countries but on a global level. Reasons are international knowledge spillover effects, like the import of goods that embody new technologies, FDI flows, joint ventures and the migration of key personnel (Klenow, Rodriguez-Clare 2004, p. 11). Especially, trade-related new-goods externalities could be central in swiftly transmitting new technologies from one country to another. New goods of higher quality are introduced and then imitated by other companies worldwide. Accordingly, in the spirit of the RBC model, it may be argued that national monies are highly synchronized after a positive global technology shock: National output and hence domestic money demand rise across countries. International capital flows are therefore not the driving force of the simultaneous change in monetary aggregates. Instead, money is regarded as an endogenous and exclusively domestic variable driven by common technological innovations.

Further examples of such global disturbances are cost-push shocks and sudden non-monetary changes on international capital markets. The classic example of a cost-push disturbance is a surprising and rapid rise in the oil price. The emphasis here is on the source but not on the transmission of the shock, as spillover effects of aggregate demand conditions are not required (Rüffer, Stracca 2006, p. 12). Instead, the oil price affects each economy directly by increasing firms' marginal costs. If such domestic price pressure is accommodated by national central banks, a positive co-movement of domestic money supplies may be observed. Financial crises are another type of common disturbance. A steep decline in asset prices worldwide may lead to interest rate cuts and the provision of additional liquidity by central banks. Again, the result is a highly synchronized pattern in monetary aggregates even in the absence of direct spillover effects.[11]

The second approach is called *"fears of floating"*. Accordingly, countries with de jure flexible regimes do not allow their exchange rate to move freely all the time. For example, the monetary authority sometimes intends to move the exchange rate towards a certain level more expeditiously than investors envisage. The central bank can also attempt to dampen exchange rate fluctuations. Both goals may be achieved by interventions on foreign exchange markets. Since currencies become substitutes on the supply side again (cf. chapter 2.1.1), direct international monetary spillover effects occur via capital flows. The central bank sacrifices its monetary independence for an

[11] Of course, financial turbulence can also trigger substantial international capital flows, thereby reinforcing the positive co-movement. Hence, distinguishing between these two different transmission channels might be especially challenging during financial turmoil.

exchange rate target. The reasons for this behavior can be manifold. Undesirable exchange rate pass-throughs and foreign-currency liabilities might play an important role in emerging markets (Frankel, Schmukler, Servén 2004, p. 703). Moreover, the monetary authority's lack of credibility may trigger fears of floating, as unwarranted exchange rate movements could fuel rising inflation expectations. In such cases, there exists an open economy dilemma – and not a trilemma as suggested by monetarism: The choice for policymakers is to have monetary independence or open capital markets (Shambaugh 2004, p. 302). A further cause for fears of floating could be the rapid speed of globalization. Due to lower transportation costs and the reduction of tariffs, international trade has become more and more important for national business cycles. Transactions in goods and services serve as the major channel for the transmission of economic fluctuations from one country to another. National policymakers are therefore increasingly concerned about the exchange rate and its impact on national competitiveness (Borio, Filardo 2007, p. 7). As a result, significant monetary interdependence remains even under a de jure flexible exchange rate regime.

"Common beliefs" refer to the idea that various monetary authorities share the same or at least similar policy objectives. Not only structural relationships like international trade or capital flows are therefore binding economies but also a similar interpretation of economic events. Policymakers in different central banks hold consensus views about what decisions are appropriate in a given situation. The result is a similar response to shocks across countries, implicitly equaling international policy coordination (Kuszczak, Murray 1986, p. 117). Common beliefs can be strenghtened by the continuous information exchange between central banks through official meetings, conferences and publications. Even peer pressures may arise on top of monetary authorities. The spread of the inflation targeting strategy in the early 1990s could be an example for such a behavior. An additional channel may occur, if monetary authorities converge to relative rather than to absolute benchmarks of success (Cicarelli, Mojon 2005, p. 10). For example, a bad inflation record seems to be more tolerable, if others also perform badly, thereby leading to more uniform monetary conditions across countries.

Although the phenomenon of common beliefs appears reasonable, one cautionary remark is appropriate. A similar monetary response is only optimal in the case of symmetric shocks and comparatively similar transmission mechanisms. If countries are affected differently, it is hardly conceivable that policymakers react in a similar manner (Papanyan 2010, p. 67).

"There is no good reason to believe that policymakers attach the same importance to a given size deviation from target in the upward as they do in the downward direction."

(Cukierman 2004, p. 2)

2.2 ASYMMETRIC CENTRAL BANK BEHAVIOR AND INFLATION BIAS

The theories presented in the previous chapter pay comparatively little – if any – attention to a microeconomic explanation of central bank behavior in open economies. In the MFD model, it is implicitly assumed that monetary policy has an inflationary bias, thereby creating excess money. Without giving further details, central banks are supposed to pursue a beggar-thy-neighbor policy. The NOEM even implicitly regards central banks as selfless entities (VanHoose 2004, p. 201). In the following, a theoretical framework is presented in which the reaction function of monetary policy is examined in more detail. This theory is based on asymmetric behavior of central banks and has been developed by Cukierman (2002) and Cukierman, Gerlach (2003). A proposal is made how the Cukierman approach can be transformed into an open economy setting characterized by financial globalization and international monetary spillover effects. It is shown that not only the (conditional) mean of foreign money possibly matters for national policymakers but also its (conditional) variance. A simple equation is derived in which the combination of uncertainty about foreign money supply shocks and asymmetric preferences leads to an inflation bias of monetary policy.

As a starting point in the theoretical analysis, the classic explanation of creating excess money and positive inflation rates by central banks is used: the framework developed by Kydland, Prescott (1977) and Barro, Gordon (1983), shortly KPBG. Policymakers have domestic target levels of unemployment (up^*) and inflation (π^*). Any deviation from these targets is costly for them, i.e. it does not make any difference whether there are positive or negative deviations from up^* and π^*. In technical terms, the central bank loss function (L) is assumed to have quadratic summands:

(2.2.1) $$L = \frac{(up_t - up^*)^2}{2} + \frac{(\pi_t - \pi^*)^2}{2}$$

If unemployment is too high ($up_t > up^*$), monetary policy tries to create inflation surprises in order to push the unemployment rate below its natural level, the Non-Accelerating Inflation Rate of Unemployment (NAIRU). The private sector understands the temptation of policymakers and, assuming rational expectations, correctly forecasts the rise in inflation on average. Consequently, inflation is sub-optimally high but without any corresponding decline in unemployment. The result is the well-known dynamic inconsistency of monetary policy under discretion.

The approach of KPBG is criticized by McCallum (1995, p. 208). Since monetary policy understands the futility of systematically reducing unemployment by inflation surprises, central banks refrain from such attempts even under discretion. In addition, the described inflation bias seems only reasonably realistic if monetary policymaking is dominated by political authorities. In the meantime, many central banks are legally independent and have a mandate of focusing on price stability (Cukierman, Gerlach 2003, p. 542).

More importantly, the KPBG explanation postulates a quadratic loss function. A similarly sized deviation from target is considered to be evenly costly for central banks irrespective of whether the deviation is positive or negative. According to Cukierman (2004, p. 2), such a specification misses elements of real life policymaking. In general, central banks have asymmetric preferences, since they place greater weight on the most imminent risk of loss. Cukierman and Muscatelli (2002, p. 5) call this behavior “framing”, i.e. policymakers develop subjective notions of risk versus inflation and unemployment targets. These risk assessments can change over time. For instance, when inflation is high and the buildup of credibility is a major concern, central banks are more averse to upward deviations of inflation from its target than to downward deviations. Conversely, during periods when price stability is not at risk and reputation is high, asymmetric preferences with respect to unemployment evolve. Policymakers are more averse to negative output gaps than to expansions. In this case, the loss function of the central bank (L) can be described by the following two equations (Cukierman 2004, p. 4f.):

(2.2.2) $$L = \frac{(Y_p - Y)^2}{2} + \frac{\pi^2}{2} \quad \text{when } Y_p > Y$$

(2.2.3) $$L = \frac{\pi^2}{2} \quad \text{when } Y_p \leq Y$$

with Y_p as potential output, Y as actual output and π as inflation rate.

The central bank dislikes recessions ($Y_p > Y$) as well as inflation.[12] As soon as Y becomes larger than or equal to Y_p, losses from the output gap are zero. The loss function of the central bank is therefore asymmetric in the output gap. Hence, not only the size but also the sign of a deviation affects L. Such a characteristic is called sign asymmetry, i.e. the central bank's response to a deteriorating economy is larger than the reaction to an improving one. In contrast, under quadratic preferences, the loss is solely determined by the size of the deviation (Dolado, Pedrero, Ruge-Murcia 2004, p. 4).

Although policymakers do not create any monetary surprises and the KPBG time inconsistency problem vanishes, Cukierman (2002) and Cukierman, Gerlach (2003) show that a new type of inflation bias may appear. Besides asymmetric concerns, they additionally assume that policymakers have only an imperfect forecasting ability of future shocks (e) hitting the economy. This disturbance can be decomposed as follows:

(2.2.4) $$e = e_1 + e_2$$

where e_1 is the central bank forecast of e at the time policy is chosen and e_2 is the forecast error independent of the forecast. Both components have zero means μ_1 and μ_2, standard deviations σ_1 and σ_2 and distribution functions $G(e_1)$ and $F(e_2)$, respectively. The forecasting ability of the central bank can vary and is monotonically rising in $(1-\iota)$. For illustration purposes, two extreme cases are distinguished. In the first one, with $\iota = 1$, the future shock e is completely unforecastable. Hence, policymakers cannot stabilize the economy. In the second one, assuming $\iota = 0$, the forecasting ability is perfect:

[12] Cukierman uses potential and actual output instead of the natural and actual unemployment rate. Independent of the concise specification, the qualitative results are the same (Cukierman 2000, p. 5). In contrast to the KPBG approach (cf. equation 2.2.1), Cukierman and Gerlach (2003, p. 547) assume that the central bank dislikes inflation and not the deviation of inflation from an inflation target.

(2.2.5) $\sigma_1^2 = (1-\iota)\sigma^2$

(2.2.6) $\sigma_2^2 = \iota\sigma^2$

with $0 \leq \iota \leq 1$ and σ as the standard deviation of the future shock e. In the work of Cukierman (2004, p. 7), e is a temporary supply shock affecting the national output gap. Foreign disturbances are not explicitly mentioned. However, besides domestic influences, spillover effects from abroad may be another source for the imperfect forecasting ability of monetary policy. For instance, sudden changes in foreign central bank behavior and their impact on international capital flows could increase the uncertainties with which domestic policymakers are confronted. For reasons of simplicity, assume that only one shock e occurs in form of a positive money supply disturbance from abroad. In reality, monetary policy might observe foreign money demand shocks and a multitude of other domestic and international disturbances. Furthermore, the exchange rate does not isolate the economy completely as suggested by monetarist theory. Domestic money cannot perfectly be controlled by central banks and is hence partly endogenous. Foreign capital starts flowing in, thereby potentially affecting domestic monetary aggregates (via money and credit creation) and the national inflation rate:

(2.2.7) $\pi = m_{CB} + de$

with π as domestic inflation rate and m_{CB} as the rate of inflation envisaged by the central bank. The parameter d determines the effect of the foreign money supply shock (e) on π. Both policymakers and the private sector are uncertain about the magnitude of the disturbance to inflation, since the size of the shock is unknown. Although timely information about changes in foreign monetary aggregates might be available, it is not clear how international investors will reallocate their portfolios. Some countries could be more affected by capital flows than others, depending on various parameters like preferences and return expectations of market participants. Furthermore, there might be uncertainty about the parameter d and hence about the size of the endogenous money and credit creation process. If the latter is small, the impact of the foreign money supply shock on domestic monetary aggregates and inflation is negligible.[13]

[13] An additional source of uncertainty not taken into account by Cukierman consists of structural changes in form of a frequently varying d parameter. The process of financial globalization may not only

The combination of uncertainty about shocks (from abroad) and asymmetric preferences of policymakers can lead to an inflationary bias. This is even true if the central bank does not systematically attempt to push output above its potential level as suggested by KPBG. The only two further conditions to be met are high central bank credibility and low inflation rates. In this case, policymakers may be more sensitive to policy errors in which monetary policy is too tight than to policy errors in which the stance is too expansionary. Both legal and economic developments over the past twenty years might have – involuntarily – contributed to this new type of inflationary bias. Today, central banks' legal independence in many countries is substantially higher than it was in the 1970s and the 1980s. Price stability has become their primary objective (Cukierman 2008, p. 722ff.). As a result, the credibility of policymakers has risen. Furthermore, globalization of goods markets limits the pricing power of companies and labor unions' room to negotiate higher wages. The risk of high and persistent inflation periods seems to be lower than previously. Consequently, central banks may devote more attention to the stabilization of the output gap.

The inflation bias is higher the larger the variability of the foreign monetary disturbance hitting the domestic economy. Put it differently, the greater the standard deviation of the international shock, the more likely it is that the domestic output gap will become negative. Hence, the short-term interest rate (i_t) controlled by the central bank depends negatively on the standard deviation of the disturbance from abroad:

(2.2.8) $$i_t = b\sigma_{e,t}^2 + \psi_t \text{ with } b < 0$$

where $\sigma_{e,t}^2$ is the (conditional) variance of the foreign monetary disturbance e_t, b is a coefficient measuring the size of the inflation bias and ψ_t is an error term.[14] An example shall clarify this relationship further. Assume that positive and negative money supply disturbances in country B regularly affect the national monetary aggregates in A. Due to the conjunction of asymmetric objectives and the uncertainty about the size of the shock, the central bank in A swiftly lowers the interest rate in each case. Otherwise,

increase the international shock size. Additionally, the propagation mechanism of how foreign disturbances are transmitted to the domestic economy could change. In chapter 7.2.7, it will be shown that the factor loadings, and hence the sensitivity of national monetary aggregates to the global liquidity force, have risen over time in some countries or regions.

[14] In principle, both conditional and unconditional variances can be used for estimating (2.2.8). Cukierman and Gerlach (2003) use unconditional standard deviations of real GDP growth. Ruge-Murcia (2004) applies a GARCH model for estimating the conditional variance of unemployment.

policymakers run the risk of being too restrictive and causing a negative output gap, since a lack of monetary liquidity occurs in economy A. More generally spoken, equation (2.2.8) implies that countries facing more volatile international shocks to domestic monetary aggregates should have, on average, lower short-term interest rates.

In this context, two important things should be noted. First, a symmetric distribution of foreign monetary disturbances around their mean is a sufficient but not a necessary condition for expression (2.2.8) to hold (Cukierman 2004, p. 11). If more positive than negative money supply shocks from abroad occur, the inflationary bias lessens but does not completely vanish. This would only be the case if central bank A can exclude foreign liquidity-dampening effects on the domestic economy with absolute certainty. Under the regime of financial globalization, this case does not seem to be realistic. Even if foreign central bank behavior is completely anticipated, there is still the possibility of unforeseen negative international money demand disturbances.

Second, expression (2.2.8) implies that certainty equivalence does not hold any longer as assumed in the linear-quadratic framework such as KPBG. In addition to analyzing the mean, evaluating the effects of second moments is also important for understanding monetary policy behavior. Since central bankers exhibit a prudence motive, periods of highly volatile foreign money supply (or money demand) shocks will cause them to pursue an inflationary policy. In contrast, the certainty equivalence principle assumes that the uncertainty faced by policymakers takes a particularly simple form by equaling an additive white-noise error term. An optimizing policymaker can therefore ignore uncertainties about disturbances to the economy when setting the short-term interest rate and proceed as if acting in a world known by certainty.

Besides foreign money supply disturbances, there are other reasons for asymmetric central bank behavior and an inflation bias of policymakers. For instance, Borio (2006, p. 6) argues that globalization on goods markets may contribute to excessive monetary policy accommodation. Favorable supply side developments such as higher international competition and low-cost imports could lead to negative inflation rates in one country. By trying to prevent deflation central banks systematically underestimate the stimulative effects of monetary policy on the economy and accommodate the build-up of financial imbalances. The result may be pronounced boom-and-bust cycles in asset prices (Papademos 2007, para. 21).

Another explanation for asymmetries is the so-called Greenspan put. A central bank may take decisive action to prevent the stock market from falling – but not to stop it from rising (Miller, Weller, Zhang 2002, p. C171; Becchetti, Mattesini 2009, p. 99f.). This hypothesis often refers to the Federal Reserve and to its behavior in 1987, 1998, 2001 and during the most recent financial crisis. Due to the negative effects that stock market crashes can have on the real economy, the Federal Reserve systematically reacted to plunging share prices by cutting interest rates. Monetary policy was therefore providing a general downside insurance on stock values. Such a policy works like a put option, thereby potentially causing a moral hazard problem.

If one additionally assumes that central banks are uncertain about the magnitude of foreign supply shocks and domestic share price disturbances, the Borio argument and the Greenspan put can be described by transforming equation (2.2.8) into the following expression:

(2.2.9) $$i_t = b\sigma^2_{w,t} + \psi_t$$

with $\sigma^2_{w,t}$ as the variance of the foreign supply disturbance and the domestic share price shock, respectively. For reasons of notational simplicity, the two innovations are assumed to be w in (2.2.9). As has previously been the case, there should be a negative relationship between a higher volatility of the disturbance ($\sigma^2_{w,t}$) and the short-term interest rate i_t.

3 LITERATURE REVIEW OF EMPIRICAL STUDIES

In the following, a short summary of previously done research on monetary spillover effects and global liquidity is given. In order to provide a yardstick for the subsequent empirical work in this thesis, the focus is on applied econometric methods and the derived major results.

Ahmed, Ickes, Wang et al. (1993) develop a multivariate structural two-country framework of the global economy. The model consists of the US as home country and an aggregate of Japan, Western Germany, France, the UK and Canada as foreign region. GDP weights on the basis of current exchange rates are used for deriving various aggregates like foreign output and money. The approach allows for idiosyncratic supply shocks originating from the national labor market and for a common world supply disturbance representing technological innovation. Furthermore, relative fiscal, money and preference shocks affect the US and the foreign region. These fundamental disturbances are identified by imposing long-run restrictions, primarily motivated by considerations from theoretical RBC models. The effects of the structural shocks on the endogenous variables in the short run are left unrestricted. The impulse response analysis conducted in a VAR framework indicates that an exogenous rise in the ratio of domestic to foreign money supply has a negative effect on the ratio of home output to foreign output.[15] The authors conclude that either money is not even expansionary in the short run or that there are substantial spillover effects of monetary policy in one country to output in other countries. The variance decomposition analysis also suggests that the relative money supply shock is important in explaining foreign business cycle fluctuations in the short run apart from US output. No evidence of differences in transmission properties of disturbances across exchange rate regimes is found. The interaction of variables between the US and the rest of the world is the same across the pre-1973 Bretton Woods period and the post-1973 flexible-exchange-rate phase. This evidence stands in contrast to the monetarist view presented in section 2.1.1.

Baks and Kramer (1999) introduce two theoretical channels for international monetary transmission. The first one is called the "push channel": High money growth in country A leads to capital flows to country B, thereby lifting share and bond prices in

[15] Ahmed, Ickes, Wang et al. (1993) do not specify whether narrow or broad monetary aggregates are used for estimating their model.

B. According to the "pull channel", strong money growth in A causes asset price inflation in A and therefore attracts foreign capital. Since capital flows from country B to A, asset prices in B decline. In the empirical part of the analysis, the authors calculate three global money measures by using GDP weights in US dollar, market exchange rates and Divisia indices. Each method is applied to both narrow and broad money growth in the G7 countries. Principal component analysis indicates that the first principal component of global money growth generally explains a high proportion of the individual country growth rates. Global excess money growth is constructed by subtracting the aggregated growth rate of nominal GDP from the aggregated growth rate of money. The two authors also calculate G7 aggregates for short-term interest rates, long-term interest rates and stock returns. Correlation and regression analysis shows that an increase in global excess money growth is consistent with a rise in real stock returns and a decline in real interest rates on a G7 level. Furthermore, Baks and Kramer (1999) find evidence of international monetary spillover effects. Increased excess liquidity growth in one country is often consistent with a rise in real stock returns and a decline in real interest rates in other countries. From this evidence, the authors conclude that a "push channel" rather than a "pull channel" is at work. Granger causality tests between domestic and rest-of-the-world-money are conducted as well. US broad money growth Granger-causes foreign broad money growth. The same result is found for Japan but not for Germany.

Holman and Neumann (2002) estimate both a cointegration model and a recursive VAR for a system of US and Canadian variables. Since the two countries are major trading partners, monetary shocks might be transmitted strongly across borders. Among other variables, the authors include broad money, output, the exchange rate and the trade balance. The long-run analysis suggests that monetary aggregates play an important role in the equilibrium relationships between the two countries. The results from the VAR model indicate that innovations to US broad money affect real activity in Canada. In addition, Canadian monetary disturbances influence US output. As shown by both impulse response and variance decomposition analysis, many of the monetary spillover effects are similar in their impact on foreign macroeconomic variables. This result might be surprising, as Canada is usually regarded as a small open economy that has little effect on US variables.

Sousa and Zaghini (2004, 2008) analyze the impact of global excess liquidity shocks on euro area variables.[16] The global liquidity measure equals the sum of broad money in the US, Japan, the UK and Canada, using PPP exchange rates for aggregation. The authors augment VAR models by including this global money variable corrected for the effect of global output. Both a structural and a recursive VAR are estimated. The impulse response analysis shows that a positive shock to global excess liquidity leads to a permanent rise in euro area M3 and the price level. Furthermore, a temporary increase in real output and a short-lived appreciation of the euro real effective exchange rate occur. The forecast error variance decomposition analysis suggests that global excess liquidity plays an important role in explaining EMU variables.

Rüffer and Stracca (2006) collect narrow and broad monetary aggregates for 15 countries including the G7 plus the euro zone and some emerging markets. The national excess money measures are computed as the ratio between money (narrow and broad) and nominal GDP. The two authors examine whether excess liquidity developments in individual countries contain some common "global" component by applying factor analysis. The common factor explains on average approximately one third of the variance of national excess money. The variance share rises to about 50% when only narrow monetary aggregates are used for the G7 plus the EMU. Granger causality tests between national excess liquidities suggest only limited evidence of international spillover effects. Additionally, Rüffer and Stracca (2006) estimate a global recursive VAR model based on G7 aggregates including the euro area. PPP exchange rates are used for constructing the global variables. The impulse response analysis indicates that a common money supply disturbance temporarily increases global output. The effect on the price level of the G7 aggregate is permanent, whereas the impact on a global real asset price measure including property and share prices is statistically insignificant. Rüffer and Stracca (2006) also estimate national recursive VARs for the US, the EMU and Japan augmented by the following global aggregates excluding the respective country or region: money, prices and output. In contrast, Sousa and Zaghini (2004, 2008) solely include global excess liquidity in their models. Such an approach may complicate the interpretation of the impulse responses, since money responds to other shocks stemming from economic activity and prices. For the EMU and Japan, Rüffer

[16] The terms euro area, euro zone and EMU are used synonymously in the following.

and Stracca (2006) find that a global liquidity innovation leads to a temporary increase of domestic output and a permanent rise of the national price level. Only for the US, the responses are statistically insignificant. The two authors conclude that the US economy may be relatively insulated from global money supply shocks. Another explanation could be the US central bank actively countering foreign monetary developments. In a final step, a variance decomposition analysis is conducted. The impact of global money disturbances on domestic variables is smallest in the US, medium in Japan and largest in the euro zone.

Giese and Tuxen (2007a) estimate a cointegrated VAR (CVAR) model on a global level. In order to obtain aggregates for the world economy, national data for the G7 countries (but not for the euro zone as a whole) are converted into a common currency by using actual US dollar exchange rates. The authors find some evidence that goods and house prices increase as broad monetary liquidity expands. In contrast, the impact on global share prices is limited. A structural break in the cointegration relationships seems to have occurred in 2001 which is attributed to exceptionally loose monetary policy worldwide. Giese and Tuxen (2007b) also use the CVAR framework on a country level. The models for the US, the EMU, Japan and the UK are combined to build a Global VAR (GVAR) approach in line with the methodology developed by Dées, Holly, Pesaran et al. (2007). The obtained empirical results are qualitatively the same as in Giese and Tuxen (2007a).

D'Agostino and Surico (2007, 2009) investigate whether global money has marginal predictive power for US inflation. The mean and the first principal component of broad money growth across the G7 economies are used as global liquidity proxies. The authors estimate a simple AR specification for US inflation augmented by the respective global liquidity measure. As yardstick for comparison, alternative forecasting models such as a univariate approach based on lags of the price index with and without US broad money growth are applied. In addition, a model based on a Phillips curve relationship is estimated. In all cases, the global-liquidity-augmented approach delivers significantly more accurate US inflation forecasts. The marginal predictive power is particularly large at horizons beyond two years. In contrast, domestic money growth has no information content for future inflation. However, the results for the US seem to be more the exception than the rule. In other G7 countries, global money only delivers superior domestic inflation forecasts when also national money has predictive power.

Sousa and Zaghini (2007) estimate a non-recursive structural VAR on a global level. The variables are aggregated by PPP exchange rates, using data from the US, the EMU, Japan, the UK and Canada. Impulse response analysis suggests that a global liquidity shock positively impacts global GDP in the short run. As for global prices, the effect is negligible in the beginning, but then becomes significantly positive and permanent. The results from the variance decomposition show that global money disturbances markedly contribute to output and price fluctuations from the second and third year onwards, respectively. Since the results may be influenced by the time series' aggregation procedure, Sousa and Zaghini (2007) conduct robustness tests by estimating VAR models for each country or region separately. The identification pattern of the global model is adopted for domestic variables as well. Overall, the national impulse responses are comparatively similar to the results on basis of the global approach.

Belke, Orth (2007) and Belke, Orth, Setzer (2008a, 2008b, 2010) study the impact of global liquidity shocks on a number of macroeconomic and financial variables at the level of the world economy. They use both PPP exchange rates and market exchange rates to aggregate national time series of major OECD countries. The authors estimate recursive VAR models and analyze the responses to an unexpected rise in global broad money. Aggregated house prices at the wordwide level and commodity prices rise relatively fast. In contrast, a significantly positive reaction of the global GDP deflator occurs only after a considerable time lag. Belke, Orth and Setzer (2010, p. 1935f.) explain this pattern by different price elasticities on asset and goods markets. For instance, the supply on the residential property market cannot easily be expanded in the short run. Additional demand stemming from excess money is then fully reflected in increasing house prices. The authors also find a negative response of the short-term interest rate to a positive global liquidity shock which is consistent with the interpretation as a money supply disturbance. Furthermore, there is an initially positive response of output before the effect dies out. This non-permanent effect is in line with the theoretical assumption that money is neutral for the real economy in the long run. Belke, Orth and Setzer (2010) augment their VAR models by including the gold price and a globally aggregated share price index. A global money supply shock triggers a fast and significantly positive response of the gold price. In contrast, the share price index does not show any significant reaction. A forecast error variance decomposition analysis suggests that global monetary variables (money and the short-term interest rate) are responsible for nearly half of the volatility in residential property prices. Furthermore, after 16 quarters, house prices contribute over 40% to consumer price volatility.

Dreger and Wolters (2009) examine the impact of broad money shocks on real share and house prices by estimating three different VARs: two individual country models for the US and the EMU with five variables each and one global approach in order to control for international spillover effects. The authors refrain from aggregating national data but include all US and euro area variables in their global model. Furthermore, it is assumed that the US variables can affect those from the EMU contemporaneously and vice versa. Generalized impulse response and variance decomposition analysis are used for comparing the results across the three models. The evidence turns out to be broadly similar regardless of which model is used. For instance, US liquidity shocks have some positive impact on US house prices. The authors take this as evidence that spillover effects are not substantial.

Alessi and Detken (2009) examine real and financial variables to ascertain their suitability as early warning indicators of high-cost asset price boom/bust cycles across 18 OECD countries. Among others, the financial variables are the term spread, the real effective exchange rate, real and nominal short-term and long-term interest rates, real narrow and broad money and real credit. Real money and credit growth rates are corrected for endogenous business cycle and asset price components by means of recursive VAR models. Besides domestic variables, seven global financial aggregates are calculated by using GDP weights and PPP exchange rates: private credit, narrow and broad money all as ratios to GDP, nominal short-term interest rates and the VAR shocks of M1, M3 and private credit growth. The high-cost asset price boom/bust episodes are mechanically defined on the basis of domestic real aggregate asset price indices (including share prices as well as residential and commercial real estate prices). The results suggest that over the average of all countries, the global M1 gap and the global private credit gap are the best early warning indicators of domestic asset price boom/bust periods. The two global gaps equal deviations from a slowly adjusting

Hodrick-Prescott (HP) trend of the M1 and the private credit ratio to GDP. According to the authors, the result reflects the large simultaneity of the identified asset price cycles.[17]

Belke, Bordon, Hendricks (2009, 2010a, 2010b) estimate a variety of CVAR models to examine the interaction between broad money, commodity prices and goods prices on a global level. The authors use PPP exchange rates to aggregate national time series of major OECD countries. The following results are found. Global consumer prices are cointegrated with global output and global money. Cointegration also exists between commodity prices on the one hand and global money and global output on the other hand. There is a long-run proportional relationship between money and prices on a global level. It is controlled for worldwide short-term interest rate changes and hence for different monetary policy stances. Global liquidity remains a key factor in determining the long-run homogeneity of commodity and goods prices. The short-run dynamics are analyzed by accounting for the error correction terms in a vector error correction model (VECM). Overall, broad monetary aggregates across OECD countries convey useful information about the future development of commodity prices which matter for aggregate demand and consumer price inflation.

Berger and Harjes (2009) criticize the use of the ratio between money and nominal GDP as excess liquidity measure. Instead, they adjust each broad monetary aggregate in the US, the EMU and Japan for long-term movements in domestic real GDP and the short-term interest rate by estimating HP filtered series. In order to forecast EMU inflation rates, the authors apply autoregressive models augmented by the derived excess liquidity measures. The approach based on US excess money produces significantly better forecasts up to 12 quarters ahead than the AR(4) benchmark equation. However, the marginal predictive power of Japanese and euro zone excess liquidity is small or even turns negative. Furthermore, Berger and Harjes (2009) examine whether monetary policy is less effective in the presence of global excess liquidity. In each of the three countries or regions, excess liquidity regimes are defined. Afterwards, the authors estimate a Cholesky VAR for the EMU, conditioning the short-term interest rate components of the model on the presence or absence of the regime

[17] Gerdesmeier, Reimers and Roffia (2009) also examine the properties of monetary and financial indicators for detecting asset price misalignements. However, they do not use global variables but a pooled probit-type approach for OECD countries and the euro area. The authors uncover that credit aggregates and nominal long-term interest rates help to forecast asset price busts.

states. Impulse response analysis indicates that during periods of US excess money the interest rate channel is impeded in the euro area. In contrast to the no-excess-liquidity regime, the output reaction to an interest rate shock is not different from zero, while the price level barely moves.

Bagliano and Morana (2009) study international co-movements among a broad data set of real and nominal variables from the US, the euro area, the UK, Japan and Canada. Besides broad monetary aggregates, the data include real GDP, CPI indices, share prices, the oil price and short-term and long-term interest rates. The authors estimate a recursive Factor Augmented VAR (FAVAR) developed by Stock and Watson (2005a). Instead of aggregating national data via exchange rates or GDP weights, principal component analysis is used for estimating global factors. International co-movement is not only found for GDP growth but also for stock market returns, inflation rates, interest rates and, to a smaller extent, growth of broad monetary aggregates. Additionally, Bagliano and Morana (2009) find evidence of a common global force driving inflation, money and interest rates, labeled as "inflation factor". In order to assess the relative importance of global and idiosyncratic disturbances for domestic variables, a variance decomposition analysis is applied. In all countries or regions, the shocks to the common factors explain a sizeable proportion of the forecast error variance of all variables except for the exchange rate. This outcome is nearly entirely due to the output and inflation factors. In contrast, the impact of common stock price and oil price disturbances is negligible. Impulse response analysis suggests that innovations to the global output and inflation forces significantly influence major domestic variables in the US and the euro zone. The authors conclude that both common sources of disturbances and similar transmission mechanisms across countries or regions explain international co-movements.

To sum up, the majority of empirical studies display the following results. Global (excess) money influences real GDP and prices positively both on a worldwide and national level. In line with theoretical considerations, the GDP effect is shortlived and occurs first, whereas prices are affected permanently over medium- and longer-term horizons. Additionally, some authors find global liquidity to influence or precede developments on real estate and commodity markets. From an econometric viewpoint, the majority of studies applies global and national VAR models for the G7 (including the EMU) or OECD countries. Some authors link the global level with the national one by augmenting open economy country VARs with global money. The latter is typically derived by aggregating domestic broad monetary aggregates on the basis of GDP weights and/or PPP and market exchange rates. Global excess liquidity is usually defined as the ratio of the so obtained global money aggregate in relation to global GDP. In a few cases, factor analysis is applied for deriving a common liquidity force.

"[...] one can't make much sense out of [...] changes in purely national monetary aggregates [...]."

(McKinnon 1982, p. 320)

4 HYPOTHESES FOR EMPIRICAL EXAMINATION

Before presenting the concrete hypotheses, the general motivation for this work is shortly outlined by coming back to the theory section in chapter 2. Besides the previously found empirical evidence for the importance of global money, there are four theoretical reasons for going beyond established models like monetarism, the MFD approach and the NOEM.

First, when dealing with international monetary spillover effects, conventional theories focus exclusively on exchange rates, goods prices and interest rates. For instance, in the MFD approach, the exchange rate and the trade balance are the major transmission channels, while the NOEM model highlights the role of the world real interest rate. Cross-border portfolio shifts are only relevant in the sense of causing variations in exchange rates, long-term interest rates, etc. Foreign money supplies do not play any *direct* role in transmitting monetary shocks across countries, even as international capital flows have risen strongly in recent years.

Second, some theories embrace – or implicitly make – assumptions which might not hold empirically. For example, in the monetarist and the MFD framework, it is assumed that the money supply is exogenous. The central bank operates through the money supply and has perfect control over it. Direct spillover effects in monetary aggregates across countries are therefore excluded by definition. In reality, money might be partly endogenous, at least in the short run. Central banks usually set the key interest rate as their main policy instrument and let money adjust endogenously to it in the first place. Capital inflows from abroad may therefore influence national monetary aggregates via a money and credit creation process in the domestic economy.

The same type of critique might be applied to the uncovered open interest rate parity which is the cornerstone of the monetarist open economy model. According to this theory, a currency whose interest rate is high tends to depreciate. The current forward exchange rate is an unbiased predictor of the future spot exchange rate (cf. equation 2.1.1.3). The freely fluctuating nominal exchange rate acts as a buffer and perfectly insulates countries from foreign money supply shocks. However, the uncovered open interest rate parity hypothesis is often rejected empirically, as currencies with high interest rates are found to appreciate further. This commonly established empirical phenomenon is called the forward discount puzzle (Bacchetta, van Wincoop 2006, p. 1) and has often been found both by practitioners on financial markets and in academic empirical studies (Cavallo 2006, p. 2f.). It implies that excess returns on foreign currency investments like carry trades are predictable. In the probably most common version of the carry trade strategy, investors borrow an amount in a low-interest-rate currency ("funding currency"). The received funds are then converted and invested in a high-interest-rate currency ("target currency"). In recent years, especially the so-called yen carry trade has played a prominent role on international financial markets. Since the Bank of Japan has set exceptionally low short-term interest rates, the yen has become a major "funding currency". As a result, monetary aggregates in Japan as well as abroad might have been influenced (Belke, Ort, Setzer 2010, p. 1934).

Third, even if the uncovered open interest rate parity holds, it remains doubtful whether the exchange rate automatically plays a crucial role in warding off monetary spillover effects from abroad. The reason is that the global perspective is typically missing in standard open economy models. Since only two countries are assumed to interact with each other, the exchange rate as relative price is a "natural" candidate for preventing international monetary policy disturbances. However, if one switches from the two-country perspective to the global level, additional complexities may arise. For example, assume a similar expansionary behavior of major central banks.[18] Since it is not possible that each currency depreciates against other currencies, the expansionary monetary policies cancel each other out. No country achieves the short-term benefits of a weaker currency as assumed in the MFD model (Sachs 1985, p. 193). Instead, all countries suffer in the medium-term from exceedingly high money supplies which lead to goods and asset price inflation.

Fourth, many open economy theories lack a microeconomic and realistic explanation of central bank behavior. This is especially true in the light of rapidly

[18] Of course, one might ask why monetary authorities should act simultaneously in such a way. One explanation could be an inflation bias due to uncertainty about foreign money supply shocks (cf. chapter 2.2). Another explanation is provided by the common-beliefs approach outlined in section 2.1.5. According to Borio (2006, p. 6), central banks simultaneously try to prevent negative inflation rates which are caused by price-dampening effects of globalization on goods markets.

increasing financial globalization in recent years. In the MFD model, the monetary authority is assumed to pursue a beggar-thy-neighbor policy without taking the possibly endogenous reaction of international investors and cross-border portfolio shifts into account. Another example is the NOEM in which central banks are considered as selfless entities. However, unexpected changes in international capital flows and their impact on domestic variables may influence the overall macroeconomic environment of monetary policy. New incentives for pursuing a specific strategy, especially in form of rising uncertainties, could emerge, thereby requiring a reconsideration of central bank reaction functions in open economies.

Given these theoretical shortcomings, four hypotheses for empirical testing in this work are presented:

1. Despite flexible exchange rates, there are direct cross-border spillover effects between domestic (excess) monies. International capital flows lead to a global (excess) money factor and to a positive co-movement of national monetary aggregates across countries. The reason behind this pattern is financial globalization as described in section one. A global money force exists, even though there are differing strategies of central banks and various institutional setups in countries or regions.

2. Global monetary liquidity is not only a pervasive force for domestic monies but also influences various macroeconomic and financial variables both on a global and national level. As can be seen in table 4.1 in a stylized way, global money supply shocks are supposed to have a short-lived positive impact on economic activity and asset prices (house, share and commodity prices). In contrast, the level of goods prices should be lifted permanently, while the short-term interest rate is expected to fall temporarily. Furthermore, differences shall materialize across variables regarding the timing of the responses. For instance, financial variables like asset and commodity prices are supposed to react immediately to a common money supply disturbance. As suggested by Belke, Orth and Setzer (2010, p. 1935), house prices should respond faster than goods prices, as the residential property supply cannot be expanded easily in the short run.

   Global monetary liquidity has "unique" and hence superior characteristics, as it should be more important for national real and financial variables than domestic monies and short-term interest rates. As a result, the leeway of central banks in conducting independent monetary policy is limited. The trilemma view does not hold. Flexible exchange rate regimes cannot preserve completely the independence of national monetary policies. This is true irrespective of whether small open or big and rather closed economies are considered. For instance, the US economy does not show clear evidence of higher monetary independence than the UK and Canada. The reason is that US financial markets are deep and liquid, thereby attracting international capital and increasing the likelihood of monetary spillover effects from other countries.

Common monetary liquidity shocks are also "unique" in comparison to other global disturbances like sudden changes in worldwide demand, technology, long-term interest rates ("global savings glut") and commodity prices. The latter shocks should only play a relatively small role, whereas global liquidity is supposed to be a driving force of the world economy and international financial markets.

Table 4.1: Expected responses to global money supply disturbances

Response of ...	... to positive global money supply shock	Effect	Start of impact
Economic activity*	+	Temporary	Delayed
Goods prices*	+	Permanent	Delayed
House prices*	+	Temporary	Immediate
Money**	+	Permanent	Immediate
Short-term interest rate*	–	Temporary	Immediate
Exchange rate**	+	Temporary	Immediate
Share prices*	+	Temporary	Immediate
Commodity prices	+	Temporary	Immediate

* global and national level; ** national level

3. The importance of the common liquidity force for global and domestic variables has increased from the 1990s onwards. There are structural breaks both in the shock component of global (excess) money and in the propagation mechanism. The reasons for the structural change in the 1990s are rising financial globalization and increasing cross-border capital flows.

4. Sudden changes in international capital flows increase the uncertainties with which domestic policymakers are confronted. Global liquidity disturbances therefore lead to an inflation bias of central banks. The inflation bias is higher the larger the variability of the foreign or common monetary disturbances. Hence, the short-term interest rate controlled by the central bank depends negatively on the variance of the global money supply shocks.

„No agreement exists [...] on the proper measurement of liquidity. Rather, the body of available research is characterized mostly by explanations of limitations."

(Fernandez 1999, p. 7)

5 DATA AND VARIABLES

In recent years, buzzwords like "global excess liquidity" and "global liquidity glut" have been en vogue among investors and in the financial press alike. However, there is often little clarity about what these terms actually mean (Hatheway, Donovan, Cates et al. 2006, p. 3). This is hardly surprising, given that there are different types of liquidity and various yardsticks. In this work, the focus is on monetary liquidity. After explaining this concept and corresponding measurement issues, major differences to two other liquidity types – market and funding liquidity – will shortly be presented. Furthermore, it is shown how these three concepts are related to each other. Finally, the selection of countries, sample periods and additional variables used in the empirical work is explained.

While a comparatively simple concept at first sight, the proper measurement of monetary liquidity is not straightforward. One major reason is that central bank-created high-powered money often represents only a tiny fraction of monetary aggregates (Rüffer, Stracca 2006, p. 7). Accordingly, any relevant definition of monetary liquidity cannot exclusively be related to monetary policy behavior but also reflects the endogenous choice of private households, companies and investors. In addition, besides money aggregates, other measures for representing the monetary environment of a country are conceivable as well. For instance, credit data could be used for empirical examination.

Sometimes, global monetary liquidity is directly approximated by foreign exchange reserves (excluding gold) of major countries. The presumption is that foreign exchange interventions are not sterilized. The accumulation of foreign exchange (FX) reserves therefore increases the national money supply.[19] However, this was only a good approximation in the 1970s and 1980s (Hatheway, Donovan, Cates et al. 2006, p.

[19] Darius and Radde (2010) add FX reserves in US dollar to US base money, arguing that this measure is a yardstick for the speed with which an asset can be converted into a medium of exchange on a global level.

4). In the meantime, interventions are usually sterilized. Furthermore, policymakers in industrialized countries have become far less active in intervening on FX markets. Given recent developments, one may nevertheless argue in favor of using global foreign exchange reserves as proxy for international liquidity. In the last few years, the global monetary system has been intermediating excess savings from emerging markets and oil-producing countries to the US (Bretton Woods II). The result was a strong increase in global FX reserves. However, from a practical viewpoint, there is still an important argument against the use of this yardstick, even if the rise in foreign exchange reserves is associated with increasing money holdings. The data provided by the IMF cover only official FX reserves. Large asset volumes increasingly held by quasi-public institutions like oil stabilization funds and reserve agencies in emerging markets are not registered (Magnus 2007, p. 16f.). With central banks seeking to let their reserves be managed more actively by other institutions, such statistical issues may become even more important in the future.

In this work, broad monetary aggregates of the G7 countries and the euro zone are used for proxying monetary liquidity and testing the hypotheses presented in the previous chapter. To be more concrete, the data are M2 for the US and Canada, M2 plus certificates of deposit for Japan (M2CD), M3 for the EMU and M4 for the UK.[20] There are two reasons for this approach. First, a comparison of the obtained results to previous empirical work is possible. Former studies on global monetary liquidity like Rüffer, Stracca (2006) and Belke, Orth, Setzer (2010) also use broad monetary aggregates. Second, the effects of international capital flows and portfolio shifts on domestic money shall be examined. Hence, focusing on a narrow definition of money does not seem to be adequate. In the majority of countries, M1 only consists of currency in circulation and demand deposits. However, using M2 or M3 is not without difficulties either. As can be seen in table 5.1, the composition of monetary aggregates broader than M1 varies substantially across countries or regions. This point is illustrated by foreign currency deposits which are included in euro area M3 and M2 for Japan. For instance, a euro area resident acquires US dollars by selling foreign securities to a non-euro area resident. The amount is transfered from a foreign bank to an overnight deposit of a monetary and

[20] Based on IMF PPP data, 48.9% of world GDP in 2007 is represented by these countries and regions (source: own calculations). Some authors also label these countries including the euro zone the G5. For reasons of simplicity, the term "G7" is kept in the following.

financial institution (MFI) in the EMU. As a result, the stock of broad money in the euro zone expands.[21] In contrast, broad monetary aggregates in the US, Canada (each M2) and the UK (M4) do not include foreign currency deposits.[22] Direct effects of international portfolio shifts are excluded by definition. Nevertheless, and more importantly, an indirect impact of international portfolio shifts on domestic monetary developments is still possible. Assume that capital is flowing in from abroad, thereby stimulating lending activity of commercial banks. Since an endogenous money and credit creation process sets in, national monetary aggregates could increase as well. The only prerequisite for these "second-round effects" is that domestic money is not completely exogenous, i.e. not under the perfect control of monetary policy.

In the following, two other liquidity types and their differences to monetary liquidity are presented: market and funding liquidity.

Market liquidity relates to the ability of buyers and sellers to make transactions without triggering marked price variations. The more transactions take place within a given time period, the higher is market liquidity. Although being illustrative, this definition and its measurement are far from clearcut. For example, a foreign exchange market may be described as liquid when currency trades occur every few seconds. Purchasing a house, in contrast, may take days or weeks, even with a willing buyer and seller. The example suggests that the appropriate metric for market liquidity is asset-specific (O'Hara 2004, p. 1f.). Additionally, it is not clear what precisely constitutes a "marked" price effect. For instance, one might refer to bid-ask spreads and has to define "unusually" high or low levels.

[21] Besides cross-border portfolio investments, international mergers and acquisitions of non-financial corporations can also influence euro zone M3 directly (Papademos 2007, para. 15).

[22] Since the Bank of England reports M1, M2 and M3 in the ECB definition, foreign currency deposits are part of M3 in the UK. In contrast, M4 includes only deposits and financial instruments denominated in pound sterling. O'Brien (2007, p. 4ff.) gives a detailed overview of various monetary aggregates and their concise definition.

Table 5.1: Definition of broad monetary aggregates used in this work

	US	EMU	Japan	UK	Canada
M1	Currency in circulation, demand deposits, other checkable deposits, non-bank traveler's checks	Currency in circulation, overnight and similar deposits	Currency in circulation, deposit money	Currency in circulation, overnight and similar deposits	Currency in circulation, net demand deposits
M2=M1 plus ...*	Saving deposits, small-denomination time deposits, retail money market mutual funds	Short-term saving deposits, short-term time deposits	Quasi-money including certificates of deposit	Short-term saving deposits, short-term time deposits	Personal saving deposits and term deposits at banks, non-personal notice deposits at banks
M3=M2 plus ...		Money market fund shares and units, repurchase agreements, debt securities with an original maturity of up to 2 years		Money market fund shares and units, repurchase agreements, debt securities with an original maturity of up to 2 years	
M4=M3 plus ...**				Deposits and short-term securities from two to five years of original maturity	
Including foreign currency deposits	No (M2)	Yes (M3)	Yes (M2CD)	No (M4)	No (M2)

* For Japan M2CD; ** UK M4: Private sector deposits with agencies of the central government are part of the UK/ECB M3, but these deposits are not included in UK M4. Public corporations and local governments are also excluded from UK M4.
Source: O'Brien (2007)

There are two important differences between market and monetary liquidity (The Bank Credit Analyst 2007, p. 9f.). First, in contrast to monetary liquidity, there is not necessarily a positive relationship to asset prices. Abundant market liquidity can be associated with gradually increasing or declining asset prices. An overall loose monetary policy should drive up prices for goods, assets or both. Second, a decoupling between monetary and market liquidity can take place temporarily via leveraging. By using derivatives, leveraged positions require only a small cash transaction in the beginning. If the position is closed, the higher market liquidity is brought again in line with monetary liquidity. Despite these differences, there is also some kind of overlap between the two types of liquidity, since market liquidity can be influenced by central bank behavior. As indicated by the recent crisis after the collapse of Lehman Brothers in September 2008, financial and economic shocks can cause market liquidity to dry up quickly. By cutting key rates and injecting additional monetary liquidity into the system, central banks ensured the proper functioning of asset markets.

There is also no definition of funding liquidity universally agreed on. For example, the IMF defines it as "the ability of a solvent institution to make agreed-upon payments in a timely fashion" (IMF 2008a, p. xi). According to the Basel Committee of Banking Supervision (BCBS 2008, p. 1), it equals "the ability [...] to fund increases in assets and meet obligations as they come due, without incurring unacceptable losses". Strahan (2008, p. 1) defines funding liquidity as the ability to raise cash at short notice either via asset sales or new borrowing. According to Drehman and Nikolaou (2009, p. 8), a bank is liquid as long as at each point in time outflows of money are smaller or equal to inflows and the stock of money held by the bank.

Funding liquidity is both related to monetary and market liquidity. Large value payment and settlement systems rely on central bank money as the ultimate settlement asset. The ability to settle therefore also depends on monetary policy behavior. During crisis time, a downward spiral between funding and market liquidity is possible (Drehmann, Nikolaou 2009, p. 21f.). Assume a bank which is forced to massively sell assets, as it cannot obtain funding liquidity neither from the central bank nor from the interbank market. Since asset prices fall strongly, the banking system has to post higher margins and liquidity outflows increase. In order to remain liquid, other banks start selling assets as well. Given the lack of buyers and market liquidity drying up, asset prices will be further depressed. This in turn is leading to a renewed round of margin calls and so forth. The downward spiral might only be interrupted by central bank intervention.

In the following, further details on relevant data issues in this work are given. The empirical part concentrates on the G7 countries (US, Canada, Japan, UK) plus the euro zone. In principle, one could argue that emerging markets should be included as well, since they have become increasingly important for the global economy and international financial markets. However, it is opted for a focus on major industrialized countries, as the majority of emerging markets has a fixed or managed floating exchange rate regime. Assuming no capital account restrictions, this makes monetary spillovers likely according to the traditional trilemma view. However, the motivation of this study is to examine whether global capital flows also influence domestic macroeconomic variables under flexible exchange rates. Furthermore, some emerging markets currencies are still not fully convertible. With a host of capital controls being in place, it is difficult to interpret national monetary aggregates in a truly global context (Berger, Harjes 2009, p. 36). Finally, there are data availability problems even for bigger emerging markets like China or India.

The data for the G7 plus euro area are on a quarterly and seasonally adjusted basis available from Q1 1973 to Q4 2007 with T=140 observations. There is a potential trade off between using long samples and the increasing number of structural breaks. Accordingly, the time span is shortened in some cases. For instance, the VAR and FAVAR models are estimated from Q1 1984 to Q4 2007 with T=96. A more detailed explanation of employing this specific sample can be found in chapter 7. Besides broad monetary aggregates, various other macroeconomic data like GDP, CPI, short-term interest rates, exchange rates, etc. are used for estimation purposes. In the empirical sections 6 and 7, the time series and variables are listed in greater detail. The data are drawn from a variety of sources, including national statistical offices, central banks and the OECD. Most of the time series are provided by professional databases like Thomson Datastream, Feri and Bloomberg. In a few cases, only non-seasonally adjusted data are available. In order to eliminate the seasonal pattern, the Census X-12 approach is applied. Since EMU series at a quarterly frequency are often available only for a relatively short time span, it is partly relied on the Area-Wide Model database by Fagan, Henry and Mestre (2001) who provide backdated time series. The authors note that some caution is warranted here, as there are methodological differences across euro zone countries in collecting the data. Moreover, data availability on a national level becomes increasingly scarce when moving back in time. The series for historical house prices in euro area countries stem from Gros (2007) and various national sources. The house price data are aggregated to an EMU-wide variable by using PPP weights provided by the IMF. A complete data list including sources and the used mnemonics in the applied EViews programs can be found in appendix A.26.

In the following empirical part, a "general-to-specific" approach is pursued. In chapter 6, autoregressive processes are estimated for global and national monetary liquidities. In chapter 7, structural approaches in form of VAR and FAVAR models are introduced.

"Economists have made increasing use of dynamic factor analysis [...] to estimate 'underlying' processes. These processes may correspond more closely than measured data to the economic concept economists use when building models."

(Gilbert, Pichette 2003, p. 6)

6 A GLOBAL MONEY FACTOR

In this chapter, dynamic factor analysis is shortly explained and then applied in order to derive a global factor for monetary excess liquidity. Granger causality tests are used to examine the interaction between global and national excess monies. The section concludes with an examination of global excess liquidity's autoregressive law of motion and some structural break tests.

6.1 FACTOR ANALYSIS

The rationale underlying factor models is that the behavior of a set of variables is driven by two distinct forces (Favero, Marcellino, Neglia 2005, p. 605). The first one equals a few factors common to all of the series. The second force has an idiosyncratic and country-specific nature. Accordingly, it solely drives one specific variable. Factor analysis provides a formal way of defining what type of variation is (more) relevant for the panel of data as a whole. Especially in an international context, the ability to separate between common and idiosyncratic movements is an appealing characteristic. The increasing interconnectedness within the global economy may mean that variables across countries have developed tighter linkages and therefore exhibit common patterns (Bai 2003, p. 158). Besides changes in structural propagation, global disturbances, which hit many countries simultaneously, could also have become more important over time. As a result, an unexpected money supply change in one major country directly spilling over to several other economies can be understood as a global shock. As increasing cross-border capital flows may occur swiftly, national monetary aggregates then display similar patterns. This is especially true, since not high-frequency data but quarterly figures are used for empirical examination in this work. If such common characteristics in monetary liquidity prevail, then international capital flows and the similar effects of globalized financial markets matter more than differences in national economic policies and institutional settings.

On a formal level, the distinction between common and idiosyncratic changes can be described by the following stylized model. For reasons of simplicity, money instead of excess money is used here.

(6.1.1) $$\Delta M_{A,t} = \alpha_A \Delta M_{A,t-1} + \varepsilon_{A,t} + c_A \eta_{ft}$$

where $\Delta M_{A,t}$ is the change in money in country A at time t, α_A is an autoregressive coefficient and $\varepsilon_{A,t}$ is the idiosyncratic shock in A at time t. c_A measures the impact of the global liquidity disturbance from abroad (η_{ft}) on $\Delta M_{A,t}$ at time t. A similar equation with the corresponding variables holds for country B:

(6.1.2) $$\Delta M_{B,t} = \alpha_B \Delta M_{B,t-1} + \varepsilon_{B,t} + c_B \eta_{ft}$$

It is assumed that the foreign liquidity shock (η_{ft}) does not stem from A or B but from other countries (i.e. from the rest of the world):

(6.1.3) $$f_t = \alpha_f f_{t-1} + \eta_{ft}$$

with f_t as global money force derived by factor analysis and measuring the co-movement of national monies caused by cross-border capital flows. α_f is an autoregressive coefficient. In this highly stylized approach, the global liquidity shock (η_{ft}) affects money growth in countries A and B directly and at the same time, although the magnitude of that effect might differ (c_A and c_B). The reason for this may be differences in the national transmission mechanism like the endogenous money and credit creation process or in central bank behavior. The idiosyncratic shocks only have an impact in their own country.[23] The two equations (6.1.1) and (6.1.2) above contain more disturbances than observable variables (Stock, Watson 2003, p. 38): one sudden change common to A and B (η_{ft}) and two country-specific ones ($\varepsilon_{A,t}$ and $\varepsilon_{B,t}$). Factor models are one way of dealing with this identification problem by enabling an estimate of f_t and a separation between common and idiosyncratic shocks.

[23] Some authors choose a different terminology, since idiosyncratic shocks may spill over through cross-country linkages as well. Despite causing co-movement between national variables, these shocks are still labeled as 'idiosyncratic' movements (Moneta, Rüffer 2006). For reasons of clarity, this terminology is not used in the following.

In order to allow for a common-idiosyncratic decomposition, several identifying assumptions have to be made in factor analysis (Justiniano 2003, p. 12; Johnson, Wichern 2007, p. 482f.). In a "strict or classical" factor model, it is assumed that the idiosyncratic errors $\varepsilon_{A,t}$ and $\varepsilon_{B,t}$ are independent and identically distributed over time (iid). Moreover, they are orthogonal to each other ($\varepsilon_{A,t} \perp \varepsilon_{B,t} \forall A, B = 1,\ldots,N$ and $A \neq B$). The global factors are also orthogonal ($f_{qt} \perp f_{lt} \forall l, q = 1,\ldots,r$ and $q \neq l$).[24] Thus, the variance-covariance matrix of both the idiosyncratic disturbances and the common forces is diagonal. The idiosyncratic errors are orthogonal to the factors (for instance $\varepsilon_{A,t} \perp f_{qt}$). Finally, classical factor analysis assumes that the number of variables (N) is much smaller than the number of observations (T).

Since these assumptions are fairly restrictive for economic time series data, Chamberlain and Rothschild (1983) introduce the "approximate" factor model which differs from the classical one in two important ways (Bai 2003, p. 138; Boivin, Ng 2006, p. 170). First, the number of observations is large in both the cross-section (N) and the time dimension (T). Second, it allows for weakly serial and cross-section correlation of the idiosyncratic shocks. For large N and T, there can be some cross-correlation among the idiosyncratic elements, since on average these distorting effects will be zero (Helbling, Bayoumi 2003, p. 19). If, in contrast, N is rather small, there is the risk of contaminating the estimated global factors with country-specific noise.

Approximate factor structures have been further developed by Stock and Watson (1998, 2002b) and have increasingly been used in empirical studies since then. Stock and Watson show that common factors can be consistently estimated in large panels using principal components. The latter depend solely on the covariance matrix of a given set of variables. For instance, if national monetary aggregates are correlated, they possibly measure the same concept in the form of global liquidity. Principal component analysis (PCA) explains such a covariance structure through a few linear combinations of these variables. PCA is therefore a variable reduction procedure. The idea is to

[24] For reasons of simplicity, only one global money factor (f_t) is assumed in equation (6.1.3). However, in factor analysis, it is possible that there are $q = 1,\ldots,r$ orthogonal factors which are common to national monetary aggregates. Later in this chapter, it will be examined empirically whether solely one factor in form of the first principal component ($PC1$) exists or whether also $PC2$, $PC3$, etc. qualify as global forces.

reduce the size of the data set (N) to r common – and "artificial" – factors called principal components which represent the key features of the data set as a whole. Then, these components can "replace" the original variables without much loss of information. In contrast, if the off-diagonal elements of the sample covariance matrix are small, the variables are not related and a factor analysis will not prove useful (Johnson, Wichern 2007, p. 488). In PCA, the factors are extracted in a sequential way with the first principal component explaining the most variation in the data set, the second principal component explaining the next most variation not explained by the first principal component and so on. The estimated factors can be thought of as a weighted average of the variables in the data set. The eigenvectors are the weights, since they measure the importance of each variable to the corresponding principal component irrespective of other variables. The weights are chosen in a way such that the sum of squared idiosyncratic components is minimized (Mönch 2005, p.16f.).

Using PCA for deriving the factors, Stock and Watson (1998, 2002b, 2005a) develop an approach which is labeled dynamic factor model in static form and comprises two equations:

(6.1.4) $$X_t = \Lambda F_t + D(L)X_{t-1} + v_t$$

with X_t as N-variate vector of observable variables (national monetary excess liquidities, i.e. each domestic money in relation to domestic nominal GDP) and F_t as r-variate vector of unobserved common static factors f_{qt} (global monetary excess liquidities) obtained by PCA with $q = 1,...,r$ and $r < N$. Λ is a $N \times r$ matrix of factor loadings which measures the impact of F_t on X_t, $D(L)$ is a $N \times N$ matrix lag polynomial of order k and v_t is a N-variate vector of idiosyncratic shocks.

(6.1.5) $$F_t = \Phi(L)F_{t-1} + \eta_t$$

with $\Phi(L)$ as $r \times r$ matrix lag polynomial of order p and η_t as r-variate vector of global shocks driving the common factors. Global and country-specific shocks are mutually uncorrelated, that is $E(\eta_{qt} v_{is}) = 0$ for all i, q, t, s with $i = 1,..., N$.[25]

[25] Please note that F_t now equals the vector of global *excess* money forces and η_t is the vector of global *excess* liquidity shocks (instead of global money factor and global liquidity disturbance in 6.1.3). It

In the first equation (6.1.4), an explanation of the covariation in X_t is provided by the common factors instead of the possible $N(N+1)/2$ parameters in the variance-covariance matrix of X_t. In contrast to a simple regression, the independent variables contained in the vector F_t cannot be observed but have to be estimated (generated regressors). As a result, an errors-in-variables problem may emerge, making statistical inference difficult (Pagan 1984). However, the uncertainty in the factor estimates is negligible if the data set N is large. Since the variance of the factor estimate is of order $1/N$, using many variables ($N \to \infty$) substantially reduces the uncertainty in the latent factors (Boivin, Giannoni 2006, p. 13f.). Static principal components are underlying the Stock and Watson approach, i.e. linear combinations of only contemporaneous variables (X_t) are used (Favero, Marcellino, Neglia 2005, p. 606). F_t appears in (6.1.4) without any lags. However, as can be seen in (6.1.5), this static formulation is not restrictive, since F_t can be interpreted as including a number of lags of the global factors. The two equations above are therefore called the *dynamic* factor model in *static* form.[26]

A dynamic factor model in static form is an appropriate tool for estimating international spillover effects. If a change in monetary liquidity in one (major) country has a swift and significant impact on liquidity conditions in other countries, the resulting pattern is picked up by a factor model. The spillover effects are so strong that they generate a common trend in national excess monies across countries and regions, thereby enabling the separation between global and country-specific developments. Alternatively, if global variables are derived by simple sum aggregation of national data using GDP weights, such a distinction is blurred. Any idiosyncratic disturbance stemming from one major country without spilling over to other economies will influence the global aggregate, therefore being counted as global shock (Elliot, Fatás 1996, p. 367). Global and idiosyncratic innovations are presumed to have the same impact, although country-specific changes should not influence the common movement in an economic sense. For instance, assume a purely idiosyncratic disturbance in a

implies that only money in excess of nominal GDP leads to international spillover effects. This assumption will be discussed later in this chapter.

[26] Justiniano (2003, p. 7) nevertheless argues that such factor models are introduced under strong restrictions. Since the dynamics are exclusively driven by autoregressions in the factors themselves, no heterogeneity in dynamics across the underlying variables is permitted. For instance, assuming price-stickiness, domestic goods prices may not respond contemporaneously to the factors but only fast-moving series like exchange rates or share prices.

comparatively large economy like Japan. Although other countries are not affected, the global aggregate will change as an arithmetic implication of its construction, since Japan has a relatively high GDP weight within the G7. In general, the same type of critique applies, if PPP or market exchange rates are used for sum aggregation.

Using factor analysis on a global level provides additional advantages. Sum aggregation implicitly assumes that the included national variables are perfect substitutes. However, given differences in country-specific measurement and other characteristics, this does not need to be true. For example, the monetary aggregate M2 in the US is not a perfect substitute for M3 in the euro zone (cf. chapter 5). Hence, it may be argued that global (excess) liquidity should not be measured directly by aggregation. Instead, estimates of it are derived by factor analysis without taking a stand on arbitrarily chosen weights. For instance, national monetary aggregates can be converted into one global measure by using weights basing on PPP or market exchange rates. If PPP is chosen, one has to decide whether the relative or the absolute version is used. In contrast to direct measures, the estimated factors are latent variables and reflect the "underlying process" (Gilbert, Pichette 2003, p. 6). In this respect, the idea of "global liquidity" closely resembles the concept of "potential output". The latter is a cornerstone of many models but cannot directly be observed and has to be estimated.

Another advantage of using factor analysis may stem from an economically more meaningful interpretation. A common money factor reflects similar movements in domestic monetary aggregates caused by international capital flows across countries. In contrast, the interpretation of global liquidity derived by simple sum aggregation is ambiguous, as a classic identification problem occurs. On the one hand, such a global money measure may reflect "true" international spillover effects. On the other hand, a global liquidity variable obtained by aggregation could also be a statistical artefact, since it simply equals the sum of individual national monies. What the researcher observes at the global level may therefore not reflect financial globalization. Instead, it could solely be the result of adding up separate non-interacting domestic variables.

However, one severe problem in identifying spillover effects by applying factor analysis still persists. If monetary policy in country A increases its national money supply, the central bank in B may do this as well to avoid a beggar-thy-neighbor pattern. As a result, the common liquidity force reflects similar behavior of central banks without capital flows from A to B actually taking place. This identification problem can be solved neither by sum aggregation nor factor models.

Moreover, at this early stage of empirical analysis, it is important to note that a global liquidity factor may not only contain monetary spillover effects but also other macroeconomic developments such as a change in the oil price or in the global business cycle. Structural models like VARs or FAVARs are needed to disentangle common monetary shocks from other global disturbances (cf. chapter 7 for more details).

As a first step in the empirical application of PCA, national monetary excess liquidity measures are derived for the G7 countries and the euro zone by dividing broad monetary aggregates by nominal GDP. It is not controlled for the influence of changes in the domestic short-term or long-term interest rate. Furthermore, for the sake of simplicity, a unit coefficient on nominal GDP is assumed. In reality, the private sector does not only demand real balances for financing actual output. Instead, there are additional motives of holding money. For instance, due to positive wealth effects, increases in nominal money might exceed nominal output growth (Polleit, Gerdesmeier 2005, p. 6). Hence, at this stage, the used yardstick for excess liquidity is a relatively rough one, thereby providing a starting point for the empirical work.

In order to make the obtained series stationary, three different methods of detrending are employed: log first order differencing, a linear time trend and a HP filter (Rüffer, Stracca 2006, p. 17). In Appendix A.1, three corresponding unit root test statistics for each series (Augmented Dickey-Fuller, Phillips-Perron, Kwiatkowski-Phillips-Schmidt-Shin) can be found. Apart from Canadian excess money on basis of a linear time trend, all detrended variables are stationary at significance levels of less than 10%.

As is common in factor models, the series are additionally standardized by subtracting the mean and dividing by the standard deviation (Eickmeier 2007, p. 525). Otherwise, the results may systematically be affected by cross-country differences in the size of money and output variability. For example, variables with large variance unduly influence the determination of factor loadings (Johnson, Wichern 2007, p. 489). For the first principal component ($PC1$) to suitably qualify as a global factor, three requirements have to be met. First, $PC1$ should explain a "sufficiently" large fraction of the variance of all national monetary excess liquidities relative to additional principal components ($PC2$, $PC3$, etc.).[27] Second, the relevance of $PC1$ should not be limited to only one or two countries but should be evenly spread across countries. Third, the explanatory power of $PC1$ for single domestic monetary excess liquidities should be higher than the explanatory power of any other single national excess money.

As can be seen in Table 6.1, the first condition is not unequivocally met for the whole data sample ranging from Q1 1973 to Q4 2007. Regardless of the detrending method, comparing the explanatory content of $PC1$ and $PC2$ shows rather small differences. For instance, the variance share of $PC1$ using log first differences is 27.3% compared to 23.0% for $PC2$. Even the third and fourth principal component is still relatively important in explaining national liquidity fluctuations across countries (19.6% and 17.4%, respectively). Since financial globalization may have become more important in the past two decades, an attempt is made to explore the temporal stability of the results by shortening the data sample to Q1 1990 – Q4 2007. Besides rising international capital flows, additional structural breaks probably took place in the 1970s and 1980s: two oil price shocks and a regime shift in the behavior of the Federal Reserve from 1979 to 1982 (Huizinga, Mishkin 1986). Hence, using the long sample contains the risk of contaminating the results with structural change apart from financial globalization.[28] From Q1 1990 to Q4 2007, the explanatory content of $PC1$ rises for all three methods of detrending. However, apart from the HP filter, this is also true for the second principal component. Hence, all in all, it is not unambiguously clear whether the obtained empirical evidence for $PC1$ can be taken as an indication of a truly global excess liquidity factor.

Besides this problem, it remains the question how to determine whether the first principal component explains a "sufficiently" large fraction of the variance. A share of around 30% appears rather small, but this is a matter of judgement. Since a yardstick for comparison is missing, a PCA is also applied to other macroeconomic and financial data which may share common variations across countries. Given international trade on goods markets, this may be true for national activity and price measures like GDP and CPI. Domestic share prices could also exhibit a common trend due to globalization in the real economy and on financial markets alike. Three month interest rates are also

[27] Of course, the meaning of "sufficiently" is not unambiguously clear and open to interpretation. With this problem is dealt in more detail in the following.
[28] With this issue is dealt in greater detail in section 6.3 by applying structural break tests.

included, although they are usually interpreted as purely national phenomena. However, domestic monetary policy may react to global shocks, thereby leading to a synchronized movement of national short-term interest rates.[29]

Table 6.1: Variance share of national excess liquidities explained by principal components, in %

1973 Q1 - 2007 Q4	PC1	PC2	PC3	PC4	PC5
Log first difference	27.3	23.0	19.6	17.4	12.7
Linear time trend	30.6	25.4	18.2	15.9	9.9
HP filter	29.0	25.7	18.1	16.8	10.4
1990 Q1 - 2007 Q4	PC1	PC2	PC3	PC4	PC5
Log first difference	31.5	25.2	18.6	15.8	9.0
Linear time trend	34.7	32.7	15.9	11.6	5.1
HP filter	36.8	25.3	21.2	11.7	4.9

Note: Sum of PCs may not add up to 100% due to rounding effects

In the following, solely log first differences as detrending method are used for each of the additional variables. The only exemption is the short-term interest rate with first differences. The reason for this procedure is to keep the presented results as parsimonious as possible. Moreover, factor analysis usually concentrates on first differences. The $PC1$'s explanatory power for the newly included time series is markedly higher than for monetary excess liquidity. For example, the variance share of real GDP across the G7 countries plus the euro zone amounts to 41.0% (cf. table 6.2). For consumer prices, it is even 77.7%. However, these results have to be put into perspective. The estimated share of 27.3% for the whole sample is based on excess money and not on national monetary aggregates itselves. From an economic viewpoint, such an approach implicitly suggests that only monetary liquidity in abundance of nominal GDP in one country leads to excess liquidity in another one. If the outstanding money stock equals nominal GDP, international capital flows are assumed to come to a halt. However, this does not need to be true. Portfolio allocations of investors may lead to capital outflows in one country with domestic money falling below national nominal GDP. It therefore makes sense to examine whether monetary aggregates which are not adjusted for real activity and prices exhibit a higher co-movement. The PCA in table 6.2

[29] A more elaborated view on the reasons for interpreting national variables as global phenomena can be found in chapter 7.2.1 where the FAVAR model is presented.

shows that this is the case. From Q1 1973 to Q4 2007, $PC1$'s variance share of broad monetary aggregates is 55.6% ($PC2$: 15.1%).[30]

Table 6.2: Share of variance explained by principal components, in % (global factors)

	PC1	PC2	PC3	PC4	PC5
Excess broad money	27.3	23.0	19.6	17.4	12.7
Broad money	55.6	15.1	12.6	9.9	6.8
3M interest rate	40.6	27.6	15.6	10.5	5.7
Real GDP	41.0	20.5	15.7	13.4	9.4
CPI	77.7	8.6	6.3	4.2	3.2
Share price	68.7	12.1	8.6	6.9	3.7

Note 1: Calculations based on first standardized differences (1973 Q1 - 2007 Q4)

Note 2: Sum of PCs may not add up to 100% due to rounding effects

The second condition to be met is that the relevance of global excess liquidity in form of $PC1$ should be evenly spread across countries or regions. Hence, the first common factor is supposed to load to a pronounced and comparable extent on all national monetary excess liquidities. When the whole data sample is analyzed, the factor loadings of $PC1$ are positive and significantly different from zero (cf. table 6.3).[31] However, there are strikingly large differences in the size of the impact coefficients. For example, the factor loading on US excess money is 0.676, whereas it is only a low 0.229 for the euro zone. These results suggest that the common excess liquidity factor has a different impact across countries. The underlying reasons may be various institutional settings like the bigger size and the comparatively higher attractiveness of financial markets in the US. Furthermore, differences in central bank behavior and the national transmission mechanism like the endogenous money and credit creation process could play an important role.

The impact coefficients of the second principal component on national monetary excess liquidities do not share the same sign. It is significantly negative for the US and

[30] As an alternative approach of comparing GDP and the three month interest rate to excess liquidity, one may also rely on the concept of output gap and the natural interest rate hypothesis postulated by Wicksell. Both approaches set the corresponding actual figure in relation to a steady state condition (potential output, natural interest rate). Accordingly, measures for "excessive" movements can then be derived in form of output and interest rate gaps. However, the concise estimation of the steady state conditions poses additional problems and remains a matter of dispute.

[31] Signs of heteroskedasticity and autocorrelation are found in a few equations of the form $X_t = \Lambda^{PC1} PC1_t + e_{Xt}$ with Λ^{PC1} as the N-variate factor loading vector measuring the impact of $PC1_t$ on X_t. Hence, the Newey-West estimator is used for obtaining the standard errors of the factor loadings. Otherwise, the standard errors tend to be underestimated by OLS.

Canada and significantly positive for the euro zone, Japan and the UK. Accordingly, the second factor appears to capture asymmetries among countries, whereas $PC1$ may be interpreted as a common force.

The shortening of the sample to Q1 1990 – Q4 2007 shows two additional features of the global excess liquidity force. $PC1$'s factor loading for Japan turns negative albeit not at conventional significance levels. The insignificant impact coefficient probably reflects the special circumstances in Japan after the bursting of the equity and housing bubble at the beginning of the 1990s. Moreover, it is important to note that the size of the remaining factor loadings changes considerably while remaining significant. The impact coefficients ($PC1$s) for the euro zone, the UK and Canada rise markedly, whereas the US loading falls substantially from 0.676 to 0.492. This evidence may be interpreted as an indicaton of a less asymmetric global excess money factor which influences countries in a more balanced way. However, caution in interpreting the results is warranted, as the timing of the structural break is chosen in an ad-hoc manner. In chapter 6.3, more sophisticated tests of structural change will be applied. Moreover, and independent of whether the full sample or a shorter one is used, an errors-in-variables problem may exist when estimating the factor loadings. Since the number of national monetary aggregates is comparatively small ($N = 5$), the variance of the factor estimate which is of order $1/N$ may not be negligible. As a result, an attenuation bias could emerge with downward biased estimates of the factor loadings.

Table 6.3: Factor loadings

1973 Q1 - 2007 Q4	PC1	PC2	PC3	PC4	PC5
US	0.676 (0.067)	-0.218 (0.091)	-0.016 (0.103)	0.163 (0.086)	-0.685 (0.121)
EMU	0.229 (0.082)	0.518 (0.065)	0.582 (0.093)	0.555 (0.117)	0.179 (0.110)
Japan	0.450 (0.089)	0.247 (0.098)	-0.717 (0.071)	0.196 (0.103)	0.429 (0.130)
UK	0.355 (0.074)	0.479 (0.105)	0.179 (0.094)	-0.782 (0.084)	0.006 (0.099)
Canada	0.403 (0.083)	-0.627 (0.064)	0.340 (0.078)	-0.119 (0.115)	0.561 (0.098)
1990 Q1 - 2007 Q4	PC1	PC2	PC3	PC4	PC5
US	0.492 (0.099)	0.578 (0.085)	0.000 (0.119)	-0.144 (0.092)	-0.634 (0.123)
EMU	0.426 (0.097)	-0.003 (0.164)	-0.846 (0.073)	0.109 (0.112)	0.302 (0.166)
Japan	-0.151(0.125)	0.771 (0.044)	0.145 (0.159)	0.313 (0.152)	0.514 (0.149)
UK	0.463 (0.068)	-0.253 (0.164)	0.317 (0.091)	0.785 (0.087)	-0.051 (0.100)
Canada	0.582 (0.055)	-0.080 (0.165)	0.404 (0.135)	-0.501 (0.124)	0.489 (0.167)

Note 1: Estimates based on first standardized differences

Note 2: Standard errors in paranthesis (using Newey-West)

The third and final condition for interpreting the first principal component as a truly global force is as follows: The explanatory power of $PC1$ for single domestic monetary excess liquidities should be higher than the explanatory power of any other single national excess money.[32] Otherwise, the common factor cannot be regarded as pervasive force across countries. In order to examine this prerequisite, two simple regressions are estimated. In the first equation, the dependent variable is the respective national monetary excess liquidity figure and the independent variable is $PC1$. In the second equation, the common excess liquidity factor is replaced by national excess monies stemming from other countries. For reasons of notational simplicity, it is referred to the previously used two-country case with the countries A and B:

(6.1.6) $$X_{A,t} = \Lambda_A^{PC1} PC1_t + v_{A,t}$$

with $X_{A,t}$ as monetary excess liquidity (money in relation to nominal GDP) in country A, Λ_A^{PC1} as factor loading, $PC1_t$ as first principal component derived by PCA and $v_{A,t}$ as idiosyncratic shock

(6.1.7) $$X_{A,t} = \alpha_B X_{B,t} + \varepsilon_{A,t}$$

with $X_{B,t}$ as national monetary excess liquidity (money in relation to nominal GDP) in country B, α_B as regression coefficient and $\varepsilon_{A,t}$ as residual

As can be seen in table 6.4, the condition that $PC1$ is a pervasive force is only met partly for the whole data sample. The explanatory power (R-squared) of the first principal component for US excess liquidity is 62.4% but 27.7% for Japan, 22.2% for Canada and 17.2% for the UK.[33] $PC1$ can explain only 7.2% of the total variance in EMU excess liquidity. However, it should be noted that the R-squared measures for the regressions between purely domestic figures are even lower. For example, a negligible 0.5% of excess liquidity in the euro zone is explained by its US counterpart. Similar results are also obtained for other regressions. Moreover, and interestingly, these results seemingly stand in contrast to the assumption that the US is pre-eminent in shaping monetary liquidity conditions abroad.

[32] The explanatory power of the first principal component is defined as $(\Lambda_i^{PC1})^2 \text{var}(PC1_t)/\text{var}(X_{it})$ with $(\Lambda_i^{PC1})^2$ as the squared factor loading of $PC1_t$ on the national excess money X_{it} for $i = 1,\ldots,N$ (Ciccarelli, Mojon 2010, p. 526).

[33] In some equations, signs of positive autocorrelation are found. However, as noted by Woolridge (2009, p. 410), the R-squared measures are not biased upwards, provided the data are stationary and weakly dependent (which is the case).

When the sample size is shortened to Q1 1990 – Q4 2007, the influence of the first common factor becomes even more asymmetric across countries. Only in case of the US, the R-squared measure increases markedly to 71.6%. For the euro zone and Canada, the figure rises marginally to 7.8% and 25.7%, respectively. For Japan and the UK, the variance share even decreases (18.1% and 12.2%, respectively). The result for Japan is another hint that the extraordinary circumstances since the 1990s led to a strong idiosyncratic pattern. Again, the extent of spillover effects solely between two countries seems to be very subdued in general. US excess liquidity can still only explain 5.2% of the total EMU variation. For Canada, the ratio is somewhat higher with 8.7%.

In this context, one note of caution seems to be appropriate. The estimates are derived mechanically without postulating structural – and hence economic meaningful – relationships between variables. For instance, the explanatory content of the regression between the US and Canada is 8.7% in the shorter sample independent of which causal relation is postulated. From an economic viewpoint, it may make sense to assume that US monetary excess liquidity drives its Canadian counterpart and not vice versa.[34] The same is true for the regression results between the first principal component and national figures. A share of 71.6% may indeed indicate that US liquidity conditions are heavily influenced by global developments. However, the opposite could hold as well: Given the predominance of the US economy and US financial markets, $PC1$ may largely be driven by US developments and not symmetrically by several countries.

Table 6.4: R-squared, in % (in left column independent variables)

1973 Q1 - 2007 Q4	US	EMU	Japan	UK	Canada
PC1 (global)	62.4	7.2	27.7	17.2	22.2
US	---	0.5	4.2	0.8	6.9
EMU	0.5	---	0.1	1.5	0.2
Japan	4.2	0.1	---	1.0	0.1
UK	0.8	1.5	1.0	---	0.0
Canada	6.9	0.2	0.1	0.0	---
1990 Q1 - 2007 Q4	US	EMU	Japan	UK	Canada
PC1 (global)	71.6	7.8	18.1	12.2	25.7
US	---	5.2	6.8	0.9	8.7
EMU	5.2	---	1.5	1.5	0.9
Japan	6.8	1.5	---	1.7	2.9
UK	0.9	1.5	1.7	---	1.6
Canada	8.7	0.9	2.9	1.6	---

[34] In contrast, Holman and Neumann (2002, p. 1851ff.) find that Canadian monetary disturbances influence US variables as well (cf. chapter 3).

To sum up, the obtained results may give a first indication of a global excess liquidity factor in form of the first principal component. However, the models are kept simple yet. Furthermore, all three prerequisites for $PC1$ to qualify as pervasive force across countries are not met unambiguously. Some caution is therefore warranted when using $PC1$ as global excess liquidity measure.

Finally, the empirical analysis deals with a rather limited data set with only five variables (one broad monetary aggregate in the US, the EMU, Japan, the UK and Canada). However, in factor analysis, it is only allowed for some cross-correlation among the idiosyncratic elements for a large number of variables (N). As a final step, it is therefore tested for the orthogonality of the country-specific errors ($v_{A,t} \perp v_{B,t}$) by estimating simple correlation coefficients. As can be seen in table 6.5, the correlation coefficient between the US and the UK amounts to -0.42 and is highly significant. Comparable results can also be found for some other country pairs. Since the majority of country-specific errors is not orthogonal to each other, the derived global excess money force in form of the first principal component should once again be interpreted with some caution. There is the risk that the common-idiosyncratic decomposition is distorted and that the estimated factor is to some extent contaminated with country-specific noise.

Table 6.5: Correlation of idiosyncratic errors

	US	EMU	Japan	UK	Canada
US	---	---	---	---	---
EMU	-0.23***	---	---	---	---
Japan	-0.40***	-0.14*	---	---	---
UK	-0.42***	0.01	-0.16*	---	---
Canada	-0.20**	-0.20**	-0.37***	-0.25***	---

Note 1: Correlation coefficients (Q1 1973 - Q4 2007)

Note 2: *** Indicates significance at 1% level, ** at 5% level, * at 10% level

6.2 GRANGER CAUSALITY TESTS

The applied factor model picks up the co-movement of broad monetary aggregates (in relation to nominal GDP) within one quarter. Such a procedure is appropriate, as cross-border capital flows might occur rather quickly. However, time lags in the transmission process of international monetary spillover effects are still possible. Assume that excess money is created by the central bank in A. Investors allocate some of these additional funds abroad. A money and credit creation process in country B sets in. However, it takes more than a quarter before a significant impact can be registered on B's monetary aggregate. In this context, the assumption of time lags is appropriate.

Since Granger causality tests are indicative of whether one variable precedes another, they are a suitable tool for examining lagged spillover effects. Excess money in country A is said to be Granger-caused by excess liquidity in B if the past development in B helps predicting the current patterns in A. In this case, the coefficients on the lagged excess liquidities in B (β_j) are different from zero at statistically significant levels (Maddala 2001, p. 379; EViews 6 User's Guide I 2007, p. 410f). Consider the following equation:

$$X_{A,t} = \sum_{j=1}^{K} \alpha_j X_{A,t-j} + \sum_{j=1}^{K} \beta_j X_{B,t-j} \qquad (6.2.1)$$

with $X_{A,t}$ and $X_{B,t}$ as national excess monies in countries A and B and K as lag length

If $\beta_j = 0$ for $j = 1,2,...,K$, $X_{B,t}$ fails to Granger-cause $X_{A,t}$.[35]

In the following, three different versions of Granger causality tests are applied. The first one is between global and domestic excess liquidities in the G7 and the euro area. The first principal component is used as global excess money measure. The second battery of tests is based on the common excess liquidity factor ($PC1$) excluding one country. For instance, in the case of the EMU, PCA is used for deriving global excess money without taking the euro area excess liquidity into account. Afterwards, it is tested for Granger causality between the common factor excluding the EMU and the euro zone excess money figure. Such a procedure may be appropriate, since there is some risk that the estimated principal component is contaminated with country-specific noise (cf. previous chapter). The third series of tests focuses on the detection of Granger causality between purely national excess liquidity measures as in equation (6.2.1). This version is suitable for uncovering systematic patterns in the precedence of monetary spillover

[35] Critically, it may be argued that Granger causality tests are misleading, if expectation effects play an important role. Assume the following constellation. The banking sector in country A anticipates a monetary expansion in B and therefore a capital inflow from abroad. An endogenous money and credit creation process in A starts in order to meet future demand for currency A. Consequently, excess money in country A rises before its counterpart in B. In this case, excess money in A Granger-causes excess money in B.

effects. For example, one may suspect asymmetries, as excess money from the US could be particularly important in influencing monetary conditions abroad. However, other constellations are conceivable as well. Given the existence of carry trades, Japan's expansionary monetary policy could also be a driving force of international monetary spillover effects. Even a "liquidity cluster" may exist. Given the large and deep financial markets in the US and the euro zone, monetary spillover effects could be concentrated between the US and the EMU.

For all Granger causality tests, $K = 4$ is chosen. This lag length proves to be large enough to avoid autocorrelation in the residuals. The results remain robust when other lag specifications are applied. Tests for heteroskedasticity (White tests) suggest that the residuals are homoskedastic. As has been the case in the previous chapter, the national excess monies are in log first differences and standardized. Table 6.6 which shows the results reads as follows. In the left column, the variables can be found which are tested for preceding the others. For example, when the whole sample ranging from Q1 1973 to Q4 2007 is used, global excess money ($PC1$) Granger-causes domestic excess liquidity in the US and Canada at conventional significance levels. However, the null hypothesis of Granger noncausality cannot be rejected in case of the euro area, Japan and the UK. When the common liquidity force excluding the respective country or region is used, Granger causality is only found for Canada. The empirical evidence of bilateral spillover effects is also rather limited. The US influences the euro area and Canada. In addition, some significant precedence is found from Japan to the US and Canada. To sum up, in only 10 of 40 possible cases, Granger causality is detected.

Instead of using data from 1973 to 2007, shortening the sample might provide an interesting testing alternative. As described in chapter one, the volume of international capital flows has risen markedly since the 1990s. One might therefore suspect that cross-country liquidity spillover effects have become more important over time. Accordingly, the same Granger causality tests are conducted again for the sub-sample ranging from Q1 1990 to Q4 2007. However, no evidence is found that international monetary spillover effects have become more important. In fact, the number of Granger causality cases even declines from 10 to 7. Rüffer and Stracca (2006, p. 19) find a similar result.

Table 6.6: Granger causality tests between global and national excess monies

1973 Q1 - 2007 Q4	Global (PC1)	Global ex respective country (PC1)	US	EMU	Japan	UK	Canada
Global (PC1)	—	—	2.36*	0.58	0.16	1.05	5.60***
Global ex respective country (PC1)	—	—	1.35	0.72	0.14	0.99	5.50***
US	0.15	1.40	—	2.00*	0.62	1.50	2.07*
EMU	0.96	1.43	0.97	—	1.49	0.45	0.76
Japan	0.64	2.49**	2.48**	0.38	—	1.93	2.00*
UK	1.76	2.07*	0.72	1.15	0.89	—	2.57**
Canada	0.51	0.90	0.82	0.79	1.22	0.27	—
1990 Q1 - 2007 Q4	Global (PC1)	Global ex respective country (PC1)	US	EMU	Japan	UK	Canada
Global (PC1)	—	—	1.35	0.81	0.29	0.11	1.80
Global ex respective country (PC1)	—	—	2.98**	0.85	0.26	0.16	2.23*
US	1.04	0.74	—	0.98	1.14	0.63	0.81
EMU	1.83	3.35**	1.61	—	0.28	1.19	2.48*
Japan	0.41	2.71**	3.35**	1.26	—	0.60	1.44
UK	1.47	1.26	1.20	0.42	0.52	—	0.77
Canada	2.50*	0.90	1.56	0.53	1.05	0.34	—

Note: F-statistics; based on four lags; *** indicates significance at 1% level, ** at 5% level, * at 10% level

Overall, the evidence of statistically significant precedence between excess liquidity measures is rather sparse. Neither the US nor Japan or the EMU seems to dominate monetary conditions abroad. However, the results should be put into perspective. As previously discussed, capital flows may occur rather quickly within one quarter. Additionally, the Granger causality tests are conducted in a simple bivariate system and not in a structural model. Besides monetary spillover effects, a multitude of other international influences may play a role, thereby hampering the identification of clear-cut Granger-causal relationships. Examples of such non-identified variables are a global business cycle or fluctuating commodity prices. Furthermore, Granger causality tests are sensitive to structural breaks (Bakbekh, Osborn, Sensier et al. 2007, p. 8). Simply splitting the sample at the beginning of the 1990s and comparing the results might not be appropriate, since it is an ad-hoc procedure and arbitrary. Although the sum of stocks of foreign assets and liabilities rose markedly since the 1990s, the concise time of structural change is still unknown.[36] Given these problems, alternative procedures may provide additional insights. In the following chapter, autoregressive approaches of global and national excess monies are estimated. After comparing the obtained persistence parameters ("law of motion"), Quandt-Andrews tests are applied in order to test for structural change and to determine its concise timing.

[36] Another candidate for a breakpoint date could be the mid-1990s, as the process of financial globalization has accelerated markedly since then (cf. chapter one). However, using 1995 for the Granger causality tests does not yield significantly different results either.

"Nothing endures but change."

(Heraclitus)

6.3 STRUCTURAL BREAKS

In the last few decades, the global economy went through a number of significant changes. It is therefore rather unlikely that the data generating process in the year 1973 at the beginning of the sample is the same as in 2007 when the series end (Del Negro, Otrok 2003, p. 4). The phenomenon of global excess liquidity may especially be prone to structural breaks for three reasons.

First, the rapid increase in financial globalization has led to strong rises of international capital flows over time. This in turn may have strengthened common trends in monetary aggregates, while country-specific elements have lost importance in explaining national developments. In this respect, the timing of structural changes is of some interest. If breaks in national excess liquidities occur uniformly at the same time, a "big bang" in financial globalization may have occurred. For instance, it is conceivable that a sharp structural break took place in the 1990s. Possible reasons are the capital account liberalization in a multitude of countries and the improvement of technology used in managing financial cross-border transactions.

Second, there might have been regime switches in central bank behavior. According to Borio (2006, p. 6), globalization on goods markets contributes to excessive monetary policy accommodation. Favorable supply side developments in the global economy lead to very low inflation rates or even deflation. Consequently, central banks ease their policy considerably, thereby accommodating the build-up of financial imbalances.

Third, the variance of exogenous structural shocks in the global economy could have changed as well. The discussion about the so-called "Great Moderation" on a country level may serve as an illustration. Some empirical studies support the hypothesis of "good luck" as explanation for the decline in domestic real GDP volatility (Stock, Watson 2002a). Accordingly, the higher macroeconomic stability can neither sufficiently be explained by changes in the structure of the economy ("propagation") nor by improved policy. Instead, smaller shocks, i.e. the "impulses", largely account for the observed reduction in volatility. However, this finding remains a matter of dispute

(Benati, Surico 2009, p. 1636). Interestingly, Sensier and van Dijk (2004, p. 834) find that, in contrast to real variables, some nominal series in the US even experienced a temporary increase in volatility. The same could be true for global excess liquidity, since several episodes of international financial crisis may have led both to common money supply and money demand shocks. Examples are the emerging markets crisis in 1997 and 1998 with possibly severe spillover effects to industrialized countries. Another example is the bursting of the equity bubble in spring 2000.[37] It is therefore an interesting empirical issue to see whether global excess liquidity disturbances have been increasing ("bad luck" instead of "good luck").

In dynamic factor analysis in static form (cf. equations 6.1.4 and 6.1.5), the following types of structural breaks are conceivable: instability in the factor dynamics, in the factor loadings, in the dynamics of national variables, in the global shocks and in the idiosyncratic disturbances. Accordingly, if a *single* sharp break occurs in both the factor dynamics and the global shocks, the factor evolution equation is as follows:

$$F_t = \Phi(L)F_{t-1} + \eta_t \text{ where } \Phi(L) = \begin{cases} \Phi_1(L), t \leq \kappa \\ \Phi_2(L), t > \kappa \end{cases}, \text{ var}(\eta_t) = \begin{cases} \sigma_1^2, t \leq \tau \\ \sigma_2^2, t > \tau \end{cases} \quad (6.3.1)$$

where $\Phi(L)$ is a matrix lag polynomial and κ and τ are the break dates of the factor dynamics and the conditional variance, respectively. The formulation allows for the conditional mean (that is the autoregressive lag coefficients) and the conditional variance to break at potentially different dates (Stock, Watson 2002a, p. 11).[38] The pursued testing strategy is to look first for a structural change in the conditional mean. Then, it is proceeded with testing for instability in the conditional standard deviation by controlling for a break in the mean. Otherwise, if instability in the conditional mean is neglected a contaminated issue is addressed when testing for structural changes in the variance (Batbekh, Osborn, Sensier et al. 2007, p. 10).

[37] Structural breaks caused by the most recent financial crisis should only play a minor role in this work, as the sample ends in Q4 2007.

[38] Furthermore, the intercept may undergo structural change as well. The global excess liquidity factor is based on standardized variables with a mean of zero over the whole sample. However, the applied Quandt-Andrews test for structural breaks exclude observations, thereby possibly leading to a non-zero constant (cf. the following explanations in this work for more details). According to Perron (1989), the failure to account for structural change in the constant (or trend) can result in spuriously high estimates of the autoregressive coefficients.

A single break in the factor loading matrix Λ and in the variance of the idiosyncratic shock v_t can be found in the following equation:[39]

$$X_t = \Lambda F_t + D(L)X_{t-1} + v_t \tag{6.3.2}$$

$$\text{where } X_t = \begin{cases} \Lambda_1 F_t + D(L)X_{t-1} + v_t, t \le \upsilon \\ \Lambda_2 F_t, + D(L)X_{t-1} + v_t, t > \upsilon \end{cases} \text{ and } \operatorname{var}(v_t) = \begin{cases} \sigma_1^2, t \le o \\ \sigma_2^2, t > o \end{cases}$$

with υ and o as break date of the factor loadings and the country-specific disturbances, respectively.

In the following, the procedure and results for estimating structural breaks in the factor dynamics are shown first. Afterwards, the outcomes for the factor loadings and the global and idiosyncratic shocks are presented.

From an economic viewpoint, changes in the factor dynamics in a univariate setting equal variations in the persistence of the common liquidity force. The latter is assumed to be the first principal component. Persistence is the speed with which global excess liquidity ($PC1_t$) converges to equilibrium after a shock (η_t^{PC1}). Consider the following equation:

$$PC1_t = \sum_{s=1}^{K} \phi_s PC1_{t-s} + \eta_t^{PC1} \tag{6.3.3}$$

with assuming $\left|\sum \phi_s\right| < 1$ for convergence

Expression (6.3.3) can be transformed into the following equation (Levin, Piger 2003, p. 9) which equals the augmented Dickey-Fuller regression:

$$PC1_t = \rho PC1_{t-1} + \sum_{s=1}^{K-1} \beta_s \Delta PC1_{t-s} + \eta_t^{PC1} \tag{6.3.4}$$

with $\rho \equiv \sum \phi_s$ as the so-called persistence parameter which equals the sum of coefficients on the lagged dependent variables. The coefficients β_s in (6.3.4) are simple transformations of the AR coefficients ϕ_s in equation (6.3.3). If $\rho = 1$, the data-generating process is infinitely persistent, since after a shock global excess liquidity never returns to its initial level (no convergence). If $\rho = 0$, the shock dies away

[39] Structural change in the autoregressive dynamics of national monetary excess liquidities ($D(L)X_{t-1}$) is also conceivable but not included in (6.3.2).

immediately and the common liquidity force is serially uncorrelated (Pivetta, Reis 2007, p. 5). Persistence and mean reversion are therefore reversely related: Higher persistence (ρ) equals lower mean reversion and vice versa. This concept is also linked to the impulse response function (IRF) in VAR models which are applied in section 7.1. However, ρ cannot distinguish between two series in which one shows a large initial rise and then a quick pronounced fall in the IRF, while the other exhibits a small increase in the beginning and a subsequent gradual decline in the IRF (Marques 2004, p. 11.).

In order to detect changes in persistence, equation (6.3.4) has to be estimated first. Afterwards, structural break tests can be applied. It is well known that estimating expression (6.3.4) by OLS can yield substantial problems in finite samples. The standard asymptotic distribution of the OLS coefficients and t-statistics become systematically poorer approximations to their true finite-sample distributions as the true value of ρ increases. In particular, OLS point estimates of ρ get increasingly downward-biased and their distributions become more skewed to the left when the persistence parameter rises towards a unit root (O'Reilly, Whelan 2005a, p. 712). This problem can be rectified by using mean- and median-unbiased estimators pioneered by Andrews (1993) and Andrews, Chen (1994) and described in detail by Tanizaki (2000). The procedure essentially consists of a Monte Carlo simulation in which equation (6.3.4) is estimated 10,000 times by OLS. Afterwards, the mean and the median of the simulated OLS coefficients of ρ are calculated and interpreted as the true unbiased persistence parameters. In order to ensure stability of the estimates, Tanizaki (2000, p. 502) implements an additional convergence criterion. The simulated ρ is not allowed to deviate more than 0.001 from the previous value. Otherwise, the simulation with 10,000 draws is repeated.[40]

In table 6.7, the results for estimating (6.3.4) can be found. Both OLS and mean- and median-unbiased estimators are applied. The estimates are based on the whole data sample ranging from Q1 1973 to Q4 2007. The lag order (K) is equal to the lag length chosen by the Akaike Information Criterion (AIC). Besides using the global factor ($PC1$) as variable, the estimates are also done separately for each excess liquidity figure

[40] Instead of a Monte Carlo simulation, a standard residual bootstrap procedure as described in Enders (2004, p. 234ff.) is used (cf. program 2 in the EViews program appendix).

on a national level (X). The motivation for this approach lies in getting a yardstick for comparison. Accordingly, with 0.471, the persistence of the common liquidity force estimated by OLS is the highest apart from the UK ($\rho = 0.630$). Another extreme is the EMU, where the excess liquidity shock dies rather quickly away ($\rho = 0.124$), albeit not at conventional significance levels.[41] The obtained results are indicative of a world factor which captures most of the persistent, or low-frequency, co-movement across countries. The national excess liquidities seem to replicate more high-frequency fluctuations. In this context, it is important to note that the country-specific estimates of ρ may also implicitly include a global component. Hence, the result that the persistence of the common factor is nevertheless higher (apart from the UK) may signal the "unique" characteristic of global excess liquidity.

The obtained findings are broadly in line with other empirical research both on a national and global level. For example, Boivin, Giannoni and Mihov (2009, p. 360f.) find that the average persistence of common inflation factors in the US is high, whereas individual inflation series exhibit strong mean-reversion. According to Kose, Otrok and Whiteman (2003, p. 1225), the world factor in the business cycle is much more persistent than the fluctuations in individual countries.

The results for the mean- and median-unbiased estimators indicate that the downward distortions are of minor importance. For example, on a global level and in the case of the US, the UK and Canada, the median-unbiased estimate even lies slightly below the level obtained by OLS. For Japan and the EMU, the median-unbiased estimator is only somewhat above the OLS coefficient. This outcome is supported by the fact that the data-generating processes are I(0) (cf. unit root tests in appendix A.1).

[41] The Newey-West heteroskedasticity and autocorrelation consistent estimator is used for deriving the standard deviations. In the following, it is shown on the basis of several tests that signs of heteroskedasticity emerges, thereby possibly leading to an underestimation of the "true" standard deviations.

Table 6.7: Persistence parameters[42]

	Lags	OLS	Mean-unbiased	Median-unbiased
Global	3	0.471 (0.098)	0.450	0.460
US	1	0.383 (0.111)	0.372	0.376
EMU	1	0.124 (0.138)	0.125	0.131
Japan	3	0.184 (0.150)	0.194	0.205
UK	2	0.630 (0.115)	0.614	0.626
Canada	4	0.447 (0.155)	0.428	0.441

Note 1: Lags are selected by AIC

Note 2: Standard errors of OLS coefficients in paranthesis (using Newey-West estimator)

In the next step, structural break tests on basis of equation (6.3.4) are estimated. Besides global excess liquidity, the national figures are also used again. In order to test whether the null hypothesis of parameter stability – and hence unchanged persistence – can be rejected, Quandt-Andrews tests are applied. In contrast to the traditional Chow test, the Quandt-Andrews procedure does not assume any prior knowledge about potential breakdates. Severe problems in splitting arbitrarily the sample therefore do not arise (Hansen 1992, p. 518f.). The Quandt-Andrews sup-F statistic is the maximum of a sequence of traditional Chow-style χ^2 tests for parameter stability at each of the different points in time. This idea is pioneered by Quandt (1960) and its asymptotic distribution is derived by Andrews (1993).[43] However, the largest value of the Chow test sequence is only a good estimator for a structural break when the covariance matrix of the residuals has a homoskedastic form (Hansen 2001, p. 121). If there is heteroskedasticity, the distribution of the lagged dependent variable in an autoregressive model can change at some point in the sample. As a result, there is the risk that Type I errors falsely indicating structural breaks occur too often. Given that heteroskedasticity is a common feature especially in autoregressive models, O'Reilly and Whelan (2005b) propose a wild bootstrapping approach for generating alternative critical values of the Quandt-Andrews sup-F statistic. On the basis of simulations, they show that their

[42] The standard deviations of the mean-unbiased and median-unbiased are not estimated. Andrews, Chen (1994, p. 192) and Tanizaki (2000, p. 503) propose additional simulation procedures to derive these statistics.

[43] An alternative method is the test developed by Bai and Perron (1998). In contrast to the Quandt-Andrews approach which assumes a single break, it is possible to detect *multiple* structural change. The Bai-Perron test is sequential, starting by looking for a single structural break. If the test rejects the null hypothesis of parameter stability, the data sample is split in two and the procedure is repeated in each sub-sample. This sequence continues until each sub-sample test cannot reject the null hypothesis any longer (Hansen 2001, p. 120f.).

procedure leads to tests with approximately the correct size, i.e. the risk of Type I errors is reduced substantially.

In the following, the wild bootstrapping approach is shortly explained in the context of global excess liquidity. First, the autoregressive model in equation (6.3.4) is estimated via OLS. Afterwards, the obtained residuals and hence the global excess liquidity shocks ($\hat{\eta}_t^{PC1}$) are stored. Then, W new time series ($PC1_t^*$) are generated on the basis of the estimated no-break model:

$$PC1_t^* = \hat{\rho}PC1_{t-1}^* + \sum_{s=1}^{K-1} \hat{\beta}_s \Delta PC1_{t-s}^* + g_t \tag{6.3.5}$$

where $\hat{\rho}$ and $\hat{\beta}_s$ are OLS estimates with $W = 10{,}000$. The g_t are pseudo-disturbances randomly drawn with replacement from the estimated $\hat{\eta}_t^{PC1}$ according to the following rule:

$$g_t = \begin{cases} \hat{\eta}_t^{PC1} & with \quad probability \quad 0.5 \\ -\hat{\eta}_t^{PC1} & with \quad probability \quad 0.5 \end{cases} \tag{6.3.6}$$

For each of the 10,000 simulated series, a sup-F test statistic is calculated. The Quandt-Andrews test includes the Lagrange Multiplier (LM) form of the χ^2 test as well as the alternative Wald or Likelihood Ratio tests. O'Reilly and Whelan (2005b, p.4) use the Wald (sup-W) test statistic for which the $\alpha - th$ percentile of the resulting distribution is taken as the $1-\alpha$ percent critical value. The same approach is followed here. On the basis of sup-W test statistics, critical values are derived for excess liquidities both on a global and national level. Besides the problem of heteroskedasticity, high persistence of explanatory variables can also lead to poor performances when applying asymptotics-based sup-F tests. O'Reilly and Whelan (2005b, p. 10f.) therefore propose a bias-adjusted wild bootstrapping approach by including a median-unbiased estimator. However, given that the persistence parameters found for excess liquidities are comparatively low, simple OLS estimates are applied here. O'Reilly and Whelan (2005b, p. 10) report that size biases are negligible for values of ρ less than 0.9.

The distribution of the Quandt-Andrews statistic becomes degenerate when the structural break approaches the beginning or the end of the sample. It is theferore usual convention in the literature to eliminate the first and last 15 percent of the observations from consideration (van Dijk, Osborn, Sensier 2002, p. 5). It is important to note that such an approach yields a trade-off between sound econometrics and the researcher's interest of including recent data. The phenomenon of global excess liquidity may have played an increasingly important role when moving towards the end of the sample. However, by using the Quandt-Andrews test on basis of the usual convention, the period from Q4 2002 to Q4 2007 is excluded.

Three heteroskedasticity tests are applied for each autoregressive model of global and national excess liquidities: White, Breusch-Pagan-Godfrey (BPG) and ARCH. The lags for the ARCH procedure (n; cf. table 6.8) are obtained by using the AIC. Accordingly, apart from the UK and Canada, significant signs of heteroskedasticity among the residuals are found. The results of the wild bootstrapping procedure indicate that sharp breaks in the persistence parameters occur but not frequently and uniformly across countries. This argues against a big bang in financial globalization which would have led to a concentration of structural breaks possibly in the 1990s. Global excess liquidity shows significant signs of structural change in the persistence parameter (ρ) in Q4 1981. The question whether the instability in ρ is due to increasing capital flows or caused by other global developments like the second oil price shock cannot be answered at this stage. Instead of simple autoregressive approaches, structural models are needed to shed further light on this issue (cf. chapter 7). With respect to national excess liquidities, a structural break in ρ is only found for the EMU in Q3 1992. Additionally, it is tested for structural change in the intercept (μ) which has been added to equation (6.3.4).[44] Instability in the constant is not found for global excess money but for the domestic excess liquidities in the EMU and the UK at different dates: Q3 2001 and Q1 1980, respectively.

[44] Cf. also the remarks in footnote 38.

Table 6.8: Quandt-Andrews breakpoint tests for intercept and persistence parameter

	White	BPG	ARCH (n)	Break date (μ)	Sub-Wald F (μ)	Break date (ρ)	Sub-Wald F (ρ)
Global	0.98	2.28*	6.88 (2)***	2000 Q3	2.79	1981 Q4	9.15**
US	0.45	1.73	3.31 (2)**	1997 Q3	2.85	1982 Q1	2.65
EMU	4.96***	1.78	8.23 (1)***	2001 Q3	14.27***	1992 Q3	9.07*
Japan	8.56***	2.19*	2.64 (3)*	1981 Q1	1.94	1990 Q3	2.48
UK	0.12	1.44	0.07 (1)	1980 Q1	9.81*	1982 Q1	4.00
Canada	1.01	0.61	1.50 (1)	1991 Q2	6.41	1983 Q2	4.60

Note 1: Critical values for sup-Wald F-statistic based on wild bootstrapping approach
Note 2: *** Indicates significance at 1% level, ** at 5% level, * at 10% level

Since there are signs of instability in the persistence of global excess liquidity, the sample is divided into the time before and after the structural break. Two estimates are done with ρ_1 before Q4 1981 and ρ_2 afterwards. Given the problem of heteroskedasticity, the Newey-West covariance estimator is again used for deriving the standard deviations. The results indicate rising persistence over time, as, with -0.446, ρ_1 is even negative, albeit not at significant levels ($S.D. = 0.32$). Some caution is warranted in interpreting theses results, since the sample size for estimating ρ_1 is comparatively small. The obtained evidence could therefore be prone to outliers. In contrast, ρ_2 amounts to 0.53 with a standard deviation of 0.10.

As mentioned above, only persistence of UK excess liquidity is higher than the comparable figure for the common factor. However, the failure to account for structural breaks in the intercept can result in spuriously high estimates of ρ. If one accounts for changes in the constant, the process may factually be less persistent. The Quandt-Andrews test indicates instability of the UK constant (μ) in Q1 1980 but no break in ρ. The persistence for the UK is therefore re-estimated including a dummy for μ equaling zero before Q1 1980 and one afterwards. Accordingly, conditioning on the break in the constant reduces the estimated persistence parameter substantially: ρ drops from 0.630 to 0.355. The heteroskedasticity-robust standard errors are 0.115 and 0.108, respectively. This result seems to be in line with the idea of global excess liquidity having "unique" characteristics.

The Quandt-Andrews test for structural change looks for simple one-off breaks. However, it is conceivable that the form of instability is gradual over time. In light of this possibility, a rolling regression for the global excess liquidity factor is applied (cf. equation 6.3.4). Such a procedure may have the advantage of allowing for greater flexibility in detecting structural changes. Each rolling sample can estimate a completely different global excess liquidity process, thereby potentially capturing gradual time variation in the intercept and the persistence parameter. In the following, a rolling window of 15 years is used. For reasons of simplicity, the previously chosen lag length (K) of one for the whole sample (cf. table 6.7) is also applied to the rolling regression. The solid line in figure 6.1 equals the persistence parameter of the global factor and the constant. For instance, the estimate for Q1 1988 is the result based on the rolling regression from Q1 1973 to Q4 1987. The two dashed lines are the 95 percent intervals obtained by a simple residual percentile bootstrap as described in Enders (2004, p. 234ff.) with 10,000 draws.[45] O'Reilly and Whelan (2005a, p. 715) suggest focusing on median-unbiased estimators for the persistence parameter, since the finite-sample biases for OLS estimates get larger as the sample sizes declines. However, as can be seen in figure 6.1 on the left hand side, the rolling OLS estimates are still substantially below 0.9, thereby signaling no risk of a downward distortion. The results are in line with a gradual increase in ρ at the beginning of the sample. The persistence parameter increases from 0.34 in 1988 to about 0.60 in 1997, thereby implying that mean reversion of global excess liquidity has gradually been getting smaller over time. However, ρ is only significantly different from zero on basis of the derived 95 percent confidence intervals from the mid-1990s onwards.[46] Afterwards, ρ fluctuates within a relatively narrow range from about 0.5 to 0.7, indicating a rather stable pattern in the autoregressive law of motion. Nevertheless, given the comparatively small sample size, the 95 percent confidence intervals are wide, as they range from slightly above zero to about one.

Overall, the obtained empirical evidence is indicative of a temporary trend break in persistence instead of the suggested one-off structural change implied by the Quandt-Andrews test. However, it is important to note that rolling regressions do not allow an unambiguous distinction between sharp and gradual structural change. For instance, assume several sharp rises in the global persistence parameter over time. In this case,

[45] As indicated in table 6.8, signs of ARCH effects are found in the residuals of global excess liquidity. Goncalves and Kilian (2004) note that using a standard residual bootstrap in the presence of conditional heteroskedasticity contains the risk of less accurate confidence bands.

[46] There are two short time spans in 1998 and 2002 in which the lower confidence band falls again below zero (cf. figure 6.1).

the rolling regression approach would also indicate a gradually increasing coefficient size as implication of its construction.

The results for the intercept on basis of the rolling regression reveal no structural instability. As can be seen in figure 6.1 on the right hand side, the fluctuations are relatively small. Moreover, the bootstrapped 95 percent confidence intervals indicate a non-significant influence of the constant over time. Hence, a spuriously high estimate of the persistence parameter does not seem to be the case.

Figure 6.1: Rolling regression for global persistence parameter (upper chart) and intercept (lower chart)

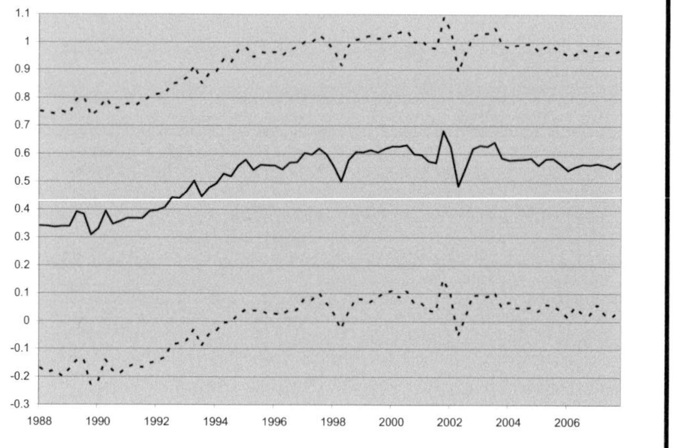

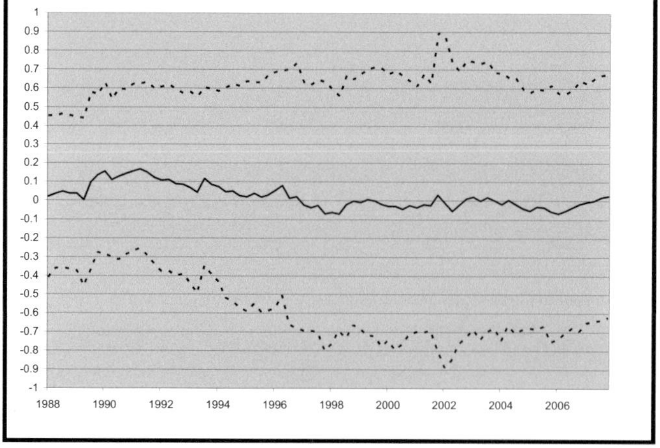

Besides structural instability in global excess liquidity, there may be time-variation in the factor loadings as well. Caused by financial globalization and rising international capital flows, the sensitivity of national excess liquidities (X_t) to changes in the common liquidity factor ($PC1_t$) could have risen. The Quandt-Andrews test is therefore repeated on basis of the following equation:

(6.3.7) $$X_t = \Lambda^{PC1} PC1_t + D(L)X_{t-1} + v_t^{PC1}$$

$$\text{where } X_t = \begin{cases} \Lambda_1^{PC1} PC1_t + D(L)X_{t-1} + v_t^{PC1}, t \le \upsilon^{PC1} \\ \Lambda_2^{PC2} PC1_t + D(L)X_{t-1} + v_t^{PC1}, t > \upsilon^{PC1} \end{cases}$$

with Λ^{PC1} as N-variate factor loading vector measuring the impact of global excess money in form of $PC1_t$ on the national excess liquidities X_t. υ^{PC1} is the break date of the factor loadings and v_t^{PC1} is the N-variate idiosyncratic disturbance vector at time t. Since substantial signs of heteroskedasticity are found by applying the White and the Breusch-Pagan-Godfrey test (cf. table 6.9 below), the wild bootstrapping approach with OLS is used again on basis of the sup-LR test to derive critical values.[47] The order k of the lag polynomial $D(L)$ is derived by the AIC. Sharp structural breaks occur between the common excess liquidity force and national excess liquidities in the EMU, the UK and Canada. However, the timing of structural variation is not concentrated in the 1990s as one may expect in the light of a big bang in financial globalization. The break date is Q1 1982 for the UK, Q2 1983 for Canada and Q2 1994 for the euro area. These results could point in the direction of other common factors or shocks behind the variation of national monetary aggregates.

Table 6.9: Quandt-Andrews breakpoint tests for factor loadings

	Lags (k)	White	Breusch-Pagan-Godfrey	Break date	sup-LR F
US	1	3.53**	3.85**	1979 Q3	3.65
EMU	1	5.08***	1.73	1994 Q2	5.9*
Japan	1	4.96***	0.95	1978 Q4	3.20
UK	4	6.99***	1.49	1982 Q1	12.36***
Canada	3	4.27***	2.74**	1983 Q2	6.40*

Note 1: Lags were selected by AIC
Note 2: *** Indicates significance at 1% level, ** at 5% level, * at 10% level

[47] The sup-W and sup-LR test are equivalent to each other in linear equations (EViews 6 User's Guide II 2007, p. 168).

In order to look whether Λ^{PC1} increases in cases where significant structural time variation is found, sub-sample estimates of the factor loadings are derived. An example shall clarify the procedure. The Quandt-Andrews test signals a break in the EMU factor loading in Q2 1994. Hence, OLS estimates for obtaining the size of the factor loadings and the Newey-West approach for deriving the corresponding standard deviations are applied for Q1 1973 to Q1 1994 (Λ_1^{PC1}) and for Q2 1994 to Q4 2007 (Λ_2^{PC2}). As previously suspected, the factor loading after the structural break is higher than before the instability occurrs. In case of the EMU, Λ_2^{PC1} is 0.387 with a standard deviation ($S.D.$) of 0.102, whereas Λ_1^{PC1} amounts to only 0.079 ($S.D. = 0.106$). Even more pronounced is the gap for Canada with $\Lambda_2^{PC1} = 0.479$ ($S.D. = 0.062$) and $\Lambda_1^{PC1} = 0.176$ ($S.D. = 0.113$). However, and surprisingly, the opposite is true in the UK. The sensitivity of national excess liquidity to the global factor before the break amounts to 0.566 ($S.D. = 0.155$). Afterwards, the factor loading drops to 0.183 but remains significant ($S.D. = 0.068$). The economic reason behind this pattern is not clear at this stage, given that simple univariate models which cannot take structural relationships into account are estimated.

Table 6.10: Comparison of factor loadings for sub-samples

	Break date	Λ_1^{PC1}	Λ_2^{PC1}
US	---	---	---
EMU	1994 Q2	0.079 (0.106)	0.387 (0.102)
Japan	---	---	---
UK	1982 Q1	0.566 (0.155)	0.183 (0.068)
Canada	1983 Q2	0.176 (0.113)	0.479 (0.062)

Note 1: Only break dates with significance of at least 10%

Note 2: Standard errors of factor loadings in paranthesis (using Newey-West estimator)

As has been the case above, rolling regressions for the factor loadings are an interesting alternative to the Quandt-Andrews test. However, such a procedure is not implemented here but later in a FAVAR environment (cf. chapter 7). This proceeding allows the direct comparison of factor loadings and potential structural instabilities across major variables. For instance, apart from monetary aggregates, it is possible to examine whether the relationship between national and global GDP has changed over time (for further details, please refer to chapter 7.2.7). Instead of factor loadings, it is concentrated here on another important yardstick for equation (6.3.7): R-squared. The latter reports the variance share of national excess liquidity which is explained by the common factor ($PC1_t$) and the domestic autoregressive dynamics (X_{t-1}). If global excess liquidity is rising in importance, its share of explanatory power for national excess monies (R^{PC1}-squared) should increase over time.[48] The complement is $1-R^{PC1}$-squared and equals the sum of the explained idiosyncratic variance share due to X_{t-1} and the unexplained variance share due to the country-specific error v_t^{PC1}.

The R^{PC1}-squared measures are calculated on basis of a rolling 15-year window as described above. Not surprisingly, they fluctuate strongly over time. However, the results seem to indicate an upward trend in the common factor's explanatory power for the EMU, Canada and the US (cf. figure 6.2 on the left hand side). Especially the case of the euro zone is conspicuous. R^{PC1}-squared tends to be very small until 2001 before rising strongly within a short time period. In Q4 2007, R^{PC1}-squared is 0.247, i.e. the global force explains 24.7% of the variance share in EMU excess liquidity over the past 15 years. In the US, the comparable figure at the end of the sample is a high 74.9%. At this stage, it is not unambiguously clear whether the global force drives US excess money or vice versa. In Canada, R^{PC1}-squared is 0.384.

In contrast, an unchanged or even declining role of the global factor is registered for Japan and the UK (cf. figure 6.2 on the right hand side). As already mentioned, the special circumstances in Japan can explain why idiosyncratic patterns still dominate. However, such an argumentation can hardly be maintained for the UK. The latter is a comparatively small open economy with London as one of the most important financial centers in the world. Hence, at least from a theoretical viewpoint, international capital flows should play a more prominent role for national monetary conditions.

48 R_i^{PC1}-squared is defined as $(\Lambda_i^{PC1})^2\,\mathrm{var}(PC1_t)/\mathrm{var}(X_{it})$ with $(\Lambda_i^{PC1})^2$ as the squared factor loading of $PC1_t$ on the national excess money X_{it} for $i=1,\dots,N$.

Figure 6.2: R^{PC1}**-squared on basis of rolling regressions**

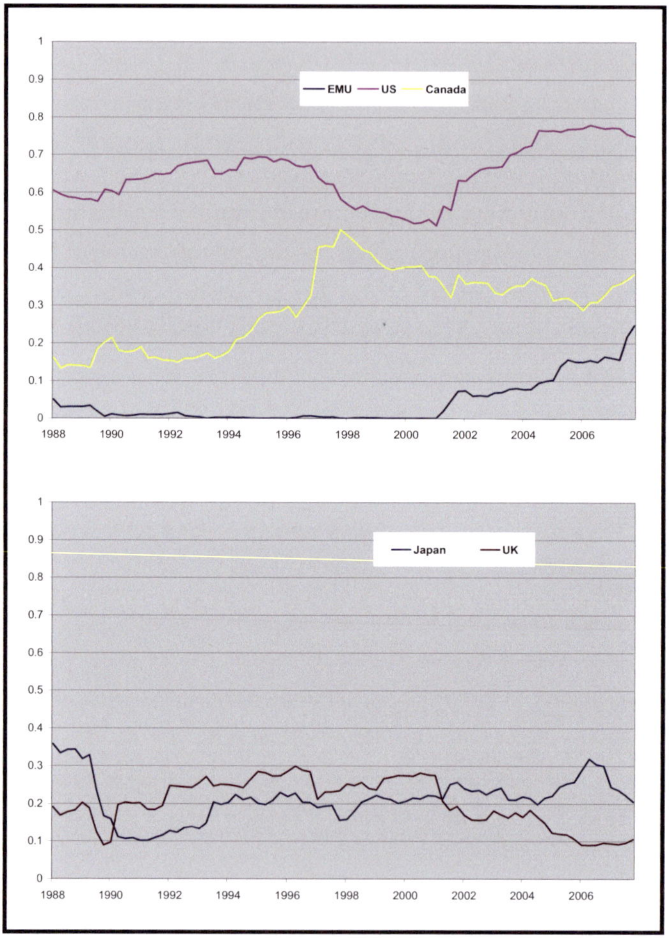

In a final step, structural break tests are applied for both global and idiosyncratic excess liquidity shocks. The global disturbance η_t in the dynamic factor model is derived from equation (6.3.1) which has been described in detail above and is briefly presented again for convenience:

$$F_t = \Phi(L)F_{t-1} + \eta_t \text{ where } \Phi(L) = \begin{cases} \Phi_1(L), t \leq \kappa \\ \Phi_2(L), t > \kappa \end{cases}, \text{ var}(\eta_t) = \begin{cases} \sigma_1^2, t \leq \tau \\ \sigma_2^2, t > \tau \end{cases} \quad (6.3.1)$$

The formulation allows for the conditional mean and the conditional variance to break at potentially different dates (Stock, Watson 2002a, p. 11). This is important, since the Quandt-Andrews breakpoint test based on the wild bootstrapping approach found instability in the persistence parameter ρ in Q4 1981 (cf. table 6.8). In order not to confound breaks in propagation (ρ) and shocks (η^{PC1}) for $PC1$, a dummy variable d_t for ρ is constructed. Equation (6.3.4) is then transformed and re-estimated as follows:

(6.3.8) $$PC1_t = \rho PC1_{t-1} + \rho^d d_t PC1_{t-1} + \sum_{s=1}^{K-1} \beta_s \Delta PC1_{t-s} + \eta'^{PC1}_t$$

where d_t takes the value zero from Q1 1973 to Q3 1981 and one afterwards. The persistence parameter is equal to ρ from Q1 1973 to Q3 1981 and to $\rho + \rho^d$ thereafter. The global shock η'^{PC1}_t denotes the error when ρ breaks in Q4 1981. The same procedure is followed for testing whether the idiosyncratic elements v^{PC1}_t derived from equation (6.3.7) are prone to instability. This is necessary, since the Quandt-Andrews test finds breaks in the factor loadings for the EMU, the UK and Canada (cf. table 6.9). Accordingly, equation (6.3.7) is augmented with the dummy variable l_t:

(6.3.9) $$X_t = \Lambda^{PC1} PC1_t + \Lambda^{PC1}_l l_t PC1_t + D(L) X_{t-1} + v'^{PC1}_t$$

with v'^{PC1}_t as idiosyncratic disturbance vector when some of the factor loadings included in vector Λ^{PC1} break at the corresponding dates. Two examples shall clarify the procedure. In case of the EMU, the Quandt-Andrews test indicates a structural break in the factor loading in Q2 1994. The dummy variable l_t is therefore zero from Q1 1973 to Q1 1994 and one afterwards. In case of the US and Japan, the Quandt-Andrews test does not report significant instability in the factor loadings. The estimate (6.3.9) therefore reduces to the above-presented expression (6.3.7) with v^{PC1}_t as idiosyncratic disturbance vector:

(6.3.7) $$X_t = \Lambda^{PC1} PC1_t + D(L) X_{t-1} + v^{PC1}_t$$

In a final step, the absolute values of the global and idiosyncratic shocks (η'^{PC1}_t, v'^{PC1}_t and v^{PC1}_t) in equations (6.3.7), (6.3.8) and (6.3.9) are regressed against a constant c. For instance, the null hypothesis of no structural break in the global excess liquidity shocks is as follows:

$$(6.3.10) \qquad E\,|\,\eta'^{PC1}_t(\kappa^{PC1})\,|= c$$

where $\eta'^{PC1}_t(\kappa^{PC1})$ denote the residuals when there is a break in the persistence parameter of global excess liquidity in form of the first principal component at date κ^{PC1} (cf. also expression 6.3.1). Under the alternative hypothesis that there is instability in the global excess liquidity shocks at date τ^{PC1} (cf. expression 6.3.1), the following expression is true:

$$(6.3.11) \qquad E\,|\,\eta'^{PC1}_t(\kappa^{PC1})\,|= c_{1p} + \varsigma(t \geq \tau^{PC1})$$

with c_{1p} as the first period shock and ς as the difference between the disturbance before and after the break.

The Quandt-Andrews test based on equation (6.3.10) indicates no sharp break of global excess liquidity shocks on conventional significance levels of less than 10 percent (cf. table 6.11).[49] Hence, neither the result of a "Great Moderation" sometimes found in the business cycle literature nor the hypothesis of a "Great Acceleration" in global excess liquidity disturbances can be postulated.

In contrast, when regressing the idiosyncratic shocks against a constant, signs of instability are partly found. This is true for the US, the EMU and Canada and may indicate that volatility breaks are essentially domestic phenomena, thereby depending on the specific conditions and policies in each country. Furthermore, there is no communality of break dates, since the three instabilities occur in Q2 1990 for the US, Q2 1993 for the EMU and Q2 1982 for Canada. However, the extent of the volatility reduction is at least partly of comparable size. Idiosyncratic excess liquidity shocks in the US decline by 42.8% after the break date compared to the disturbances occurring before. In the EMU, the shock size drops by 47.1% (Canada: -34.9%). In contrast to this work, van Dijk, Osborn and Sensier (2002, p. 8) find positive changes in volatility for nominal time series across the G7 countries. However, besides using other variables, they focus on monetary aggregates and do not deal with excess liquidities.

[49] Stock and Watson (2002a, p. 46) point out that homoskedastic standard errors are valid under the null hypothesis of no structural break in the residuals. Hence, the Quandt-Andrews test can be done on the basis of simple OLS regressions.

In addition, the observed volatility change may still mirror a trend decline. Hence, the Quandt-Andrews tests for the US, the EMU and Canada are repeated by regressing the idiosyncratic errors against a constant and an additional time trend. In all three cases, structural instability cannot be found any longer for idiosyncratic excess liquidity shocks. This evidence is indicative of a gradual decline in the country-specific disturbances instead of the assumed sudden one-off break in the Quandt-Andrews test.

Table 6.11: Quandt-Andrews breakpoint tests for shocks

	Global shock			
	Break date	sup-LR F (constant)	Change in shock, in %	sup-LR F (constant + trend)
Global	1983 Q4	4.69	---	---
	Idiosyncratic shocks			
US	1990 Q2	17.49***	-42.81	2.74
EMU	1993 Q2	16.63***	-47.06	4.22
Japan	2001 Q1	3.27	---	---
UK	1979 Q2	5.08	---	---
Canada	1982 Q2	7.74*	-34.90	5.57

Note: *** Indicates significance at 1% level, ** at 5% level, * at 10% level

The above-estimated rolling regressions for deriving the global persistence parameter and the R-squared measures (cf. equations 6.3.4 and 6.3.7) are used for comparing the two different types of shocks over time: the global excess liquidity disturbance captured by the error term η_t^{PC1} and the idiosyncratic innovations v_t^{PC1}. Figure 6.3 shows the results and is interpreted as follows. Since a moving 15-year window is used again, the values for Q1 1988 show the average errors $|\eta_t^{PC1}|$ and $|v_t^{PC1}|$ from Q1 1973 to Q4 1987. Moreover, for enabling a better comparison, the shocks are indexed with Q1 1988 equaling one. In general, both the global and the country-specific disturbances decline over time. At the end of the sample, the global excess liquidity shock is 24.5% lower compared to the starting level at the beginning. Although the magnitude differs, the same phenomenon is also found for the idiosyncratic disturbances. In Q4 2007, the strongest decreases can be found for the EMU with 43.9% and for the US with 40.2%. Even in the case of Japan, a reduction of 13.4% occurs, although the idiosyncratic shocks do not decline on average until 2005.

Figure 6.3: Comparison of global and idiosyncratic shocks (Index Q1 1988=1)

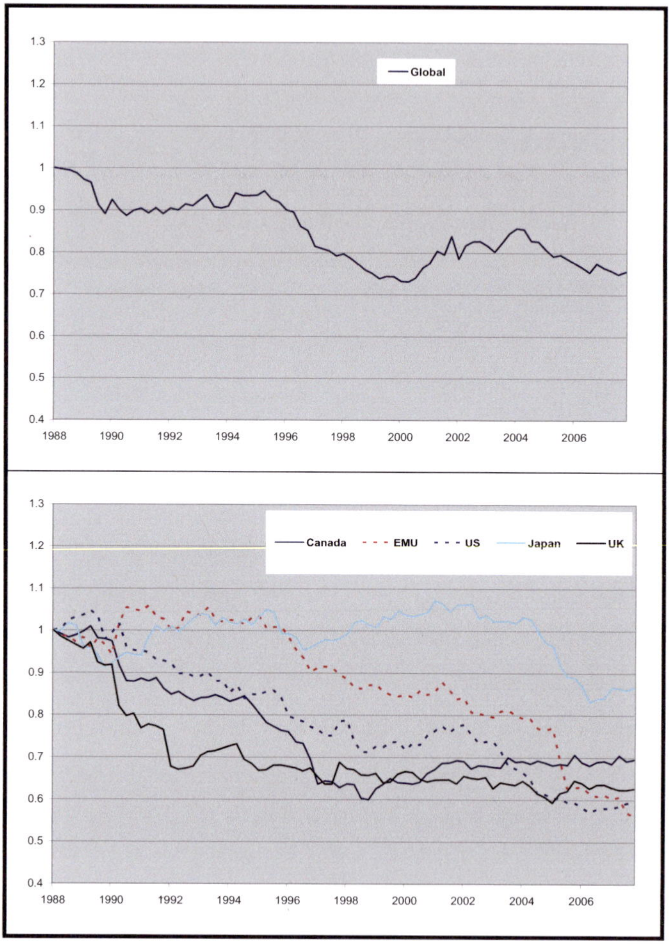

Unfortunately, these results do not provide clear-cut evidence as to whether global excess liquidity shocks have become more important in comparison to country-specific disturbances. Since v_t^{PC1} in the EMU, the US, the UK and Canada decrease stronger than η_t^{PC1}, one may be tempted to argue that the conditional variance of the common factor plays an increasingly prominent role on a national level. However, only in the theoretical ceteris paribus case, it is possible to make inferences about the changing relative importance of global and idiosyncratic shocks (Monfort, Renne,

Rüffer et al. 2003, p. 10). In reality, other factors can dominate the development of the two variances. For example, it is still conceivable that there is an autonomous decline in country-specific volatility due to a lower measurement error in broad monetary aggregates and nominal GDP. Such a finding would be merely suggestive of an increasing role of global excess liquidity shocks. In addition, it is important to keep in mind that rolling regressions implicitly assume a gradual change in coefficients and hence error terms. Alternatively, there may be temporary outbursts of volatility with the variables undergoing multiple sharp breaks. For instance, the first change is a comparatively small increase in the shocks, the second one a relatively large decline. Testing for smooth changes in such an environment can then be quite misleading.

From a general viewpoint, there is one additional critique. Inevitably, disturbances derived from only one equation each do not represent structural shocks, as the interconnectedness of variables across countries cannot be taken into account. Differences between monetary aggregates and other economic variables might be blurred in univariate autoregressive settings. In order to identify a more reasonable economic structure, VAR and FAVAR (Factor augmented VAR) models are estimated in the following. The parameters will be used to capture the structure of the system, while the residuals will be the shocks.

Before turning to the VAR and FAVAR section in the next chapter, a short summary of the so far obtained empirical evidence is given. Although the conditions for qualifying as a global factor are not met unequivocally, the results point towards the existence of a common (excess) liquidity force in the form of $PC1$. The Granger causality tests show comparatively sparse evidence of lagged international monetary spillover effects. This is also true for a shorter data sample which takes rising financial globalization since the 1990s into account. One reason might be that international capital flows occur rather quickly. The Quandt-Andrews breakpoint test in combination with a wild bootstrapping approach uncovers signs of instability in the persistence parameter of global excess liquidity. On basis of a rolling 15-year window, a gradual increase in persistence from 1988 to 1997 is found. The comparison of factor loadings for sub-samples partly shows rising impact coefficients of $PC1$ on national excess monies. Rolling regressions reveal an increasing explanatory power of the first principal component for domestic excess liquidities in the US, Canada and the EMU. Finally, both global and idiosyncratic shocks across countries and regions decline over time.

"[...] empirical work on monetary policy has reached the point where many people find it more natural to put commodity prices than money in VARs."

(Leeper, Roush 2003, p. 1218)

7 INTERNATIONAL TRANSMISSION IN STRUCTURAL MODELS

VAR and FAVAR models allow estimating monetary spillover effects in a structural context. The challenge is to find a suitable identification pattern for deriving the impact of global excess liquidity shocks on domestic variables. Impulse response and variance decomposition analysis are used to compare whether the results are in line with the hypotheses postulated in section 4.

7.1 OPEN ECONOMY VARS

The analysis starts with simple standard open economy VARs for the G7 countries and the euro zone. Afterwards, a VAR model solely for the EMU is analyzed in greater depth.

7.1.1 G7 COUNTRIES PLUS EURO ZONE

It is assumed that each G7 economy including the EMU can be described by the following structural form equation (Kim, Roubini 2000, p. 565):

(7.1.1.1) $$G(L)X_t = \varepsilon_t$$

where $G(L)$ is a $N \times N$ matrix polynomial in the lag operator L and X_t is a $N \times 1$ data vector, ε_t is a $N \times 1$ serially uncorrelated structural disturbances vector with $\mathrm{var}(\varepsilon_t) = \Theta$ and Θ as diagonal matrix where the diagonal elements are the variances of the structural shocks. Equation (7.1.1.1) can be estimated via a reduced-form VAR. The latter is a regression of the vector X_t on its own lags. Formally, the reduced-form VAR of order k can be written as

(7.1.1.2) $$X_t = A(L)X_{t-1} + u_t$$

with $A(L)$ as lag polynomial of order k and u_t as $N \times 1$ vector of reduced-form residuals. The evolution of the vector X_t depends both on a systematic component in form of the VAR coefficients $A(L)$ and on unexpected disturbances u_t. The VAR coefficients reflect the structure of the economy and determine how the shocks are propagated through the economy. While the reduced-form representation in (7.1.1.2) can consistently be estimated by OLS, the challenge is to identify the structural shocks of the VAR. The problem is that the reduced-form residuals u_t may in general be correlated, thereby constituting a linear combination of some "structural" and some "non-fundamental" disturbances. It is therefore necessary to add more structure and transform the reduced-form approach into a structural model by pre-multiplying the above equation by the $N \times N$ matrix A_0 (Enders 2004, p. 292f.; Caldara, Kamps 2008, p. 12):

(7.1.1.3) $$A_0 X_t = A_0 A(L) X_{t-1} + A_0 u_t = A_0 A(L) X_{t-1} + \varepsilon_t$$

where A_0 describes the contemporaneous relation among the variables collected in the vector X_t, thereby providing a mapping between the structural shocks and the reduced-form representations ($\varepsilon_t = A_0 u_t$). Hence, if one knows A_0, then the parameters and disturbances in the structural model can be recovered by estimating the reduced form of the VAR. A multitude of assumptions for matrix A_0 is proposed in the literature (Bracke, Fidora 2008, p. 12f.): a recursive ordering of variables (Cholesky decomposition), contemporaneous restrictions on the error term, restrictions on the long-run dynamics via cointegration, a decomposition in temporary and permanent components (Blanchard-Quah) and imposing sign restrictions on the impulse response functions.

In the following, the Cholesky factorization is used by assuming that the contemporaneous coefficient matrix A_0 is lower triangular. Since the variance-covariance matrix of the reduced-form errors contains $N(N+1)/2$ free parameters, identifying A_0 requires imposing $N(N-1)/2$ restrictions. This approach implies a recursive structure, that is a Wold-causal chain. If there is a significantly high contemporaneous co-movement between two reduced-form innovations, then the complete effect is assigned to the disturbance that comes first in the VAR ordering.[50] As

[50] According to Enders (2004, p. 277), the correlation is deemed to be significantly high when $|corr| > 0.2$ with $corr$ as correlation coefficient. This is the case in each of the estimated VARs.

can be seen in equation (7.1.1.4) below, the error terms for each country or region are assumed to follow this specific causal ordering: commodity price innovations (CP) $\triangleright$ real GDP innovations (YR) $\triangleright$ consumer price innovations (PI) $\triangleright$ broad monetary aggregate innovations (abbreviated to M3 for reasons of notational simplicity) $\triangleright$ short-term interest rate innovations (SR) $\triangleright$ real effective exchange rate innovations (ER).[51] Under this scheme, commodity prices are regarded as the most exogenous reading, since they are not influenced contemporaneously by all the other variables. For example, it is not possible that changes in national economic activity lead to variations in commodity prices within one quarter. Instead, and exclusively, it only works the other way around. This is not a critical assumption for small economies like the UK and Canada, since their demand for raw materials in general should be comparatively small. However, it could be critical in case of the US where the reverse contemporaneous causal relationship (YR $\triangleright$ CP) may hold as well.[52]

The real effective exchange rate (ER) denotes the other extreme in the causal ordering above, since ER is assumed to be the most endogenous variable. As a forward-looking asset price, it may respond very quickly to all disturbances. Hence, exchange rate shocks are modeled as a combination of all innovations included in the VAR.

Short-term interest rate disturbances (SR) have no contemporaneous impact on any of the variables apart from the effective exchange rate. For instance, economic activity and prices take at least one quarter to respond to short-term interest rate innovations. Such a pattern can be rationalized by time lags between changes in monetary policy and variations in GDP and consumer prices. Any contemporaneous correlation between SR and YR/PI is thus taken to reflect causation from output and prices to the monetary policy variable and not the other way around. Hence, the central bank is assumed to take into account the contemporaneous state of commodity prices, real activity, consumer prices and monetary aggregates before possibly changing the short-term interest rate. However, such an ordering scheme is open to debate. In many countries and regions, data on GDP, prices and monetary aggregates are not available within the respective quarter but only later. However, partial information is often available through the quarter.

[51] Please note that for commodity prices the HWWI price index converted in the respective national currency is used for each country or region.
[52] Exogeneity tests in form of Granger causality tests cannot solve this problem, since they assume time lags for the relation between US GDP and commodity prices.

The recursive ordering also implies a function for money demand which is contemporaneously dependent on commodity prices, real activity and consumer price inflation. On the one hand, it can be argued that such an identification is critical, since the CPI already includes some commodity prices. On the other hand, Sims (1992, p. 988ff.) suggests including commodity prices as proxy for future inflation pressure. This in turn may alleviate the so-called price puzzle which is explained in greater detail below. Please note that the short-term interest rate is ordered after the broad monetary aggregate, i.e. the interest elasticity of money demand is assumed to be zero.

$$\begin{bmatrix} 1 & 0 & 0 & 0 & 0 & 0 \\ a_{21} & 1 & 0 & 0 & 0 & 0 \\ a_{31} & a_{32} & 1 & 0 & 0 & 0 \\ a_{41} & a_{42} & a_{43} & 1 & 0 & 0 \\ a_{51} & a_{52} & a_{53} & a_{54} & 1 & 0 \\ a_{61} & a_{62} & a_{63} & a_{64} & a_{65} & 1 \end{bmatrix} \begin{bmatrix} u_t^{CP} \\ u_t^{YR} \\ u_t^{PI} \\ u_t^{M3} \\ u_t^{SR} \\ u_t^{ER} \end{bmatrix} = \begin{bmatrix} \varepsilon_t^{CP} \\ \varepsilon_t^{YR} \\ \varepsilon_t^{PI} \\ \varepsilon_t^{M3} \\ \varepsilon_t^{SR} \\ \varepsilon_t^{ER} \end{bmatrix} \tag{7.1.1.4}$$

with a as coefficient in the A_0 matrix.

The data sample for estimating the VAR models for the G7 and the euro zone ranges from Q1 1984 to Q4 2007. There are two reasons for shortening the time horizon in comparison to chapter 6. First, the obtained results can be compared to previous empirical work which typically starts in the 1980s (Rüffer, Stracca 2006; Sousa, Zaghini 2007; Belke, Orth, Setzer 2010). Second, as shown by the results from the autoregressive approaches in the previous chapter, a longer sample contains the risk of contaminating the results with structural breaks. In the 1970s, two oil price shocks occurred. Moreover, from 1979 to 1982, regime shifts in the behavior of the Federal Reserve took place (Huizinga, Mishkin 1986). Such instabilities have nothing to do with structural variation triggered by rising international capital flows and the phenomenon of global liquidity.

All variables included in the VARs apart from the short-term interest rate are transformed into log first differences. For the short-term interest rate, first differences are calculated. All series are standardized with a mean of zero and a variance of one. This procedure is necessary, since the impact of common excess liquidity shocks on the VAR disturbances will be analyzed later in this chapter. Please keep in mind that the global excess liquidity force is estimated by PCA on the basis of national log first differenced and *standardized* variables (cf. section 6.1). Afterwards, the series included in the VAR models are "re-constructed" in levels as follows. First, they are set equal to zero in the first quarter of 1984. Then, the cumulative sum of each variable is calculated.[53] In addition, a constant and a linear time trend are included in each VAR. Using series in levels implicitly assumes that the variables are jointly covariance-stationary. The examination of the VAR residuals by using unit root tests (Augmented Dickey-Fuller, Phillips-Perron, Kwiatkowski-Phillips-Schmidt-Shin) do not show any signs of non-stationarity (cf. appendix A.2).

There are both economic and statistical reasons for estimating the models in levels. Standard economic theory as described in chapter 2 usually refers to the variables in levels and not in first differences. Hence, deriving the VARs in first differences would make a direct connection between theory and empirical results difficult (Simon 2001, p. 15). From a statistical viewpoint, the specification in levels allows for implicit cointegrating relationships in the data (Sousa, Zaghini 2008, p. 207), although an explicit analysis of the long-run behavior of each economy is not performed in the following. In contrast, estimating the VARs in first differences could lead to a loss of information when the variables are I(1) and cointegrated.

The selection of the lag polynomial order k is based on the usual criteria such as the Likelihood Ratio test, the Final Prediction Error, the Akaike information criterion, the Schwarz criterion and the Hannan-Quinn criterion. Additionally, multivariate LM tests are implemented to detect serial correlation in the residuals. Accordingly, in case of the euro area, Japan, the UK and Canada a lag length of two seems to be appropriate. For the US, $k = 4$ is chosen. However, some minor autocorrelation in the residuals of the VAR models remains (cf. appendix A.3). This problem cannot be solved by adding more lags. Additionally, the test statistics for heteroskedasticity (White), ARCH effects (LM) and normality of the residuals (Jarque-Bera) are not always satisfactory (cf. appendix A.4-A.6). Hence, some caution is warranted when the results are interpreted in the following.[54]

[53] A comparable approach albeit for global and non-standardized variables can be found in Belke, Orth and Setzer (2010, p. 1936). The series are obtained by first choosing an initial value of 100 at the beginning of the sample. Then, the levels are calculated by multiplying with the corresponding growth rate.

[54] In the presence of autocorrelation and heteroskedasticity, the VAR coefficients estimated by OLS remain unbiased and consistent. However, they are not efficient any longer, i.e. the estimates of the

Furthermore, it is important to note that the assumption of orthogonal structural shocks in small-dimensional VARs is a strong one. The six equations in (7.1.1.4) imply that each economy in the G7 including the euro zone is only driven by six shocks. However, if the number of "true" disturbances is larger, the assumption of orthogonality does not hold and an omitted variable bias occurs. Certain considerations (or variables) are not taken into account in the VAR model and therefore end up in the error term. As a result, the omitted variables incorrectly become part of the estimated historical shocks used to derive impulse responses. In such a case, the six identified disturbances in (7.1.1.4) are linear combinations of the higher number of "true" original shocks. Key to addressing this problem is to increase the amount of information so that the innovations span the space of structural disturbances. But increasing the number of variables in a VAR inevitably creates the problem of parameter profligacy. If k lags of N variables are included, $k \times N^2$ free parameters have to be estimated. With N expanding, the degrees of freedom rapidly decline and inference becomes impossible (Eichenbaum, Evans 1995, p. 989).

A concrete example of shock mismeasurement is the price puzzle. When monetary policy disturbances are identified by innovations in the short-term interest rate, the responses of output and money supply are in line with economic theory. A monetary tightening is associated with a fall in the money supply and the output. However, the response of the price level is wrong, as a sudden increase in interest rates is associated with an increase in the price level rather than a decrease. Sims (1992) suggests that the price puzzle might be explained by an omitted variable bias and the forward-looking behavior of central banks when setting interest rates. Small-dimensional VARs do not consider variables which could be used to forecast future inflation. As a result, interest rate innovations also erroneously reflect inflationary pressures that lead to price increases. In order to identify price shocks properly, Sims (1992, p. 988ff.) suggests including commodity prices.

The problem of omitted variable bias and shock mismeasurement can especially occur in small-dimensional open economy VARs. Besides domestic influences, a multitude of other (neglected) variables from abroad may have an impact on the

standard errors will be smaller than the true standard errors. Furthermore, the violation of the i.i.d assumption can lead to inaccurate confidence bands in an impulse response analysis when a standard residual bootstrap procedure is used.

national economy as well. For instance, in the presence of increasing global capital flows, it is conceivable that changes in national monetary aggregates are not solely determined within each country. Instead, they might also be influenced by foreign monetary conditions, i.e. domestic money disturbances are not exogenous but endogenous to foreign money innovations. In order to test for such shock mismeasurements, global excess liquidity disturbances are derived by a simple AR(1) process in which the residuals are the shocks. Afterwards, heteroskedasticity-autocorrelation robust F-Wald tests are done for testing whether the monetary aggregate innovations derived from the recursive VARs above are contaminated by common excess liquidity disturbances.[55]

An example for the EMU shall clarify the procedure further. In the first step, a global excess liquidity factor excluding the euro zone is estimated by applying PCA and deriving the first principal component (GEL_exEMU_t). The PCA is based on national excess liquidities in the US, Japan, the UK and Canada. As is standard in factor analysis, the domestic variables are standardized with a mean of zero and a variance of one. In the second step, the following AR(1) process is estimated:

$$(7.1.1.5) \qquad GEL\_exEMU_t = bGEL\_exEMU_{t-1} + \vartheta_t^{GEL\_exEMU}$$

with GEL_exEMU_t as global excess money force outside the euro area at time t, equaling the first principal component ($PC1$) and b as autoregressive coefficient. $\vartheta_t^{GEL\_exEMU}$ is the global excess liquidity shock excluding the EMU at time t. Afterwards, the following estimate is applied:

$$(7.1.1.6) \qquad \varepsilon_t^{EMU\_M3} = c_0\vartheta_t^{GEL\_exEMU} + c_1\vartheta_{t-1}^{GEL\_exEMU} + c_2\vartheta_{t-2}^{GEL\_exEMU}$$

The money disturbances in the euro zone are the residuals in the recursive VAR ($\varepsilon_t^{EMU\_M3}$). Finally, a heteroskedasticity-autocorrelation robust Wald test is done by applying the Newey-West estimator. The null hypothesis assumes all of the coefficients to be jointly equal to zero, that is $c_0 = c_1 = c_2 = 0$. The null hypothesis therefore states that money shocks in the euro area are not significantly influenced by global excess liquidity disturbances. Please note that the F-test is based on a regression with only the

[55] Impulse response analysis is not done here but in the following chapter where national VAR models for the EMU will be augmented by the global excess liquidity force.

current global excess liquidity disturbance ($\vartheta_t^{GEL\_exEMU}$) and two quarterly lags ($\vartheta_{t-1}^{GEL\_exEMU}$ and $\vartheta_{t-2}^{GEL\_exEMU}$) as independent variables. The reason for only including global excess liquidity shocks up to six months is that international capital is assumed to flow rather quickly after a common money disturbance.

The above-described procedure is repeated for the US, Japan, the UK and Canada. In addition to global disturbances, national excess liquidity shocks are derived by a simple AR(1) process and tested for significance by the same type of Wald tests (cf. equation 7.1.1.6). This allows examining to what extent national monetary conditions spill over to other economies. Table 7.1 shows the results for all conceivable Wald tests.[56] Accordingly, in the case of the euro zone, the null hypothesis is rejected. The EMU money shocks are not exogenous to foreign money spillovers but also influenced by common liquidity factor disturbances. The corresponding F-statistic is 4.67 with $p \leq 0.01$. The coefficient c_0 which reflects the contemporaneous influence of global excess liquidity shocks on $\varepsilon_t^{EMU\_M3}$ is significantly different from zero and has a positive sign in line with theoretical considerations. The same is true for c_2. The excess liquidity innovations in Japan and Canada also exert a significant influence on $\varepsilon_t^{EMU\_M3}$. Apart from the euro area, an omitted variable bias can only be detected in the UK. For the US, Japan and Canada, the null hypothesis of the Wald test that the coefficients c_0, c_1 and c_2 are zero cannot be rejected for all specifications.

In addition to the disturbances derived from simple autoregressive settings, the innovations from the money equations in the recursive VAR models are used as regressors for the Wald test. For instance, it is examined whether the broad US money disturbance obtained by estimating the US VAR significantly influences the M3 shock in the EMU at time t obtained by estimating the EMU VAR:

$$\varepsilon_t^{EMU\_M3} = c_0\varepsilon_t^{US\_M2} + c_1\varepsilon_{t-1}^{US\_M2} + c_2\varepsilon_{t-2}^{US\_M2} \quad (7.1.1.7)$$

The evidence is indicative of asymmetries, since monetary spillover effects seemingly do not occur uniformly across countries or regions. In some cases, the null hypothesis of the heteroskedasticity-robust Wald test ($c_0 = c_1 = c_2 = 0$) can be rejected, in others not.

[56] Please refer to the first figure in each cell in the following. The second figure is based on additional VAR estimates which are explained later.

For example, and surprisingly, the money market in a small open economy like Canada seems to be insulated from the impact of foreign broad monies.[57] The opposite conclusion holds for the US and the euro area. Money shocks from the US, Japan and the UK have a significant impact on EMU money disturbances. Broad money innovations stemming from the euro area, the UK and Canada exert a significant influence on US liquidity shocks.[58] In each case, the contemporaneous coefficient c_0 is positive and highly significant. The results may indicate that monetary spillover effects influence particularly large countries or regions with deep and attractive financial markets. For the euro zone, this might be true at least since the start of the EMU in 1999. Another reason may be differences in the transmission channels and/or policy behavior. Japan barely seems to be affected by foreign monetary spillover effects which could be explained by the special circumstances and the strong idiosyncratic patterns since the beginning of the 1990s.[59]

Table 7.1: Testing for omitted excess liquidity shocks in G7 VARs

	Additional excess liquidity shocks					
National VARs	Global	US	EMU	Japan	UK	Canada
US	1.49	---	0.26/7.09***	1.31/0.44	1.39/2.91**	1.18/2.28*
EMU	4.67***	1.69/7.35***	---	2.87**/3.00**	1.80/3.50**	3.21**/0.81
Japan	0.12	0.62/0.92	2.00/1.40	---	0.39/0.93	0.02/1.40
UK	5.15***	3.93**/5.33***	0.79/6.20***	1.06/0.28	---	2.18*/1.38
Canada	0.12	2.03/0.52	0.24/0.07	0.18/1.29	0.11/0.51	---

Note 1: F-statistics of heteroskedasticity-autocorrelation robust Wald tests (first figure based on autoregressive approach; second figure based on VAR)

Note 2: *** Indicates significance at 1% level, ** at 5% level, * at 10% level

In order to get a yardstick for comparison, the above-described Wald tests are repeated for innovations in the short-term interest rate. More precisely, it is tested whether interest rate shocks in the "Big-3" (US, EMU and Japan) influence the VAR interest rate disturbances of other countries. Again, the error terms are derived by using simple AR(1) processes and applying recursive VAR models. The autoregressive

---

[57] This is independent of whether national or global disturbances from autoregressive estimates or VAR models are used.

[58] Hence, augmenting national VAR models by global excess liquidity seems to be an interesting issue for empirical examination. This is done for the EMU in the next chapter.

[59] The overall results remain robust when different specifications for the recursive VAR models are tried. In appendix A.7, an example can be found where two changes in comparision to (7.1.1.4) are implemented. First, commodity prices are ordered last in the system. Since participants on commodity markets price in all available information, commodity prices may also be regarded as the most endogenous variable. Second, money is ordered after the short-term interest rate, thereby assuming a non-zero interest elasticity of money demand. When this identification pattern is used, global excess liquidity shocks derived from a AR(1) model significantly influence not only money disturbances in the EMU and the UK but also in the US.

estimates are done both for nominal and real short-term interest rate shocks. The latter are based on the difference between the nominal short-term interest rates and the corresponding yearly increases in domestic consumer prices. The results suggest that monetary spillover effects between countries or regions do not occur exclusively in form of international capital flows. Spillover effects between monetary aggregates are therefore not "unique". Instead, an international interest rate channel also seems to be at work. For instance, interest rate innovations in the US and Japan influence short-term interest rate shocks in all the other countries. At the same time, the euro zone "exports" short-term interest rate disturbances abroad. One explanation for this cross-border pattern could be that unexpected changes in foreign short-term interest rates lead to exchange rate variations. This in turn may have undesirable effects on domestic output and prices, thereby leading to changes in the national monetary policy stance via the short-term interest rate.

Table 7.2: Testing for omitted interest rate shocks in G7 VARs

	Additional 3M interest rate shocks		
National VARs	US	EMU	Japan
US	---	1.59/0.34/2.23*	2.78**/1.46/16.40***
EMU	0.72/3.37**/2.09	---	3.92**/0.72/2.21*
Japan	2.10/0.75/5.30***	1.60/2.35*/2.16*	---
UK	3.31**/2.49*/1.20	1.72/1.41/6.80***	1.52/2.62*/3.94**
Canada	7.99***/5.00***/1.51	1.33/6.06***/3.16**	9.90***/3.32**/7.08***

Note 1: F-statistics of heteroskedasticity-autocorrelation robust Wald tests; the first two figures are based on autoregressive approaches (nominal and price-adjusted shocks), the third figure is based on VAR
Note 2: *** Indicates significance at 1% level, ** at 5% level, * at 10% level

However, there are two important caveats to such an interpretation and to the simple Wald tests in general independent of whether money or interest rate disturbances are examined. First, other global forces apart from money or short-term interest rates could still be behind these effects. For example, central banks may react simultaneously to sudden changes in global GDP or commodity prices, i.e. monetary spillover effects actually do not take place but only reflect other common shocks. Second, the results are not unambiguous. For instance, money and interest rate shocks from the EMU influence the corresponding innovations in the US and vice versa.

In the next chapter, a different approach is pursued for the euro area: a global liquidity-augmented VAR.

7.1.2 EMU

As suggested by the Wald tests, international liquidity spillover effects seem to play a role for the euro area. The assumption that the central bank responds to exogenous national money which is not influenced by foreign monetary conditions may therefore not be valid. Instead, monetary policy reacts to endogenous disturbances, since national liquidity is influenced by developments on foreign money markets. Kim (2001, p. 342) suggests a "marginal method" to exclude systematic responses of central banks to shocks from abroad. A variable that reflects the state of the global economy in the monetary reaction function is added to the model. Accordingly, the Cholesky VAR for the EMU presented in the previous chapter is augmented by the global excess liquidity factor exluding money in the euro area (GEL_exEMU). The latter is derived by PCA in form of the first principal component. A block exogeneity test is strongly rejected, i.e. it seems to be useful to incorporate global excess liquidity into the VAR. This general approach – augmenting a VAR by estimated factors, then performing standard identification – is also pursued by Favero, Marcellino (2004) and Favero, Marcellino and Neglia (2005).

The concrete identification form of the recursive global-liquidity augmented VAR is as follows:

$$\begin{bmatrix} 1 & 0 & 0 & 0 & 0 & 0 & 0 \\ a_{21} & 1 & 0 & 0 & 0 & 0 & 0 \\ a_{31} & a_{32} & 1 & 0 & 0 & 0 & 0 \\ a_{41} & a_{42} & a_{43} & 1 & 0 & 0 & 0 \\ a_{51} & a_{52} & a_{53} & a_{54} & 1 & 0 & 0 \\ a_{61} & a_{62} & a_{63} & a_{64} & a_{65} & 1 & 0 \\ a_{71} & a_{72} & a_{73} & a_{74} & a_{75} & a_{76} & 1 \end{bmatrix} \begin{bmatrix} u_t^{CP} \\ u_t^{GEL\_exEMU} \\ u_t^{YR} \\ u_t^{PI} \\ u_t^{M3} \\ u_t^{SR} \\ u_t^{ER} \end{bmatrix} = \begin{bmatrix} \varepsilon_t^{CP} \\ \varepsilon_t^{GEL\_exEMU} \\ \varepsilon_t^{YR} \\ \varepsilon_t^{PI} \\ \varepsilon_t^{M3} \\ \varepsilon_t^{SR} \\ \varepsilon_t^{ER} \end{bmatrix} \quad (7.1.2.1)$$

It is assumed that global excess liquidity excluding the euro zone ($\varepsilon_t^{GEL\_exEMU}$) contemporaneously influence all the other variables apart from commodity prices (ε_t^{CP}).[60] However, and clearly, such a recursive identification scheme has a low degree of flexibility, thereby not fully reflecting the complexities in the arena of international policy interdependence. For example, Cushman and Zha (1997, p. 434), Kim and

[60] In the following SVAR, it is alternatively assumed that global money affects commodity prices contemporaneously but not vice versa.

Roubini (2000, p. 564) and Faust and Rogers (2003, p. 1409) argue that in the era of increasingly integrated goods and capital markets, open economies are vulnerable to external shocks. Not allowing central banks to react contemporaneously to some crucial foreign variables can therefore cause a misidentification of central bank behavior and result in an erroneous measure of the monetary policy disturbance. In this context, it is typically referred to a recursive VAR which does not allow the short-term interest rate and the exchange rate to react simultaneously to each other. As a result, exchange rate puzzles can occur, since small open economies might often be concerned about the effects of a depreciation of their currencies on inflation.

The extension of global excess liquidity to the basic recursive system can add to these misspecification problems. In particular, the Cholesky VAR simply implies that the central bank looks at global excess liquidity before setting its key interest rate ($GEL\_exEMU \triangleright SR$). This scheme does not take into account possible feedback effects from the euro zone to the rest of the world. Ceteris paribus, a higher EMU short-term interest rate contemporaneously attracts international capital flows to the euro zone and therefore may have an impact on global excess liquidity ($SR \triangleright GEL\_exEMU$). In other words, the common liquidity force might be less exogenous than assumed in equation (7.1.2.1). The same is true for the relationship between national money and global excess liquidity. In the Cholesky approach, a simple one-directional causal ordering is assumed ($GEL\_exEMU \triangleright M3$), although feedback effects are also conceivable ($M3 \triangleright GEL\_exEMU$).

Leeper and Roush (2003, p. 1231) point to an additional problem, since the recursive identification scheme takes an extreme stand on the contemporaneous interaction between national money and the short-term interest rate. Either the interest elasticity of money demand or the interest elasticity of money supply is constrained to be zero. In equation (7.1.2.1) above, national money is predetermined for the interest rate ($M3 \triangleright SR$). Accordingly, the interest elasticity of money demand is implicitly assumed to be zero. In the opposite case ($SR \triangleright M3$), national money does not play any role in explaining contemporaneous central bank behavior. The interest rate cannot directly respond to disturbances in the monetary aggregate and is therefore inelastic to money supply changes. The omission of simultaneity between the two variables may result in a misspecification of the model.

Since complex economic relations cannot be described fully appropriately in the recursive approach, an additional structural VAR (SVAR) is estimated for comparison. The SVAR allows to postulate more reasonable contemporaneous interactions among variables (cf. expression 7.1.2.2 below). For instance, in the spirit of Leeper and Roush (2003), the interest elasticities of money supply and demand are determined freely, thereby implying that SR and $M3$ are simultaneous phenomena. The monetary authority reacts to the exchange rate and global excess liquidity but not to economic activity (YR) and prices (PI) due to publication lags.[61] In addition, the contemporaneous impact of commodity prices (CP) on central bank behavior is constrained to be zero. Otherwise, the VAR model is not locally identified and the matrix of disturbances cannot be derived. Obviously, it is not possible to estimate the relation between commodity prices and the short-term interest rate when simultaneously an identification between SR and GEL_exEMU is chosen. Feedback effects are allowed between $M3$ and GEL_exEMU, i.e. global excess liquidity can have a contemporaneous impact on the national monetary aggregate and vice versa. The same is true for the relation SR-GEL_exEMU. The central bank takes global excess liquidity outside the euro zone into account before setting its key interest rate. At the same time, it is possible that changes in the short-term interest rate have an impact on GEL_exEMU. In contrast to the Cholesky VAR, an alternative specification is also implemented for the relation between global excess liquidity and commodity prices: GEL_exEMU contemporaneously influences CP but not vice versa. In line with the concept of currency substitution (cf. chapter 2.1.2), $M3$ can be influenced by the effective exchange rate (ER). Economic activity (YR) is not affected at the same time by any other variables, given time lags in the transmission mechanism. Consumer prices (PI) are only contemporaneously influenced by changes in commodity prices and the exchange rate. As has been the case before, the exchange rate is regarded as a forward-looking asset price which responds to all other variables in the model. The following equation shows the complete structural disturbances matrix:

[61] As mentioned before, the central bank may have partial information on GDP and consumer prices within the quarter. However, in order to get an alternative to the recursive VAR, this identification is implemented.

$$(7.1.2.2)\qquad \begin{bmatrix} 1 & a_{12} & a_{13} & 0 & 0 & 0 & 0 \\ 0 & 1 & 0 & 0 & a_{25} & a_{26} & 0 \\ 0 & 0 & 1 & 0 & 0 & 0 & 0 \\ a_{41} & 0 & 0 & 1 & 0 & 0 & a_{47} \\ 0 & a_{52} & a_{53} & a_{54} & 1 & a_{56} & a_{57} \\ 0 & a_{62} & 0 & 0 & a_{65} & 1 & a_{67} \\ a_{71} & a_{72} & a_{73} & a_{74} & a_{75} & a_{76} & 1 \end{bmatrix} \begin{bmatrix} u_t^{CP} \\ u_t^{GEL\_exEMU} \\ u_t^{YR} \\ u_t^{PI} \\ u_t^{M3} \\ u_t^{SR} \\ u_t^{ER} \end{bmatrix} = \begin{bmatrix} \varepsilon_t^{CP} \\ \varepsilon_t^{GEL\_exEMU} \\ \varepsilon_t^{YR} \\ \varepsilon_t^{PI} \\ \varepsilon_t^{M3} \\ \varepsilon_t^{SR} \\ \varepsilon_t^{ER} \end{bmatrix}$$

Since the SVAR includes 22 zero restrictions when only 21 are needed ($N(N-1)/2$ with $N=7$), the SVAR is overidentified. However, the corresponding Likelihood Ratio (LR) test suggests that the specified short-run restrictions cannot be rejected at conventional significance levels. The LR statistic equals 0.08 and the p-value is 0.77.

In order to determine the lag length of the global-liquidity augmented recursive VAR approach and the SVAR, the usual criteria, like the Final Prediction Error, the Akaike Information criterion, etc. are applied. Some of these criteria point at a lag length of two, some at a lag length of even eight. The Lagrange Multiplier (LM) test for detecting autocorrelation is performed additionally. A lag length of two seems to be appropriate to prevent strong autocorrelation among the residuals. However, a multivariate LM test suggests that some minor serial correlation remained. This problem cannot be solved by including more lags in the VAR. Furthermore, signs of heteroskedasticity in the residuals are found (White test), whereas ARCH effects do not play a significant role. The Jarque Bera test indicates that the null hypothesis of jointly normally distributed residuals is rejected (cf. appendix A.8). Overall, some caution is warranted when the results will be interpreted in the following.

As has been the case in the previous chapter, apart from the short-term interest rate, all euro area variables are transformed into log first differences. For the short-term interest rate, first differences are calculated. Afterwards, the series are standardized with a mean of zero and a variance of one and "re-constructed" in levels by setting them equal to zero in the first quarter of 1984. Finally, the cumulative sum of each series is calculated. The same is done for the common excess liquidity factor derived from PCA.

The two VARs each contain seven variables with two autoregressive lags plus a constant and a linear trend.[62] Hence, in each equation, a total of 16 free parameters has to be estimated. Since the sample covers the time period between Q1 1984 and Q4 2007, there are 96 quarterly observations available. This shall be enough to ensure sufficient degrees of freedom. Rüffer and Stracca (2006) use a comparably long sample and estimate 18 free parameters per equation.

In the following, impulse response analysis is used to shed light on possible effects and transmission mechanisms in the EMU after a positive one standard deviation shock to global excess liquidity. In each figure, the solid line represents the response. Since all variables are standardized, the responses are also expressed in standard deviations. The dashed lines are the 95% confidence intervals bootstrapped by a standard residual bootstrap procedure with 500 draws (Enders 2004, p. 234ff.). The time horizon of the impulse response analysis is 20 quarters.

After a global excess liquidity shock, the EMU monetary aggregate rises significantly from quarter two to quarter six in the recursive model. This may reflect an endogenous money and credit creation process triggered by international capital flows. However, in the SVAR, the response of euro zone M3 is persistently negative from quarter one to quarter fifteen, albeit not at significant levels.

[62] Unit root tests (Augmented Dickey-Fuller, Phillips-Perron and Kwiatkowski-Phillips-Schmidt-Shin) suggest that the obtained residuals are stationary (cf. appendix A.9).

Figure 7.1: Response of EMU money to global excess liquidity shock (Cholesky VAR in the upper chart; SVAR in the lower chart)

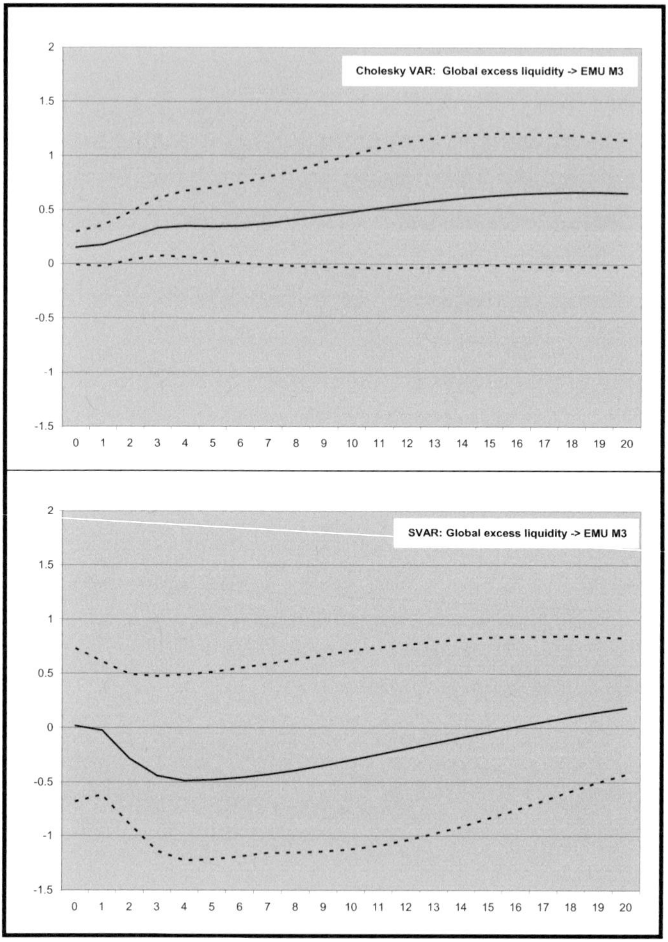

In both VAR models, a global excess liquidity shock has no significant impact on real GDP and consumer prices in the EMU (cf. figure 7.2). At the same time, it is important to note that a price puzzle does not occur either. In many empirical studies with small-scale VARs, the response of the price level to an interest rate or money supply disturbance is not in line with theoretical considerations. Monetary expansion is associated with a decline in the price level rather than an increase and vice versa.

Figure 7.2: Response of EMU GDP and CPI to global excess liquidity shock (Cholesky VAR in the upper chart; SVAR in the lower chart)

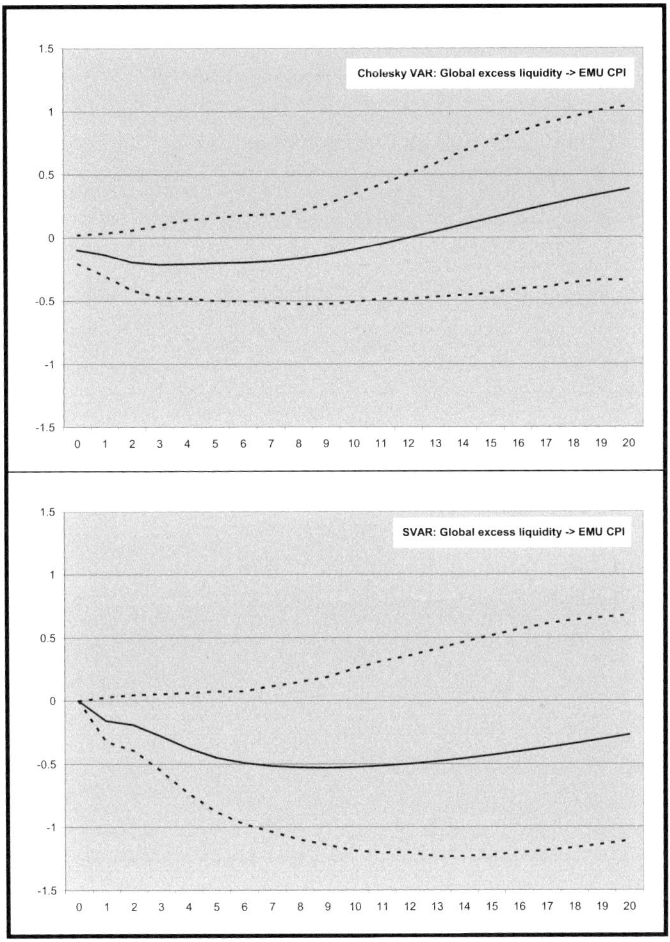

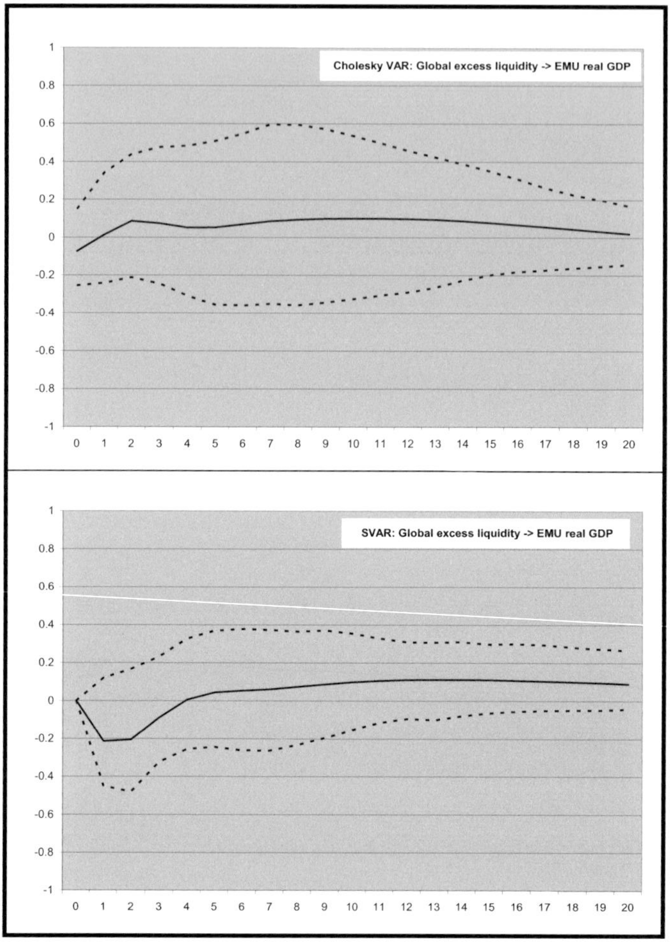

An interesting topic is the direct comparison of how the effective exchange rate and the short-term interest rate respond to a global excess liquidity shock. Besides an endogenous money and credit creation process in one country, there could be other mechanisms which are central in transmitting a global excess money shock to domestic variables. Consider again the monetarist model (chapter 2.1.1) and the Mundell-Fleming-Dornbusch (MFD) approach (2.1.3). In the spirit of these two theories, one may argue that a sudden change in monetary conditions abroad will primarily be reflected on foreign exchange markets. For instance, a positive global excess liquidity disturbance outside the euro zone leads to an appreciating EMU exchange rate and a beggar-thy-neighbor effect (MF model). The NOEM highlights the real interest rate as major transmission channel (chapter 2.1.4). Since prices remain initially sticky, a rise in global excess liquidity outside the euro zone may trigger a reduction in the foreign real interest rate. As a global capital market exists, the real interest rate in the EMU would also decline and cause a prosper-thy-neighbor effect.

The derived results seem to be somewhat more compatible with the monetarist approach and the MFD model than with the NOEM. At least, the Cholesky VAR indicates an immediate strengthening of the effective euro exchange rate. However, no pronounced overshooting or transitory effect occurs as suggested by theoretical considerations (Dornbusch, 1976). Instead, the impact is rather persistent over the time horizon of 20 quarters. This stands in contrast to the research done by Rüffer and Stracca (2006, p. 42) who find a comparatively short-lived influence. Other impulse responses in the Cholesky VAR also suggest that the empirical evidence in this work does not present a textbook version of the MFD model. Although the exchange rate in the EMU rises significantly, a beggar-thy-neighbor effect in terms of real GDP does not materialize (cf. the previous figure 7.2). A possible explanation is that global excess liquidity shocks have two offsetting effects on economic activity in the euro area. The first one is in form of a higher availability of monetary liquidity, thereby stimulating real GDP. The second one dampens economic activity at the same time via an appreciating euro exchange rate. However, such a conclusion is far from certain. In the SVAR, global excess liquidity shocks do not lead to a significant response of the exchange rate.

Figure 7.3: Response of EMU real effective exchange rate to global excess liquidity shock (Cholesky VAR in the upper chart; SVAR in the lower chart)

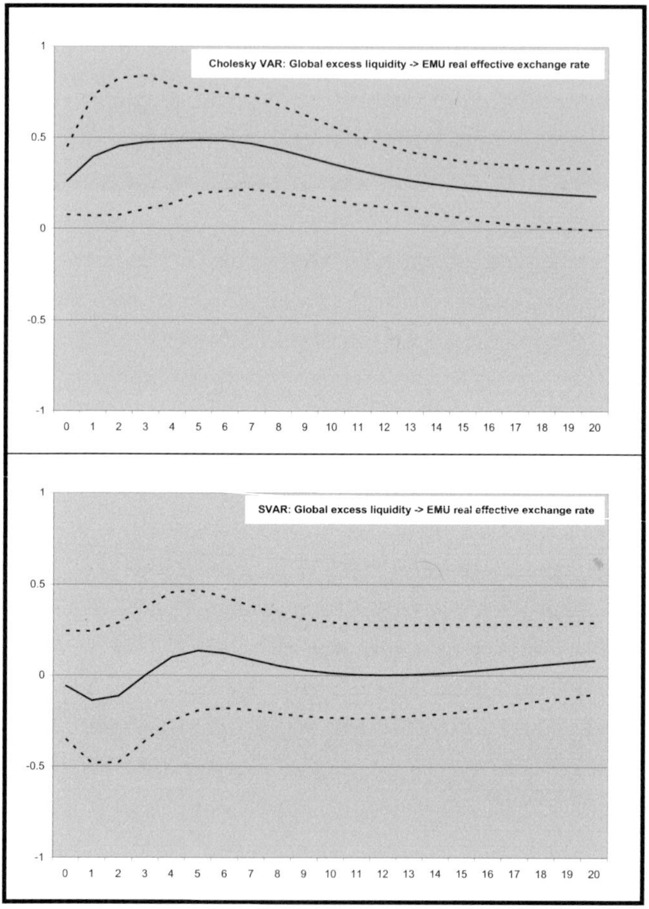

Seemingly, the impulse response analysis in both VARs is not compatible with the transmission channel stressed in the NOEM either. A global excess liquidity shock abroad does not lead to a significantly declining short-term interest rate in the euro area (cf. figure 7.4). However, it is important to note that the New Open Economy Macroeconomics focuses on long-term interest rates instead of money market rates. Hence, an outright rejection of the NOEM hypothesis is not possible. Furthermore, the results could also stem from a misspecification of the two VAR models in form of a classic identification problem. The global excess liquidity shock derived within the VAR framework may not only contain global money supply disturbances but sudden shifts in international money demand as well. If one assumes that a positive common money demand shock abroad also lifts money demand in the EMU, the interest rate in the euro area increases. For instance, Rüffer and Stracca (2006, p. 24) find a rising short-term interest rate. However, the authors do not consider this pattern as indicative of misspecification. They argue that it reflects the reaction of the monetary authority in the euro zone, trying to offset the expansionary disturbance from abroad.

Figure 7.4: Response of EMU 3 month interest rate to global excess liquidity shock (Cholesky VAR in the upper chart; SVAR in the lower chart)

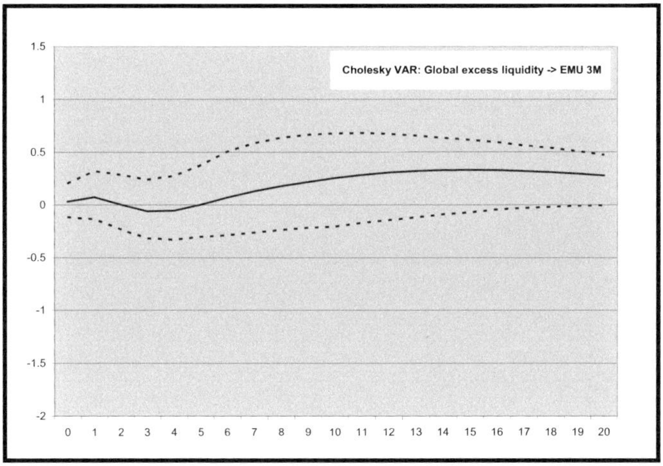

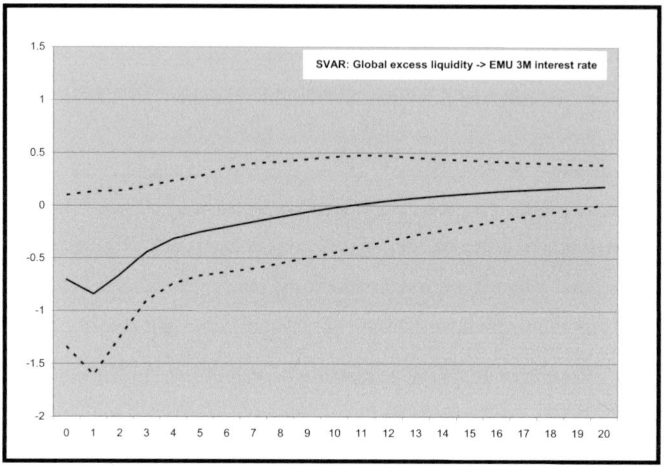

In order to get a better overview of the derived VAR results, the responses to all three possible monetary condition shocks – global excess liquidity, national short-term interest rate and domestic money – are subsumized in the following table 7.3. In each case, the impact of a positive disturbance is analyzed. The sign in paranthesis indicates whether the variable increases or declines significantly after the disturbance.[63] There is no evidence that the common excess liquidity force has independent information value above national variables like the short-term interest rate and broad money. In contrast, the latter two variables are at least partly important in the Cholesky VAR. For example, a domestic money innovation leads to a significantly positive and persistent response of EMU consumer prices. Perhaps the most striking pattern can be found for the outcomes of the SVAR. All responses apart from one prove to be non-significant independent of whether it is a domestic or global disturbance.[64] Since the SVAR possibly takes interdependencies in an open economy better into account than a recursive model, this evidence may point to the negligible role of monetary influences in general and global excess money in particular.

[63] The corresponding figures for the impulse responses can be found in appendix A.10.

[64] Only the response of the three month interest rate after a domestic money shock is significant but has a positive and therefore "wrong" sign (liquidity puzzle).

Table 7.3: Comparison of impulse responses in the two EMU VARs

Positive disturbance	Cholesky VAR	SVAR
Global excess liquidity -> EMU GDP	no significant response	no significant response
Global excess liquidity -> EMU CPI	no significant response	no significant response
Global excess liquidity -> EMU money	(+) Q2 to Q6	no significant response
Global excess liquidity -> EMU 3M interest rate	no significant response	no significant response
Global excess liquidity -> EMU exchange rate	(+) Q3 to Q19	no significant response
EMU money -> EMU GDP	no significant response	no significant response
EMU money -> EMU CPI	(+) from Q4 onwards	no significant response
EMU money -> EMU 3M interest rate	(+) Q2 to Q11	(+) Q9 to Q19
EMU money -> EMU exchange rate	no significant response	no significant response
EMU 3M -> EMU GDP	no significant response	no significant response
EMU 3M -> EMU CPI	(+) from Q5 onwards	no significant response
EMU 3M -> EMU money	(+) Q2 to Q12	no significant response
EMU 3M -> EMU exchange rate	no significant response	no significant response

Note: Significant responses based on 95% confidence bands (bootstrap procedure with 500 draws)

However, substantial caution in interpreting the results in this specific way is warranted for two reasons. First, the presence of puzzles can serve as a strict criterion for judging the validity of the empirical model. As both the recursive approach and the SVAR contain a liquidity puzzle after a national money innovation, it is not possible to say that the identified disturbances are close to the "true" monetary policy shocks. The results may only be rationalized by the existence of money demand disturbances instead of money supply innovations. Accordingly, clear-cut conclusions about the appropriateness of economic theories should not be drawn. Second, as already pointed out, simply augmenting VARs by a common liquidity force runs the risk of confounding global money supply and global money demand disturbances. From a theoretical viewpoint, a separation between these two innovations is conceivable in a VAR. Further global factors or aggregates like real GDP, prices and the short-term interest rate could be included instead of only one common excess liquidity force. The interaction between global variables could then be taken into account. However, such a model would consist of up to ten variables, thereby limiting the degrees of freedom and leading to substantial practical problems. Further structural models on a global level like FAVARs are needed to disentangle global money supply and demand shocks (cf. the following chapter 7.2). Only then, economically meaningful conclusions for national economies can be derived.

Besides an omitted variable bias caused by neglected global variables, another concern in VAR models is the possibility of structural breaks in the coefficients and the shocks. For example, if there are signs of variation in the VAR coefficients due to increasing financial globalization, the impulse responses might be unstable. Clear-cut conclusions about the propagation mechanism are therefore not possible. The EMU economy reacts differently to a global excess liquidity shock depending on when exactly being hit by the disturbance. Hence, as has been the case in chapter 6.3, Quandt-Andrews tests are applied both for the VAR coefficients and the error terms.

With respect to the VAR coefficients, two versions of the Quandt-Andrews test are implemented.[65] The first one covers all coefficients in the respective VAR equation. The second one concentrates on the interaction between the common liquidity factor (GEL_exEMU) and the respective dependent variable. For example, in the equation with the short-term interest rate (SR_t), only the coefficients b_1 and b_2 in (7.1.2.3) below are examined for structural variation. This allows concentrating on breaks in bivariate relationships which may be overlooked when the Quandt-Andrews test is applied simultaneously to all coefficients.

$$SR_t = b_1 GEL\_exEMU_{t-1} + b_2 GEL\_exEMU_{t-2} \quad (7.1.2.3)$$

Table 7.4 shows the results. The general propagation mechanism in the VARs appears to be stable. The Maximum LR test does not detect structural breaks when being used for all coefficients in each equation. Furthermore, the signs of instability in the bivariate relationships are limited. There is only one structural break in the coefficient measuring the relation between EMU economic activity at time t and lagged global excess liquidity. The structural break occurs in Q2 1992. Unfortunately, given the limited size of the data sample, it is not possible to re-estimate the two equations and examine how and to what extent the VAR coefficients change. Otherwise, the degrees of freedom decline strongly.

[65] Since signs of heteroskedasticity are found, a heteroskedasticity-robust estimator (Newey-West) is used. Otherwise, there is the risk that Type I errors falsely indicating structural breaks occur too often (cf. chapter 6.3). Stock and Watson (2002a, p. 11) also use heteroskedasticity-robust Quandt-Andrews tests for deriving structural breaks in autoregressive approaches.

Table 7.4: Quandt-Andrews breakpoint tests for propagation in VARs

	All coefficients		Global excess liquidity	
VAR equations	Date	Max LR F	Date	Max LR F
Commodity prices	1990 Q3	1.80	1994 Q2	4.12
Global excess liquidity	1991 Q4	4.51	1990 Q1	9.17
EMU real GDP	1990 Q1	6.71	1992 Q2	12.21**
EMU CPI	1994 Q2	2.57	1988 Q3	4.44
EMU M3 money supply	2000 Q2	2.88	2001 Q1	5.82
EMU 3M interest rate	1991 Q4	5.22	1990 Q1	8.78
Real effective exchange rate	1992 Q4	3.99	1992 Q4	5.58

Note 1: Heteroskedasticity and autocorrelation robust version (Newey-West) of Maximum LR test
Note 2: *** Indicates significance at 1% level, ** at 5% level, * at 10% level

The Quandt-Andrews test is repeated for the structural shocks in the recursive model and the SVAR. As has been the case in chapter 6.3 in the univariate setting, the disturbances are regressed against a constant (cf. equation 6.3.10). When signs of instability are found, an additional time trend is included, reflecting the possibility of gradual change. Again, the number of detected instabilities is limited (cf. table 7.5). In the recursive approach, only the GDP disturbances and the short-term interest rate shocks appear to be unstable with the break occuring in Q4 1990 and Q2 1996, respectively. In the SVAR, structural change is also detected for these two variables, although the timing of the breaks is different. It is Q2 1993 for the economic activity disturbances and Q3 1993 for the short-term interest rate innovations. In addition, the global excess liquidity shocks seem to be unstable (Q4 2003). However, independent of which VAR model and disturbance is looked at, when including a time trend, the null hypothesis of no change cannot be rejected any longer. This evidence is indicative of a gradual decline in the shocks instead of the assumed sudden one-off break in the original Quandt-Andrews test.

Table 7.5: Quandt-Andrews breakpoint tests for VAR shocks

	Shocks Cholesky VAR			Shocks SVAR		
VAR equations	Date	Max LR F	Max LR F (trend)	Date	Max LR F	Max LR F (trend)
Commodity prices	1989 Q2	3.40	---	1988 Q2	2.89	---
Global excess liquidity	2003 Q4	3.93	---	2003 Q4	7.58*	6.90
EMU real GDP	1990 Q4	10.05**	3.30	1993 Q2	11.66**	4.12
EMU CPI	1988 Q2	2.51	---	1989 Q2	2.30	---
EMU M3 money supply	2003 Q4	3.40	---	2003 Q4	4.76	---
EMU 3M interest rate	1996 Q2	11.54**	4.33	1993 Q3	9.10**	4.87
Real effective exchange rate	2003 Q4	5.12	---	2003 Q4	4.86	---

Note 1: Sign of trend, if significant, in parentheses
Note 3: *** Indicates significance at 1% level, ** at 5% level, * at 10% level

Apart from some variation, the majority of VAR coefficients and shocks appear to be stable over time. However, besides structural breaks, there is still another important issue, possibly influencing the derived impulse responses: the set of assumptions in the identification scheme.[66] In the following, robustness checks are done to examine how sensitive the results are to various specifications. For both VARs, there is a multitude of different identification patterns conceivable. For example, in the recursive approach, global excess liquidity (GEL_exEMU) could be ordered first before commodity prices (CP). This implies the causal relationship $GEL\_exEMU \triangleright CP$ and not vice versa as previously assumed. Alternatively, the common excess liquidity factor could be ordered last, therefore be regarded as the most endogenous variable in the system (cf. 7.1.2.4 below). Such an ordering has some appeal for two reasons. First, it is an extreme assumption, being suitable for a statistical sensitivity analysis. Second, from an economic viewpoint, contemporaneous feedback effects of the EMU variables on global excess liquidity can implicitly be taken into account. Since the euro zone is not a classic small open economy, it may also influence monetary conditions abroad via its domestic interest rate or money aggregate ($SR \triangleright GEL\_exEMU$ and $M3 \triangleright GEL\_exEMU$, respectively).

$$(7.1.2.4)\qquad \begin{bmatrix} 1 & 0 & 0 & 0 & 0 & 0 & 0 \\ a_{21} & 1 & 0 & 0 & 0 & 0 & 0 \\ a_{31} & a_{32} & 1 & 0 & 0 & 0 & 0 \\ a_{41} & a_{42} & a_{43} & 1 & 0 & 0 & 0 \\ a_{51} & a_{52} & a_{53} & a_{54} & 1 & 0 & 0 \\ a_{61} & a_{62} & a_{63} & a_{64} & a_{65} & 1 & 0 \\ a_{71} & a_{72} & a_{73} & a_{74} & a_{75} & a_{76} & 1 \end{bmatrix} \begin{bmatrix} u_t^{CP} \\ u_t^{YR} \\ u_t^{PI} \\ u_t^{M3} \\ u_t^{SR} \\ u_t^{ER} \\ u_t^{GEL\_exEMU} \end{bmatrix} = \begin{bmatrix} \varepsilon_t^{CP} \\ \varepsilon_t^{YR} \\ \varepsilon_t^{PI} \\ \varepsilon_t^{M3} \\ \varepsilon_t^{SR} \\ \varepsilon_t^{ER} \\ \varepsilon_t^{GEL\_exEMU} \end{bmatrix}$$

In the following, the focus is on analyzing the responses to a global excess liquidity shock. The obtained results for the identification scheme (7.1.2.4) above indicate comparatively little change. For instance, the reaction of economic activity and prices in the EMU to a disturbance in the common liquidity factor remains insignificant. Further figures can be found in the appendix A.11.

[66] Using different lag lengths yields comparatively little change in the impulse responses and is therefore not reported.

Figure 7.5: Response of EMU GDP and CPI to global excess liquidity shock in Cholesky VAR (GEL_exEMU ordered last)

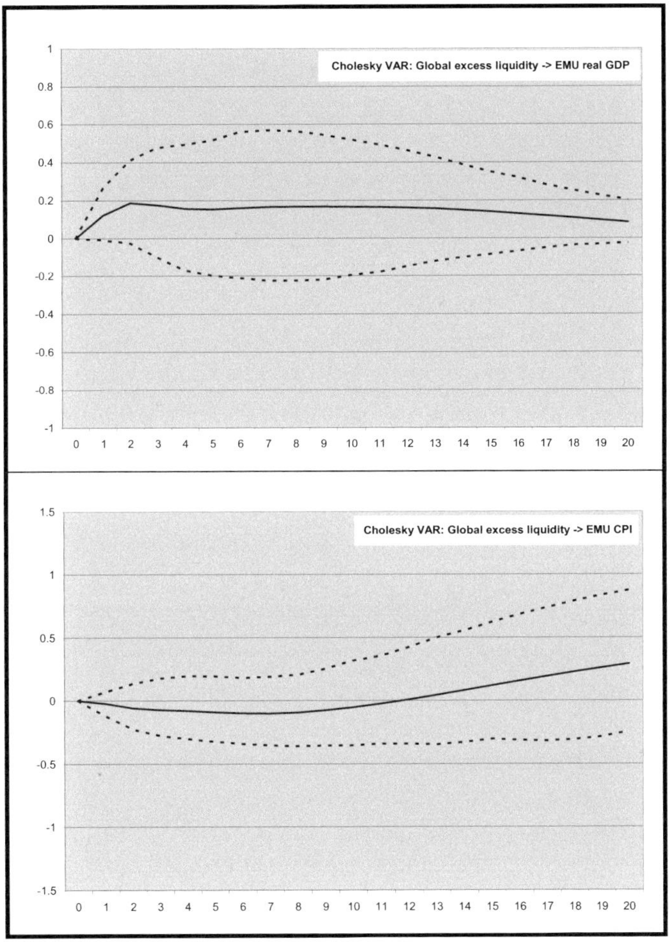

The SVAR is overidentified (cf. expression 7.1.2.2), as 22 restrictions are imposed while only 21 are needed. A just-identified scheme might therefore be an interesting alternative to check for the robustness of the results. The following changes are made in the identification matrix (7.1.2.5) below. It is not allowed for currency substitution effects in money demand, i.e. there is no contemporaneous interaction between the broad monetary aggregate ($M3$) and the effective exchange rate (ER). The restrictions in the monetary policy reaction function are relaxed, since a contemporaneous reaction of the short-term interest rate to real GDP and prices can take place. In addition, the central bank looks at commodity prices but not at global excess liquidity outside the EMU.

$$(7.1.2.5)\quad \begin{bmatrix} 1 & a_{12} & a_{13} & 0 & 0 & 0 & 0 \\ 0 & 1 & 0 & 0 & a_{25} & a_{26} & 0 \\ 0 & 0 & 1 & 0 & 0 & 0 & 0 \\ a_{41} & 0 & 0 & 1 & 0 & 0 & a_{47} \\ 0 & a_{52} & a_{53} & a_{54} & 1 & a_{56} & 0 \\ a_{61} & 0 & a_{63} & a_{64} & a_{65} & 1 & a_{67} \\ a_{71} & a_{72} & a_{73} & a_{74} & a_{75} & a_{76} & 1 \end{bmatrix} \begin{bmatrix} u_t^{CP} \\ u_t^{GEL\_exEMU} \\ u_t^{YR} \\ u_t^{PI} \\ u_t^{M3} \\ u_t^{SR} \\ u_t^{ER} \end{bmatrix} = \begin{bmatrix} \varepsilon_t^{CP} \\ \varepsilon_t^{GEL\_exEMU} \\ \varepsilon_t^{YR} \\ \varepsilon_t^{PI} \\ \varepsilon_t^{M3} \\ \varepsilon_t^{SR} \\ \varepsilon_t^{ER} \end{bmatrix}$$

The new identification scheme leads to minor changes in the timing and dynamics of the impulse responses. As is the case in the baseline SVAR, major macroeconomic variables in the EMU do not show any significant reaction to a common excess liquidity disturbance. For example, this is true for domestic economic activity and consumer prices (cf. figures below). Further results can be found in the appendix A.12.

Figure 7.6: Response of EMU GDP and CPI to global excess liquidity shock in SVAR

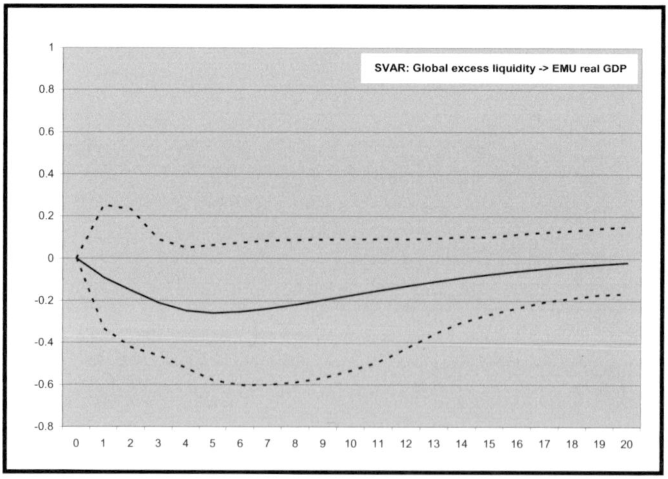

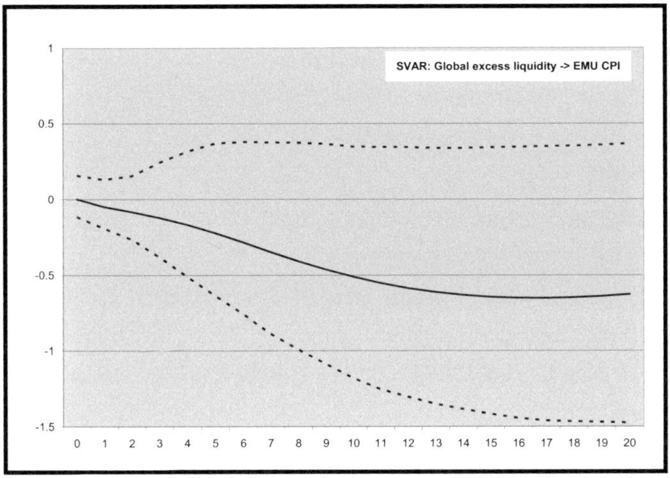

In the following, major results of the VAR analysis in chapter 7.1 are shortly summarized. Wald tests indicate that domestic money shocks in the G7 countries and the euro area are contaminated by disturbances to foreign monies and the common excess liquidity force. However, augmenting EMU VARs by a global excess liquidity factor yields little results. The so far obtained empirical evidence for the euro area rejects the hypothesis that financial globalization has led to a new channel in monetary transmission which can affect domestic real quantities and prices. This finding is independent of the chosen identification matrix for the residuals. One major reason for this result could be a general problem implied with the use of small-scale VARs in an international context. Since such models cannot take global interdependencies fully into account, they are only partly suitable for deriving the impact of global shocks on national variables (cf. the following chapter for a more detailed critique). Moreover, simply including common factors in national VAR models clearly comes at a cost. This procedure blurs the difference between global and idiosyncratic innovations. In contrast, factor models distinguish strictly between these two types of disturbances, since the common factor is not influenced by individual national time series. In the two VARs above, however, both domestic variables and the global excess liquidity force are modeled in a fully endogenous setting. In the following, a new type of model is presented which can deal with this problem and may alleviate some shortcomings: a FAVAR.

"Considering how to capture the major features of the global economy is truly a daunting task. [...] In total there will be at least two billion decision makers, all interacting, throughout the globe."

(Granger, Jeon 2007, p. 980f.)

7.2 A GLOBAL SFAVAR

A Structural Factor Augmented VAR (SFAVAR) allows examining the interaction between global variables. Furthermore, it is possible to analyze the impact of global (money) shocks on various domestic economies in a structural context. Examining spillover effects of the common liquidity force on a multitude of national variables is especially relevant for central banks. In the following, the SFAVAR model is shortly explained and then estimated.

7.2.1 METHODOLOGY

Conventional VAR analysis is afflicted by the curse of dimensionality, as the number of parameters grows with the square of the model dimension. With often rather small samples at hand, the degrees of freedom can decline rapidly (Kose, Otrok and Whiteman 2005, p. 16). Typically, standard VARs rarely employ more than six to eight variables. This small number is especially a problem when open economies are analyzed. Then, the researcher faces a trade-off between plausible economic considerations and technical feasibility. On the one hand, given increasing globalization, a multitude of foreign influences may have a significant impact on national variables. On the other hand, simply expanding the external sector in the model or analyzing the interaction of several economies is not possible, since it leads to an overparametrization problem. The risks of an omitted variable bias and a misspecification of the VAR are therefore looming high. Key to solving the trade-off is to increase the amount of information in the model by common factors summarizing the information contained in a set of variables across countries. The specific combination of a standard VAR model with factor analysis is labeled factor augmented VAR or briefly FAVAR. Hence, although the FAVAR copes with many variables and exploits a lot of information, it still achieves parameter reduction and does not run into problems of scarce degrees of freedom. Bernanke, Boivin and Eliasz (2005, p. 405f.) even find that the inclusion of factors alleviates price and liquidity puzzles traditionally found in empirical studies. Another advantage of FAVAR models is the possibility to obtain impulse response functions for any variable included in the data set, even if the number of variables is high. This is an especially appealing feature in the light of spillover effects across countries and common shocks. Usually, the ambiguities surrounding the origins and propagation of foreign disturbances are high and difficult to analyze. The FAVAR methodology allows both examining the interaction of global variables and their effects on national open economies in a completely structural setting. It is possible to distinguish between structural common and structural idiosyncratic shocks without blurring them as in a conventional VAR analysis augmented by global variables. Furthermore, the relevance of a large number of disturbances and transmission channels can be assessed simultaneously. Various theories are therefore put to compete in a "horse race" to see which ones are best supported by the data (Justiniano 2003 p. 8; Eickmeier 2007, p. 522). For instance, the question can be answered how important a common money supply shock is for both global and national economic activity compared to a commodity price disturbance.

Given these obvious advantages, it is surprising that the majority of researchers neglects the international context and focuses on national economies instead when implementing FAVAR models. Examples are the work by Bernanke, Boivin and Eliasz (2005), Stock and Watson (2005a) and Boivin, Giannoni and Mihov (2009). In contrast, Boivin and Giannoni (2008) examine whether the rapid globalization of financial markets weakens the ability of US monetary policy to influence the domestic economy. A further exemption is the work of Bagliano and Morana (2009). They specify international latent factors and examine the implications of global shocks on national variables.

In the following, a general and more detailed formulation of the FAVAR model is derived in line with Stock and Watson (2005a). Recall the dynamic factor model in static form from chapter 6.1:

(7.2.1.1) $$X_t = \Lambda F_t + D(L)X_{t-1} + v_t$$

(7.2.1.2) $$F_t = \Phi(L)F_{t-1} + \eta_t$$

with X_t as N-variate vector of observable variables and F_t as r-variate vector of unobserved common static factors f_{qt} with $q = 1,...,r$, $r < N$. Λ is a $N \times r$ matrix of factor loadings. η_t is a r-variate vector of global shocks driving the common factors and v_t equals a N-variate vector of idiosyncratic disturbances. Global and country-specific shocks are mutually uncorrelated, that is $E(\eta_{qt} v_{is}) = 0$ for all i, q, s, t with $i = 1, \ldots, N$. $D(L)$ is a $N \times N$ matrix lag polynomial of order k and $\Phi(L)$ is a $r \times r$ matrix lag polynomial of order p with the roots outside the unit circle in each case:[67]

$$(7.2.1.3) \qquad D(L) = \begin{bmatrix} \delta_{1,1}(L) & \ldots & \delta_{1,N}(L) \\ \vdots & \ddots & \vdots \\ \delta_{N,1}(L) & \ldots & \delta_{N,N}(L) \end{bmatrix} \text{ and } \Phi(L) = \begin{bmatrix} \phi_{1,1}(L) & \ldots & \phi_{1,r}(L) \\ \vdots & \ddots & \vdots \\ \phi_{r,1}(L) & \ldots & \phi_{r,r}(L) \end{bmatrix}$$

Substituting the factor evolution equation (7.2.1.2) into (7.2.1.1) and collecting terms yields the complete FAVAR form (Stock, Watson 2005a, p. 9):

$$(7.2.1.4) \qquad \begin{bmatrix} F_t \\ X_t \end{bmatrix} = \begin{bmatrix} \Phi(L) & 0 \\ \Lambda\Phi(L) & D(L) \end{bmatrix} \begin{bmatrix} F_{t-1} \\ X_{t-1} \end{bmatrix} + \begin{bmatrix} \varepsilon_{Ft} \\ \varepsilon_{Xt} \end{bmatrix} \text{ where } \begin{bmatrix} \varepsilon_{Ft} \\ \varepsilon_{Xt} \end{bmatrix} = \begin{bmatrix} I \\ \Lambda \end{bmatrix} \eta_t + \begin{bmatrix} 0 \\ v_t \end{bmatrix}$$

The evolution of the factors is modeled as in a VAR. The FAVAR contains the exclusion restriction implied by factor analysis, i.e. X does not predict F given $\Phi(L)F_{t-1}$. Such restrictions resemble the assumption of exogenous world variables which are used to identifiy global shocks in open economy VARs.[68] If the matrix lag polynomial $\Phi(L)$ and/or the factor loading matrix Λ equal zero, the system boils down to a standard national VAR model of the form $X_t = D(L)X_{t-1} + \varepsilon_{Xt}$. If $\Phi(L) = 0$, the common factors do not interact with each other, thereby making the estimation of a global model impossible. At least theoretically, the condition $\Lambda = 0$ could hold for big countries. For example, the US economy may be independent of developments abroad, while setting the macroeconomic trend for the rest of the world.

In principle, all FAVAR coefficients can be estimated by a quasi-maximum likelihood approach. However, since this is computationally cumbersome, Bernanke,

[67] Since $D(L)$ is assumed to be a $N \times N$ matrix, all variables X_t are modeled as endogenous from the outset, i.e. there are feedback effects possible between national economies (Bagliano, Morana 2009, p. 435). However, using a large data set, the degrees of freedom can rapidly decline and pose substantial practical problems when estimating the FAVAR. More details and an alternative approach can be found in chapter 7.2.3.

[68] This exclusion restriction will be tested in chapter 7.2.5. In the FAVAR approach developed by Bernanke, Boivin and Eliasz (2005), common factors and variables are allowed to interact endogenously, i.e. a zero restriction does not exist.

Boivin, Eliasz (2005, p. 398 ff.) and Stock, Watson (2005a, p. 16) propose a two-step approach. In the first step, the common forces are derived. Stock and Watson (2005a, p. 29) apply the PCA directly to the whole data set. Although this approach exploits all available information, this makes the economic interpretation of the factors difficult or even impossible (Bagliano, Morana 2009, p. 434). For example, it is not clear what the first principal component actually represents when X_t is heterogenous and covers economic activity, prices, financial markets etc. An economic more meaningful approach is the division of the data set into categories of variables, thereby capturing r dimensions of each economy ($X_{1t}, X_{2t}, ..., X_{rt}$). The following categories are chosen for the G7 and the EMU with $r = 7$ before doing the PCA:

- broad economic activity reflected by real GDP;
- overall inflation which includes consumer prices, producer prices, import prices and the GDP deflator;
- commodity markets reflected by the HWWI and the CRB commodity price indices in domestic currency;
- the residential property market (house prices)[69];
- monetary liquidity including broad monetary aggregates, like M2 or M3;
- short-term interest rates which include 3-month interest rates and
- stock markets represented by the MSCI share price index in domestic currency.

For each category, an estimate of the global factor f_{qt} is obtained as the first principal component with $q = 1,...,r$. Each segment of X_t is therefore explained by exactly one factor (cf. 7.2.1.5). $PC1$ exclusively loads on the specific category of national variables, i.e. each first principal component drives the contemporaneous value of domestic variables apart from an idiosyncratic error v_t. In contrast, the national variables exert their influence only with a time lag. Given this procedure, a total of $r = 7$ global forces is derived: an economic activity factor, an inflation factor, a commodity price factor, a

[69] In some countries like the US, residential property prices are also included in the CPI. Hence, some overlap in the data may exist. However, such an effect should play only a comparatively small role in this work, since the global inflation factor is based on four price variables.

house price factor, a money factor, a short-term interest rate factor and a share price factor.

$$\begin{bmatrix} X_{1t} \\ X_{2t} \\ \dots \\ X_{rt} \end{bmatrix} = \begin{bmatrix} \Lambda_1 & 0 & \dots & 0 \\ 0 & \Lambda_2 & \dots & 0 \\ \dots & \dots & \dots & \dots \\ 0 & 0 & \dots & \Lambda_r \end{bmatrix} \begin{bmatrix} f_{1t} \\ f_{2t} \\ \dots \\ f_{rt} \end{bmatrix} + \begin{bmatrix} X_{1t-1} \\ X_{2t-1} \\ \dots \\ X_{rt-1} \end{bmatrix} + \begin{bmatrix} v_{1t} \\ v_{2t} \\ \dots \\ v_{rt} \end{bmatrix} \tag{7.2.1.5}$$

In the literature, there is often a focus on business cycles and real GDP when defining global co-movement across countries (Canova, Ciccarelli and Ortega, 2007; Kose, Otrok and Whiteman 2008). In addition, Cicarelli and Mojon (2010) find a common pattern among inflation rates. However, it may also make sense to think in terms of other macroeconomic and financial variables as global ones. More specifically, common patterns could also concern variables which have usually been regarded as exclusively national phenomena. One example is the residential property market. Housing is a non-traded good for which price arbitrage across countries is not achievable. However, the IMF (2004, p. 84) conducts a factor analysis, estimating that about 40% of domestic house price developments can be explained by global factors. The outcome is explained by arbitrage relationships between residential property prices and globally traded securities like shares. Since common shocks have an impact on these securities, house prices across countries are also affected simultaneously. Furthermore, the most recent financial and economic crisis can be understood and modeled as a global demand shock which is characterized by a synchronous downturn of house prices (Federal Reserve Bank of Kansas City, 2009). Vansteenkiste and Hiebert (2009) empirically assess the co-movement of residential property prices in euro area countries. The authors find evidence of spillovers, although they are limited in size. Fratzscher, Juvenal and Sarno (2009) argue that one of the striking features of the global economy in the past 15 years has been the pronounced cycles on equity and housing markets. They find that relative global asset price changes may be an important source of adjustment in international current account positions.

Even national short-term interest rates may exhibit common patterns across countries. Of course, there is no world central bank which sets the short-term interest rate for many countries. However, from this quite trivial insight, it cannot be concluded that interest rate shocks are not identifiable on a global level (Belke, Rees 2009, p. 8). If a global cycle exists in economic activity and on housing markets, the money market rates should move synchronously as well. The reason for this is that national monetary policies react directly or indirectly to global developments. Directly in the sense that global variables enter the central bank's reaction function via world GDP and/or global excess liquidity. Indirectly, if monetary policy does not react until global variables have an effect on national patterns. "Global interest rate shocks" can then be interpreted as unexpected changes in this reaction pattern. In the literature, common beliefs and peer pressure are mentioned as additional reasons for a similar reaction pattern of central banks (cf. chapter 2.1.5). National monetary policies react quite similarly via meetings and the exchange of information among central banks (implicit policy coordination). For example, the establishment of inflation targeting regimes in many industrialized countries might serve as an example of "common beliefs" in this respect.

When variables like short-term interest rates, broad money and house prices are not exclusively domestic phenomena but also contain a common component across countries, deriving a SFAVAR model might prove useful. All factors are regarded as endogenous, thereby allowing the estimate of the structural relationships between these global variables. Since a total of seven common forces $(f_{1t}, f_{2t}, \ldots, f_{rt})$ is used, it is possible to disentangle international relationships and get a better understanding of the global economy. In addition, recent topics discussed among academics and policymakers are open for investigation. For instance, the extent to which global variables contributed to the strong rise in property prices across countries until the start of the latest financial crisis can be analyzed. In this respect, the presented FAVAR approach expands previous empirical research done by Bagliano and Morana (2009, p. 437ff.). The authors concentrate on only four common forces which they label "inflation factor", "output growth factor", "stock return factor" and "oil price factor". For example, the inflation factor contains not only prices but also interest rates as well as monetary aggregates. Their approach therefore does not allow for examing the interaction between single common forces.

After deriving the global factors, the FAVAR is estimated as follows in the second step. The obtained common forces $\hat{F}_t$ are regressed onto the desired number of lags p to obtain the estimator of $\Phi(L)$. $\hat{\Lambda}$ and $\hat{D}(L)$ are derived by estimating regressions of X_t on $(F_t, X_{t-1,}..., X_{t-k})$ with k as lag length (Stock, Watson 2005a, p. 13). Afterwards, $\hat{\Phi}(L)$, $\hat{\Lambda}$ and $\hat{D}(L)$ are used to construct the complete restricted coefficient matrix in expression (7.2.1.4):

$$(7.2.1.4) \qquad \begin{bmatrix} F_t \\ X_t \end{bmatrix} = \begin{bmatrix} \Phi(L) & 0 \\ \Lambda\Phi(L) & D(L) \end{bmatrix} \begin{bmatrix} F_{t-1} \\ X_{t-1} \end{bmatrix} + \begin{bmatrix} \varepsilon_{Ft} \\ \varepsilon_{Xt} \end{bmatrix}$$

The structural disturbances have to be derived from the FAVAR innovations ε_{Ft} and ε_{Xt} with $\begin{bmatrix} \varepsilon_{Ft} \\ \varepsilon_{Xt} \end{bmatrix} = \begin{bmatrix} I \\ \Lambda \end{bmatrix} \eta_t + \begin{bmatrix} 0 \\ v_t \end{bmatrix}$. The procedure starts with identifying η_t. As is the case in standard VAR analysis, the shocks η_t are reduced-form error terms. The only difference is that η_t represents disturbances to the common factors and not to the macroeconomic variables X_t. For example, global GDP shocks capture innovations to business cycle co-movements like common demand disturbances. Let ϖ_t denote the r structural global innovations which are linearly related to the reduced-form shocks η_t as follows:

$$(7.2.1.6) \qquad \varpi_t = H\eta_t$$

with H as an invertable $r \times r$ matrix. Structural FAVAR analysis requires identifying the elements of the H matrix for which several approaches are available. For instance, Bagliano and Morana (2009, p. 435) propose a simple recursive ordering based on the relative speed of adjustment to global shocks. They order the output and inflation factor first, followed by interest rates and money. Share prices, exchange rates and the oil price are ordered last, as these common forces are assumed to be fast-moving variables. The H matrix can then be written as

$$(7.2.1.7) \qquad H = \begin{bmatrix} h_{11} & & \\ \vdots & \ddots & \\ h_{r1} & \dots & h_{rr} \end{bmatrix}$$

Of course, alternative identification schemes are also available as is the case in standard VAR analysis. One might argue that a Wold-causal chain is not appropriate in a fully international context, therefore using an economically less restrictive approach. In any case, exact identification is reached when $r(r-1)/2$ restrictions are imposed.[70]

It is important to note that the second step of the FAVAR procedure implicitly makes one crucial assumption. As previously discussed in chapter 6.1, the *estimated* global factors are treated as if they are data and hence perfectly observable in reality. Consequently, there may be a generated regressor problem (Bernanke, Boivin, Eliasz 2005, p. 399). The uncertainty in the factor estimates is only negligible when the data set N is large. The reason for this is based on a key property of factor models: The variances of the factor estimates are of order $1/N$. Hence, using many macroeconomic variables ($N \to \infty$) markedly reduces the uncertainty and thus the variance of the latent factors (Boivin, Giannoni 2006, p. 13f.).

As final part of the second-step procedure, the structural idiosyncratic shocks have to be derived from the reduced-form innovations v_t. Estimating $X_t = \Lambda\Phi(L)F_{t-1} + D(L)X_{t-1}$ obtains ε_{Xt} as residual with $\varepsilon_{Xt} = \Lambda\eta_t + v_t$. Less technically spoken, each country is hit both by disturbances stemming from the global economy (η_t) and by national innovations (v_t). However, since ε_{Xt}, Λ, η_t and ϖ_t ($\varpi_t = H\eta_t$) are available, the country-specific shocks v_t can easily be determined and then transformed into the structural idiosyncratic disturbances ξ_t. Operationally, Bagliano and Morana (2009, p. 435) propose regressing the N innovations ε_{Xt} on ϖ and hence on the r global structural shocks. The obtained residuals equal the N idiosyncratic disturbances v_t for which the usual restrictions have to be implemented ($\xi_t = Qv_t$ with Q as invertable $N \times N$ matrix). As a result, one gets the structural moving average polynomial $B^1(L)$ and hence the impulse response function with respect to the structural country-specific disturbances ξ_t. Adding the moving average polynomial $B^2(L)$ of the structural global innovations ϖ_t yields the complete impulse response function of the SFAVAR (Bagliano and Morana 2009, p. 434):

$$X_t = B^1(L)\xi_t + B^2(L)\varpi_t \qquad (7.2.1.8)$$

---

[70] In the following chapter, a non-recursive structural disturbances matrix will be introduced and discussed.

The identification problem typically found in open economy analysis is solved by distinguishing between structural global and structural idiosyncratic shocks for each variable and country included in the model.

7.2.2 IMPULSE RESPONSE ANALYSIS (I): GLOBAL FACTORS

Before starting the impulse response analysis, some preparatory work is necessary. First, the global factors have to be estimated. Second, it will be examined whether each of the first principal components qualify as pervasive force of the global economy. Third, the global structural shocks have to be identified.

In the beginning, the global factors across different categories of national variables $(X_{1t}, X_{2t}, ..., X_{rt})$ are estimated by PCA. As is standard in factor model applications, the variables are initially detrended. Apart from the short-term interest rates, all series are log first differenced. For the short-term interest rates, first differences are calculated. Afterwards, all the detrended variables are standardized so that each of them has a mean of zero and a variance of one. Otherwise, the results would have systematically been affected by cross-country differences in variability.

The FAVAR model is based on variables which are at least partly regarded as national phenomena in previous empirical studies. It is therefore important to examine whether the estimated first principal components ($PC1$) suitably qualify as factors capturing international co-movement. Three conditions have to be met (cf. chapter 6.1). First, $PC1$ should explain a "sufficiently" large fraction of the total variance of the data set in comparison to the remaining principal components of higher order. Second, the relevance of the first principal component should evenly be spread across countries or regions. Third, the explanatory power of $PC1$ for single national variables should be higher than the explanatory power of any other single national variable. Otherwise, the first principal component cannot be regarded as a pervasive force across countries.

In order to examine whether the first condition is met, the proportion of the total variance of the series attributable to $PC1$ to $PC3$ is calculated for each common factor. In the case of national monies, a significant part of the whole variance (48.6%) can be explained by the first principal component. In contrast, $PC2$ accounts for only 18%. The first principal component's share of the short-term interest rate variance is somewhat lower than the share of $PC1$ with respect to money (42.8%; $PC2$: 19.7%).

For the inflation factor which includes four different measures of inflation for each country or region (CPI, PPI, import prices and the GDP deflator), the $PC1$ statistic is 31.8% compared to 16.9% for $PC2$. Even for house prices, the share of the first principal component is 33.2%. With 55.9% and 74.3%, the $PC1$ statistic for commodity and share prices is the highest. From this evidence, it is concluded that the first prerequisite is met by all first principal components.

Table 7.6: Share of variance explained by the first three principal components, in %

	PC1	PC2	PC3
Real GDP	36.5	23.0	17.0
Inflation	31.8	16.9	9.6
Commodity prices	55.9	27.8	7.9
House prices	33.2	26.9	15.5
Broad money	48.6	18.0	15.0
3M interest rate	42.8	19.7	18.5
Share prices	74.3	12.1	6.4

Note: Estimates based on first standardized differences

The second condition is that the relevance of $PC1$ should evenly be spread across countries or regions in contrast to $PC2$ and $PC3$. The factor loadings are estimated for the first three principal components of each variable. In table 7.7, the results are presented for real GDP, inflation, house prices, broad money, the short-term interest rate and share prices.[71]

The first common factor loads positively and to a significant extent on national variables. The only exemption from this pattern is Japan in which non-signicant impact coefficients for GDP and house prices are detected. This evidence suggests that country-specific developments play a more important role in Japan than in the rest of the world. Despite positive factor loadings in general, there are some differences in the coefficient size across countries and categories of variables. For example, the impact coefficients of the share price factor are of comparatively similar magnitude, whereas the factor loading sizes of other first principal components are more heterogenous. In order to get a yardstick for comparison, the impact coefficients of $PC2$ and $PC3$ on national variables are additionally estimated. They do not share the same positive sign and the number of insignificant coefficients rises. From this evidence, it is concluded that $PC2$

[71] Commodity prices are excluded from the estimates, since they apply to all countries apart from the variations in the respective exchange rate.

and *PC*3 primarily reflect idiosyncratic patterns. In contrast, the first principal components may be interpreted as common forces.

Table 7.7: Factor loadings

GDP	PC1	PC2	PC3
US	0.557 (0.047)	-0.248 (0.106)	0.220 (0.150)
EMU	0.297 (0.108)	0.587 (0.130)	-0.567 (0.215)
Japan	0.054 (0.109)	0.703 (0.103)	0.707 (0.135)
UK	0.500 (0.058)	0.167 (0.146)	-0.268 (0.100)
Canada	0.589 (0.035)	-0.268 (0.127)	0.242 (0.129)
Money	PC1	PC2	PC3
US	0.281 (0.093)	0.899 (0.082)	0.310 (0.173)
EMU	0.367 (0.079)	-0.404 (0.148)	0.834 (0.130)
Japan	0.502 (0.050)	-0.024 (0.129)	-0.218 (0.174)
UK	0.522 (0.043)	-0.168 (0.148)	-0.306 (0.178)
Canada	0.512 (0.052)	-0.010 (0.156)	-0.245 (0.143)
3M interest rates	PC1	PC2	PC3
US	0.530 (0.061)	-0.484 (0.115)	-0.002 (0.105)
EMU	0.385 (0.087)	0.601 (0.114)	-0.322 (0.125)
Japan	0.272 (0.064)	0.154 (0.111)	0.926 (0.050)
UK	0.453 (0.060)	0.456 (0.111)	-0.058 (0.074)
Canada	0.539 (0.048)	-0.415 (0.123)	-0.185 (0.105)
House prices	PC1	PC2	PC3
US	0.394 (0.128)	-0.399 (0.136)	0.794 (0.165)
EMU	0.513 (0.073)	0.466 (0.117)	0.023 (0.171)
Japan	0.144 (0.110)	0.718 (0.063)	0.158 (0.189)
UK	0.467 (0.073)	-0.324 (0.116)	-0.569 (0.197)
Canada	0.586 (0.060)	-0.059 (0.121)	-0.140 (0.115)
Inflation	PC1	PC2	PC3
US	0.348 (0.026)	-0.026 (0.070)	-0.099 (0.108)
EMU	0.261 (0.033)	0.235 (0.066)	0.101 (0.091)
Japan	0.174 (0.043)	0.295 (0.050)	0.144 (0.083)
UK	0.246 (0.049)	0.210 (0.088)	-0.097 (0.079)
Canada	0.227 (0.040)	0.153 (0.070)	-0.228 (0.075)
Share prices	PC1	PC2	PC3
US	0.478 (0.019)	-0.238 (0.161)	0.092 (0.231)
EMU	0.464 (0.031)	-0.098 (0.164)	-0.403 (0.256)
Japan	0.357 (0.049)	0.916 (0.116)	0.145 (0.204)
UK	0.466 (0.026)	-0.097 (0.178)	-0.509 (0.233)
Canada	0.449 (0.039)	-0.272 (0.147)	0.734 (0.240)

Note 1: Estimates based on first standardized differences

Note 2: Standard errors in paranthesis (using Newey-West)

Note 3: Factor loadings of global inflation in relation to domestic CPI

For examining the third and final condition, two simple regressions are run. In the first equation, the dependent variable is the respective national time series and the independent variable is $PC1$. This estimate is the same one for obtaining the factor loadings in table 7.7. In the second regression, the first principal component is replaced by national variables. In order to get a parsimonious procedure as much as possible, exclusively US variables are used. The US economy is the largest one in the world, thereby possibly influencing other national economies and rivaling the impact of global factors on other countries. For instance, a regression is done between house prices in the UK as dependent variable and the global house price factor as independent one. Afterwards, the estimate is repeated. However, this time, not $PC1$ but US house prices are the independent variable.

The comparison of the obtained two R-squared measures indicates that each first principal component may be regarded as pervasive force (cf. table 7.8). Apart from Japan, the explanatory power of the regressions with $PC1$ as independent variable is always higher than the estimates with the corresponding US variable. For example, R-squared in the regression with the global house price factor amounts to 36.2% for the UK. The latter figure reduces to only 5.1% when US house prices are included as independent variable. An even more pronounced drop in explanatory power can be observed for the EMU with declining from 43.7% to nearby zero percent. Comparable effects also take place with respect to real GDP, broad money and short-term interest rates. Only for share prices, the differences in the two R-squared measures are less pronounced in general. This finding suggests that spill over effects from the US stock market on share prices in other countries play an important role.

Taking the obtained evidence for all three prerequisites together indicates that each $PC1$ may be regarded as a global factor picking up similarities across countries. Of course, this does not mean that all domestic variables are dominated by international developments. Overall, idiosyncratic events are seemingly still an important force in the G7 and the EMU. For instance, in many cases, the explanatory power of the first principal component is not above but below the threshold of 50%. However, the common patterns found by PCA seem to be worth further exploiting in empirical analysis.

Table 7.8: R-squared, in %

Real GDP	US	EMU	Japan	UK	Canada
PC1	56.5	16.2	0.0	45.8	63.4
US	---	1.9	0.0	5.3	26.6
Inflation	US	EMU	Japan	UK	Canada
PC1	77.8	43.8	19.4	39.1	33.1
US	---	32.7	13.9	25.7	29.7
House prices	US	EMU	Japan	UK	Canada
PC1	25.9	43.7	3.5	36.2	57.0
US	---	0.0	1.5	5.1	5.2
Broad money	US	EMU	Japan	UK	Canada
PC1	39.2	32.7	61.1	66.2	63.4
US	---	1.4	6.3	3.6	6.9
3M interest rates	US	EMU	Japan	UK	Canada
PC1	60.1	31.7	15.8	44.0	62.3
US	---	3.3	4.4	8.2	41.3
Share prices	US	EMU	Japan	UK	Canada
PC1	85.6	80.8	47.8	81.6	75.5
US	---	61.8	26.6	67.2	66.3

Note 1: Estimates based on first standardized differences

Note 2: R-squared for global inflation/US CPI with national CPI as dependent variable

The seven global factors $(f_{1t}, f_{2t}, ..., f_{7t})$ are used for estimating a FAVAR in levels including a constant and a time trend.[72] As the global factors have been obtained in first differences, they are "re-constructed" in levels by setting each global factor equal to zero in the first quarter of 1984 and calculating the cumulative sum of the first principal components.

The global innovations in the H matrix (cf. 7.2.1.6) can be identified by applying standard procedures like a Cholesky decomposition. However, a simple recursive ordering may not be appropriate in an international context. Given its low level of flexibility, one inevitably has to make extreme assumptions about the interaction between global variables. Moreover, the complexities of international policymaking are not appropriately reflected in a Wold-causal chain (cf. chapter 7.1.2).

[72] Unit root tests (Augmented Dickey-Fuller, Phillips-Perron and Kwiatkowski-Phillips-Schmidt-Shin) suggest that the derived reduced-form residuals are stationary (cf. appendix A.13).

Hence, in order to identify the global structural shocks, the following assumptions are made in the SFAVAR:[73]

$$(7.2.2.1)\qquad \begin{bmatrix} 1 & 0 & 0 & 0 & 0 & 0 & 0 \\ 0 & 1 & a_{23} & 0 & 0 & 0 & 0 \\ a_{31} & 0 & 1 & a_{34} & a_{35} & a_{36} & a_{37} \\ 0 & 0 & 0 & 1 & 0 & 0 & 0 \\ a_{51} & a_{52} & 0 & 0 & 1 & a_{56} & 0 \\ 0 & 0 & a_{63} & a_{64} & a_{65} & 1 & 0 \\ a_{71} & a_{72} & a_{73} & a_{74} & a_{75} & a_{76} & 1 \end{bmatrix} \begin{bmatrix} \eta_t^{YR} \\ \eta_t^{PI} \\ \eta_t^{CP} \\ \eta_t^{HP} \\ \eta_t^{M} \\ \eta_t^{SR} \\ \eta_t^{SP} \end{bmatrix} = \begin{bmatrix} \varpi_t^{YR} \\ \varpi_t^{PI} \\ \varpi_t^{CP} \\ \varpi_t^{HP} \\ \varpi_t^{M} \\ \varpi_t^{SR} \\ \varpi_t^{SP} \end{bmatrix}$$

with η_t as the vector of errors in the reduced-form equations and ϖ_t as the common structural shocks. It is assumed that the global GDP (YR) and the global house price factor (HP) are not influenced contemporaneously by any other global variable due to lags in the transmission mechanism. The common inflation force (PI) is affected within the same quarter only by the commodity price factor (CP). The latter is influenced at the same time by all other common factors apart from inflation. The global money factor (M) is determined contemporaneously by the GDP and inflation force as well as by the short-term interest rate (SR). The same assumption is made by Sousa and Zaghini (2007, p. 413) when estimating a global SVAR. For the reaction function of central banks' worldwide, it is assumed that they react within the same quarter to commodity prices, global house prices and global money, but not to economic activity and inflation due to time lags in publication. Of course, residential property prices are often not timely available either. However, given their usually high persistence, this assumption does not seem to be overly critical. Share prices (SP) are assumed to respond to all other global variables at the same time, as available information is quickly priced in by market participants.

To determine the lag length, the usual criteria such as the Likelihood Ratio test, the Final Prediction Error, the Akaike information criterion, the Schwarz criterion and the Hannan-Quinn criterion are applied. Most of the criteria point to a lag length of two which is also sufficient to avoid serial correlation among the residuals and seems to be appropriate in order to estimate a model that is as parsimonious as possible. The White

---

[73] Since some structure on the global economy is imposed, the notion of a Structural FAVAR (SFAVAR) is introduced instead of a pure FAVAR analysis.

test suggests that the reduced-form innovations are jointly homoskedastic. However, in some single equations, signs of heteroskedasticity still emerge. The null hypothesis of jointly normally distributed residuals in the Jarque-Bera test is rejected (cf. appendix A.14 for the corresponding statistics).[74] Since there is some misspecification, caution is appropriate when the results are interpreted in the following.

The LR test for overidentified VARs suggests that the short-run restrictions cannot be rejected at any conventional significance level. The statistic is equal to 5.1 and the corresponding p-value is 0.17.

The major result of the impulse response analysis is that common money shocks significantly influence the global economy. The outcomes of the empirical analysis are in line with economic theory. For example, the price puzzle and the liquidity puzzle do not appear. As can be seen in figure 7.7 below, a global liquidity innovation has a significant positive impact on global GDP after six quarters. As before, the solid line in each figure represents the response to a one standard deviation shock measured in standard deviations. The dashed lines represent the 95% confidence intervals based on a standard residual bootstrap procedure with 500 draws. Furthermore, global inflation significantly responds with a considerable time lag of 11 quarters to a global liquidity shock, showing a persistently positive effect afterwards. This result suggests that a higher common money force drives up the level of goods prices in the medium-term. Strong responses can also be found for the house price and the short-term interest rate factor. Global house prices rise strongly without any delay, albeit the response is only temporarily significant in line with the postulated hypothesis in chapter 4 (cf. table 4.1). The outcome may indicate that excess liquidity on a worldwide level had contributed to the phase of exceptionally high increases in residential property prices across countries before the recent financial crisis set in. Moreover, the different reaction patterns in the common inflation and house price force are in line with different price elasticities on asset and goods markets as suggested by Belke, Orth and Setzer (2010, p. 1938f.). Temporarily, global money shocks drive short-term interest rates down strongly by up to one standard deviation. Accordingly, the derived common liquidity innovations can be interpreted as global money supply disturbances.

[74] Furthermore, LM ARCH tests are conducted. The detailed results can be found in chapter 7.3 where the asymmetric behavior of central banks is examined (cf. table 7.25). ARCH effects are found in the global money, global house price and global short-term interest rate equations.

Figure 7.7: Impulse response analysis in SFAVAR (global money supply shock)

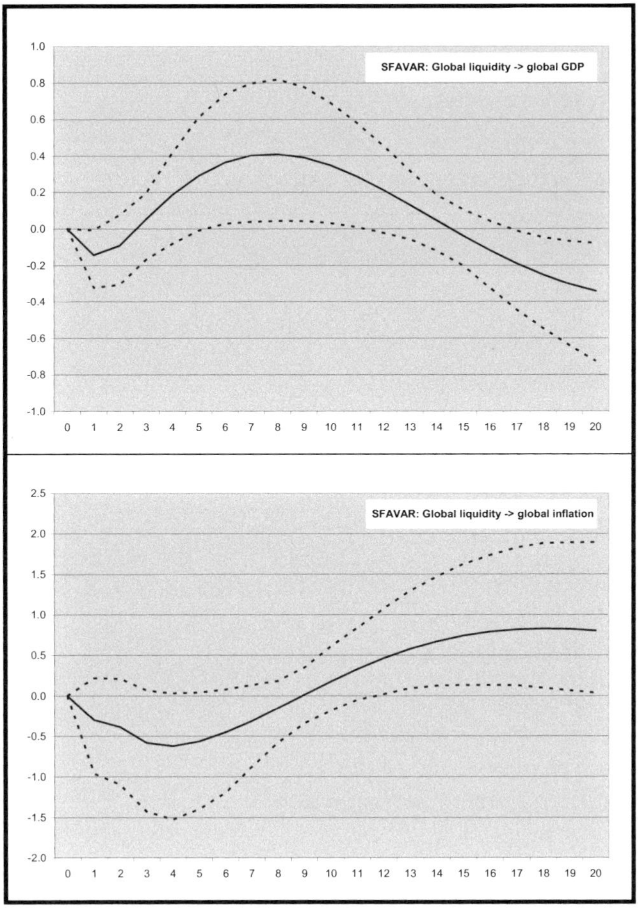

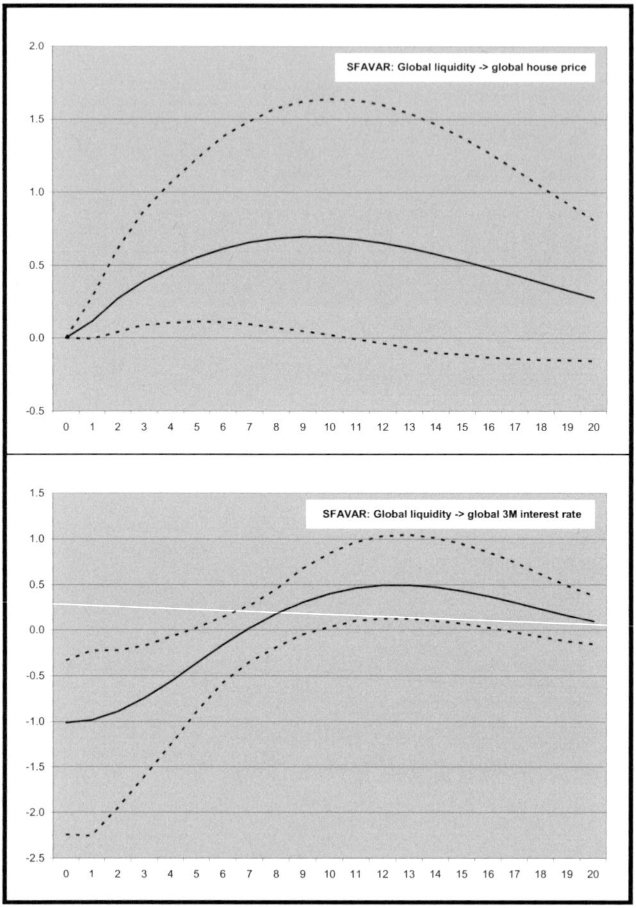

All in all, the impulse response analysis seems to confirm the results found by Rüffer and Stracca (2006) and Belke, Orth and Setzer (2010) on the basis of global VARs: Common liquidity disturbances influence major macroeconomic variables on an international level. However, with respect to asset prices, the results show some marked differences compared to previous empirical work. Furthermore, some of the hypotheses postulated in chapter 4 can be rejected. A significantly positive impact both on commodity and share prices is not found (cf. figure 7.8)[75], whereas Belke, Orth and

[75] A money demand channel is also not at work, since global money does not react positively and to a significant extent to a global share price and commodity price shock. This effect can only be found after a common house price disturbance (cf. appendix A.15 for the full set of impulse responses).

Setzer (2010, p. 1939) report a significantly positive response of commodity prices to a global liquidity shock. A study conducted by Alessi and Detken (2009) finds that global measures of liquidity, like the M1 gap and the private credit gap, are useful early warning indicators of asset price booms in OECD countries. Their asset price measure includes house prices as well as commercial property and share prices.

Figure 7.8: Response of commodity and share prices to a global money supply shock

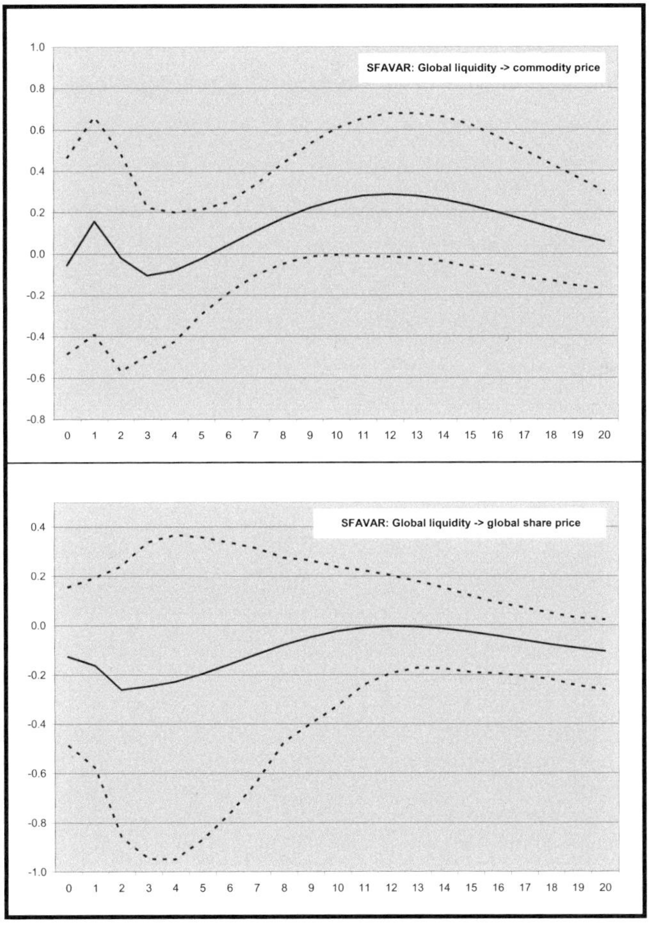

Apart from the common liquidity force, global economic activity and house price disturbances prove to be significant as well (cf. figure 7.9). For example, a sudden change in the GDP innovation leads to higher inflation from quarter two to quarter eleven. Hence, and in contrast to the response to a global money supply shock, the inflationary effect is only temporary. Significant responses of common factors to a global house price shock can also be found. In contrast, the common short-term interest rate is not a driving but a driven force. For example, an interest rate shock does not trigger any significant response of the common house price factor. Instead, a sudden change in the disturbance of residential property prices leads to an increasing short-term interest rate in the beginning. Belke, Orth and Setzer (2008b, p. 416f.) argue that monetary policymakers had not directly reacted to house price developments until the subprime crisis. Instead, they propose that residential property prices are correlated with inflation expectations. Furthermore, changes in house prices may induce wealth effects and therefore variations in private households' propensity to purchase consumer goods.

The same insignificant results are found after shocks to the inflation factor and commodity and share prices (see appendix A.15 for the full set of impulse responses). Especially the outcome that commodity price disturbances do not play any significant role in the global economy is a surprising one. Both in theoretical and empirical research, they are usually regarded as *the* classic example of a common shock which applies to many countries simultaneously.

Figure 7.9: Impulse response analysis in SFAVAR (various global shocks)

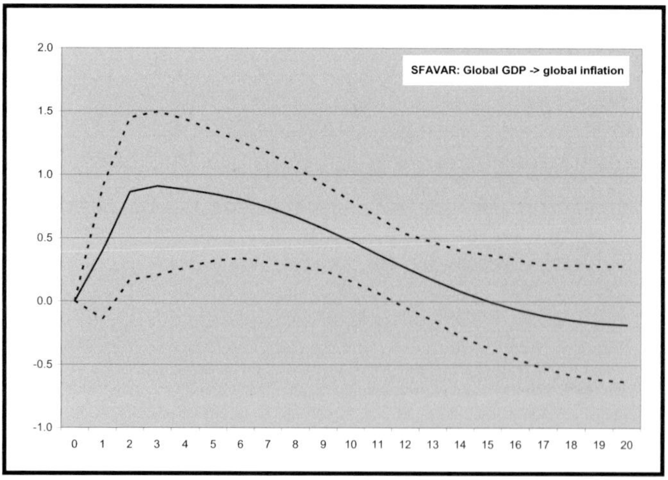

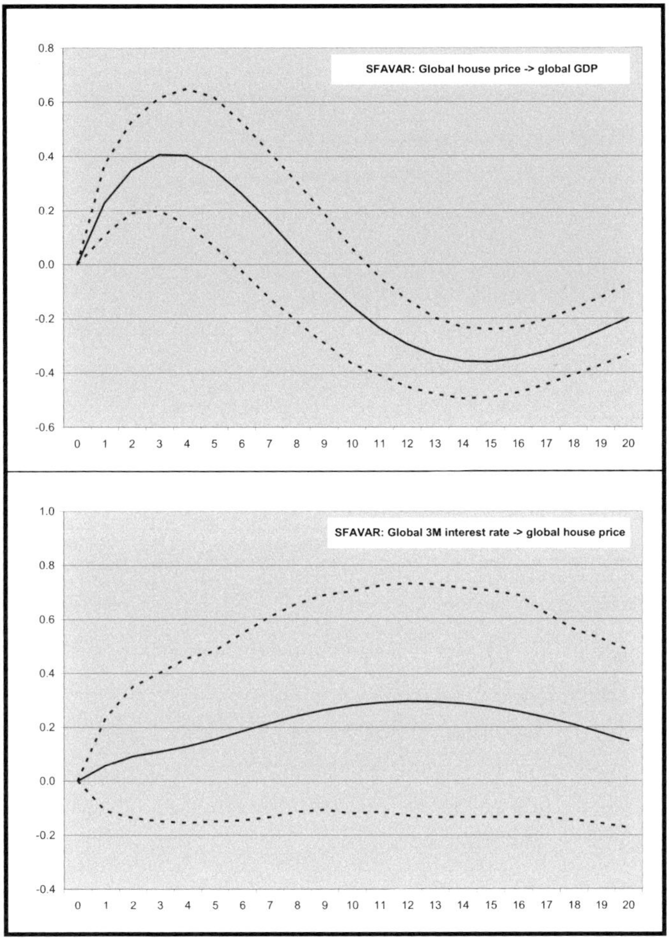
SFAVAR: Global house price -> global GDP
0.8
0.6
0.4
0.2
0.0
-0.2
-0.4
-0.6
0 1 2 3 4 5 6 7 8 9 10 11 12 13 14 15 16 17 18 19 20
SFAVAR: Global 3M interest rate -> global house price
1.0
0.8
0.6
0.4
0.2
0.0
-0.2
-0.4
0 1 2 3 4 5 6 7 8 9 10 11 12 13 14 15 16 17 18 19 20

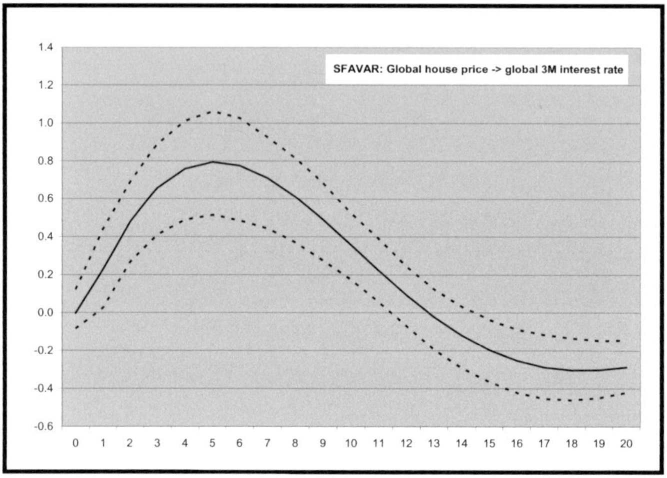

7.2.3 IMPULSE RESPONSE ANALYSIS (II): NATIONAL VARIABLES

In order to investigate the effects of global and idiosyncratic structural shocks on national economies, the equation $X_t = \Lambda\Phi(L)F_{t-1} + D(L)X_{t-1} + \varepsilon_{Xt}$ has to be estimated. However, since $D(L)$ is a $N \times N$ matrix lag polynomial with $N = 55$, a completely endogenous setting in which all variables can interact across countries yields substantial practical problems. Please keep in mind that for each of the analyzed five countries or regions eleven variables are included in the dataset (real GDP, four inflation measures, two commodity price indices in domestic currency, house prices, broad money, short-term interest rate and share prices). In addition, the seven global factors also have to be added to each equation. Accordingly, the strong decline in the degrees of freedom makes estimating the SFAVAR on a national level not feasible any longer. Even if only a lag length of one is chosen for both common forces and national variables, each equation contains a total of 62 parameters (64 parameters if a constant and a deterministic trend are included). Although using a smaller dataset, Bagliano and Morana (2009, p. 439) nevertheless estimate 43 coefficients on the basis of a sample ranging from Q1 1980 to Q2 2005. Once again, the typical empirical trade-off between economic considerations and technical feasibility emerges.

Given these problems, an alternative approach is pursued in the following. Instead of a fully endogenous setting, separate VARs for each country or region are derived. Hence, it is possible to examine spillovers from global factors to national variables. At the same time, idiosyncratic spillover effects between countries are intentionally neglected. More technically spoken, the fully endogenous and unrestricted $N \times N$ matrix lag polynomial $D(L)$ (cf. 7.2.1.3) is transformed into a restricted diagonal $o \times o$ matrix lag polynomial $K(L)$. In the first step, the N elements of X_t are stacked into o national sub-vectors. Each sub-vector contains m elements which are exclusively country-specific variables like national GDP, prices, money, the short-term interest rate etc.[76] In the second step, the matrix lag polynomial $K(L)$ is obtained by imposing the following zero restrictions:

(7.2.3.1) $$K(L) = \begin{bmatrix} k_1(L) & 0 & 0 & 0 & 0 \\ 0 & k_2(L) & 0 & 0 & 0 \\ 0 & 0 & k_3(L) & 0 & 0 \\ 0 & 0 & 0 & k_4(L) & 0 \\ 0 & 0 & 0 & 0 & k_5(L) \end{bmatrix}$$

where $k_o(L)$ with $o = 1...5$ represent the m-variate lag polynomials of the national VARs.[77] In this setting, national variables in one country are allowed to interact with each other but not with variables from another country. The FAVAR expression $X_t = \Lambda\Phi(L)F_{t-1} + D(L)X_{t-1} + \varepsilon_{Xt}$ is then converted into the following equation:

(7.2.3.2) $$X_t = \Lambda\Phi(L)F_{t-1} + K(L)X_{t-1} + \varepsilon_{Xt}$$

The national VARs for the G7 and the euro zone with the lag polynomials $k_o(L)$ have a reduced-form and can be transformed into a structural model. The procedure works as follows. The national variables in levels are again "re-constructed" by calculating the cumulative sum of the standardized national variables.[78] This is necessary to be fully consistent with the approach on the global level. Since a national economy can be hit by both common and idiosyncratic shocks, one has to distinguish between these two effects. The error term ε_{Xt} which consists of global and idiosyncratic disturbances is regressed on the global structural innovations (ϖ_t). On the basis of the

[76] The concise data set for the national sub-vectors can be found in the expression (7.2.3.3) and will then be explained in more detail.
[77] This exclusion restriction will be tested in chapter 7.2.5.
[78] Beforehand, all variables apart from the short-term interest rates are transformed into log first differences. For the short-term interest rates, first differences are calculated.

obtained country-specific components, $m(m-1)/2$ restrictions can be imposed for exact identification on a national level. However, and again, it is refrained from using a Cholesky decomposition. Instead, structural relationships between the respective variables are implemented as follows:

$$\begin{bmatrix} 1 & 0 & 0 & 0 & 0 & 0 & 0 \\ 0 & 1 & 0 & 0 & 0 & a_{26} & 0 \\ 0 & 0 & 1 & 0 & 0 & 0 & 0 \\ a_{41} & a_{42} & 0 & 1 & a_{45} & a_{46} & 0 \\ 0 & 0 & a_{53} & a_{54} & 1 & a_{56} & 0 \\ a_{61} & a_{62} & a_{63} & a_{64} & a_{65} & 1 & a_{67} \\ a_{71} & a_{72} & a_{73} & a_{74} & a_{75} & a_{76} & 1 \end{bmatrix} \begin{bmatrix} v_t^{YR} \\ v_t^{PI} \\ v_t^{HP} \\ v_t^{M} \\ v_t^{SR} \\ v_t^{ER} \\ v_t^{SP} \end{bmatrix} = \begin{bmatrix} \xi_t^{YR} \\ \xi_t^{PI} \\ \xi_t^{HP} \\ \xi_t^{M} \\ \xi_t^{SR} \\ \xi_t^{ER} \\ \xi_t^{SP} \end{bmatrix} \tag{7.2.3.3}$$

with v_t as the vector of country-specific reduced-form errors and ξ_t as the vector of idiosyncratic structural disturbances. The restrictions on a national level resemble the assumptions made for global variables. For example, GDP (YR) and house prices (HP) are not influenced contemporaneously by other national variables. By using the short-term interest rate (SR), the central bank is supposed to react at the same time to money (M), the exchange rate and house prices. The inflation figure (PI) equals consumer prices and is only affected by the real effective exchange rate (ER) at the same time. The latter variable and share prices (SP) are assumed to respond contemporaneously to all other variables.

Please note that not all available national variables used for deriving the global factors are implemented in (7.2.3.3) for identifying the m structural idiosyncratic shocks. There are both statistical and economic reasons for this approach. From a statistical viewpoint, using all domestic variables for one country would still lead to a classic degrees-of-freedom problem despite the implementation of the restricted $K(L)$ matrix. Hence, for instance, only one domestic inflation measure in form of the CPI is used, whereas producer prices, import prices and the GDP deflator are not considered in (7.2.3.3). Since central banks typically focus on the development of consumer prices, this procedure seems to be justified. Furthermore, innovations to the two commodity price indices (HWWI and CRB) are interpreted as global phenomena and excluded from the idiosyncratic disturbances matrix. Otherwise, the difference between global and country-specific shocks might be blurred, thereby hampering proper identification as has possibly been the case for the EMU VARs in chapter 7.1.2. The applied setting still allows disturbances to the commodity price factor to influence national variables via the lagged common forces ($\Phi(L)F_{t-1}$).

Finally, the real effective exchange rate is added to the set of domestic variables in equation (7.2.3.3) and used for the identification of the country-specific disturbances. The reason for this is that the exchange rate may play a role in the national transmission mechanism of open economies. Bagliano and Morana (2009, p. 437) pursue a different approach by estimating a common real exchange rate factor for the G7 and the EMU. However, the economic meaning of this global exchange rate factor is dubious. Exchange rate variations are changes in relative prices of currencies, thereby canceling out each other on a global level. For instance, a weaker euro exchange rate automatically equals appreciating currencies of other countries or regions.

Before presenting the structural impulse responses on a national level, two cautionary remarks in interpreting the results seem to be appropriate. First, both the variables included in the VAR and the identification patterns are the same for all countries, although the countries differ markedly in economic size. For instance, the exchange rate might play an important role for comparatively small open economies like Canada and the UK but not for the US. Second, despite trying to derive national VAR models as parsimonious as possible, analyzing the impact of global shocks on national variables is still rather costly in terms of degrees of freedom. Since the whole SFAVAR contains seven factors and seven national variables with two lags each, 30 parameters (including a constant and a deterministic component) have to be estimated per equation.[79]

In the following, the effects of global money supply shocks on national variables are analyzed. As has been the case before, the 95 percent confidence bands are derived from a residual bootstrap with 500 draws. Accordingly, global liquidity disturbances have a significant impact on broad national monetary aggregates in the EMU, the US (cf. figure 7.10) and Canada. This may reflect an endogenous money and credit creation

[79] For each of the national sub-models, a lag length of two is chosen. Otherwise, too many degrees of freedom would have been lost. *LM* tests indicate that serial correlation among the residuals is of minor importance. However, there are signs of heteroskedasticity (apart from the Canadian model) and ARCH effects. Furthermore, the null hypothesis of jointly normally distributed residuals is rejected in each sub-model (cf. appendix A.16 for the detailed test statistics).

process triggered by international capital flows. However, the responses differ in their magnitude and persistence, thereby indicating that various national transmission mechanisms are at work. In the UK and Japan, there are no significant effects of common liquidity shocks on domestic monetary aggregates.

Figure 7.10: Response of EMU and US money to a global money supply shock

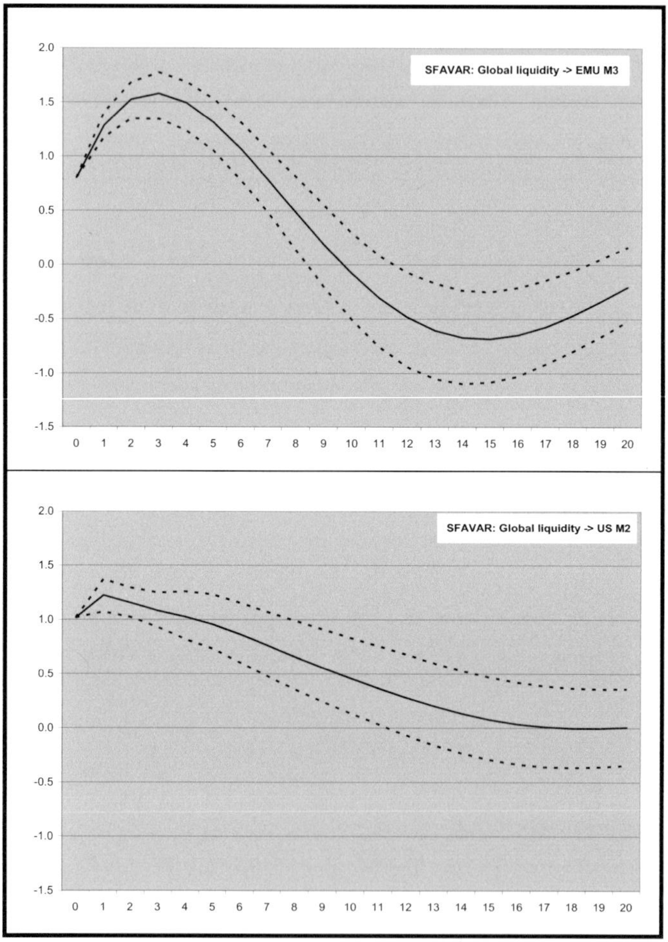

As can be seen in table 7.9 below, innovations to global money supply also trigger significant responses of other major national variables like real GDP, consumer prices, house and share prices across countries.[80] However, and surprisingly, these effects do not occur primarily in comparatively small open economies such as the UK and Canada but in the US and the EMU. Of the seven national variables included in the US VAR, five are significantly influenced. Only the exchange rate and share prices do not respond on basis of the bootstrapped 95 percent confidence intervals. In the euro area, four variables react significantly. This is at odds with theoretical considerations which suggest that foreign shocks in economies of large size should only play a negligible role. One explanation for this pattern could be the huge and deep financial markets in the US and the EMU, thereby attracting cross-border capital flows and making monetary spillover effects more likely.

What is also conspicuous is that there are some puzzles on the national level, whereas this is not the case for the global impulse response analysis done before. In total, of the 35 responses (seven variables for each of the five countries or regions), six puzzles are detected: one with respect to the exchange rate in the euro area and the UK, one in Canada (GDP) and three in Japan (GDP, CPI, house prices). The latter might have to do with the special circumstances in Japan since the beginning of the 1990s. Nevertheless, this evidence could also indicate that neglecting the interaction between countries yields some drawbacks in form of atheoretical results.

Furthermore, the persistence and the timing of the responses to a global money supply disturbance are not always in line with the postulated hypotheses in chapter 4 (cf. table 4.1). For instance, it is expected that a positive innovation to the common liquidity force causes a permanent rise in the domestic price level. However, only a temporary effect can be found in case of the US. Another example is the reaction of the US short-term interest rate. Although the temporary negative response is in line with expectations, it does not occur immediately but only after a considerable time lag of 9 quarters. US GDP reacts positively as postulated, albeit without any delay.

[80] A set of impulse responses on a country level in chart form is included in appendix A.17.

Table 7.9: Overview of significant responses to positive global money supply shocks (sign of responses in paranthesis)

	US	EMU	Japan	UK	Canada
GDP	(+) T I	(+) T D	(–) T D	---	(–) T D
Inflation	(+) T D	---	(–) T D	---	---
House prices	(+) T D	---	(–) T D	---	---
Broad money	(+) T I	(+) T I	---	---	(+) P I
Short-term interest rates	(–) T D	---	(–) T D	---	---
Exchange rate	---	(–)/(+) T I	---	(–) T D	(+) T I
Share prices	---	(+) T D	---	(+) T I	---

Note 1: Significant responses based on bootstrapped 95 percent confidence interval

Note 2: T=temporary; P=permanent; D=delayed; I=immediate

In the following, the outcomes for the EMU and partly for the US are explained in more detail. Economic activity in the euro area reacts positively with a time lag of seven quarters to a global money supply shock. In order to get a yardstick for comparison, the response of euro zone GDP to a structural idiosyncratic money supply shock is derived as well (cf. figure 7.11).[81] The impulse response function displays a rather similar dynamic but is somewhat more pronounced in its impact on domestic economic activity.[82] This stands in contrast to the results derived from the two conventional EMU VARs in chapter 7.1.2. In both models, the global excess liquidity disturbance does not trigger a significant response of domestic economic activity. One conceivable reason for this result is that global money supply and global money demand shocks are confounded in open economy VARs. The concise distinction between common and country-specific innovations is also not possible.

In contrast to economic activity, no significant effect on EMU CPI can be found after a global common liquidity shock. Consumer prices in the euro area show a positive reaction to an idiosyncratic money innovation after eleven quarters. However, the effect is not persistent. Moreover, a temporary price puzzle occurs in the beginning after the disturbance sets in. This might indicate a misspecification in the euro zone, as the identification seems to work well on a global level. At this stage, it is not clear whether the missing interaction between countries or regions is responsible for this pattern.

[81] EMU money shocks are interpreted as money *supply* innovations, since the domestic short-term interest rate declines after a positive country-specific disturbance to EMU money.

[82] In Appendix A.18, further comparisons between the impact of global and country-specific money disturbances can be found. Besides domestic economic activity, the comparison is done for the following national variables across the G7 countries plus the EMU: CPI, house prices and the short-term interest rate. Overall, the effects of idiosyncratic broad money innovations on domestic variables in Japan, the UK and Canada are negligible.

Another explanation could be that there are nevertheless other global forces at work which are not explicitly considered in the FAVAR. For instance, technology disturbances on a national or global level may occur as suggested by the real business cycle theory. With this topic will be dealt in more detail in chapter 7.2.6.

Figure 7.11: Response of EMU GDP and EMU prices to global and idiosyncratic money supply shocks

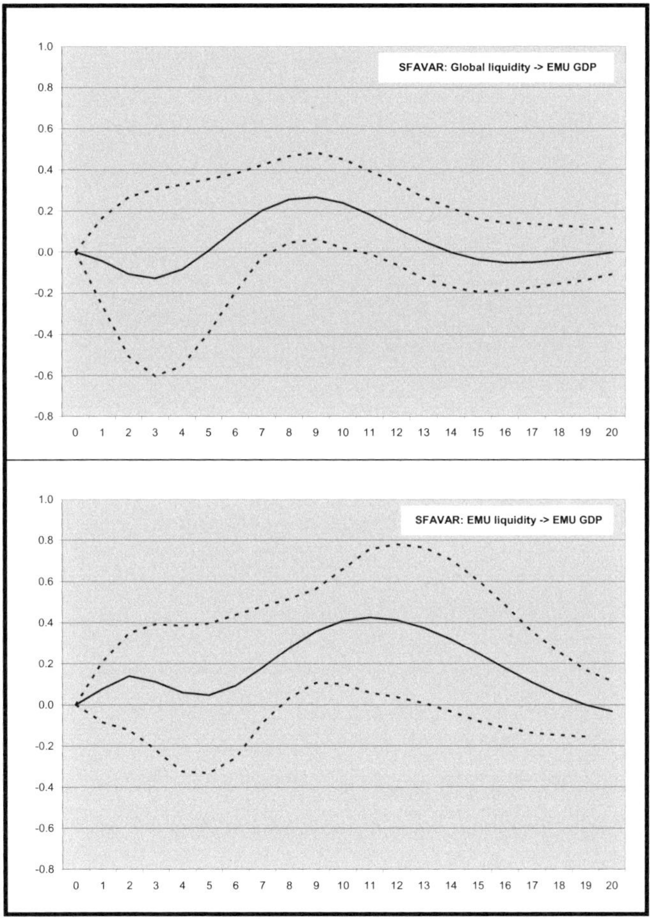

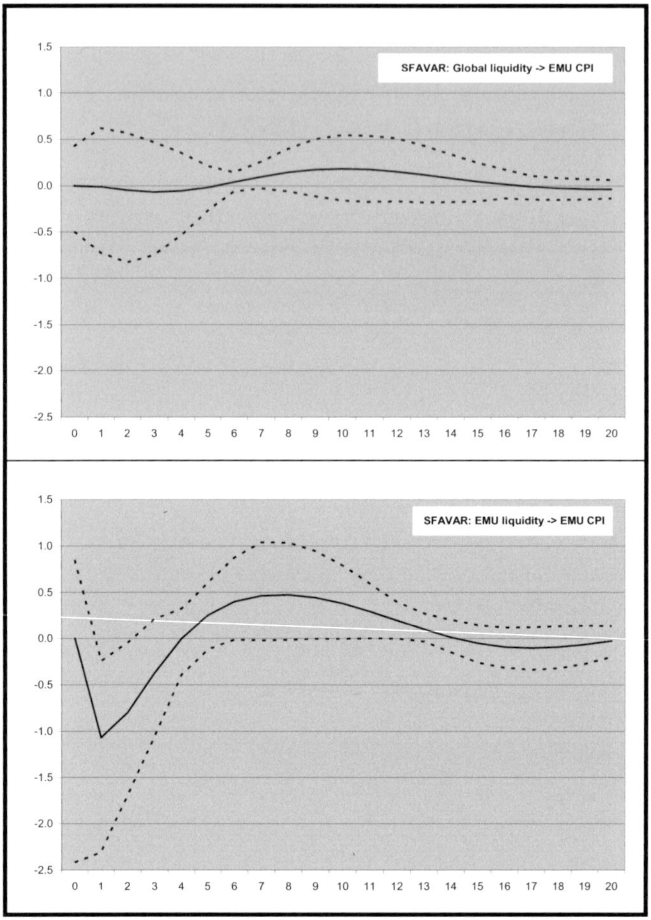

As has been discussed in chapter 7.1.2, an interesting issue is whether interest rates (NOEM) or exchange rates (MFD) are central in transmitting foreign money supply shocks to domestic macroeconomic variables. After a global liquidity shock, the short-term interest rate in the euro area does not react significantly. Furthermore, the common monetary expansion leads to a temporary exchange rate puzzle, i.e. the effective euro exchange rate declines strongly before an appreciation sets in. From this evidence, it may be concluded that both the interest rate and exchange rate channel play a less important role than suggested by established open economy models. However, at the same time, substantial caution is appropriate, since the existence of a puzzle may point towards misspecification. Additionally, the New Open Economy Macroeconomics focuses on long-term interest rates instead of money market rates. Hence, an outright rejection of the NOEM hypothesis is not possible.[83]

[83] In chapter 7.2.6, the influence of the long-term interest rate will be examined in detail by including long-term interest rates both on a global and national level.

Figure 7.12: Response of EMU interest rate and exchange rate to a global money supply shock

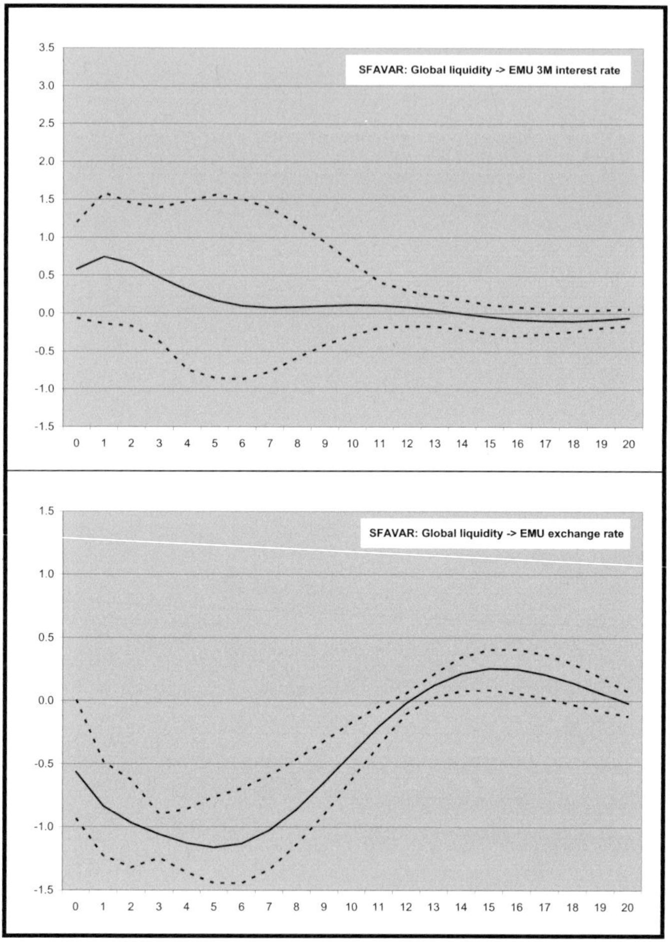

With respect to house prices in the euro zone, the empirical evidence indicates that idiosyncratic innovations are more important than global ones (cf. figure 7.13). After a country-specific money supply disturbance, house prices rise significantly from quarter 4 to 14. In contrast, the response to a common money supply shock is less pronounced and not different from zero. This stands in contrast to the evidence obtained for the US where house prices are driven by both forces. The positive impact from the global money supply shock is even stronger than the one from the idiosyncratic shock.[84] Hence, the bubble in the US residential property market in recent years may not only be explained by a rising domestic money supply or exceptionally low short-term interest rates but by excessive global liquidity as well.

Figure 7.13: Response of EMU and US house prices to global and idiosyncratic money supply shocks

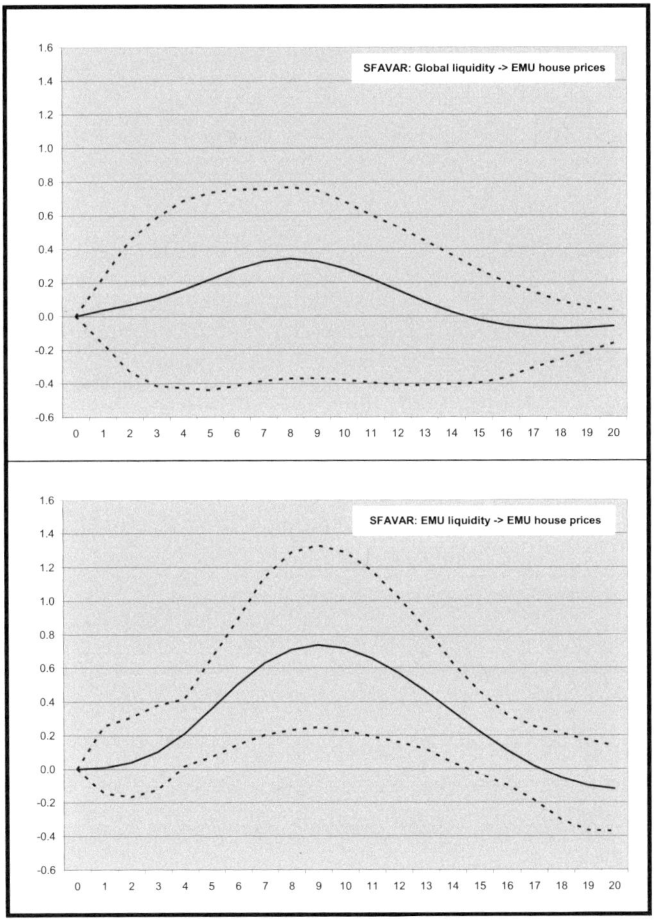

[84] US money shocks are interpreted as money *supply* innovations, since the domestic short-term interest rate declines after a positive country-specific disturbance to US money.

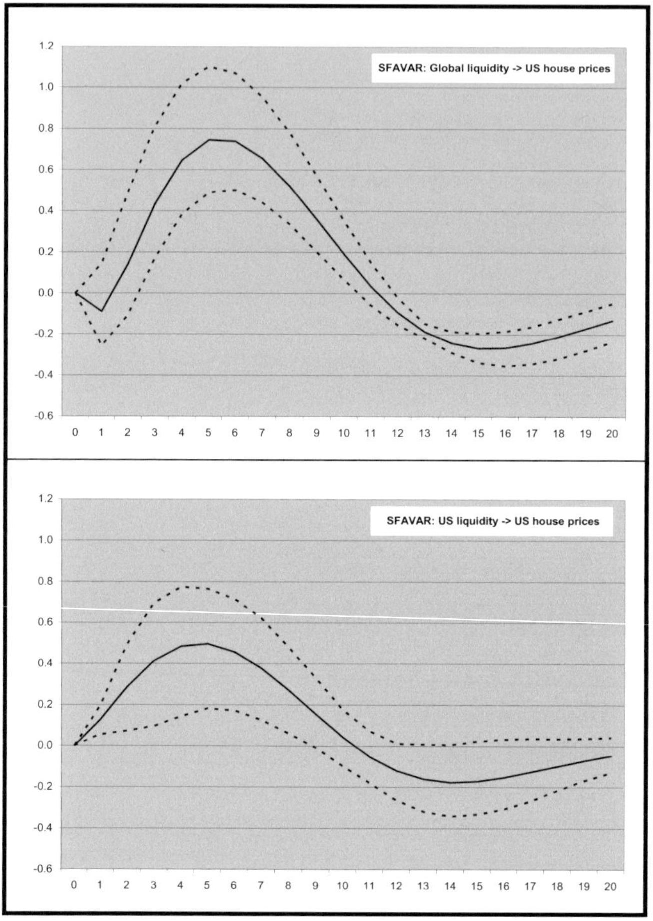

To sum up, the results allow conclusions about the sources of co-movement. Although the US and the euro area are hit by the same global excess liquidity shock, the responses sometimes differ substantially. Common disturbances are only a necessary but not a sufficient condition for generating co-movement in economies and on financial markets across countries and regions. Only if similar or at least comparable transmission mechanisms are at work, the impulse provided by the global shock triggers a likewise response (Bagliano, Morana 2010, p. 2327ff.). This is seemingly not the case for the housing market but for economic activity. Despite some differences in the size and speed of the responses, a common money supply shock leads to a temporary higher path of real GDP both in the US and the euro zone (cf. appendix A.18 for the US impulse response in chart form).

7.2.4 VARIANCE DECOMPOSITION ANALYSIS

The impulse response analysis in the previous two sections quantifies the reaction of global and domestic variables to common exogenous shocks. Implications about the propagation mechanism between the global and national level can be derived. An alternative method for examining the effects of disturbances on endogenous variables is the forecast error variance decomposition. It separates the variation in an endogenous variable into the component shocks to the VAR, thereby providing information about the relative importance of each random innovation. In the SFAVAR setting, the forecast error variance analysis can be done both for global factors and domestic variables over specific time horizons. Furthermore, it is possible to compare the importance of common and idiosyncratic shocks for each country or region.

First, it is concentrated on the interaction of global factors. The chosen time horizon contains 20 quarters. The left column of table 7.10 shows the endogenous common forces for which the variance decomposition analysis is conducted. In the remaining columns, the global factor shocks contributing to the variation of each common force are to be found. Accordingly, common money supply shocks are the driving force of house prices on a global level. The variance share is a high 52.3%. In contrast, the short-term interest factor contributes only 8.5% to the variation in residential property prices. Global money is also important in explaining movements in the short-term interest rate (36.5%). However, with respect to economic activity and prices, the relevance is rather limited with variance shares of only 9.3% and 6.0%, respectively. Here, the impact of the interest rate factor is far higher (31.1% and 51.0%). This suggests that, in contrast to the hypotheses in chapter 4, global money is not "unique" but rivaled by other variables. With respect to commodity and share prices, neither money supply disturbances nor other shocks play an important role. This confirms the results obtained from the impulse response analysis. After 20 quarters, shocks to commodity prices are still responsible for 70% of the variation in commodity prices. For share prices, the ratio is 71.2%.

Table 7.10: Forecast error variance decomposition of global factors at period 20 (in %)

	GDP	Goods prices	Commodity prices	House prices	Money	Interest rate	Share prices
GDP	21.1	6.4	6.1	3.5	9.3	31.1	22.4
Goods prices	5.2	19.5	8.9	6.5	6.0	51.0	2.7
Commodity prices	5.6	3.1	70.0	4.0	1.1	5.6	10.5
House prices	0.6	21.3	7.1	5.8	52.3	8.5	4.4
Money	1.0	14.0	10.3	4.2	24.9	31.7	13.8
Short-term interest rate	4.9	10.9	7.2	7.5	36.5	18.8	14.2
Share prices	0.4	3.7	18.5	2.5	0.5	3.2	71.2

Note: Sum may not add up to 100% due to rounding effects

In a second step, the general importance of common and country-specific structural innovations is compared for the following national variables: real GDP, CPI, house prices, broad money and the short-term interest rate. Again, the time horizon is 20 quarters. The variance decomposition analysis shows that global shocks in general are an important driver of domestic variables in the G7 countries and the EMU (cf. table 7.11). The forecast error variance shares typically range between 40% and 55%. This is also true for national broad monies and short-term interest rates. Common disturbances are even relevant for the variation in domestic house prices. The figure for the US is 49.1% and for the euro zone 53.4%. The only exemptions are national consumer prices with comparatively low shares (US: 30.7%; EMU: 37.2%).

Interestingly, the classic distinction between (comparatively) small open economies and large rather closed countries made in economic literature is not supported by the data. In most of the cases, global innovations are as important for domestic variables in the US as in the EMU, Canada and the UK. Only in Japan, the variance share of global shocks is lower. The outcome that both small and large economies are markedly impacted or sometimes even dominated by common forces is also found by Bagliano and Morana (2009, p. 440f.) who apply a global FAVAR as well. In contrast, according to Rüffer and Stracca (2006, p. 26), the effect of common disturbances on domestic variables is the smallest in the US, medium in Japan and largest in the euro area. The results are derived from national VAR models augmented by global aggregates.

The reason why global innovations are found to be more important for the US economy in this work could be a purely statistical one. Since only five countries or regions are included in the dynamic factor analysis, global shocks may be confounded with domestic disturbances in the US.[85] However, an economically more meaningful interpretation is also conceivable. For example, deep and liquid US financial markets attract international capital, thereby increasing the likelihood of monetary spillover effects from other countries.

Table 7.11: Forecast error variance decomposition of domestic variables at period 20 (in %)

	Total global shocks	Total idiosyncratic shocks
US GDP	50.5	49.5
EMU GDP	48.2	51.8
Japan GDP	41.3	58.7
UK GDP	48.9	51.1
Canada GDP	46.5	53.5
US CPI	30.7	69.3
EMU CPI	37.2	62.8
Japan CPI	41.6	58.4
UK CPI	34.5	65.5
Canada CPI	28.9	71.1
US house prices	49.1	50.9
EMU house prices	53.4	46.6
Japan house prices	44.8	55.2
UK house prices	46.5	53.5
Canada house prices	50.0	50.0
US broad money	43.8	56.2
EMU broad money	46.6	53.4
Japan broad money	41.3	58.7
UK broad money	55.1	44.9
Canada broad money	54.2	45.8
US short-term interest rate	55.3	44.7
EMU short-term interest rate	45.7	54.3
Japan short-term interest rate	41.2	58.8
UK short-term interest rate	49.6	50.4
Canada short-term interest rate	44.7	55.3

In the following, a more detailed analysis of the variance decomposition is done by focusing on the importance of global broad money compared to a variety of country-specific variables in the US and the euro zone. Again, the time horizon is 20 quarters. In the left column of table 7.12, the domestic variables for which the variance decomposition analysis is conducted can be found. In the remaining columns, the global and idiosyncratic shocks contributing to the variation of each national variable are shown. Five major results can be uncovered. First, global liquidity influences domestic broad money to a non-negligible extent. In the euro area, the variance share is 11.2%, in

[85] The robustness of the results for the US is examined in Chapter 7.2.8.

the US even 23.4%. Second, in the majority of cases, common liquidity plays a more important role in explaining domestic patterns than national monies and short-term interest rates do. For instance, the variance share of global money for EMU GDP is 8.7% compared to 3.5% and 1.3% in case of domestic money and the domestic short-term interest rate, respectively. Third, the variability of country-specific variables is partly affected to a greater extent by common money than by idiosyncratic developments excluding national money and the short-term interest rate. For example, global money contributes 8.2% to the variability of EMU consumer prices. This compares to 7.8% for domestic GDP and 6.4% for the effective exchange rate. Fourth, although global monetary liquidity is an important factor, other common forces in the SFAVAR significantly affect the variability of national variables. Again, global money is not "unique". Only in the case of US money, the variance share of common liquidity (23.4%) is higher than the sum of variances for all other global disturbances (20.4%). Fifth, and finally, there are some marked differences between the US and the EMU, thereby confirming the previous finding of the impulse response analysis that rather different transmission mechanisms are at work.

Table 7.12: Forecast error variance decomposition for the US and the euro area at period 20 (in %)

	Global money	Other global	Domestic money	Domestic GDP	Domestic interest rates	Exchange rate	Other domestic
US GDP	16.3	34.2	3.9	18.3	5.0	2.5	19.8
US CPI	9.9	20.8	1.2	5.1	16.6	5.5	40.9
US house prices	13.3	35.8	6.5	6.8	1.9	8.2	27.5
US money	23.4	20.4	19.8	9.1	11.2	1.5	14.6
US short-term interest rate	16.6	38.7	11.5	7.7	6.2	4.2	15.1
US exchange rate	5.6	41.2	0.9	12.8	6.8	25.8	6.9
US share prices	14.9	46.7	1.8	7.3	18.1	5.2	6.0
EMU GDP	8.7	39.5	3.5	8.9	1.3	17.1	21.0
EMU CPI	8.2	29.0	7.9	7.8	2.3	6.4	38.4
EMU house prices	3.9	49.5	10.6	0.4	0.8	16.5	18.3
EMU money	11.2	35.4	30.9	9.8	6.7	4.5	1.5
EMU short-term interest rate	4.7	41.0	4.6	11.3	13.5	9.2	15.7
EMU exchange rate	5.6	44.6	0.7	14.0	1.1	24.0	10.0
EMU share prices	1.7	39.5	0.6	5.5	2.8	23.1	26.8

Note: Sum may not add up to 100% due to rounding effects

7.2.5 EXCLUSION RESTRICTIONS

The FAVAR presented in chapter 7.2.1 implies two major exclusion restrictions. The first one states that X does not predict F given lagged F. According to the second one, X_j does not forecast X_i given lagged F for $i, j = 1,...,N$ and $i \neq j$. The testing of these two restrictions is necessary, as a rejection of the respective null hypothesis would indicate a misspecification of the applied FAVAR.

The first restriction is that X does not predict F given lagged F. More technically, the upper right block in equation (7.2.5.1) equals zero:

$$(7.2.5.1) \qquad \begin{bmatrix} F_t \\ X_t \end{bmatrix} = \begin{bmatrix} \Phi(L) & 0 \\ \Lambda\Phi(L) & D(L) \end{bmatrix} \begin{bmatrix} F_{t-1} \\ X_{t-1} \end{bmatrix} + \begin{bmatrix} \varepsilon_{Ft} \\ \varepsilon_{Xt} \end{bmatrix}$$

This exclusion restriction can be examined by sequentially including lagged national variables X_j in the factor evolution equation (Stock, Watson 2005a, p. 33f.):

$$(7.2.5.2) \qquad F_t = \Phi(L)F_{t-1} + \Psi_j(L)X_{jt-1} + \varepsilon_{Ft}$$

where $\Psi_j(L)$ is a r-variate vector lag polynomial with $r = 7$ and order $p = 2$ as is the case in the baseline SFAVAR. The null hypothesis is that $\Psi_j(L) = 0$ for $j = 1,...,35$.[86] One example shall shed further light on the procedure. The common money factor derived by PCA as the first principal component is interpreted as one pervasive force driving the global economy. Lagged national variables like monetary aggregates (X_{jt-1}) should therefore not Granger-cause the global liquidity factor f_t^L. Otherwise, the obtained impulse responses and the variance decompositions contain both global and idiosyncratic components and cannot be interpreted as reactions to a truly common money supply shock.

The exclusion restriction of $\Psi_j(L) = 0$ is examined via chi-squared tests and presented in table 7.13. Since some signs of heteroskedasticity are found in the global

---

[86] $\Psi_j(L)$ is a 7×1 vector lag polynomial in order to match the seven global factors. The number of national variables N reduces from 55 in the unrestricted $D(L)$ matrix to 35 in the restricted $K(L)$ matrix. Furthermore, the following variables are excluded from the idiosyncratic disturbances matrix in order to save degrees of freedom: producer prices, import prices, the GDP deflator and the two commodity price indices. In contrast, the real effective exchange rate is added to the set of country-specific variables (cf. chapter 7.2.3).

residuals, a heteroskedasticity (and autocorrelation) robust version is chosen by applying the Newey-West estimator.[87] Given that a total of 35 national variables are used, 35×7 tests can be conducted. For instance, lagged national monetary aggregates may not only Granger-cause the common liquidity force but the global GDP or inflation factor as well. In order to enable a comparison of all possible tests, Stock and Watson (2005a, p. 33f.) calculate the percentiles of the marginal empirical distribution of the p-values which is also done in this work. Under the null hypothesis, 5% of the p-values are expected to be less than 0.05. However, empirically, there are many more rejections. 5% of the p-values are less than 0.003 and 25% are still below 0.069.

Table 7.13: Percentiles of p-values from Granger causality tests ($X_{jt-1} \to F_t$)

	Percentile								
	0.010	0.050	0.100	0.250	0.500	0.750	0.900	0.950	0.990
National variables	0.000	0.003	0.012	0.069	0.276	0.589	0.816	0.902	0.969

Overall, these results suggest that the exclusion restriction of $\Psi_j(L) = 0$ is not appropriate, thereby signaling some misspecification of the FAVAR.[88] In the next step, Granger causality tests are conducted for selected country-specific variables and the common forces by neglecting "cross-variable" cases. For instance, chi-squared values are estimated for the relation between broad money in the euro area and the global liquidity factor but not for EMU GDP and the common money force. In addition, the two commodity price indices (HWWI and CRB future) expressed in domestic currency are not considered. These are global factors by definition apart from variations in the exchange rate.

The p-values (first figure in each cell of table 7.14) below show that the Granger causality tests between national and global liquidities are rejected in four of five cases at conventional significance levels of less than 10%. Only M3 in the euro area does not Granger-cause the common liquidity force. From an economic policy viewpoint, this might be an interesting result. Global liquidity is not dominated by the US but influenced by several countries independent of economic size. However, when the respective domestic money variables are included in the equation, the additional explanatory power tends towards zero (second figure in each cell of table 7.14). The

[87] The extent of serial correlation among the residuals is negligible.

[88] However, in the further course of this chapter, it will be shown that the consequences of this misspecification are of minor importance.

latter figures are derived by simply comparing the adjusted R-squared measure in the domestic-variable-augmented approach in expression (7.2.5.2) with the adjusted R-squared in the baseline FAVAR (assuming $\Psi_j(L)=0$). A similar outcome is found for the relationship between the national and common short-term interest rates. In three cases, the Granger causality tests are rejected. But again the marginal adjusted R-squared statistics are very small, i.e. the lagged domestic variables cannot explain the global factors.

Table 7.14: p-values of chi-squared tests and marginal adjusted R-squared ($X_{jt-1} \rightarrow F_{jt}$)

Global factors	US	EMU	Japan	UK	Canada
GDP	0.604/0.000	0.054/0.000	0.125/0.000	0.335/0.000	0.819/0.000
Inflation	0.134/0.000	0.353/0.000	0.747/0.000	0.356/0.000	0.026/0.000
House prices	0.957/0.000	0.429/0.000	0.015/0.000	0.457/0.000	0.191/0.000
Broad money	0.007/0.000	0.361/0.000	0.046/0.000	0.032/0.000	0.019/0.000
Short-term interest rates	0.062/0.001	0.079/0.001	0.022/0.009	0.419/0.000	0.216/0.000
Share prices	0.433/0.000	0.601/-0.002	0.481/-0.001	0.217/0.002	0.454/0.000

Note: First figure refers to the p-value, the second one to the marginal adjusted R-squared

In a final step, one special "cross-variable" case is examined. From an economic viewpoint, it might be interesting to see whether there are feedback effects from domestic short-term interest rates to global money. Major central banks like the Federal Reserve and the ECB could exert influence on common liquidity by setting their national key interest rates. The Granger causality tests indicate that the null hypothesis of no influence can be rejected for monetary policy in the US and Japan but not for the euro area. Especially conspicuous is the very high significance level of the Japanese short-term interest rate which may reflect the existence of carry trades. However, and once again, the marginal adjusted R-squared measures are zero.[89]

Table 7.15: p-values of chi-squared tests and marginal adjusted R-squared (domestic short-term interest rates $\rightarrow$ global money)

	US	EMU	Japan	UK	Canada
p-value	0.025	0.785	0.000	0.896	0.216
Marginal adjusted R-squared	0.000	0.000	0.000	0.000	0.000

[89] The question whether the magnitude of global liquidity can be influenced by national central bank behavior should be distinguished from the aspect of how the common money force is allocated across countries. The applied tests do not say anything about the second issue. Besides other variables, the allocation might depend on interest rate differentials between countries.

All in all, the tests dealing with the first exclusion restriction show two things. First, the assumption of $\Psi_j(L)=0$ is not appropriate in principle, thereby signaling some misspecification of the FAVAR. Second, and more important, the concise extent of the misspecification seems to be negligible. In the considered cases, the marginal adjusted R-squared measures are very small. Hence, the factors can nevertheless be interpreted as pervasive forces of the global economy which are only marginally explained by idiosyncratic patterns.

In the following, the second restriction is presented and tested. Since X_j does not forecast X_i given lagged F, it is true that $E(X_{it} \mid F_{t-1}, F_{t-2}...X_{it-1}, X_{it-2},..., X_{jt-1}, X_{jt-2},...) = E(X_{it} \mid F_{t-1}, F_{t-2}...X_{it-1}, X_{it-2}...)$. In order to test this restriction, expression (7.2.5.3) is formulated:

$$(7.2.5.3) \qquad X_{it} = \Lambda_i \Phi(L) F_{t-1} + k_{io}(L) X_{it-1} + \delta_{ij}(L) X_{jt-1} + \varepsilon_{Xt}$$

with $k_{io}(L)$ as lag polynomial in the national VAR model (cf. also expression 7.2.3.1). The exclusion restriction is that the additional lag polynomial $\delta_{ij}(L)=0$ for $o=5$, $i,j=1,...,35$ and $i \neq j$. Theoretically, 35×34 heteroskedasticity-autocorrelation robust Granger causality tests can be done. If the null hypothesis is rejected for a multitude of variables X_{jt-1}, the assumption of a restricted and diagonal $K(L)$ matrix in equation (7.2.3.1) is not appropriate. In an extreme case, the $K(L)$ matrix becomes an unrestricted and fully endogenous $D(L)$ matrix as assumed by Bagliano and Morana (2009). Idiosyncratic shocks spill over directly from one country to another besides the existence of global factors.

In the following, the exclusion restriction is not tested for all conceivable 35×34 cases. Instead, it is concentrated on the influence of US variables (X_{jt-1}) on each of the remaining economies in the G7 plus the euro area (X_{it}). As the US is the largest economy in the world, idiosyncratic spillovers from the US are more likely than from any other country or region. Furthermore, such specific and individual testing allows for examining whether there are systematic patterns in rejecting the null hypothesis. Again, "cross-variable" cases are not considered in the first step. For instance, it is tested whether US broad money Granger-causes monetary liquidity in

Canada but not Canadian economic activity. The obtained results indicate that idiosyncratic shocks from the US play at least partly a role. This seems to be particularly the case in the euro area in which four of the six chi-squared tests are rejected at conventional significance levels. However, in each case, the marginal adjusted R-squared measures are small or even negative.

Table 7.16: p-values of chi-squared tests and marginal adjusted R-squared ($X_{jt-1} \rightarrow X_{it}$)

	EMU	Japan	UK	Canada
US GDP -> ... GDP	0.006/0.008	0.137/-0.037	0.289/-0.020	0.020/-0.065
US CPI -> ... CPI	0.070/-0.054	0.233/-0.031	0.047/-0.062	0.391/-0.063
US house prices -> ... house price	0.748/-0.026	0.005/-0.034	0.192/-0.097	0.000/-0.025
US money -> ... money	0.247/-0.032	0.056/-0.026	0.717/-0.036	0.601/-0.039
US 3M -> ... 3M	0.023/0.014	0.114/-0.028	0.647/-0.007	0.115/-0.088
US share prices -> ... share price	0.090/-0.027	0.164/0.000	0.257/0.028	0.255/0.009

Note: First figure refers to the p-value, the second one to the marginal adjusted R-squared

In the second step, “cross-variable” cases are examined for national monetary aggregates. More precisely, it is tested to what extent US variables (GDP, CPI, house prices, etc.) influence broad money in the remaining G7 countries and the EMU. This step allows for analyzing whether national monetary liquidity is additionally affected besides the influences from domestic variables and the global forces. Again, this seems to be partly the case for the euro zone. Both US CPI and US house prices Granger-cause broad money in the EMU. The null hypothesis is also rejected for the following three relationships: US house prices $\rightarrow$ Japanese money; US money $\rightarrow$ Japanese money; US short-term interest rates $\rightarrow$ UK money. However, in each case, the marginal adjusted R-squared measures are negative.

Table 7.17: p-values of chi-squared tests and marginal adjusted R-squared ($X_{jt-1} \rightarrow X_{it}$)

	EMU	Japan	UK	Canada
US GDP -> ... money	0.335/-0.032	0.252/-0.027	0.278/-0.035	0.634/-0.039
US CPI -> ... money	0.047/-0.030	0.247/-0.027	0.867/-0.036	0.623/-0.039
US house prices -> ... money	0.020/-0.029	0.000/-0.023	0.550/-0.035	0.264/-0.038
US money -> ... money	0.247/-0.032	0.056/-0.026	0.717/-0.036	0.601/-0.039
US 3M -> ... money	0.976/-0.033	0.434/-0.028	0.034/-0.033	0.131/-0.037
US exchange rate -> ... money	0.451/-0.032	0.895/-0.028	0.577/-0.036	0.238/-0.038
US share prices -> ... money	0.791/-0.033	0.649/-0.028	0.522/-0.036	0.466/-0.039

Note: First figure refers to the p-value, the second one to the marginal adjusted R-squared

Overall, the empirical evidence seems to suggest some misspecification in the applied FAVAR, albeit with very modest consequences in terms of additional explanatory power for global factors and national variables. Hence, the assumptions of common forces not influenced by lagged national variables and a restricted $K(L)$ matrix on a country level seem to be justified. However, it is important to note that only simple Granger causality tests between two variables (or one variable and one factor) are used. The augmentation of the FAVAR by interacting national variables could have painted a different picture. For example, one may have made a comparison of the structural impulse responses between a new augmented version of the FAVAR and its baseline counterpart in chapter 7.2.3. Unfortunately, as explained previously, such an approach is difficult to achieve, given the limited degrees of freedom.

In the following, another issue is examined which could lead to misspecification problems: the omission of global factors.

7.2.6 ADDITIONAL GLOBAL SHOCKS

The SFAVAR focuses on global forces like monetary liquidity, GDP and inflation. However, there could be other neglected variables which also play a role in the global economy. The result would be an omitted variable bias as is often the case in open economy VAR models. Hence, it is looked for three other forces which may influence the factors in the SFAVAR approach: technology, long-term interest rates and credit aggregates.

The importance of technology shocks is stressed in the real business cycle theory (RBC) and in the literature on endogenous growth. In contrast to monetary policy disturbances impacting the aggregate demand curve, technology innovations influence aggregate supply. In the Solow model, all companies in the economy have the same level of total factor productivity (TFP), i.e. technology is freely accessible to all. Knowledge externalities within one country or even in an international context are not considered. An example for the diffusion of knowledge also across countries is the extension of the Solow model by Mankiw, Romer and Weil (1992, p. 410ff.). International knowledge spillover effects are conceivable in various forms. The imports of goods can embody new technologies as well as FDI flows, joint ventures, the local presence of multinationals and the migration of key personnel (Klenow, Rodriguez-Clare 2004, p. 11ff.). Especially trade-related new-good externalities could be central in transmitting new technologies from one country to another. New goods of higher quality are introduced and then imitated by other companies worldwide. One classic example for investigating empirically the diffusion of technology shocks across countries is the work of Backus, Kehoe and Kydland (1992, p. 756ff.).

The second potentially interesting common force is the long-term interest rate. Changes in the real interest rate affect households by generating intertemporal substitution (cf. the NOEM), wealth and portfolio allocation effects. They also alter companies' incentives for investment. Since a global capital market exists, the world real interest rate may be an important mechanism which transmits foreign shocks to open economies. Furthermore, explaining the behavior of long-term interest rates has gained substantial attraction of both academics and policymakers in recent years. For instance, instead of a global liquidity glut, a global savings glut may have emerged (Bernanke 2005a). A preference shock occurred via increased desired savings by emerging countries. The consequences have been rising capital flows to the US and unexceptionally low domestic long-term interest rates since the late 1990s, thereby driving up asset prices. In contrast, Caballero (2006, p. 7f.) argues that the shortage of financial assets have played a central role. Emerging markets' FX reserves have been surging under the so-called Bretton Woods II system. Given increasing global demand for financial assets and limited supply by industrialized countries, long-term interest rates have fallen strongly. In addition, the phenomenon of petrodollar recycling from commodity-exporting countries has exerted further downward pressure on real interest rates (Belke, Gros 2009b, p. 12ff.).

The third global factor is the co-movement of national credit aggregates instead of synchronized changes in monetary liquidity. In neoclassical models, the so-called money view dominates where money is the only financial quality meriting attention. All other assets are implicitly assumed to be imperfect substitutes for money but perfect substitutes for one another. Monetary policy operates through the liability side of banks' balance sheets. For example, central bank easing leads via rising reserves of the banking system to an additional creation of deposits by banks and to an increase in the overall money stock. This in turn lowers the nominal interest rate and heightens domestic demand (Friedman, Kuttner 1993, p. 200f.). An alternative to the neoclassical account of monetary transmission through the money market is the credit view. Independent and significant effects stem from the asset side of banks' balance sheets. Asymmetric information triggers imperfections on financial markets. For companies, the cost of external funds is higher than the cost of internal ones, since exhaustive monitoring by outsiders is not possible or too costly. As a result, bank loans and other sources of financing are not perfect substitutes. Monetary policy affects economic activity through the credit market by influencing banks' ability to grant loans to the private sector. For instance, central bank easing may influence companies' balance sheets by increasing asset prices and thus the value of collateral (Schaller, Junayed 2007, p. 2).

Given increasing globalization on financial markets, the credit channel may have a role of its own to play in the international transmission of monetary shocks. As shown in table 7.6, the first principal component for share prices in the G7 and the EMU explains 74.3% of the total variance, i.e. there is a strong co-movement of national stock markets. For instance, assume a change in monetary conditions in one country which influences domestic share prices. This in turn also impacts share prices abroad and hence the balance sheets of foreign firms. In addition, international capital flows may not exclusively be triggered by portfolio allocation shifts. When banks operate worldwide, excessive credit availability in one country may swiftly spill over to other countries. If the global credit channel is an important part of the transmission mechanism, then international bank lending behavior warrants more attention by policymakers.

The empirical analysis starts with technology shocks derived on basis of the identification pattern proposed by Galí (1999, p. 257). This procedure has been discussed intensively in the last few years in the RBC literature. Accordingly, there are technology and non-technology shocks which are orthogonal to each other. Galí's basic identifying assumption is that technology innovations are the only disturbances which have an effect on the long-run level of labor productivity. Assuming that both variations in the log productivity ($prod_t$) and log hours ($hours_t$) are integrated of order one, one gets the following expression:

$$(7.2.6.1) \qquad \begin{bmatrix} \Delta prod_t \\ \Delta hours_t \end{bmatrix} = \begin{bmatrix} C^{11}(L) & C^{12}(L) \\ C^{21}(L) & C^{22}(L) \end{bmatrix} \begin{bmatrix} \varepsilon_t^z \\ \varepsilon_t^m \end{bmatrix}$$

where ε_t^z and ε_t^m equal the technology and the non-technology innovations at time t, respectively. $C(L)$ are lag polynomials. Since Galí (1999, p. 257) assumes that the unit root in productivity stems exclusively from technology shocks, the matrix of long-run multipliers is lower triangular ($C^{12}(1) = 0$).

In order to estimate this approach on a global level, the following five-step procedure is pursued. First, labor productivity figures for the G7 plus the euro zone are calculated by subtracting the log of total employee hours from the log of GDP for each country or region.[90] Second, the obtained figures for labor productivity and total employee hours are standardized on the basis of log first differences with a mean of zero and a variance of one. Third, global forces for labor productivity and hours worked are estimated by deriving the first principal component ($PC1$) each. Accordingly, for labor productivity the proportion of the total variance attributable to $PC1$ is 26.1% compared to 22.5% for $PC2$. For total hours worked, $PC1$'s share is 38.3% ($PC2$: 22.7%).[91] Fourth, the two first principal components are "re-constructed" in levels by setting each global factor equal to zero in Q1 1984 and calculating the cumulative sum of the $PC1$s. Fifth, unit root tests are applied for global productivity and global hours worked. Accordingly, the Augmented Dickey-Fuller and Phillips-Perron test indicate that global productivity is integrated of order one. With respect to global hours worked, the empirical evidence is more mixed, with the unit root tests indicating integration of order one or being stationary (cf. appendix A.21).[92] Hence, concerning hours, equation (7.2.6.1) is estimated both in levels and log first differences. All lag criteria (AIC, SIC, etc.) point to a lag length of one. After deriving the global technology innovation, the following equation is estimated:

$$(7.2.6.2) \qquad \varpi_t = c_0 \varepsilon_t^z + c_1 \varepsilon_{t-1}^z + c_2 \varepsilon_{t-2}^z + c_3 \varepsilon_{t-3}^z + c_4 \varepsilon_{t-4}^z$$

with ϖ_t as global structural shocks derived from the SFAVAR (cf. equation 7.2.2.1) and ε_t^z as global technology shock each at time t. Heteroskedasticity and

[90] A series of total hours worked in the EMU is not available to the knowledge of the author. The EMU figure is constructed as the sum of hours worked in the following countries: Germany, France, Italy, Spain, the Netherlands, Belgium, Ireland and Finland. On basis of PPP weights provided by the IMF, the measure covers 89% of total EMU GDP in 2007.

[91] With respect to total hours worked, $PC1_t$ loads positively and to a significant extent on all national variables apart from the Japanese series (cf. appendix A.19). The impact coefficient of the first principal component for labor productivity is significantly negative in Japan and Canada. Moreover, the explanatory power of the first principal component for domestic labor productivity in the EMU is low with only 3.0% (cf. appendix A.20). Hence, $PC1$ for labor productivity is not unambiguously identified as a global and pervasive force for individual countries or regions.

[92] More precisely, the Augmented Dickey-Fuller test signals I(0), whereas the PP test suggests I(1).

autocorrelation-robust Wald F-tests are done by applying the Newey-West estimator. The null hypothesis assumes that the technology innovations do not have an impact on the global structural shocks contemporaneously and in the past four quarters, i.e. c_0, c_1, c_2, c_3 and c_4 are jointly equal to zero. A constant in equation (7.2.6.2) is neglected, since its influence proves to be insignificant. The results indicate that the null hypothesis is rejected for five of the seven global innovations (cf. table 7.18). Apart from the global money and the short-term interest rate shock, all innovations in the SFAVAR are contaminated by technology disturbances. This is true independent of whether total hours worked are modeled as stationary time series or integrated of order one. Interestingly, the coefficient signs are not always in line with economic theory. For example, global technology shocks have a positive impact on global inflation. It is not clear whether this result is triggered by another common force behind technological innovations or due to the specification suggested by Galí (1999). Alternatively, the fact that the first principal component for labor productivity is not unambiguously a common force may prevent a proper estimation of technology disturbances on a global level.

Table 7.18: Testing for omitted global technology shocks in the SFAVAR

Global structural shocks	Hours (I(1))	Significant Coefficients	Hours (I(0))	Significant Coefficients
GDP	3.04**	c_0=-0.15**; c_1=0.14**; c_2=0.12*	3.29***	c_0=-0.16**; c_1=0.14**; c_2=0.13*
Inflation	2.04*	c_1=0.61**	2.25*	c_0=0.54**; c_1=0.64*
Commodity prices	1.95*	c_1=0.34*	2.22*	c_0=0.40**; c_1=0.35*
House prices	2.39**	c_1=-0.15**; c3=0.11*	1.96*	c_1=-0.11*
Monetary liquidity	1.82	---	1.37	---
3M interest rates	1.16	---	1.26	---
Share prices	2.96**	c_0=-0.28*; c_1=-0.40**; c_2=0.40**	2.83**	c_0=-0.30*; c_1=-0.35*; c_2=0.41**

Note 1: F-statistics from heteroskedasticity and autocorrelation-robust Wald tests (Newey-West)

Note 2: *** Indicates significance at 1% level, ** at 5% level, * at 10% level

The same type of Wald tests used in equation (7.2.6.2) is repeated for long-term interest rate shocks and credit disturbances. As a measure for long-term interest rates, ten year (10Y) government bond yields are used.[93] The credit aggregates are broad-based and contain all domestic loans of the banking system to the private and the public sector. Alessi and Detken (2009) analyze boom and bust cycles in asset prices by distinguishing between private and total domestic credit. However, in context of this work, a broad measure of loan activity seems to be more appropriate, as international spillover effects may also have an impact on credit availability to the public sector.

[93] In the case of Japan, the average maturity of outstanding government bonds is used for data availability reasons.

The credit aggregates sometimes display huge structural breaks due to changes in the official statistics. Adalid and Detken (2007, p. 49) propose the following procedure in order to get economic interpretable time series. Since the credit data stem from the IMF, detailed explanatory notes are available in form of the International Financial Statistics (IFS) published by the IMF (2008b). Whenever the IFS documentation and the econometric package TRAMO SEATS simultaneously signal a level shift, the size of the structural break is estimated. This avoids confusing "real" instability in the data with purely statistical variations.[94] Afterwards, the time series are corrected backwards.

In this work, a somewhat different approach is pursued. In the beginning, a simple AR(1) process is estimated for each of the non-standardized credit aggregates in log first differences. If the Quandt-Andrews test signals a break in the autoregressive parameter which is in line with the IFS documentation, a dummy approach is implemented. For instance, both the Quandt-Andrews approach and the IFS indicate a variation in UK domestic credit at the beginning of 1987. The distribution of the Quandt-Andrews statistic becomes degenerate when the structural break approaches the beginning or the end of the sample (cf. chapter 6.3). In order to lose as little data as possible, only the first and last five percent of the observations are eliminated instead of the usual 15 percent. A dummy is constructed which equals one in Q1 1987 and zero for the rest of the sample. Afterwards, domestic credit in the UK is regressed on the dummy. For the derived residuals, the above-described approach is repeated. An AR(1) process is estimated and the Quandt-Andrews test for the persistence parameter is done. If a second structural variation is indicated in line with the IFS notes, a new dummy is constructed. The procedure ends when either the Quandt-Andrews test signals no structural instability or the break date does not concur with the one documentated by the IFS ("true" structural change instead of a statistically induced break).

After purging the credit series of statistical changes, a PCA for the credit aggregates and the 10Y government bond yields is implemented. Beforehand, the national variables are first differenced (yields) and first log differenced (credit aggregates), respectively. Then, the series are standardized with mean zero and variance one. $PC1$ for the long-term interest rates amounts to a high 66.0% ($PC2$: 13.9%). The

[94] Furthermore, using only the IFS documentation for detecting significant structural breaks may not be appropriate, as statistical change could also be of negligible extent.

first principal component for domestic credit is markedly lower with 34.7% ($PC2$: 21.4%).[95] Again, the two $PC1$s are "re-constructed" in levels by setting the global interest rate and credit factor equal to zero in Q1 1984 and calculating the cumulative sum of the first principal components. Two equations are estimated with the common interest rate and credit factor as dependent variables. The global forces used in the baseline SFAVAR (GDP, inflation, commodity, house prices, liquidity, short-term interest rates and share prices plus constant and time trend) are the independent variables. Otherwise, the economic interpretation of the derived shocks gets difficult. For example, changes in the quantity of credit can be caused by shifts in loan demand or loan supply. Using the GDP factor and other common forces as independent variables may help disentangling the two effects and derive global credit supply shocks. In addition, autoregressive terms of the common long-term interest rate and credit force are used as independent variables. As is the case in the SFAVAR, a lag length of two is chosen in each case. The obtained residuals are taken as a proxy of the global interest rate and credit innovations for the type of Wald tests previously described in equation (7.2.6.2). Accordingly, common long-term interest rate shocks seem to play an important role in the global economy. Of the seven common disturbances in the SFAVAR, four are significantly affected by long-term interest rate shocks: GDP, inflation, commodity prices and short-term interest rates. The SFAVAR may therefore contain some additional interest-rate sensitive elements as well.[96] Again, the signs of the significant coefficients are not always in line with theoretical considerations. For example, there is a positive co-movement between long-term interest rates innovations and commodity price disturbances. Assuming a global savings glut, higher raw material prices should lead to rising petrodollar recycling and declining government bond yields in the G7 and the EMU. There are two additional results worth mentioning. Global

[95] In each case, the factor loadings of $PC1_t$ are positive and significant apart from US credit (cf. appendix A.19). The impact coefficients of the long-term interest rate factor are of relatively similar size across countries, whereas the differences for the credit force are more pronounced. The comparison of R-squared measures as described in chapter 7.2.2 shows that the explanatory power of the first principal component is higher than the R-squared statistics on basis of US figures (cf. appendix A.20). Overall, the two $PC1$s seem to represent global factors.

[96] However, these Wald tests do not allow unambiguous conclusions about causal relationships between variables. For instance, it is still possible that not only long-term interest rate shocks impact GDP disturbances but that the opposite relation (GDP $\rightarrow$ long-term interest rate) also holds. The same caveat applies to the previously presented technology shocks.

money supply disturbances are not affected by long-term interest rate errors.[97] The same is true for the common house price shocks. This is a surprising result, given the recent discussion of the interest rate conundrum and its impact on the boom and bust of residential property prices.

Overall, the credit channel seems to play a comparatively small role in the global economy. Six of the seven errors in the SFAVAR are not affected by the common credit supply disturbances. Only the structural money supply shocks are contaminated. The significant coefficients are positive and in line with theoretical expectations. However, the applied testing procedure does not allow an unambiguous answer to the question whether the money or the credit view prevails on a global level. Common credit shocks may influence common money disturbances and/or vice versa.

Table 7.19: Testing for omitted global long-term interest rates and global credit shocks in the SFAVAR

Global structural shocks	Global long-term interest rate	Significant Coefficients	Global credit	Significant Coefficients
GDP	2.39**	c_0=0.20***	0.95	---
Inflation	4.30***	c_0=0.71***; c_3=0.53**	1.66	---
Commodity prices	4.63***	c_0=0.59***; c_3=0.33**	1.69	---
House prices	1.27	---	1.55	---
Monetary liquidity	1.24	---	1.98*	c_0=0.25**; c_2=0.25**
3M interest rates	4.86***	c_0=0.33***	1.59	---
Share prices	0.97	---	1.08	---

Note 1: F-statistics from heteroskedasticity and autocorrelation-robust Wald tests (Newey-West)
Note 2: *** Indicates significance at 1% level, ** at 5% level, * at 10% level

Furthermore, one additional cautionary note seems to be appropriate. The estimated shocks to long-term interest rates and credit aggregates are reduced-form innovations and not structural disturbances. The impulse responses in the SFAVAR may change when these variables are added to the system. In the following, two further estimates are therefore done. In the first one, the common short-term interest rate factor is replaced by the long-term interest rate force in the global model. Furthermore, the short-term interest rate in the VARs for the US and the euro area is substituted by the 10Y government bond yield in the US and the EMU, respectively. Both in the global and national model, the lag length and the schemes for identifying the structural shocks (expressions 7.2.2.1 and 7.2.3.3) are left unchanged. Variations of these parameters would make a comparison to the previously obtained impulse responses difficult. For

[97] Belke and Rees (2009, p. 25f.) find that long-term interest rate shocks have an impact different from zero on five of the seven common errors including monetary liquidity. Their approach differs slightly, since they do not use lagged long-term interest rates as additional regressors in the long-term interest rate equation.

instance, a change in the identification matrix may lead to a different outcome, even if short-term and long-term interest rates are perfect substitutes.

In the following, it is concentrated on the impact of the long-term interest rate factor on the residential property market in the US and the euro area. Some authors like Glaeser, Gottlieb and Gyourko (2010) suggest for the US that exceptionally low long-term interest rates contributed to strongly rising house prices until the recent financial crisis. However, the results on basis of the SFAVAR show that disturbances to the common long-term interest rate factor do not trigger a significant response of house prices in the US. At least in this specific setting, global money supply shocks are "unique" in explaining the temporary boom on the US residential property market. The reaction of EMU house prices to a disturbance to the global long-term interest rate factor is not significant either.

Figure 7.14: Response of EMU and US house prices to a positive global long-term interest rate shock

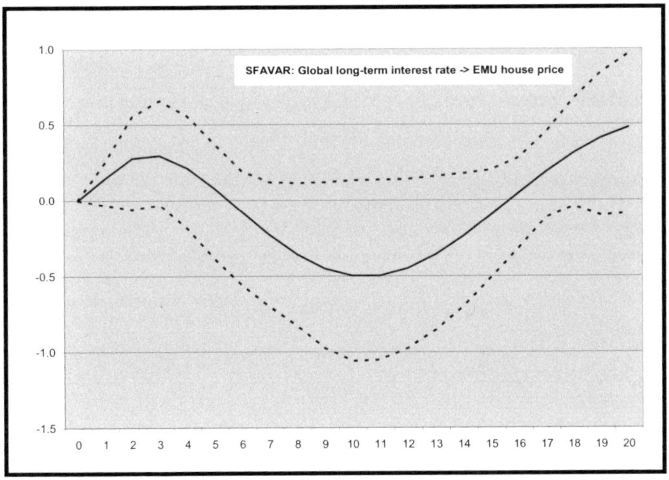

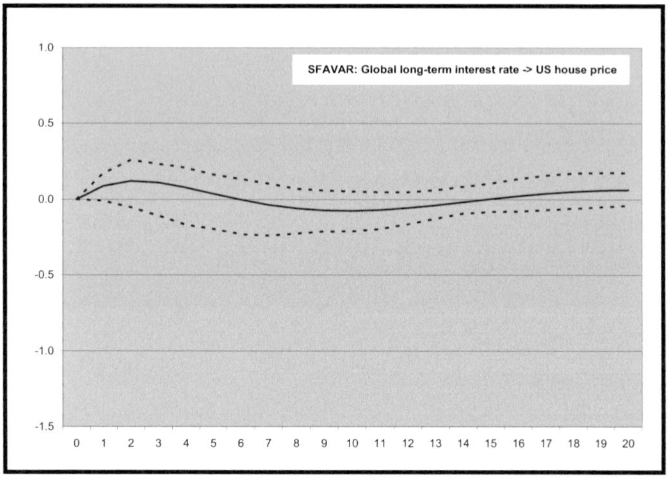

In the second estimate, the common monetary liquidity factor is replaced by the global credit force. Moreover, on a national level, the broad monetary aggregates M2 and M3 in the US and the euro zone are substituted by total domestic credit each. Again, the identification patterns on a global and national level remain the same. An innovation to the common credit force does not lead to a significant rise of economic activity in the euro area as is the case after a global money supply shock. In the US, even a puzzle emerges, as real GDP significantly declines from Q3 to Q8.

Figure 7.15: Response of EMU and US GDP to a positive global credit shock

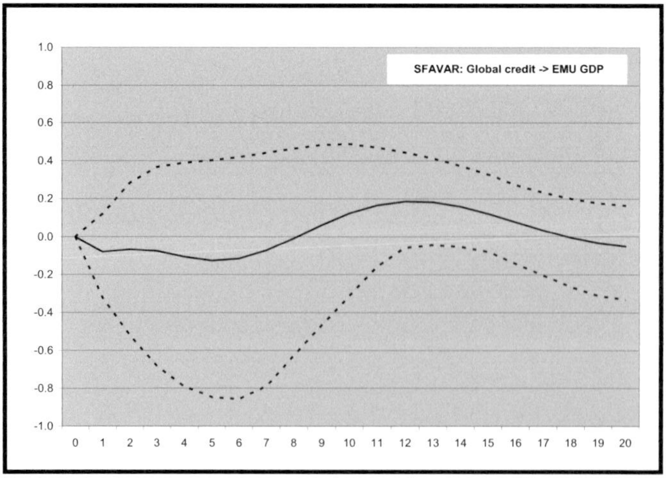

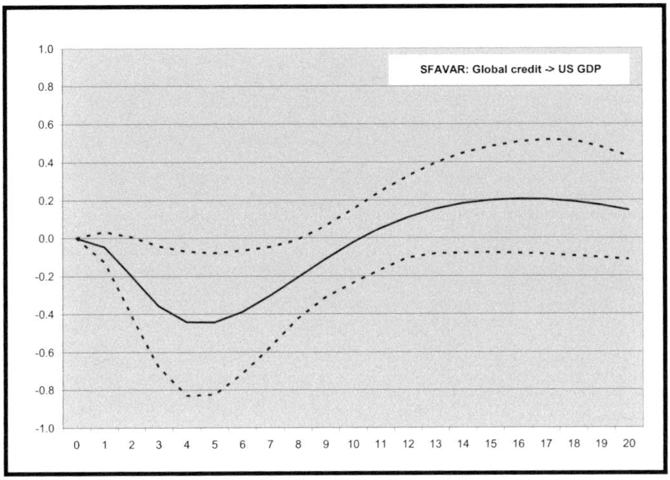

To sum up, the obtained evidence is more compatible with the global money view. Long-term interest rates and the credit channel in form of common forces seem to play a comparatively small role for residential property prices and economic activity in the US and the EMU. However, some caution is warranted when drawing conclusions, since puzzles exist.

7.2.7 STRUCTURAL BREAKS

As described in more detail in chapter 6.3, it is rather unlikely that the data generating process in 1984 is the same as in 2007. This in turn could undermine the stability of the SFAVAR. In the following, three types of structural breaks are examined, namely in the factor dynamics (Φ), in the global structural shocks (ϖ_t) and in the factor loadings (Λ).[98]

(7.2.7.1) $F_t = \Phi(L)F_{t-1} + \varepsilon_{Ft}$ with $\varepsilon_{Ft} = I\eta_t$

$$\text{where } \Phi(L) = \begin{cases} \Phi_1(L), t \le \kappa \\ \Phi_2(L), t > \kappa \end{cases}, \ \text{var}(\varpi_t) = \begin{cases} \sigma_1^2, t \le \tau \\ \sigma_2^2, t > \tau \end{cases} \text{ with } \varpi_t = H\eta_t$$

[98] The dynamics $D(L)$ on a national level and the idiosyncratic structural errors ξ_t may undergo profound changes as well. These types of time variation are neglected here. One reason is that a comparison between global and country-specific shocks does not lead to unambiguous results (cf. chapter 6.3). Structural breaks in the intercept are found to be insignificant.

Equation (7.2.7.1) allows for the global SFAVAR coefficients and the common structural shocks (ϖ_t) to break at potentially different dates (κ and τ, respectively).

(7.2.7.2) $$X_t = \Lambda\Phi(L)F_{t-1} + D(L)X_{t-1} + \varepsilon_{Xt}$$

$$\text{where } X_t = \begin{cases} \Lambda_1\Phi(L)F_{t-1} + D(L)X_{t-1} + \varepsilon_{Xt}, t \leq \upsilon \\ \Lambda_2\Phi(L)F_{t-1} + D(L)X_{t-1} + \varepsilon_{Xt}, t > \upsilon \end{cases}$$

Equation (7.2.7.2) allows for a break in the factor loadings at date υ.

It is started by jointly testing for the stability of all the coefficients on the lags of a given global variable using a heteroskedasticity (and autocorrelation) robust version of the Quandt-Andrews structural breakpoint test (Newey-West). Although the White test suggests that the residuals are jointly homoskedastic, signs of heteroskedasticity emerge in some single equations (cf. chapter 7.2.2). The range of the sample is trimmed by 15% on each side. Of the seven tests performed, none rejects the null hypothesis of stability at conventional confidence levels. Moreover, additional Quandt-Andrews tests are separately implemented for three variables as regressors in each of the seven SFAVAR equations: global monetary liquidity, global GDP and global house prices. Only in the global liquidity and global share prices equations do signs of structural variation emerge. In contrast, the null hypothesis of structural stability in the remaining equations cannot be rejected.

Table 7.20: Quandt-Andrews breakpoint tests for global SFAVAR coefficients

	All coefficients		Global liquidity		Global GDP		Global house prices	
FAVAR equations	Date	Max LR F	Date	Max LR F	Date	Max LR F	Date	Max LR F
Global GDP	1990 Q2	3.88	1988 Q2	8.09	1990 Q2	4.72	1990 Q2	6.48
Global inflation	2001 Q3	3.73	1990 Q3	3.32	1990 Q3	3.73	2001Q3	3.17
Commodity prices	1996 Q2	2.92	1998 Q1	2.90	1990 Q3	2.83	1999Q2	1.99
Global house prices	1991 Q3	3.17	1989 Q2	5.46	1989 Q2	8.05	1989Q2	5.26
Global liquidity	1997 Q3	5.46	1990 Q3	19.10***	1990 Q3	20.11***	1990 Q3	17.24***
Global 3M interest rates	1988 Q3	4.53	1988 Q3	8.08	1988 Q3	8.78	1988 Q3	3.66
Global share prices	1999 Q4	2.40	2002 Q2	8.50	1995 Q2	9.11	2002 Q2	11.11*

Note 1: Heteroskedasticity and autocorrelation robust version of Maximum LR test (Newey-West)

Note 2: *** Indicates significance at 1% level, ** at 5% level, * at 10% level

Due to the trimming exercise, 15 percent of the sample period gets lost both at the start and at the end of the sample period. Hence, the most recent years in the run-up to the global financial crisis are excluded from the Quandt-Andrews tests above. As an alternative for detecting structural breaks, it is opted for estimating the following dummy approach (Boivin and Giannoni 2008, p. 28):

(7.2.7.3) $$F_t = \Phi(L)F_{t-1} + \Phi^d(L)d_tF_{t-1} + \varepsilon_{Ft}$$

where d_t takes the value zero for the period Q1 1984 – Q4 2001 and one afterwards. The coefficients of the global factors are equal to $\Phi(L)$ for Q1 1984 – Q4 2001 and to $\Phi(L) + \Phi^d(L)$ thereafter. The dummy procedure can be regarded as an alternative to the data-consuming Quandt-Andrews tests. However, it is important to note that the sample splitting occurs arbitrarily, since there is a multitude of other break dates conceivable.

According to the implemented specific dummy approach, the effects of global liquidity shocks have seemingly become stronger from 2002 to 2007. Interestingly, the most pronounced impact can be found on global house prices (cf. figure 7.16). After three quarters, the effect of a global liquidity shock gets stronger and more persistent in comparison to the baseline SFAVAR. On average, the impact on global house prices from Q3 to Q20 increases by 50%. This is taken as a first indication that the propagation mechanism in the global economy may have changed in recent years and the importance of global money supply shocks has risen. In addition, global GDP shocks have also played a more important role as their impact on inflation has increased.

Figure 7.16: Impulse response analysis in SFAVAR (dummy approach)

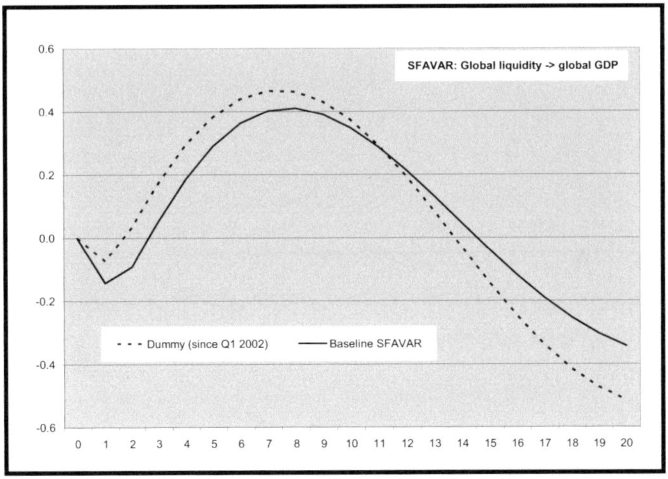

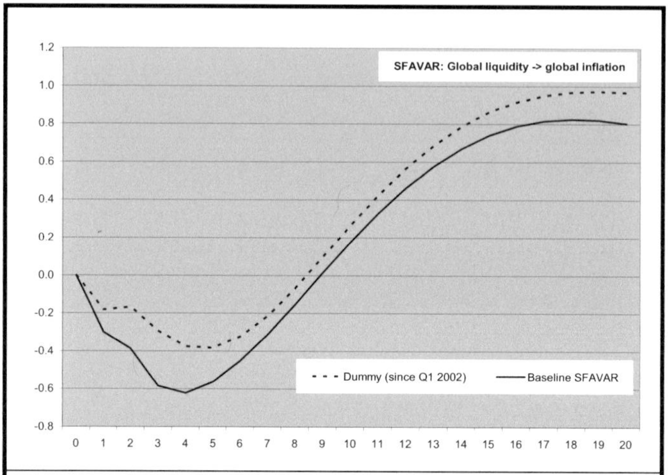
SFAVAR: Global liquidity -> global inflation
- - - Dummy (since Q1 2002)
—— Baseline SFAVAR
1.2
1.0
0.8
0.6
0.4
0.2
0.0
-0.2
-0.4
-0.6
-0.8
0 1 2 3 4 5 6 7 8 9 10 11 12 13 14 15 16 17 18 19 20

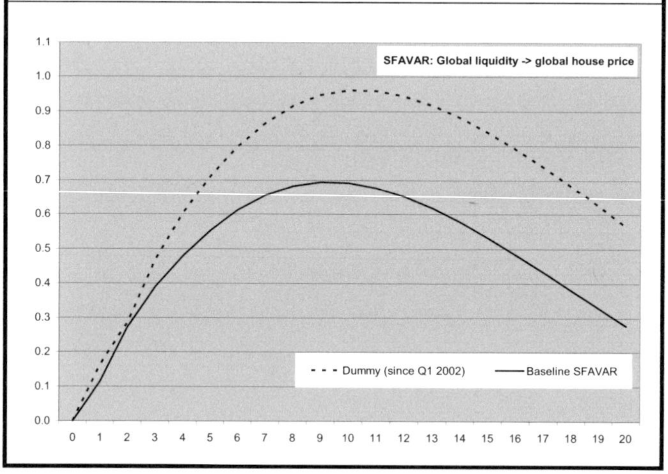
SFAVAR: Global liquidity -> global house price
- - - Dummy (since Q1 2002)
—— Baseline SFAVAR
1.1
1.0
0.9
0.8
0.7
0.6
0.5
0.4
0.3
0.2
0.1
0.0
0 1 2 3 4 5 6 7 8 9 10 11 12 13 14 15 16 17 18 19 20

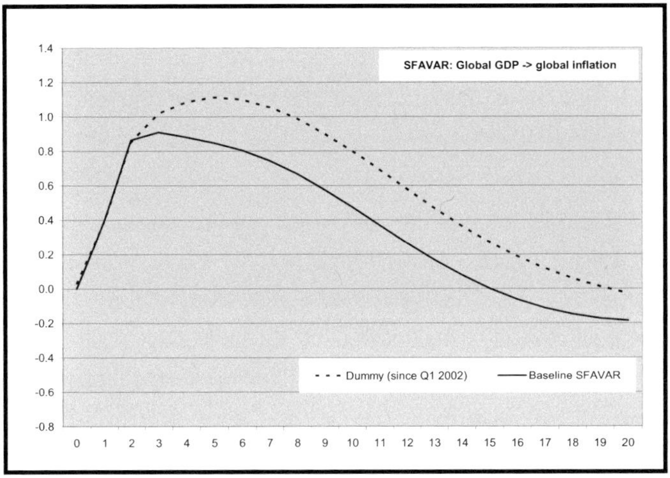

However, there are three problems associated with this simple dummy approach. First, estimating equation (7.2.7.3) is rather costly in terms of degrees of freedom. Since the SFAVAR contains seven factors and two lags, fourteen additional parameters per equation have to be estimated. Second, the procedure assumes a sharp structural break which is far from certain. From a technical viewpoint, this can easily be remedied. Instead of implementing a binary dummy which is zero or one, the variable can equal several values over time. For example, in Q1 2002, the dummy variable is 0.25; in Q2 2002, it equals 0.5 etc. However, since the concise nature of the possibly gradual structural change is not known, such an approach is not feasible. As already mentioned previously, a third problem arises in the need of selecting the timing of the instability. One could argue that the events leading to the structural variation are selected exogenously in form of a hypothesis like rising financial globalization. Unfortunately, with choosing Q1 2002, the exact timing is still arbitrary. Robustness tests are needed to derive more general conclusions.

In the following, the responses are checked with two alternative break dates: Q1 2001 and Q1 2003. For reasons of simplicity, the binary dummy variable with zero and one is used again. In both cases, global money supply shocks remain more important for the common GDP factor immediately after the disturbance in comparison to the baseline SFAVAR. However, already from Q6 onwards, the positive responses of the two alternative dummy approaches are less persistent. The reaction of the common house price factor seems to be more in favor of structural change. The dummy-augmented model with a break occurring in Q1 2003 indicates a stronger response compared to the baseline SFAVAR, albeit less pronounced than in the first dummy approach (break in Q1 2002). Assuming instability in Q1 2001, the differences are rather small and the response dies away more quickly than in the original model.

In this context, it is important to note that potentially omitted variables are not behind the changed impulse responses. In the previous chapter, it has been found that technology shocks which are neglected in the baseline SFAVAR may also play a role for the global economy. Such omitted variables can bias the estimated coefficients and disturbances in the model and hence both the propagation mechanism and the shock components. At the same time, they do not imply structural change. Model misspecification by itself cannot generate spurious structural instability (Boivin, Giannoni 2002b, p. 108).

Figure 7.17: Robustness tests for impulse response analysis in SFAVAR (dummy approach)

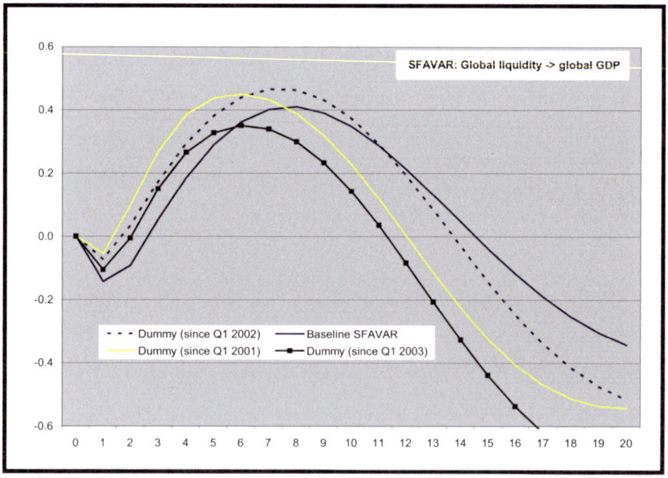

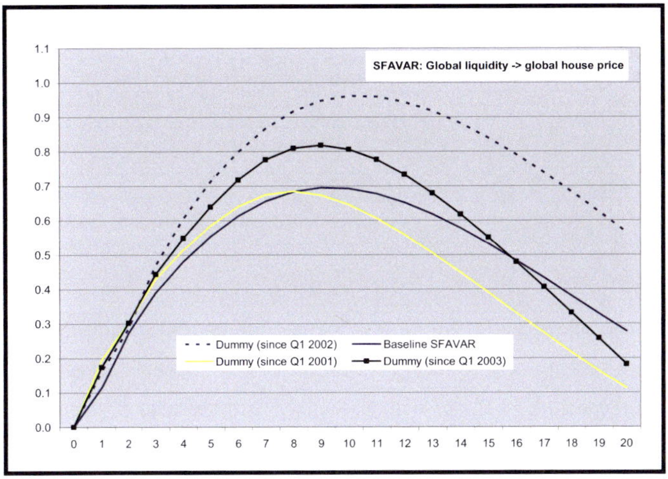

In the next step, the stability of the global structural shocks is examined. Under the null hypothesis that there is no break in the variance, $E\,|\,\varpi_t(\tau)\,|$ is constant. It is therefore tested for a break by implementing the Quandt-Andrews test in the regression of $|\,\varpi_t(\tau)\,|$ against a constant (cf. also equation 6.3.10). Accordingly, apart from the short-term interest rate innovations, there is no indication of sharp structural breaks (cf. table 7.21). The estimated break date of global interest rate shocks is Q1 1991. However, the finding of such a sharp break may still mirror a trend. Hence, it is also tested for more gradual change in the global short-term interest rate shocks by augmenting the equation with a time trend as additional independent variable. The null hypothesis of no sharp break is not rejected again. The coefficient sign of the time trend is significantly negative, thereby reflecting that the magnitude of the short-term interest rate disturbances decreases over time.

Table 7.21: Quandt-Andrews breakpoint tests for global SFAVAR shocks

Global structural shocks	Date	Max LR F	Max LR F (trend)
GDP	1988 Q2	6.20	---
Inflation	1998 Q4	2.40	---
Commodity prices	1988 Q4	3.01	---
House prices	1991 Q3	5.95	---
Monetary liquidity	2003 Q4	2.99	---
3M interest rates	1991 Q1	18.65***	6.62 (–)
Share prices	1991 Q2	3.41	---

Note 1: Sign of trend, if significant, in parentheses

Note 2: *** Indicates significance at 1% level, ** at 5% level, * at 10% level

The structural break tests are also done for the factor loadings in order to examine whether the transmission mechanism between global factors and national variables has changed. 15 of the 30 implemented heteroskedasticity and autocorrelation-robust Quandt-Andrews breakpoint tests indicate a sharp break in the respective factor loading on the basis of conventional significance levels (cf. table 7.22). Especially prone to instability is the relation between global and national GDP with breaks for the US, the EMU, Japan and the UK. Only for Canada, no structural variation is found.

The relations between global factors and national variables are also unstable in respect of money and house prices with three of five possible breaks each. It is important to note that the breaks typically do not occur approximately at the same time across countries. For example, the break between global and EMU money is in Q2 1994, whereas it is in Q1 2001 for the US. The same irregular pattern can also be found for house prices and GDP across countries. This argues against a big bang in economic and financial globalization with the G7 countries and the euro zone influenced by global forces at approximately the same time. Instead, the global factors seemingly started impacting national variables at various points in time.

Table 7.22: Quandt-Andrews breakpoint tests for factor loadings

Relation between ...	US	EMU	Japan	UK	Canada
global and national GDP	12.63*** (1994 Q4)	10.45** (1990 Q2)	11.55** (1989 Q3)	8.37* (1995 Q2)	2.40 (2000 Q2)
global inflation and national CPI	4.53 (2003 Q4)	0.81 (1989 Q2)	5.88 (1994 Q1)	7.59* (1990 Q3)	5.87 (1988 Q2)
global and national house prices	62.79*** (2004 Q1)	2.38 (1988 Q4)	9.52** (1991 Q2)	1.91 (1990 Q1)	18.77*** (1999 Q1)
global and national money	9.67** (2001 Q1)	14.81*** (1994 Q2)	8.02* (1992 Q4)	2.03 (1997 Q3)	3.42 (1999 Q1)
global and national 3M interest rates	14.07*** (2001 Q1)	4.81 (1992 Q4)	1.22 (2001 Q3)	14.38*** (1993 Q2)	3.41 (1990 Q1)
global and national share prices	2.78 (1998 Q4)	5.45 (1990 Q3)	5.91 (1992 Q3)	7.19* (1994 Q3)	9.94** (1993 Q4)

Note 1: Heteroskedasticity-robust version of Maximum LR test

Note 2: *** Indicates significance at 1% level, ** at 5% level, * at 10% level

However, as previously noted, the Quandt-Andrews test focuses on simple one-off breaks. Such an assumption is not justified, if gradual changes in coefficients and residuals occur. Rolling regressions for factor loadings are therefore estimated, concentrating on GDP, money and house prices. Given that the sample covers a comparatively short time span of 24 years, it is opted for a rolling 12-year window. The orders of the matrix lag polynomials $\Phi(L)$ and $K(L)$ are set uniformly to two as is the case in the baseline SFAVAR.

Selected results can be found in figure 7.18 in which the solid line equals the factor loading and the two dashed lines are the 95 percent intervals obtained by a simple residual bootstrap with 500 draws. For example, the data for Q1 2000 are the results based on the rolling regression from Q1 1988 to Q4 1999. The full set of figures is included in the appendix (A.22 – A.24). A clear-cut pattern across countries and variables does not emerge. In some cases, the factor loadings increase over time. In other cases, they remain unchanged or even decline. Concerning global liquidity, the factor loading for EMU M3 more than doubles from 0.15 to 0.39 at significant levels, whereas the impact on US M2 also rises but less markedly. The factor loadings for broad money in Canada and the UK decrease somewhat over time but remain at comparatively high and significant levels (0.4 and 0.5, respectively). Only in Japan, the impact coefficient declines strongly. At the end of the sample, the rolling factor loading is close to 0.1 and not significantly different from zero (cf. A.22). The same diverse pattern across countries also holds for the relation between national and global GDP and national and global house prices, respectively.

Interestingly, US variables in general seem to be increasingly influenced by common forces. For example, the US factor loadings of both global GDP and global house prices rise significantly. However, at this point, it is too early to conclude whether the US has really become more prone to influences from abroad. Given the fact that the common forces for money, GDP and house prices are estimated on basis of only five variables, the reverse causality may hold, i.e. developments in the US have recently become more important for the global economy. With this issue is dealt in the next chapter by conducting robustness checks.

In contrast, the effect from globalization on national GDP seems to have diminished for a comparatively small economy like Canada. Not surprisingly, domestic developments also play a more important role in the case of Japanese house prices, given the special circumstances after the bursting of the housing and equity bubble at the beginning of the 1990s.

Figure 7.18: Rolling regressions for factor loadings

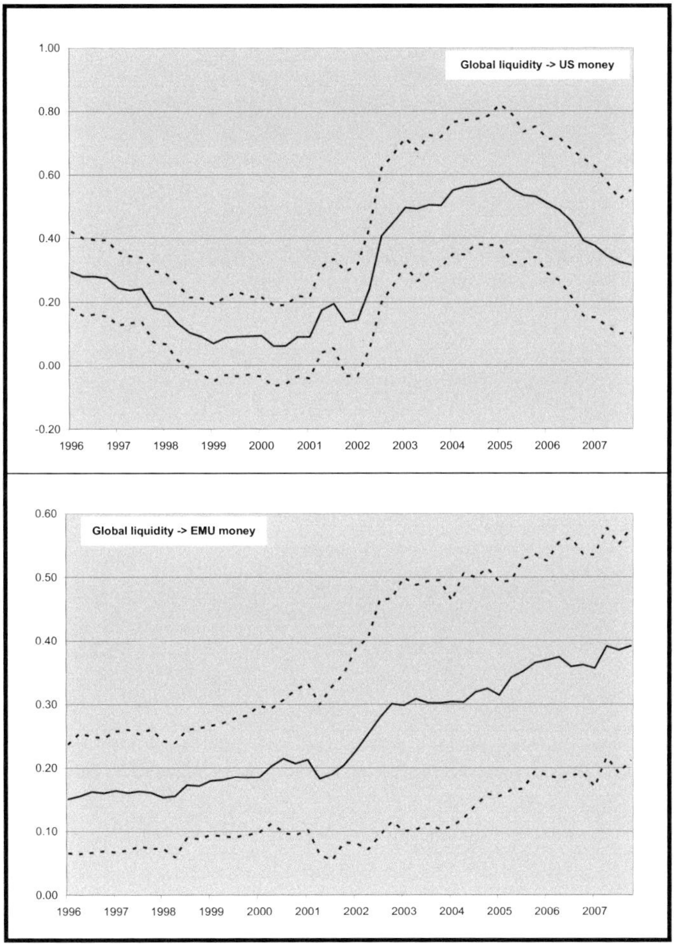

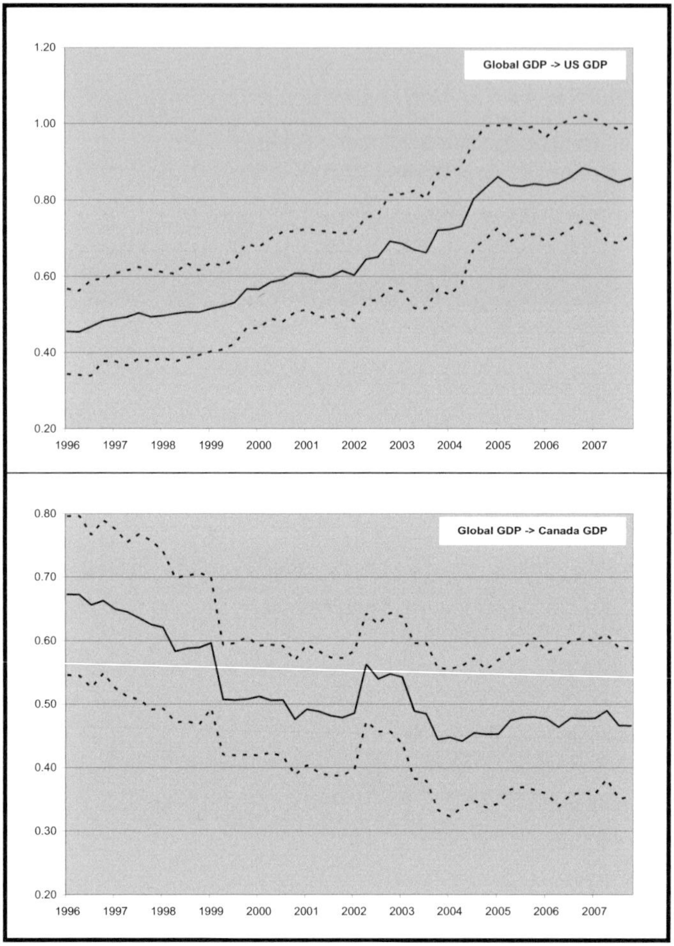
Global GDP -> US GDP
1.20
1.00
0.80
0.60
0.40
0.20
1996 1997 1998 1999 2000 2001 2002 2003 2004 2005 2006 2007
Global GDP -> Canada GDP
0.80
0.70
0.60
0.50
0.40
0.30
0.20
1996 1997 1998 1999 2000 2001 2002 2003 2004 2005 2006 2007

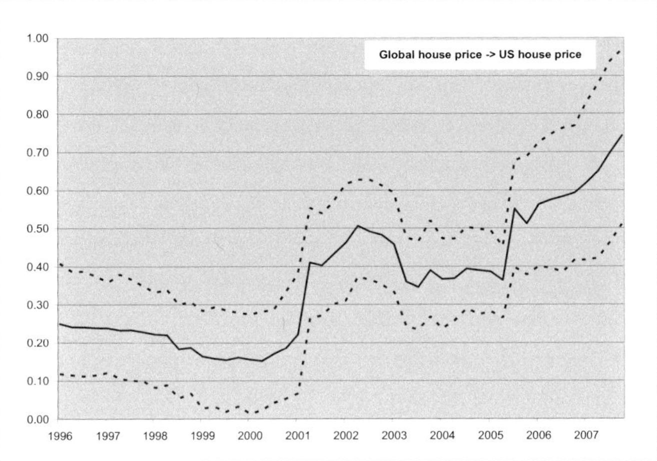

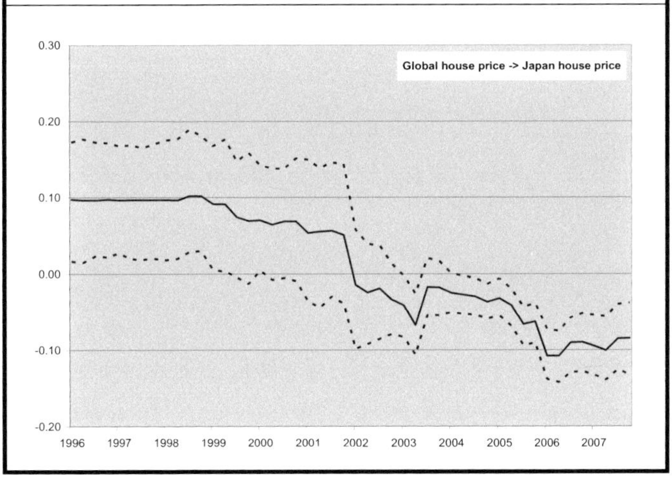

So far, the structural break tests are more indicative of instability in the propagation mechanism than in the shocks. This is especially true for the interaction between global and national variables. There are little signs that the common disturbances and hence the global impulses have changed systematically. This is a remarkable result, as several financial and political crises with worldwide implications took place between 1984 and 2007. Examples are the Asian crisis in 1997, the collapse of the hedge fund Long Term Capital Management (LTCM) in 1998, the bursting of the equity bubble in 2000 and the terrorist attack on the World Trade Center in 2001.

Another widely used method for distinguishing between shocks and propagation is the implementation of counterfactuals. Examples in a VAR setting are the work by Stock, Watson (2002a, p. 18ff.) and Boivin, Giannoni (2002b, p. 100f.). These authors investigate the sources of lower output volatility on a country level, the so-called Great Moderation, by disentangling the relative contributions of two opposing explanations: smaller disturbances or structural variations in the economy. The first view simply attributes the bulk of the lower variability to "Good Luck". According to Stock and Watson (2002a, p. 20), the 1990s in the US economy would have been almost as volatile as the 1970s, had the disturbances of the 1970s occurred in the 1990s. Advocates of the second hypothesis see changes in the transmission process and/or in the way monetary policy has been conducted ("Good policy") as major driver.

In general, such counterfactuals can also be conducted in a FAVAR framework. Consider again the following equation which describes the interaction between national variables and global factors:

$$X_t = \Lambda\Phi(L)F_{t-1} + K(L)X_{t-1} + \varepsilon_{Xt} \text{ with } \varepsilon_{Xt} = \Lambda\eta_t + v_t \tag{7.2.7.4}$$

The counterfactual VAR method consists of dividing the whole data sample into two sub-samples:

$$X_t = \Lambda_a\Phi_a(L)F_{t-1} + K_a(L)X_{t-1} + \varepsilon_{Xt} \text{ with } Var(\varepsilon_{Xt}) = \Sigma_a \tag{7.2.7.5}$$

where the subscript $a = 1{,}2$ denotes the first and second sub-sample. By estimating expression (7.2.7.5) for different Λ_a, Φ_a, K_a and Σ_a, it is possible to derive the counterfactual impulse responses for X_t. The latter equal the reaction of national variables to a shock that would have occured, if either the transmission process in the economy (Λ_a, Φ_a and K_a) or the disturbances (Σ_a) had taken on different values. An example shall further clarify the procedure of such historical counterfactuals. For instance, equation (7.2.7.5) is estimated with Λ_2 as the factor loading matrix in the second sub-sample and Σ_1 as the error covariance matrix of the first period. The same estimate is repeated for Λ_1 and Σ_1. This counterfactual exercise examines whether the common shocks from the first sub-sample generate substantially different responses of X_t when the propagation mechanism between the global factors and the national variables is the one from the second period.[99] Less technically spoken, a measure for the change in the transmission channel from the global economy to individual countries is provided in the face of unchanged common disturbances. Such an approach might be appealing, since the rolling regressions of the factor loadings indicate the rising importance of global forces for national economies. It can be dealt with the opposite case as well, i.e. Λ_1 is assumed to be valid for both sub-samples and Σ_a changes. This would be an exercise to calculate what would have happened in a country, if financial globalization, and hence a regime shift, had not occurred or had no impact on the transmission mechanism. Historical counterfactuals therefore equal rerunning economic history (Sims, Zha 2006, p. 55).

Although these features are appealing, historical counterfactuals are not feasible in this work. In the baseline SFAVAR, a total of 30 parameters have to be estimated per equation on a national level. Splitting the sample from 1984 to 2007 into two parts would drastically reduce the degrees of freedom. For example, assume that samples 1 and 2 have equal size and therefore only cover 48 observations each instead of 96 for the whole sample.

Besides these technical considerations, there are also economic objections against implementing counterfactuals in the context of global liquidity. Consider a case in which no degrees-of-freedom problems exist. The sample is split with Λ_a^L and Σ_a and $a = 1,2$. Λ_a^L denotes the factor loadings through which the common liquidity force influences national broad monetary aggregates. The rolling regressions done previously indicate rising factor loadings over time for the EMU. The counterfactual therefore consists of replacing Λ_1^L by Λ_2^L in the euro area sub-model, leaving all other parameters in the first sample (Σ_1, Φ_1, K_1 and the factor loadings Λ_1 excluding Λ_1^L) unchanged. Impulse responses to a common money supply shock are derived and compared with the ones based on Λ_1^L. The researcher is then able to find out whether the increased sensitivity of national broad money to the global liquidity force has led to significant differences in the European transmission process. Additionally, one may not solely focus on the mean of each variable but calculate confidence bands as well. If the latter

[99] In order to keep this example as simple as possible, it is assumed that the idiosyncratic disturbances v_t as part of the error covariance matrix Σ_a remain unchanged.

are getting narrower after a common liquidity shock, there is less uncertainty surrounding the impact of international capital flows on country-specific macroeconomic variables. However, counterfactuals of this type suffer from one major shortcoming: the Lucas critique. Changes of one specific parameter or equation may affect the behavior of major players in the economy. For instance, if national money is more strongly affected by developments from abroad, expectations of both the central bank and the private sector about domestic variables will probably be influenced. The result is an immediate change in the remaining coefficients of the system which are assumed to be constant in the counterfactual exercise. This problem does not materialize though if the central bank and the private sector are backward looking or if the variation in the factor loadings is small and of temporary nature. In contrast, the stronger and the more persistent the structural changes are, the more relevant becomes the Lucas critique (Boivin, Giannoni 2002a, p. 3).

7.2.8 ROBUSTNESS CHECKS

Three robustness tests are applied in order to test whether the results obtained from the impulse response and variance decomposition analysis hold in general independent of variations in the specification.

First, an alternative version of the SFAVAR is estimated by changing the lag length from two to four. Little consequences for the results are found. Common liquidity, house price and GDP innovations still significantly influence the global economy.

Second, different assumptions for identifying the global structural shocks are implemented. In contrast to equation (7.2.2.1), it is assumed that the global short-term interest rate contemporaneously reacts to global GDP and inflation but not to commodity prices, global house prices and global liquidity. This change seems to be the most obvious one, since monetary policy may have knowledge of the development of GDP and inflation within the quarter. The impulse response functions in the SFAVAR remain stable, apart from the responses to a global liquidity shock for which some changes are found. For example, the global economic activity force temporarily shrinks before increasing. The common inflation factor rises without any time delay, thereby not being in line with economic theory. In Appendix A.25, some selected figures for the baseline and the newly identified SFAVAR can be found for direct comparison.

The third robustness check examines the "cross-sectional" stability of the global forces. In approximate factor models, it is assumed that the cross-sectional dimension of the dataset is large, possibly even larger than the time dimension. Hence, the exclusion of one variable should not markedly influence the results. However, this may not be true in the SFAVAR, since it focuses on a rather limited set of countries (G7 countries plus euro zone) often with only one variable per country. For instance, for broad monetary liquidity, five time series are used to estimate the common monetary liquidity force. The same is true for other variables like house prices, share prices and real GDP. It is therefore conceivable that the exclusion of one time series may significantly alter the results obtained by PCA. This risk may especially be pronounced with respect to US variables, since the US economy and US financial markets are the largest and most important ones in the world. Furthermore, given the low number of variables per country, the global forces could be contaminated with country-specific noise (cf. also chapter 6.1). World shocks may therefore systematically be confounded with idiosyncratic US disturbances. For example, US money could have a great weight in the common liquidity factor. In an extreme case, no spillovers and common innovations across countries actually take place but solely idiosyncratic errors stemming from the US (Stock, Watson 2003, p. 11). As a result, US house prices would not be influenced by global money supply shocks as suggested by the impulse response analysis. Instead, idiosyncratic US money disturbances actually cause US residential property prices to rise.

In order to assess how vulnerable the results are, each global factor excluding one country is estimated via PCA. In a first step, the co-movement between the common force including all five countries/regions and the global factor based on four countries/regions is estimated. A comparatively little unchanged correlation coefficient is indicative of a symmetric global variable, i.e. it is not overly influenced by one country or region. The results show that this is the case, as the co-movement is relatively high across various constellations. Interestingly, this is even true when the US is not considered in the dataset. For example, the correlation coefficient between the global liquidity factor including the US and the common money force excluding the US is 0.98 (EMU: 0.96). A relatively high degree of co-movement is also observable for other variables like GDP, inflation and the short-term interest rate. This may point in the direction that the global economy is less asymmetrically influenced by the US than usually thought. The global house price factor is somewhat less robust with values of 0.81 for the EMU and Canada.

Table 7.23: Co-movement between global force and global force ex respective country

Global force excluding ...	GDP	Inflation	House prices	Liquidity	3M interest rate	Share prices
US	0.90***	0.95***	0.91***	0.98***	0.93***	0.99***
EMU	0.97***	0.98***	0.81***	0.96***	0.97***	0.99***
Japan	1.00***	0.98***	0.99***	0.98***	0.98***	0.99***
UK	0.93***	0.97***	0.86***	0.96***	0.96***	0.99***
Canada	0.86***	0.99***	0.81***	0.96***	0.93***	0.99***

Note 1: Correlation coefficients

Note 2: *** Indicates significance at 1% level, ** at 5% level, * at 10% level

The obtained evidence seemingly indicates that the global factors are not dominated by one specific country or region. However, simple correlation coefficients cannot distinguish between shocks and propagation. The obtained results are therefore only indicative of robustness. In a second step, a conditional exercise is conducted. All global factors are derived by excluding US variables and then used for estimating the SFAVAR. Afterwards, the obtained impulse responses and the variance decomposition are compared with the results for the common forces including the US (baseline model; cf. chapters 7.2.2 and 7.2.3).

In the following, it is concentrated on the reaction of US variables to a common money supply shock. For instance, a global liquidity disturbance leads to rising US house prices independent of which of the two specifications are used (cf. figure 7.19). The comparison of other impulse responses also yields robust results, although the concise response and the bootstrapped 95 percent confidence intervals differ in some cases. For example, in the baseline model, US GDP significantly reacts to a common money supply shock already from quarter one onwards. In the approach without US monetary liquidity, the pattern of US GDP is more in line with theory. The significant response starts at quarter three. However, the probability bands also get somewhat wider in the beginning, i.e. there is higher uncertainty regarding the impact of the common money supply shock on US economic activity in comparison to the baseline model.

Figure 7.19: Robustness tests for US impulse responses in SFAVAR

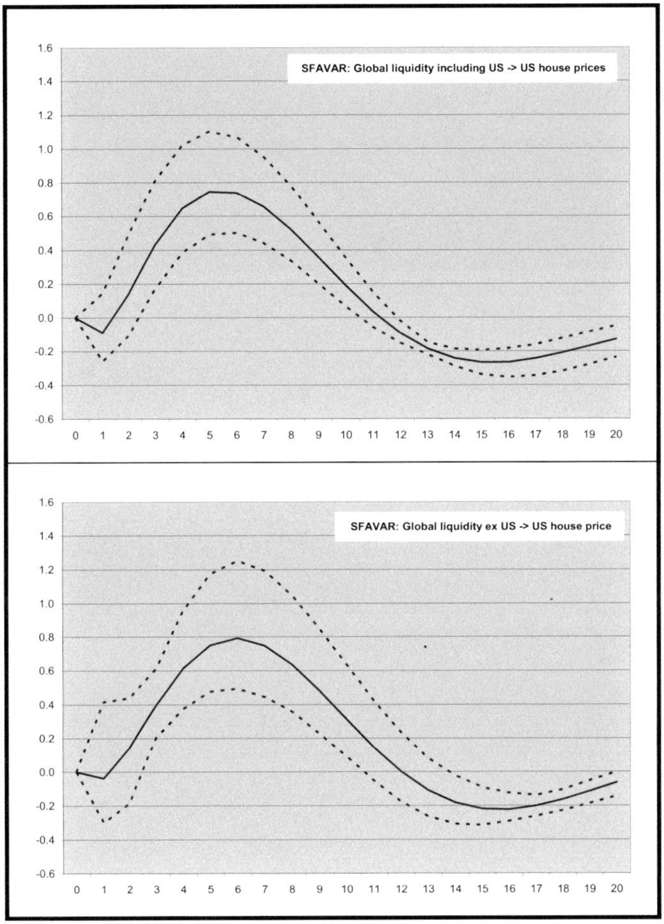

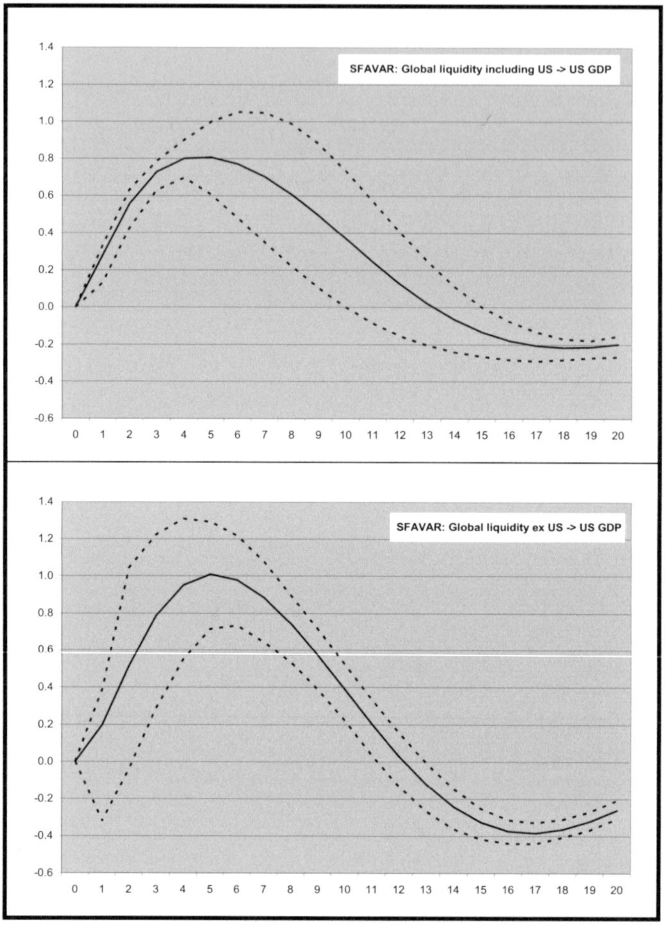

The same conditional robustness check is also done for the forecast error variance decomposition analysis implemented in chapter 7.2.4. Again, 20 quarters are chosen as time horizon. Accordingly, common forces keep playing an important role for US variables. For example, global money excluding US liquidity still contributes 12.9% to the variations in the US short-term interest rate (cf. table 7.24). Again, with 19.8%, the highest variance share is found for US money. However, in all cases, the importance of global money decreases compared to the baseline model. For instance, the common liquidity force including US money contributes 16.3% to the variability in US GDP. When the PCA is applied without US liquidity, the variance share declines to 10.7%.

Table 7.24: Robustness test for US forecast error variance decomposition (in %)

	Global money (including US)	Global money (ex US)
US GDP	16.3	10.7
US CPI	9.9	7.2
US house prices	13.3	7.9
US money	23.4	19.8
US short-term interest rate	16.6	12.9
US exchange rate	5.6	3.5
US share prices	14.9	5.0

Overall, two conclusions can be drawn from the robustness checks. First, to some extent, the importance of common money for US variables in the baseline model seems to depend on idiosyncratic elements stemming from the US themselves. Second, and however, the general results after a global money supply shock excluding US liquidity remain intact. Both on basis of the impulse response analysis and the obtained variance shares, one may argue that common money supply disturbances are worth the attention of central banks and researchers alike.

7.3 INFLATION BIAS OF MONETARY POLICY

In chapter 2.2, the following equation has been derived to test for an inflation bias of central banks under the regime of financial globalization:

(2.2.8) $$i_t = b\sigma_{e,t}^2 + \psi_t \text{ with } b < 0$$

where i_t is the short-term interest rate controlled by the central bank, $\sigma_{e,t}^2$ is the variance of the foreign money supply disturbance e_t and ψ_t is an error term. The short-term interest rate is assumed to depend negatively on the variance of the money supply shock from abroad. Hence, the inflation bias is higher the larger the variability of the foreign money disturbance hitting the domestic economy.

In general, there is a multitude of different empirical approaches conceivable for estimating the relation between i_t and $\sigma_{e,t}^2$. For example, foreign or global money shocks can be obtained by estimating autoregressive approaches where the residuals equal the disturbances. Afterwards, the variance of the foreign or global money shocks is derived and a simple regression between i_t and $\sigma_{e,t}^2$ is run as described in (2.2.8). A more sophisticated approach would be to estimate Taylor rules of various kinds for each central bank. Then, these equations could be augmented by the variance of the common liquidity force, again derived on basis of an autoregressive expression.

In the following, it is opted for a different procedure by using the FAVAR model and the included global shocks and national short-term interest rate equations. The latter consist of both idiosyncratic variables (X_{t-1}) and global forces (F_{t-1}) as independent variables, thereby representing a potentially interesting alternative to conventional central bank reaction functions. The variance of the global money shock ($\sigma_{\eta,t}^2$) derived from a GARCH model is additionally included as a regressor. The national short-term interest rate equations across countries or regions can then be written as follows:

(7.3.1) $$i_t = \Lambda\Phi(L)F_{t-1} + K(L)X_{t-1} + b\sigma_{\eta,t}^2 + \psi_{Xt} \text{ and } \psi_{Xt} = \Lambda\eta_t + v_t$$

where η_t equals the global shock and v_t is the idiosyncratic disturbance.[100] However, before estimating expression (7.3.1), one has to test for ARCH effects in the common shocks derived from the FAVAR model. The reason is that in the absence of conditional heteroskedasticity, the parameter b is not identified (Dolado, Pedrero, Ruge-Murcia 2004, p. 12; Doyle, Falk 2010, p. 535). Put it differently, $\sigma_{\eta,t}^2$ can only be part of a monetary policy rule, if the conditional variance of the global disturbances is not constant. In order to address this issue, the LM test for the presence of ARCH up to order four in the common FAVAR residuals is applied. The LM test is based on the regression of the squared residuals on a constant and one to four lags of the squared residuals. Besides global money shocks, other common disturbances like goods price innovations are examined as well. For instance, Borio (2006, p. 6) argues that the risk of falling into deflationary territory due to globalization on goods markets may lead to asymmetric central bank behavior (cf. chapter 2.2). In addition, it is also tested for ARCH effects in the effective exchange rate residuals for each country or region. In open economy theories like the MFD approach, the exchange rate is regarded as the most important transmission channel of monetary shocks.

---

[100] Since (7.3.1) contains the reduced-form innovations η_t and v_t, the equation is augmented by the variance of the global reduced-form errors ($\sigma_{\eta,t}^2$) as well. If one includes the variance of the common structural shocks derived in the baseline SFAVAR (cf. 7.2.2.1), the following results change only marginally. This evidence is indicative of robustness independent of the concise identification assumptions on a global level.

As can be seen in table 7.25, severe signs of conditional heteroskedasticity are found for global money disturbances. Independent of the order of the ARCH specification, the null hypothesis of constant variance is rejected at conventional significance levels. Some evidence of conditional heteroskedasticity is also found for the short-term interest rate and partly for house prices. Interestingly, there are no signs of ARCH effects in global inflation. This evidence seemingly stands in contrast to the extension of the Borio (2006) argument. The process of globalization on goods markets and the corresponding uncertainty about the international inflation environment do not lead to an inflation bias of central banks. Moreover, the null hypothesis cannot be rejected for global share prices which are often regarded as especially volatile. The empirical evidence with respect to the effective exchange rates is mixed. Strong signs of time-varying conditional variance are found for the EMU and the UK. However, for the US, Japan and Canada, the null hypothesis cannot be rejected.

To sum up: The majority of the analyzed error terms in the FAVAR is homoskedastic. In these cases, the uncertainty element cannot cause asymmetric central bank behavior as described in chapter 2.2. Furthermore, the heteroskedasticity found in some of the FAVAR residuals is a necessary but not a sufficient condition for an inflation bias of policymakers. In addition, there should be a significantly negative effect of the variance of global shocks on the national short-term interest rate.

Table 7.25: Testing for ARCH effects

	ARCH(1)	ARCH(2)	ARCH(3)	ARCH(4)
Global GDP	0.00	0.11	0.08	0.10
Global inflation	1.38	0.68	0.57	0.49
Global commodity prices	0.43	0.54	0.32	0.25
Global house prices	3.05*	1.59	1.00	1.90
Global broad money	7.56***	4.57**	3.25**	2.47*
Global short-term interest rates	7.14***	3.17**	1.06	0.67
Global share prices	0.00	0.29	0.24	0.18
US exchange rate	0.19	0.60	0.32	0.31
EMU exchange rate	10.82***	7.49***	7.00***	4.95***
Japan exchange rate	0.11	0.41	0.41	0.69
UK exchange rate	2.72	4.77**	3.78**	3.53**
Canada exchange rate	0.14	0.09	0.59	0.55

Note 1: F-statistics from LM test for ARCH

Note 2: *** Indicates significance at 1% level, ** at 5% level, * at 10% level

Before estimating expression (7.3.1), one additional step has to be made. The researcher now knows that some of the shocks in the FAVAR exhibit ARCH effects. However, the concise form of conditional heteroskedasticity is not clear yet. In the literature, it is suggested to implement a GARCH(1,1) model for parameterization (Dolado, Pedrero, Ruge-Murcia 2004, p. 12; Doyle, Falk 2010, p. 528). Afterwards, the GARCH(1,1) assumption has to be tested by a misspecification test. The problem is that the estimate of the conditional variance is a generated regressor which measures the true but unobserved regressor $\sigma^2_{\eta,t}$ in (7.3.1) with noise. If the conditional heteroskedasticity does not follow a GARCH(1,1) process, the estimator for $\sigma^2_{\eta,t}$ is systematically biased and the model is misspecified. A standard misspecification test for ARCH models works as follows (Dolado, Pedrero, Ruge-Murcia 2004, p. 13). The same LM test described above is repeated for the standardized residuals, i.e. the residuals of the FAVAR equations divided by the estimated conditional standard deviations. If the variance equation in form of GARCH(1,1) is correctly specified, the FAVAR residuals corrected for heteroskedasticity and squared should be serially uncorrelated.

In the following, the GARCH(1,1) specification is estimated for the residuals in which signs of ARCH effects have been found: global house prices, global money, the global short-term interest rate and the effective exchange rates in the EMU and the UK. Please recall that there are two equations included in the FAVAR. The first one represents the global economy, the second one describes the national level:

$$F_t = \Phi(L)F_{t-1} + \varepsilon_{Ft} \text{ where } \varepsilon_{Ft} = I\eta_t \tag{7.3.2}$$

$$X_t = \Lambda\Phi(L)F_{t-1} + K(L)X_{t-1} + \varepsilon_{Xt} \text{ where } \varepsilon_{Xt} = \Lambda\eta_t + v_t \tag{7.3.3}$$

with η_t and v_t as global and country-specific shocks, respectively. The GARCH(1,1) specification for both types of disturbances can be written as follows:

$$\sigma^2_{\eta,t} = \alpha_1\eta^2_{t-1} + \beta_1\sigma^2_{\eta,t-1} \tag{7.3.4}$$

$$\sigma^2_{v,t} = \alpha_2 v^2_{t-1} + \beta_2\sigma^2_{v,t-1} \tag{7.3.5}$$

In a first step, the GARCH equations (7.3.4) and (7.3.5) are estimated by using the quasi-maximum likelihood estimator, since the residuals may not be conditionally normally distributed. Otherwise, the estimates of the covariance matrix could be inconsistent, resulting in incorrect standard errors (EViews 6 User's Guide II 2007, p. 192). Afterwards, the LM tests up to order four are done for the standardized residuals in the FAVAR equations (7.3.2) and (7.3.3) on basis of the estimated standard deviations. The results indicate that the null hypothesis of no serial correlation cannot be rejected in any of the cases. Hence, it appears that the parsimonious GARCH(1,1) approach adequately captures the conditional heteroskedasticity, thereby providing support for a correct model specification.

Table 7.26: Estimating GARCH(1,1) and testing for remaining ARCH effects

	GARCH(1,1)	ARCH(1)	ARCH(2)	ARCH(3)	ARCH(4)
Global house prices	α_1=0.22*; β_1=0.71***	0.01	0.40	0.31	0.38
Global broad money	α_1=0.31**; β_1=0.39*	0.42	1.51	1.05	0.89
Global short-term interest rates	α_1=0.11; β_1=0.77***	0.12	0.29	0.84	0.77
EMU exchange rate	α_2=-0.17*; β_2=0.34	0.00	0.35	0.42	0.40
UK exchange rate	α_2=0.84***; β_2=-0.01	0.83	0.66	0.76	0.78

Note 1: F-statistics from LM test for ARCH(1) to ARCH(4)

Note 2: *** Indicates significance at 1% level, ** at 5% level, * at 10% level

Finally, the following two GARCH-M expressions are applied in order to estimate the slope coefficient b:

(7.3.6) $$i_t = \Lambda\Phi(L)F_{t-1} + K(L)X_{t-1} + b\sigma^2_{\eta,t} + \psi_{Xt}$$

(7.3.7) $$i_t = \Lambda\Phi(L)F_{t-1} + K(L)X_{t-1} + b\sigma^2_{v,t} + \psi_{Xt}$$

As can be seen in table 7.27, the obtained results are mixed. No signs of inflation bias are found with respect to global money. Although b is negative for each country or region, the impact is not significant. The same insignificant results are found for the common short-term interest rate factor disturbance. Interestingly, when the conditional variance of global house price shocks is added to the national interest rate equation, the parameter b is negative, large in size and significantly different from zero. This is independent of which country or region is considered. The slope coeffient b ranges from -0.90 for the UK to -1.33 in the case of the US. One explanation could be that central banks regard the volatility in residential house prices as yardstick for business cycle risks evolving in other countries. Variations in property markets might be more persistent and easier to anticipate than short-term fluctuations in the rest of the economy. Against the backdrop of the recent financial crisis, this result may deserve further empirical examination. Belke, Orth and Setzer (2008b, p. 416f.) argue that residential property prices are correlated with inflation expectations. Accordingly, the conditional variance of house prices is a proxy for the volatility of inflation expectations. The results may therefore be interpreted as signs of asymmetric behavior and an inflationary bias of central banks.

In contrast, the b coefficients with respect to the exchange rate in the EMU and UK are positive, albeit not at significant levels.

Table 7.27: Estimates of b coefficient

	US	EMU	Japan	UK	Canada
Global house prices	-1.33 (0.18)	-1.25 (0.18)	-1.05 (0.20)	-0.90 (0.20)	-1.02 (0.17)
Global broad money	-0.17 (0.18)	-0.06 (0.18)	-0.06 (0.19)	-0.11 (0.18)	-0.06 (0.17)
Global short-term interest rates	-0.03 (0.20)	0.01 (0.19)	0.03 (0.21)	-0.04 (0.20)	-0.05 (0.18)
EMU exchange rate	---	1.79 (1.07)	---	---	---
UK exchange rate	---	---	---	0.10 (0.06)	---

Note: Standard errors in paranthesis

Nevertheless, there are three arguments which should be kept in mind before jumping to conclusions. First, one may still argue that the results are simply a statistical artefact. In many countries, house prices are only published with a time lag. Assuming a contemporaneous relationship between the conditional variance of the global house price factor and national short-term interest rates could therefore not be in line with the information policymakers actually have.

Second, the estimated coefficients in equations (7.3.6) and (7.3.7) may be convolutions of two different phenomena: the preferences of the central bank and the structural parameters of the economy (Cukierman, Muscatelli 2002, p. 28). Instead of policymakers' asymmetric objectives leading to an inflation bias, there could also be non-linearities in the economic structure. More concretely, the negative slope coefficients found for the conditional variance of the global house price factor do not unambiguously reflect asymmetric behavior and hence an inflation bias of monetary policy. The foreign property markets themselves may react in a non-linear way to – possibly symmetric – policy shocks. In the literature, such asymmetric responses have been extensively examined for the overall economy. Frequently cited examples are the work of Cover (1992) and Karras (1999). These authors find that negative money supply disturbances have a statistically significant effect on output in the US and Europe. At the same time, the impact of positive money supply innovations is negligible. There is a multitude of reasons conceivable for these results. For instance, it is argued that the aggregate supply function is convex. As the economy approaches full capacity, an expansion in aggregate demand induced by lower interest rates or higher money supply has increasingly smaller effects on output and a larger impact on prices. Another potential source of asymmetry relates to credit constraints which are more likely to bind during recessions. In each of these two cases, the effectiveness of monetary policy measures depends on the state of the economy. Ball and Mankiw (1994) suggest a model where the existence of menu costs leads to asymmetry in price flexibility and the business cycle after monetary disturbances.

Third, even if there are no non-linearities in the economy, it is important to keep in mind that central bank preferences are not directly observable in reality. Instead, there are many alternative specifications conceivable for estimating the policy rule. For instance, in the procedure above, a GARCH(1,1) process as part of the central bank reaction function is chosen. The LM tests signal no further ARCH effects which are taken as sign for correct model specification. However, this is only true in a purely statistical sense. For instance, a GARCH(1,2) model could also have been specified. In this case, the LM tests do not indicate a misspecification of the global shocks either. The sticking point to the whole procedure is that rejecting linearity against a specific non-linear alternative does not necessarily imply the general validity of the non-linear model (Kim, Osborn, Sensier 2005, p. 622). Further research is therefore needed. One way would be to keep the equations completely unrestricted. Then, the researcher has to find out by suitable testing which form of non-linearity is best supported by the data.

8 SUMMARY OF EMPIRICAL RESULTS

In chapters 6 and 7, different econometric approaches have been implemented for testing the hypotheses presented in section 4. In the following, the main empirical results are briefly summarized. Furthermore, it is concluded whether the hypotheses have to be rejected or not.

In chapter 6, dynamic factor models in static form are estimated for the G7 countries and the EMU. Although not all prerequisites are unambiguously met, the overall results suggest that the co-movement across national excess liquidities is picked up by a global factor in form of the first principal component. The Granger causality tests show rather sparse evidence of lagged international monetary spillover effects. One reason might be that international capital flows occur rather quickly. Structural break tests applied in an autoregressive setting uncover signs of instability in the persistence parameter of global excess liquidity. On the basis of a rolling 15-year window, a gradual increase in persistence from 1988 to 1997 is found. The comparison of factor loadings for sub-samples partly shows rising impact coefficients of $PC1$ on national excess monies. Rolling regressions reveal an increasing explanatory power of the first principal component for domestic excess liquidities in the US, Canada and the EMU. Structural change is also detected for global and idiosyncratic shocks. Apart from Japan, country-specific disturbances decline more strongly over time than the common innovations, thereby possibly pointing to the greater role of global excess liquidity shocks.

Overall, the first and the third hypothesis cannot be rejected on basis of the obtained empirical evidence in section 6.[101] However, caution is warranted when interpreting the results. For instance, only in the theoretical ceteris paribus case, it is possible to make inferences about the changing relative importance of global and idiosyncratic shocks. Furthermore, not all prerequisites for applying approximate factor structures are met unequivocally. Finally, it is important to keep in mind that the models are univariate and do not allow far-reaching conclusions.

[101] According to the first hypothesis, international capital flows lead to a global (excess) money factor. The third hypothesis states that the importance of the common liquidity force for global and national variables has risen over time. As a result, there are structural breaks both in the shock component and in the propagation mechanism of global excess money.

In section 7, more economic structure is implemented by applying open economy VARs and a global SFAVAR. In recursive national VARs for the G7 and the euro area, it is tested for an omitted variable bias. The results indicate that domestic money disturbances are influenced by global excess liquidity shocks and foreign national monetary innovations. Large countries or regions like the US and the euro area also seem to be affected. Both a recursive and a structural VAR is implemented for the EMU augmented by a global excess liquidity factor. Impulse response analysis is done. Little evidence is found that the common excess liquidity force has independent information value above the national short-term interest rate and domestic money. The evidence for structural breaks in the propagation mechanism and the shock components is sparse. Seemingly, both the second and the third hypothesis can therefore be rejected.[102] However, and once again, caution is warranted when interpreting the results. Besides the emergence of puzzles, the approach runs the risk of confounding global money supply and global money demand disturbances.

Impulse response analysis on basis of a global SFAVAR uncovers that common money supply shocks significantly influence the following variables on a worldwide level: GDP, prices, the short-term interest rate and house prices. In contrast, a negligible impact is found on commodity and share prices. Innovations to the common money supply also trigger significant reactions of domestic variables like broad money, economic activity, CPI and residential property prices. These effects do not primarily occur in small open economies but in the US and the euro zone. A comparison of the impulse responses shows that primarily different national transmission mechanisms are at work. There is some evidence that global excess liquidity contributed to the strongly increasing US house prices in the run-up to the recent financial crisis. The forecast error variance decomposition analysis reveals that global money disturbances are a driving force of global house prices and the global short-term interest rate. However, with respect to worldwide economic activity and prices, the relevance is rather limited. In the majority of cases, common liquidity plays a more important role in explaining domestic patterns in the US and the EMU than national monies and short-term interest rates. Furthermore, the variability of domestic variables in the US and the EMU is partly

[102] According to the second hypothesis, global monetary liquidity influences various macroeconomic and financial variables both on a global and national level. Furthermore, global money is supposed to be "unique" and hence more important for national variables than domestic monetary conditions (or other common forces).

affected to a greater extent by global money than by idiosyncratic developments excluding national money and the domestic short-term interest rate. The testing of the exclusion restrictions suggests some misspecification in the FAVAR, albeit with rather modest consequences. Common excess liquidity does not have "unique" characteristics. Besides global GDP and house price shocks, other types of common disturbances like changes in technology seem to have some impact on a worldwide level. Structural break tests are more indicative of instability in the propagation mechanism than in the shocks. A dummy approach suggests that the effect of a common money innovation on global house prices has become stronger from 2002 to 2007. Structural breaks are also found for the factor loadings, thereby suggesting a changing transmission channel from the global economy to national variables. Rolling regressions reveal that the factor loadings between common and domestic money in the US and the EMU rise over time. Robustness checks indicate that the obtained results are comparatively stable.

Overall, the implications of the SFAVAR results for the second and third hypothesis are mixed. Global excess liquidity seemingly influences global and national variables. Furthermore, this effect has become stronger over time. However, global liquidity is not outright "unique" but rivaled by other common forces. Structural breaks can be detected for the propagation mechanism but not for the global shocks.

No signs of asymmetric national central bank behavior due to global money disturbances are found. The fourth hypothesis is therefore rejected.[103] Instead, common house price shocks may trigger an inflation bias of policymakers across countries.

To sum up, the obtained evidence in this work appears to contradict at least partly the prevalent monetary transmission mechanism in traditional models like the monetarist framework, the MFD approach and the NOEM. National variables such as short-term interest rates and money supplies may not be the sole channels by which central banks affect real quantities and prices. A new kid on the block in form of global liquidity seems to have emerged especially for large countries with huge and deep financial markets. However, there is one important reservation to all of the implemented econometric models in this work and their corresponding conclusions. The empirical concept of common money does not allow to distinguish unambiguously between the

[103] The fourth hypothesis states that the short-term interest rate controlled by policymakers depends negatively on the variance of global excess money disturbances.

following two effects, thereby leading to a classic identification problem. On the one hand, the phenomenon of global liquidity may be economically meaningful, as international capital flows and monetary spillover effects between countries occur. On the other hand, the patterns observed at a global level could still be a statistical artefact and driven by other common – and possibly not identified – forces. Direct spillover effects are only of minor importance for national monetary conditions. As a result, isolated domestic monies in individual economies are condensed into a global factor by PCA.

"The precision with which economic models can be expressed mathematically belies the fact that they cannot claim to be anything more than approximations to an unknown, and possibly unknowable, data-generating process."

(Dennis, Leitemo, Söderström 2009, p. 1604)

9 Policy implications

In this section, structural implications of global money for national policymakers are briefly discussed. Major topics are the following: decreasing influence of central banks on domestic variables, rising uncertainty due to structural change in the national monetary transmission mechanism and international policy coordination. Although the obtained empirical results in this work partly confirm previous research (cf. chapter 3), they are still preliminary. Accordingly, instead of "strong" policy conclusions, potentially interesting issues are raised, sometimes in form of open questions. Further research efforts are necessary to examine how relevant the policy suggestions may become.

Global liquidity seems to convey additional information about monetary conditions not summarized by national monies and short-term interest rates. The common liquidity factor may merit policymakers' attention in the same way as global slack in extended Phillips curve specifications and worldwide interest rates (global savings glut hypothesis). Furthermore, the influence of central banks on domestic money supply is seemingly weakening. In some countries or regions, global liquidity restricts monetary policy in its ability to impact nominal and real variables. Examples are the effects of the common money factor on national economic activity, inflation, house prices and the short-term interest rate. Floating exchange rates may therefore no longer impart complete national monetary autonomy to central banks. Globalization could not only have advantages for policymakers in form of inflation-curbing effects as primarily discussed among researchers and practitioners. Instead, international capital flows may also incur challenges and disadvantages for central banks (Belke, Orth and Setzer 2010, p. 1943). For instance, a distortion of the traditional interest rate channel could pose substantial problems. Assume a central bank hiking its policy rate to fight domestic inflationary pressure. Global excess liquidity flows into the country in order to benefit from the widening interest rate differential. As a result, the restrictive monetary policy is counteracted. The impulse response analysis conducted in section 7.2.3 suggests that this may be the case in the US (cf. table 7.9). After a global money supply shock, the US short-term interest rate declines significantly. The global liquidity force seems to mitigate the effects of national monetary policy even or especially in large countries or regions. One explanation could be that US financial markets attract huge capital flows from abroad.

Instead of concentrating primarily on domestic variables and the exchange rate, central banks may therefore also incorporate the international transmission of monetary shocks in their analysis. Optimal monetary policy behavior shall become more outward-looking. A benign neglect of foreign central bank behavior and international portfolio shifts may not be appropriate. Monetary policy needs to learn how to monitor the flows of liquidity between countries. A structural understanding of global money shocks and disturbances on financial markets may be warranted.

However, the task of taking into account international capital flows is a complicated one. Money may be shifted quickly from one economy or asset type to another. Furthermore, there is substantial data uncertainty with which central banks are confronted. Since the common money factor cannot be observed directly, PCA is necessary to distinguish between global and country-specific elements. However, other econometric methods may yield different results and could even lead to opposing policy implications in practice. If the phenomenon of global liquidity is difficult to measure accurately or in a timely fashion, the additional information contained in common money is hardly exploitable by central banks. The weight given to global liquidity should therefore also depend on how precisely it is measured.

The problem of imperfect information associated with global money is comparable to other variables playing a critical role in theoretical models. The probably most prominent examples are the concepts of potential output and the natural rate of unemployment. For instance, potential output is often defined as a trend in real GDP which has to be estimated. In New Keynesian models, potential output equals the level of economic activity occurring in the absence of any nominal price rigidities. Such a constellation is typically unobservable in reality. Data uncertainty can have severe implications for central bank behavior. According to Aoki (2003, p. 507 ff.), the optimal monetary policy response to variables including noise is attenuated relative to the case with perfect information.

Besides data uncertainty, structural changes associated with the process of globalization on financial markets could also trigger cautious policy behavior. As shown in chapter 7.2.7, the factor loadings between national monies and the common liquidity force rise over time in some countries or regions. The result may be an increase in uncertainty about how the domestic monetary transmission mechanism works. Opening the economy up to capital flows from abroad means that there are new potential routes to influence national economic activity and prices. Central banks have to face these challenges. The problem is that structural breaks might be the most difficult source of uncertainty to deal with. The extent to which the underlying structure of the economy is varying is virtually impossible to determine ex ante (Shuetrim, Thompson 1999, p. 4). Only with the benefit of hindsight, policymakers are aware of the concise change in factor loadings.

Given these structural breaks, one may question the practical significance of the certainty equivalence, according to which incomplete information does not significantly change results with respect to optimal monetary policy. Central banks can ignore uncertainties about disturbances to the economy when setting interest rates and proceed as if they were in a certain world. The knowledge that unforecastable additive shocks will occur in the future has no effect on current policy. However, certainty equivalence is based on two major critical assumptions. First, it assumes that the objective function of policymakers is quadratic. In section 2.2, it has been shown that this might not always be the case due to asymmetric preferences of central banks. Second, imperfect information takes a particularly simple form. Decision makers know the "true" model of the economy and only random additive error terms exist. In reality, uncertainty about structural parameter values in the transmission mechanism might be a key characteristic of the monetary poliy environment. This is especially true in an international context. Since there is a multitude of possibly changing parameters in the global economy, the concise impact of common shocks on national variables may differ significantly at various points of time.

As shown by Brainard (1967), policy is set differently from a world of purely additive shocks, if central banks are uncertain about the impact of the policy instrument on the economy. In contrast to simple random disturbances, imperfect information about elasticities in the transmission process creates multiplicative uncertainty. The more a specific policy is used, the more agnostic decision makers are about the consequences of their actions. For instance, if factor loadings between national and global money are not perfectly known, aggressively hiking the short-term interest rate to achieve price stability can increase the likelihood of missing the target by a large amount. In his classic work, Brainard (1967, p. 413ff.) finds that optimal monetary policy under uncertainty is a function of both the first and second central moments characterizing the model parameters. In the modified reaction function, decision makers place less weight on variables whose coefficients are more uncertain. Optimal central bank behavior is shown to be more conservative than when the "true" elasticities are equal to their point estimates (Shuetrim, Thompson 1999, p. 5).

However, already Brainard (1967, p. 415ff.) and other consecutive authors like Craine (1979, p. 71ff.) point out that this result is not universally robust. For example, imperfect information about model dynamics can lead to more aggressive monetary policy reactions. Suppose that global excess liquidity is determined by a simple AR(1) process as assumed in chapter 6.3. However, the corresponding autoregressive parameter is not precisely known by policymakers. For central banks, it will pay off to react more aggressively to a common money shock. Otherwise, there is the risk that the disturbances lead to persistently high domestic money growth, thereby causing rising prices and/or asset price inflation. This stylized example makes clear that determining the implications of multiplicative uncertainty on central bank behavior cannot be made in any ad hoc manner. Instead, it is an empirical issue and has to be carefully examined in the context of any specific model.

There is an additional objection regarding the Brainard conservatism principle and subsequent approaches modeling uncertainty by employing Bayesian decision theory. It is assumed that the central bank does not know the precise coefficient values of the transmission mechanism but the distributions from which they are drawn. Decision makers formulate a prior probability function on the model parameters and compute the policy minimizing the expected loss. Typically, the latter variable depends on unconditional squared deviations of inflation, the unemployment rate and the interest rate from target levels (Williams 2004, p. 2). This Bayesian approach might not always be a realistic setting. In structural macroeconomic models which take national and global variables into account the dimensionality of the parameter space is large. Hence, the elicitation of priors is demanded to an extent which is not practical for central banks. In addition, the most realistic form of parameter uncertainty might not be the random changes of coefficients with coefficients to be comparatively high in one period and rather low in the next. Instead, as a more plausible setting for central banks, there may be persistent parameter shifts (Rudebusch 2000, p. 10) as reflected in rising factor loadings of the common money force over time.

An alternative approach to specifying priors and minimizing the Bayes risk is robust control and the use of Knightian uncertainty, i.e. a situation where the decision maker cannot assign mathematical probabilities to random events. The central bank fears that its reference model of the economy may be subject to misspecification. A policy optimized to perform well in the model could therefore actually produce unintended and unwelcome results in reality. The decision makers acknowledge this doubt by deliberately introducing incorrect values of key parameters and assessing the consequences for monetary policy. Instead of interpreting misspecifications as random events, the central bank assumes a fictitious evil agent to be at work. This evil agent will choose parameter values to make policymakers look as bad as possible. Optimal policy tries to minimize such a worst-case result (Dennis, Leitemo, Söderström 2009, p. 1606ff.; Walsh 2004, p. 31f.). In a number of studies, the worst case consists of a larger and more persistent inflation shock. As a result, robust interest rate responses are often found to be more aggressive than the ones that would be obtained without model uncertainty (Walsh 2004, p. 25f.).

In the context of this work, further increasing cross-border capital flows may be interpreted as evil agent. The structural changes in some factor loadings between national and global money could be regarded as a sequence of non-random perturbations to the central bank's reference model in form of the FAVAR approach. Given these assumptions, an interesting research topic for the future might be whether the process of financial globalization changes the degree of policy activism. In particular, there could be two questions worth further examination. First, does a rule that was optimal in the past continue to do reasonably well if the phenomenon of common money is becoming more important over time? Second, is it more risky for central banks to underestimate factor loadings or to overestimate them? One could argue that rising cross-border capital flows make a pro-active strategy a more favorable policy option. However, at the same time, there is no guarantee for successful domestic policy responses. At least in theory, the influence of international events could be so overwhelming that aggressive central bank reaction to external money supply shocks does not pay off.

Another interesting topic in the light of global liquidity is policy coordination. The rationale stems from spillover effects that domestic monetary policy can have on other countries. For example, the extremely low short-term interest rates in Japan during the last few years led to carry trades. Financial investors took up loans in Japanese Yen and invested the proceeds in currencies with higher interest rates, thereby exporting monetary liquidity from Japan to other countries. Since foreign central banks had to bear parts of the excess money burden, a free-rider problem and negative external effects could have taken place. For example, additional monetary liquidity may increase the risk of asset price bubbles and inflationary pressure outside Japan. Such a constellation equals a non-cooperative game in which national decision makers like the Bank of Japan solely focus on maximizing the welfare function of its own country.[104] In contrast, in a cooperative equilibrium, monetary competition between national authorities does not exist. Central banks are committed to implementing policies that maximize the joint welfare of the involved countries. Since structural changes between global and national liquidity in form of rising factor loadings cannot be prevented by monetary policy, international coordination may keep global liquidity shocks as low as possible. As generally argued by Canzoneri, Cumby and Diba (2005, p. 365ff.), the gains from cooperative behavior are increasing in the size of the policy trade-offs generated by shocks. If the monetary liquidity export via carry trades poses a significant threat to financial stability abroad, international cooperation may be superior to independent decisions made by central banks.

The need for coordination could also arise for other reasons. Monetary authorities might have difficulties in forecasting the actions of policymakers in other countries. Moutot and Vitale (2009, p. 34) therefore propose the exchange of

[104] However, the game-theoretic analysis of policy coordination might have limits. Countries and monetary authorities are treated as if they were persons. Hence, the question of how to coordinate involving decisions by many agents is bypassed (Bordo, Schwartz 1988, p. 460).

information among central banks and the sharing of views about international issues. However, in their view, domestic monetary policy shall still act on its own. Policymakers solely incorporate the expected actions of other central banks into their decisions.

Finally, another argument in favor of international cooperative behavior could be the recent financial crisis. Central banks worldwide implemented "non-standard" unorthodox measures to enhance credit support. Since both financial markets and economies show signs of stabilization, the coordination of monetary exit strategies on a global level may be necessary. Otherwise, economies with central banks hiking interest rates first may find their currencies strengthening, thereby attracting capital from countries not yet strongly recovering (Belke 2009, p. 21). However, the simultaneous phasing-out of unorthodox measures also contains risks. Especially in times of high uncertainty about the prospects of the global economy, policy coordination could lead a multitude of countries choosing the wrong set of measures at the same time. International policy coordination would merely elevate the shortcomings that are apparent in domestic economies to the global level. In contrast, independent and not correlated national monetary policies lead to risk diversification. The variance of a sum of disturbances decreases when the covariance of the individual components declines (Belke 2009, p. 23; Belke, Gros 2009a, p. 101).

There are further arguments speaking against international cooperation. The welfare gains from coordination may strongly depend on the sources and the concise nature of the disturbances. Any concrete proposal has therefore to be tested for robustness to the variety of sudden changes that may hit several countries simultaneously. In chapter 7.2.6, it has been shown that besides common money shocks other disturbances like technology may also play an important role. Hence, specific and coordinated central bank behavior could be optimal for responding to sudden changes in the financial and monetary environment. However, these measures may not be particularly salutary for disturbances stemming from the real economy like global technology shocks.

Furthermore, there might be practical problems in implementing effective international coordination. Suppose that countries agree on cooperative behavior in principle. It is then still an open question *how* to coordinate central bank action in practice. Many issues that emerged in the long-standing and continuing debate on the relative merits of rules versus discretion in domestic economic policy resurface once again. For instance, simple policy rules may reduce at least some of the negotiation costs that inevitably belong to international discretionary systems. Additionally, rules are championed as providing protection against the above-discussed model uncertainty, since central banks may not agree on how global money actually responds to a discretionary policy change. Even if a consensus can be reached, a time inconsistency problem still exists under discretion. Decision makers could renege on previously reached agreements when it later becomes advantageous to do so.

However, a rule-based international monetary system also may not always be optimal. For example, the distinction between global money supply and global money demand shocks could have important implications for the specific type of coordination. When common money supply disturbances occur, central banks are directly responsible. Simple rules to unwind excess liquidity may therefore be appropriate. In contrast, global money demand disturbances could be far more difficult to deal with. As different types of investors (banks, hedge funds, pension funds, etc.) and asset classes (shares, bonds, derivatives, etc.) might be involved, each global money demand disturbance could be different in its consequences for financial markets and real economies. Accordingly, in this case, the benefits of a discretionary approach may outweigh the disadvantages such policies have.

Finally, another practical problem in implementing effective international coordination is the rising complexities associated with in the future. Additional players have emerged on the global economic scene in form of major emerging markets. Simply going forward with cooperation within the G7 might no longer be sufficient, as the excess liquidity in the BRIC countries has increased recently (Belke, Gros 2010, p. 12ff.). Although BRIC currencies like the Chinese renminbi are not yet fully convertible, this development may merit increasing attention in coming years.

"Although this paper has addressed a range of questions, this analysis is only a start."

(Forbes, Chinn 2004, p. 720)

10 CONCLUSIONS

In this work, the existence of a global money market due to financial globalization and cross-border capital flows has been examined empirically. The obtained evidence suggests that common shocks to broad monetary aggregates are an important driver of the global economy and major industrialized countries or regions. The traditional trilemma view is put further into question as has been done in previous empirical research. Even under flexible exchange rates, international liquidity spillover effects seemingly occur, influencing a variety of domestic variables like economic activity, short-term interest rates and house prices.

The obtained results also suggest that especially large countries or regions like the US and the EMU are influenced by global money supply shocks. This stands in contrast to standard economic theory in which primarily small open economies are hit by disturbances from abroad. One explanation could be the huge volume of international capital flows attracted by deep and liquid financial markets in the US and the euro zone.

Furthermore, this work stresses the importance of taking an international perspective for central banks. In contrast to the conclusions derived from the Feldstein-Horioka puzzle, monetary policy does not work exclusively through domestic channels. Although national idiosyncracies are still relevant when analyzing the monetary transmission mechanism, the global view might deliver additional insights. Central banks and researchers alike may need to go beyond simple models and widen their battery of tools by including global variables in general and the phenomenon of common money in particular. Instead of focusing on concepts like the Taylor rule, a better structural understanding of global disturbances is warranted. The applied SFAVAR is only a small step forward in this direction. Several alternative approaches are conceivable. For instance, global shocks can be identified via long-run restrictions à la Blanchard-Quah in order to separate between sudden changes in global supply and global demand. The combination of cointegration with dynamic factor models yields a

Factor Augmented Vector Error Correction model (FAVEC). Bracke and Fidora (2008) apply structural VARs for the US and Emerging Asia, using sign restrictions. They find that monetary shocks in form of money supply and short-term interest rate disturbances explain the largest part of the variation in global external imbalances. In contrast, savings shocks (savings glut hypothesis) are found to be less important. Another interesting strand of empirical research is the analysis of asset prices and the role of common money. Alessi and Detken (2009) find that the global M1 gap and the global private credit gap are the best early warning indicators for boom and bust cycles in asset prices across OECD countries.

Besides further efforts in empirical work, the inclusion of a common money factor in structural theoretical models may be worth further consideration. For example, Woodford (2007) analyzes the impact of global liquidity on the effectivness of national monetary policies in a New Keynesian two-country setting. The use of dynamic stochastic general equilibrium (DSGE) open economy models could also be a fruitful approach for examining the impact of foreign monetary shocks on domestic variables.

Apart from developing theoretical and empirical models in an international context, rather unconventional concepts like scenario building could be useful for monetary policy behavior in practice. Since cross-border capital flows may make a straightforward interpretation of domestic monetary aggregates difficult, scenarios about the use of global excess liquidity and its likely impact on domestic variables shall be formed. This in turn might allow central banks a better assessment of risks associated with various capital-flow constellations (Moutot, Vitale 2009, p. 24).

Scenario building and sophisticated models may support policymakers in their daily effort to face the challenge of structural change caused by globalization on goods and financial markets. However, looking ahead, the fog of uncertainty may even become denser. For example, financial markets may undergo profound modifications after the recent unprecedented financial crisis. For instance, tighter regulation of international capital flows is conceivable, thereby possibly limiting monetary spillover effects. Even in "normal" times, it would have been not clear whether the extent of monetary spillover effects across countries will increase or decline in coming years.

On the one hand, it could be argued that global money is only a transitory phenomenon. The enormous rise in cross-border capital flows is largely driven by a decline in the home bias (Greenspan 2005, para. 11). Meanwhile, investors do not primarily put their money in assets located in their home country but increasingly diversify by using comparable foreign opportunities. If the home bias is eliminated, the volume of international capital flows decreases. Since a new "steady state" on international financial markets is reached, the importance of monetary spillover effects for domestic variables subsides. Central banks are getting more leeway again in their decisions. The most crucial thing for policymakers is to respond to this renewed structural break in a timely manner.

On the other hand, it may also be plausible to expect some degree of convergence in the scale and characteristics of international financial integration between advanced and developing countries (Lane, Milesi-Ferretti 2008, p. 331f.). If major emerging markets like China or India open up their financial markets, the volume of international capital flows could surge further. In this scenario, the phenomenon of global money may even become more important than it seems to have been the case in recent years.

References

Adalid, R. and C. Detken (2007): *Liquidity Shocks And Asset Price Boom/Bust Cycles*, ECB Working Paper No 732, European Central Bank, Frankfurt/Main, February.

Ahmed, S., B.W. Ickes, P. Wang and B.S. Yoo (1993): *International Business Cycles*, American Economic Review, Vol. 83, pp. 335-359, June.

Alessi, L. and C. Detken (2009): *'Real Time' Early Warning Indicators For Costly Asset Price Boom/Bust Cycles. A Role for Global Liquidity*, ECB Working Paper No 1039, European Central Bank, Frankfurt/Main, March.

Andersen, T. M. and N. C. Beier (2005): *International transmission of transitory and persistent monetary shocks under imperfect information*, Journal of International Economics, Vol. 66, pp. 485-507.

Andrews, D.W.K. (1993): *Exactly Median-Unbiased Estimation Of First Order Autoregressive Unit Root Models*, Econometrica, Vol. 61, pp. 139-165, January.

Andrews, D.W.K. and H.-Y. Chen (1994): *Approximately Median-Unbiased Estimation Of Autoregressive Models*, Journal of Business and Economic Statistics, Vol. 12, pp. 187-204, April.

Aoki, K. (2003): *On the Optimal Monetary Policy Response to Noisy Indicators*, Journal of Monetary Economics, Vol. 50, pp. 501-523.

Arango, S. and M.I. Nadiri (1981): *Demand for Money in Open Economies*, Journal of Monetary Economics, Vol. 7, pp. 69-83.

Bacchetta, P. and E. van Wincoop (2006): *Incomplete information processing: a solution to the forward discount puzzle*, Federal Reserve Bank of San Francisco Proceedings, San Francisco, June.

Backus, D.K., P.J. Kehoe and F.E. Kydland (1992): *International Real Business Cycles, Journal of Political Economy*, Vol. 100, pp. 745-775.

Bagliano, F.C. and C. Morana (2009): *International macroeconomic dynamics: A factor vector autoregressive approach*, Economic Modelling, Vol. 26, pp. 432-444.

Bagliano, F.C. and C. Morana (2010): *Business Cycle Comovement in the G-7: Common Shocks or Common Transmission Mechanisms?*, Applied Economics, Vol. 42, pp. 2327-2345.

Bai, J., (2003): *Inferential theory for factor models of large dimensions*, Econometrica, Vol. 71, pp. 135-171, January.

Bai, J. and P. Perron (1998): *Estimating And Testing Linear Models With Multiple Structural Changes*, Econometrica, Vol. 66, pp. 47-78, January.

Baks, K. and C. Kramer (1999): *Global Liquidity and Asset Prices: Measurement, Implications and Spillovers*, IMF Working Paper WP/99/168, International Monetary Fund, Washington, December.

Ball, L. and N.G. Mankiw (1994): *Asymmetric Price Adjustment and Economic Fluctuations*, The Economic Journal, Vol. 104, pp. 247-261, March.

Barro, R.J. and D.B. Gordon (1983): *Rules, discretion and reputation in a model of monetary policy*, Journal of Monetary Economics, Vol. 12, pp. 101-121.

Basel Committee on Banking Supervision (2008): *Principles for Sound Liquidity Risk Management and Supervision*, Bank for International Settlements, Basel, September.

Batbekh, S., D.R. Osborn, M. Sensier and D. van Dijk (2007): *Is there causality in the mean and volatility of inflation between the US and other G7 countries?*, mimeo, April.

Batini, N., B. Jackson and S. Nickell (2005): *An open-economy new Keynesian Phillips curve for the UK*, Journal of Monetary Economcis, Vol. 52, pp. 1061-1071.

Batten, D.S. and R.W. Hafer (1984): *Currency Substitution: A Test of Its Importance*, Review, Federal Reserve Bank of St. Louis, St. Louis, pp. 5-11, August/September.

Becchetti, L. and F. Mattesini (2009): *The Stock Market and the Fed*, Applied Financial Economics, Vol. 19, pp. 99-110.

Belke, A. (2009): *Global liquidity and monetary exit strategies – options for the euro area*, Directorate General for Internal Polices, Policy Department A: Economic and Scientific Policies, European Parliament, Brussels, November.

Belke, A., I.G. Bordon and T.W. Hendricks (2009): *Global Liquidity and Commodity Prices – A Cointegrated VAR Approach for OECD Countries*, DIW Discussion Paper 898, Deutsches Institut für Wirtschaftsforschung, Berlin, May.

Belke, A., I.G. Bordon and T.W. Hendricks (2010a): *Monetary Policy, Global Liquidity and Commodity Price Dynamics*, DIW Discussion Paper 898, Deutsches Institut für Wirtschaftsforschung, Berlin, February.

Belke, A., I.G. Bordon and T.W. Hendricks (2010b): *Global liquidity and commodity prices – a cointegrated VAR approach for OECD countries*, Applied Financial Economics, Vol. 20, pp. 227-242.

Belke, A. and D. Gros (2009a): *Is a Unified Macroeconomic Policy Necessarily Better for a Common Currency Area?*, European Journal of Political Economy, Vol. 25, pp. 98-101, March.

Belke, A. and D. Gros (2009b): *A Simple Model of an Oil Based Global Savings Glut – The "China Factor" and the OPEC Cartel*, DIW Discussion Paper 911, Deutsches Institut für Wirtschaftsforschung, Berlin, July.

Belke, A. and D. Gros (2010): *Global Liquidity, World Savings Glut and Global Policy Coordination*, DIW Discussion Paper 973, Deutsches Institut für Wirtschaftsforschung, Berlin, February.

Belke, A. and W. Orth (2007): *Global Excess Liquidity and House Prices. A VAR Analysis for OECD Countries*, Ruhr Economic Papers #37, University Duisburg-Essen, Duisburg-Essen, December.

Belke, A., W. Orth and R. Setzer (2008a): *Global "excess" liquidity: does it matter for house and stock prices on a global scale?*, Journal of Financial Transformation, Vol. 24, pp. 145-154.

Belke, A., W. Orth and R. Setzer (2008b): *Sowing the seeds for the subprime crisis: does global liquidity matter for housing and other asset prices?*, International Economics and Economic Policy, Vol. 5, pp. 403-424, December.

Belke, A., W. Orth and R. Setzer (2010): *Liquidity and the dynamic pattern of asset price adjustments: A global view*, Journal of Banking and Finance, Vol. 34, pp. 1933-1945, August.

Belke, A. and T. Polleit (2009): *Monetary Economics in Globalised Financial Markets*, Berlin, Heidelberg.

Belke, A. and A. Rees (2009): *The importance of Global Shocks for National Policymakers – Rising Challenges for Central Banks*, DIW Discussion Paper 922, Deutsches Institut für Wirtschaftsforschung, Berlin, September.

Benati, L. (2007): *The time-varying Phillips correlation*, Journal of Money, Credit and Banking, Vol. 39, pp. 1275-1283.

Benati, L. and P. Surico (2009): *VAR Analysis and the Great Moderation*, The American Economic Review, Vol. 99, pp. 1636-1652.

Berger, H. and T. Harjes (2009): *Does Global Liquidity Matter for Monetary Policy in the Euro Area?*, International Finance, Vol. 12, pp. 33-55.

Bernanke, B.S. (2005a): *The Global Saving Glut and the U.S. Current Account Deficit*, Remarks at the Sandridge Lecture, Virginia Association of Economics, Richmond, Virgina, 10 March.

Bernanke, B.S. (2005b): *Monetary Policy in a World of Mobile Capital*, Cato Journal, Vol. 25, pp. 1-12.

Bernanke, B.S., J. Boivin and P. Eliasz (2005): *Measuring the Effects of Monetary Policy: A Factor-Augmented Vector Autoregressive (FAVAR) Approach*, The Quarterly Journal of Economics, Vol. 120, pp. 387-442.

Boivin, J. and M.P. Giannoni (2002a): *Has Monetary Policy Become Less Powerful?*, Staff Reports No. 144, Federal Reserve Bank of New York, New York, March.

Boivin, J. and M.P. Giannoni (2002b): *Assessing Changes in the Monetary Transmission Mechanism: A VAR Approach*, Economic Policy Review, Federal Reserve Bank of New York, pp. 97-111, May.

Boivin, J. and M.P. Giannoni (2006): *DSGE Models in a Data-Rich Environment*, NBER Working Paper 12772, National Bureau of Economic Research, Cambridge, December.

Boivin, J. and M.P. Giannoni (2008): *Global Forces and Monetary Policy Effectiveness*, NBER Working Paper 13736, National Bureau of Economic Research, Cambridge, January.

Boivin, J., M.P. Giannoni and I. Mihov (2009): *Sticky Prices and Monetary Policy: Evidence from Disaggregated US Data*, American Economic Review, Vol. 99, pp. 350-384, March.

Boivin, J. and S. Ng (2006): *Are more data always better for factor analysis?*, Journal of Econometrics, Vol. 132, pp. 169-194, May.

Bordo, M.D. and A.J. Schwartz (1988): *Transmission of Real and Monetary Disturbances under Fixed and Floating Exchange Rates*, The Cato Journal, Vol. 8, Fall.

Borio, C. (2006): *Monetary and prudential policies at a crossroads? New challenges in the new century*, BIS Working Papers No 216, Bank for International Settlements, Basel, September.

Borio, C. and A. Filardo (2007): *Globalisation and inflation: New cross-country evidence on the global determinants of domestic inflation*, BIS Working Papers No 227, Bank for International Settlements, Basel, May.

Borondo, C. (2000): *International Transmission of Monetary Shocks with Interest Rate Rules*, Working Paper, Asociación Española de Economía y Finanzas Internacionales, Valladolid, September.

Bowman, D. and B. Doyle (2003): *New Keynesian, Open-Economy Models and Their Implications for Monetary Policy*, International Finance Discussion Paper 762, Board of Governors of the Federal Reserve System, Washington, March.

Bracke, T. and M. Fidora (2008): *Global Liquidity Glut Or Global Savings Glut? A Structural VAR Approach*, ECB Working Paper No 911, European Central Bank, Frankfurt/Main, June.

Brainard, W., (1967): *Uncertainty and the Effectiveness of Monetary Policy*, The American Economic Review, Papers and Proceedings, Vol. 57, pp. 411-425, May.

Caballero, R.J. (2006): *On The Macroeconomics Of Asset Shortages*, NBER Working Paper No. 12753, National Bureau of Economic Research, Cambridge, December.

Caldara, D. and C. Kamps (2008): *What Are The Effects of Fiscal Policy Shocks? A VAR-Based Comparative Analysis*, ECB Working Paper No 877, European Central Bank, Frankfurt/Main, March.

Canova, F., M. Ciccarelli and E. Ortega (2007): *Similarities and convergence in G-7 cycles*, Journal of Monetary Economics, Vol. 54, pp. 850-878, April.

Canzoneri, M.B., R.E. Cumby and B.T. Diba (2005): *The Need for International Policy Coordination: What's Old, What's New, What's Yet to come?*, The Journal of International Economics, Vol. 66, pp. 363-384, July.

Cavallo, M. (2006): *Interest Rates, Carry Trades, and Exchange Rate Movements*, Federal Reserve Bank of San Francisco Economic Letter, Number 2006-31, San Francisco, November.

Chamberlain, G. and M. Rothschild (1983): *Arbitrage, Factor Structure, and Mean-Variance Analysis on Large Asset Markets*, Econometrica, Vol. 51, pp. 1281-1304, September.

Ciccarelli, M. and B. Mojon (2005): *Global Inflation*, ECB Working Paper No 537, European Central Bank, Frankfurt/Main, October.

Ciccarelli, M. and B. Mojon (2010): *Global Inflation*, The Review of Economics and Statistics, Vol. 92, pp. 524-535, August.

Corden, W.M. and S.J. Turnovsky (1983): *Negative International Transmission Of Economic Expansion*, European Economic Review, Vol. 20, pp. 289-310, January.

Cover, J.P. (1992): *Asymmetric Effects Of Positive And Negative Money Supply Shocks*, The Quarterly Journal of Economics, Vol. 107, pp. 1261-1282, November.

Craine, R (1979): *Optimal monetary policy with uncertainty*, Journal of Economic Dynamics and Control, Vol. 1, pp. 59-83, February.

Cukierman, A. (2000): *The Inflation Bias Result Revisited*, Working Paper, Tel-Aviv University, April.

Cukierman, A. (2004): *Non Linearities in Taylor Rules – Causes, Consequences and Evidence*, Keynote Lecture presented at the 19th Economic Annual Meetng of the Central Bank of Uruguay, October 5.

Cukierman, A. (2008): *Central bank independence and monetary policymaking institutions – Past, present and future*, European Journal of Political Economy, Vol. 24, pp. 722-736, December.

Cukierman, A. and S. Gerlach (2003): *The Inflation Bias Revisited: Theory and Some International Evidence*, The Manchester School, Vol. 71, pp. 541-565, September.

Cukierman, A. and V. A. Muscatelli (2002): *Do Central Banks have Precautionary Demands for Expansions and for Price Stability?* – Theory and Evidence, CESifo Working Paper No. 764, Munich, August.

Cushman, D.O. and T. Zha (1997): *Identifying monetary policy in a small open economy under flexible exchange rates*, Journal of Monetary Economics, Vol. 39, pp. 433-448, August.

D'Agostino, A. and P. Surico (2007): *Does Global Liquidity Help to Forecast U.S. Inflation?*, MPRA Paper No. 6283, Munich, November.

D'Agostino, A. and P. Surico (2009): *Does Global Liquidity Help to Forecast U.S. Inflation?*, Journal of Money, Credit and Banking, Vol. 41, pp. 479-489.

Darius, R. and S. Radde (2010): *Can Global Liquidity Forecast Asset Prices?*, IMF Working Paper, International Monetary Fund, Washington, August.

Dées, S., S. Holly, M.H. Pesaran and L.V. Smith (2007): *Long-run macroeconomic relations in the global economy*, ECB Working Paper No 750, European Central Bank, Frankfurt/Main, May.

Dellas, H. (2006): *Monetary policy in open economies*, European Economic Review, Vol. 50, pp. 1471-1486.

Del Negro, M. and C. Otrok (2003): *Time-varying European Business Cycles,* mimeo, February.

Dennis, R., K. Leitemo and U. Söderström (2009): *Methods for robust control*, Journal of Economic Dynamics and Control, Vol. 33, pp. 1604-1616, August.

Dolado, J., R.M.-D. Pedrero and F.J. Ruge-Murcia (2004): *Nonlinear Monetary Policy Rules: Some New Evidence for the US*, Studies in Non-Linear Dynamics and Control, Vol. 8, pp. 1-32.

Dornbusch, R. (1976): *Exchange rate expectations and monetary policy*, Journal of International Economics, Vol. 6, pp. 231-244, August.

Doyle, B.M. and B. Falk (2010): *Do Asymmetric Central Bank Preferences Help Explain Observed Inflation Outcomes?*, Journal of Macroeconomics, Vol. 32, pp. 527-540.

Drehman, M. and K. Nikolaou (2009): *Funding Liquidity Risk. Definition And Measurement*, ECB Working Paper No 1024, European Central Bank, Frankfurt/Main, March.

Dreger, C. and J. Wolters (2009): *Liquidity and Asset Prices – How Strong Are the Linkages?*, DIW Discussion Paper 860, Deutsches Institut für Wirtschaftsforschung, Berlin, February.

Eichenbaum, M. and C.L. Evans (1995): *Some Empirical Evidence on the Effects of Shocks to Monetary Policy on Exchange Rates*, Quarterly Journal of Economics, Vol. 110, pp. 975-1009, November.

Eickmeier, S. (2007): *Business Cycle Transmission from the US to Germany – a Structural Factor Approach*, European Economic Review, Vol. 51, pp. 521-555, April.

Elliot, G., A. Fatás (1996): *International business cycles and the dynamics of the current account*, European Economic Review, Vol. 40, pp. 361-387, February.

Enders, W. (2004): *Applied Econometric Time Series*, New York, 2nd edition.

EViews 6 User's Guide I, Irvine, California, 2007.

EViews 6 User's Guide II, Irvine, California, 2007.

Fagan, G., J. Henry and R. Mestre (2001): *An Area-Wide Model (AWM) For The Euro Area*, ECB Working Paper No 42, European Central Bank, Frankfurt/Main, January.

Faust, J. and J.H. Rogers (2003): *Monetary policy's role in exchange rate behavior*, Journal of Monetary Economics, Vol. 50, pp. 1403-1424, October.

Favero, C.A. and M. Marcellino (2004): *Large Datasets, Small Models and Monetary Policy in Europe*, Working Paper, Innocenzo Gasparini Institute for Economic Research, Bocconi University, Milan, September.

Favero, C.A., M. Marcellino and F. Neglia (2005): *Principal components at work: the empirical analysis of monetary policy with large datasets*, Journal of Applied Econometrics, Vol. 20, pp. 603-620.

Federal Reserve Bank of Kansas City (2009): *Proceedings of the Symposium on Financial Stability and Macroeconomic Policy*, Federal Reserve Bank of Kansas City, Kansas City, August.

Feldstein, M. and Horioka, C. (1980): *Domestic Saving And International Capital Flows*, The Economic Journal, Vol. 90, pp. 314-329, June.

Fernandez, F.A. (1999): *Liquidity Risk. New Approaches To Measurement And Monitoring*, Working Paper, Securities Industry Association, New York, December.

Forbes, K.J. and M.D. Chinn (2004): *A Decomposition of Global Linkages in Financial Markets Over Time*, The Review of Economics and Statistics, Vol. 86, pp. 705-722, August.

Fratzscher, M., Juvenal, L. and L. Sarno (2009): *Asset Prices, Exchange Rates And The Current Account*, European Economic Review, Vol. 54, pp. 643-658, July.

Frankel, J., S.L. Schmukler and L. Servén (2004): *Global transmission of interest rates: monetary independence and currency regime*, Journal of International Money and Finance, Vol. 23, pp. 701-733, September.

Frenkel, J.A. and A. Razin (1987): *The Mundell-Fleming Model: A Quarter Century Later*, NBER Working Paper No. 2321, National Bureau of Economic Research, Cambridge, July.

Friedman, B.M. and K.N. Kuttner (1993): *Economic Activity and the Short-term Credit Markets: An Analysis of Prices and Quantities*, Brookings Papers on Economic Activity, Vol. 2, pp. 193-283.

Galí, J. (1999): *Technology, Employment, and the Business Cycle: Do Technology Shocks Explain Aggregate Fluctuations?*, The American Economic Review, Vol. 89, 249-271.

Galí, J. and T. Monacelli (2005): *Monetary Policy and Exchange Rate Volatility in a Small Open Economy*, Review of Economic Studies, Vol. 72, pp. 707-734

Gerdesmeier, D., H.-E. Reimers and B. Roffia (2009): *Asset Price Misalignments And The Role Of Money And Credit*, ECB Working Paper No 1068, European Central Bank, Frankfurt/Main, July.

Giese, J.V. and C.K. Tuxen (2007a): *Global Liquidity and Asset Prices in a Cointegrated VAR*, mimeo, July.

Giese, J.V. and C.K. Tuxen (2007b): *Global Liquidity and Asset Prices: Cross-Country Linkages in a GVAR model*, mimeo, August.

Gilbert, P.D. and L. Pichette (2003): *Dynamic Factor Analysis for Measuring Money,* Working Paper 2003-21, Bank of Canada, Ottawa, July.

Glaeser, E., J. Gottlieb and J. Gyourko (2010): *Can interest rates explain the US housing boom and bust?*, Online comment available at http://www.voxeu.org/index.php?q=node/5445, August.

Goncalves, S. and L. Kilian (2004): *Bootstrapping autoregressions with conditional heteroskedasticity of unknown form*, Journal of Econometrics, Vol. 123, pp. 89-120, November.

Granger, C.W.J. and Y. Jeon (2007): *Evaluation of global models*, Economic Modelling, Vol. 24, pp. 980-989, November.

Greenspan, A. (2005): *Stability and Economic Growth: The Role of the Central Bank*, Remarks before the Banco de Mexiko's 80th Anniversary International Conference, November 14.

Gros, D. (2007): *Bubbles in real estate? A Longer-Term Comparative Analysis of Housing Prices in Europe and the US*, CEPS Working Document No. 276, Centre for European Policy Studies, Brussels, October.

Hansen, B.E. (2001): *The New Econometrics of Structural Change: Dating Breaks in U.S. Labor Productivity*, Journal of Economic Perspectives, Vol. 15, pp. 117-128, Autumn.

Hansen, B.E. (1992): *Testing for Parameter Instability in Linear Models*, Journal of Policy Modeling, Vol. 14, pp. 517-533, August.

Hatheway, L., P. Donovan, A. Cates and S. Bancroft (2006): *Lack of Liquidity*, Global Economic Perspectives, UBS Investment Research, London, 18 May.

Helbling, T. and T. Bayoumi (2003): *Are They All in the Same Boat? The 2000-2001 Growth Slowdown and the G-7 Business Cycle Linkages*, IMF Working Paper, International Monetary Fund, Washington, March.

Holman, J.A. and R.M. Neumann (2002): *Evidence on the cross-country transmission of monetary shocks*, Applied Economics, Vol. 34, pp. 1837-1857, October.

Huizinga, J. and F.S. Mishkin (1986): *Monetary Policy Regime Shifts And The Unusual Behavior Of Real Interest Rates*, NBER Working Paper 1678, National Bureau of Economic Research, Cambridge, August.

International Monetary Fund (2004): *The Global House Price Boom*, World Economic Outlook – The Global Demographic Transition, Chapter II, pp. 71-89, Washington, September.

International Monetary Fund (2008a): *Containing Systemic Risks and Restoring Financial Soundness*, Global Financial Stability Report, World Economic and Financial Surveys, Washington, April.

International Monetary Fund (2008b): *International Financial Statistics. World & Country Notes*, Washington, September.

Johnson, R.A. and D.W. Wichern (2007): *Applied Multivariate Statistical Analysis*, 6th edition, Upper Saddle River, New Jersey.

Justiniano, A. (2003): *Sources and Propagation Mechanisms of Foreign Disturbances in Small Open Economies: A Dynamic Factor Analysis*, Working Paper, Department of Economics, Princeton University, January.

Karras, G. (1999): *Openness and the effects of monetary policy*, Journal of International Money and Finance, Vol. 18, pp. 13-26, January.

Kim, S. (2001): *International transmission of U.S. monetary policy shocks: Evidence from VAR's*, Journal of Monetary Economics, Vol. 48, pp. 339-372, October.

Kim, D.H., D.R. Osborn and M. Sensier (2005): *Nonlinearity In The Fed's Monetary Policy Rule,* Journal of Applied Econometrics, 20, pp. 621-639.

Kim, S. and N. Roubini (2000): *Exchange rate anomalies in the industrial countries: A solution with a structural VAR approach*, Journal of Monetary Economics, Vol. 45, pp. 561-586, June.

Klenow, P.J. and A. Rodriguez-Clare (2004): *Externalities And Growth*, NBER Working Paper 11009, National Bureau of Economic Research, Cambridge, December.

Kose, M.A., C. Otrok and C.H. Whiteman (2003): *International Business Cycles: World, Region, and Country-Specific Factors*, The American Economic Review, Vol. 93, pp. 1216-1239, September.

Kose, M.A., C. Otrok and C.H. Whiteman (2005): *Understanding the Evolution of World Business Cycles*, IMF Working Paper WP/05/211, International Monetary Fund, Washington, November.

Kose, M.A., C. Otrok and C.H. Whiteman (2008): *Understanding the Evolution of World Business Cycles*, Journal of International Economics, Vol. 75, pp. 110-130, May.

Kuszczak, J., J.D. Murray (1986): *A VAR Analysis of Economic Interdependence: Canada, the United States, and the Rest of the World*, Federal Reserve Bank of St. Louis Review, pp. 77-131, December.

Kydland, F.E. and E.C. Prescott (1977): *Rules Rather Than Discretion: The Inconsistency of Optimal Plans*, Journal of Political Economy, Vol. 85, pp. 473-491, June.

Lane, P.R. (2001): *The new open economy macroeconomics: a survey*, Journal of International Economics, Vol. 54, pp. 235-266, August.

Lane P.R. and G.M. Milesi-Ferretti (2007): *The external wealth of nations mark II: Revised and extended estimates of foreign assets and liabilities, 1970-2004*, Journal of International Economics, Vol. 73, pp. 223-250, November.

Lane P.R. and G.M. Milesi-Ferretti (2008): *The Drivers of Financial Globalization*, The American Economic Review, Papers and Proceedings, Vol. 98, pp. 327-332, May.

Leeper, E.M. and J.E. Roush (2003): *Putting 'M' Back in Monetary Policy*, Journal of Money, Credit and Banking, Vol. 35, pp. 1217-1256, December.

Levin, A.T. and J.M. Piger (2003): *Is Inflation Persistence Intrinsic in Industrial Economies*, Working Paper, Federal Reserve Bank of St. Louis, St. Louis, November.

Magnus, G. (2007): *The Credit Cycle and Liquidity: Have we arrived at a Minsky Moment?*, Economic Insights – By George, UBS Investment Research, London, 6 March.

Mankiw, N.G., D. Romer and D.N. Weil (1992): *A Contribution to the Empirics of Economic Growth*, Vol. 107, pp. 407-437, May.

Marques, C.R. (2004): *Inflation Persistence: Facts or Artefacts?*, ECB Working Paper No 371, European Central Bank, Frankfurt/Main, June.

McCallum, B.T. (1995): *Two Fallacies Concerning Central-Bank Independence*, The American Economic Review, Papers and Proceedings, Vol. 85, pp. 207-211, May.

McKinnon, R.I. (1981): *The Exchange Rate and Macroeconomic Policy: Changing Postwar Perceptions*, Journal of Economic Literature, Vol. XIX, pp. 531-557, June.

McKinnon, R.I. (1982): *Currency Substitution and Instability in the World Dollar Standard*, The American Economic Review, Vol. 72, pp. 320-333, June.

Miles, M.A. (1978): *Currency Substitution, Flexible Exchange Rates, and Monetary Independence*, The American Economic Review, Vol. 68, pp. 428-436, June.

Miller, M., P. Weller and L. Zhang (2002): *Moral Hazard and the US Stock Market: Analysing the 'Greenspan put'*, The Economic Journal, Conference Papers, Vol. 112, C171-C186, March.

Mönch, E. (2005): *Forecasting The Yield Curve In A Data-Rich Environment. A No-Arbitrage Factor-Augmented VAR Approach*, ECB Working Paper No 544, European Central Bank, Frankfurt/Main, November.

Moneta, F. and R. Rüffer (2006): *Business Cycle Synchronisation In East Asia*, ECB Working Paper No 671, Frankfurt/Main, August.

Monfort, A., J-.P. Renne, R. Rüffer and G. Vitale (2003): *Is Economic Activity In The G7 Synchronized? Common Shocks Versus Spillover Effects*, CEPR Discussion Paper Series, Discussion Paper No. 4119, Brussels, November.

Moutot, P. and G. Vitale (2009): *Monetary Policy in a Global Environment*, ECB Occasional Paper No 106, European Central Bank, Frankfurt/Main, January.

Neanidis, K.C. and C.S. Savva (2006): *The Effects of Uncertainty on Currency Substitution and Inflation: Evidence from Emerging Economies*, Economics Discussion Paper EDP-0609, The University of Manchester, March.

Neri, S. and A. Nobili (2006): *The transmission of monetary policy shocks from the US to the euro area,* Banca D'Italia Temi di discussione del Servizio Studi Number 606, December.

O'Brien, Y-Y. C (2007): *Measurement of Monetary Aggregates Across Countries*, Working Paper 2007-02, Finance and Economic Discussion Series, Divisions of Research & Statistics and Monetary Affairs, Federal Reserev Board, Washington.

O'Hara (2004): *Liquidity and Financial Market Stability*, Working Paper No. 55, National Bank of Belgium, Brussels, May.

O'Reilly, G. and K. Whelan (2005a): *Has Euro-Area Inflation Persistence Changed Over Time?*, The Review of Economics and Statistics, Vol. 87, pp. 709-720, November.

O'Reilly, G. and K. Whelan (2005b): *Testing Parameter Stability: A Wild Bootstrap Approach*, Research Technical Paper 8/RT/05, Central Bank & Financial Services Authority of Ireland, Dublin, December.

Pagan, A. (1984): *Econometric Issues in the Analysis of Regressions with Generated Regressors*, International Economic Review, Vol. 25, pp. 221-247, February.

Papademos, L. (2007): *The effects of globalization on inflation, liquidity and monetary policy*, Speech held at a conference on the "International Dimensions of Monetary Policy", S'Agaró, Girona, 11 June.

Papanyan, S. (2010): *The Transmission of Shocks between Europe, Japan and the United States*, Journal of Forecasting, Vol. 29, pp. 54-70, November.

Perron, P. (1989): *The Great Crash, the Oil Price Shock, and the Unit Root Hypothesis*, Econometrica, Vol. 57, pp. 1361-1401, November.

Pivetta, F. and R. Reis (2007): *The Persistence of Inflation in the United States,* mimeo.

Polleit, T. and D. Gerdesmeier (2005): *Measures of Excess Liquidity*, Working Paper No. 65, HfB Business School of Finance & Management, Frankfurt/Main, August.

Quandt, R.E. (1960): *Tests of the hypothesis that a linear regression system obeys two separate regimes*, Journal of the American Statistical Association, Vol. 55, pp. 324-330.

Rajan, R.G. (2005): *Has Financial Development Made the World Riskier?*, NBER Working Paper 11728, National Bureau of Economic Research, Cambridge, November.

Rogoff, K. (2006): *Impact of Globalization on Monetary Policy*, paper prepared for symposium sponsored by the Federal Reserve Bank of Kansas City on "The New Economic Geography: Effects and Policy Implications, Jackson Hole, August.

Rüffer, R. and L. Stracca (2006): *What is global excess liquidity, and does it matter?*, ECB Working Paper No. 696, European Central Bank, Frankfurt/Main, November.

Rudebusch, G.D. (2000): *Is the Fed Too Timid? Monetary Policy in an Uncertain World,* mimeo, June.

Ruge-Murcia, F.J. (2004): *The inflation bias when the central bank targets the natural rate of unemployment*, The European Economic Review, Vol. 48, pp. 91-107, February.

Sachs, J.D. (1985): *Is There a Case for More Managed Exchange Rates,* Proceedings, Federal Reserve Bank of Kansas City, pp. 185-226,

Sarno, L. (2001): *Toward a New Paradigm in Open Economy Modeling: Where Do We Stand?*, Federal Reserve Bank of St. Louis Review, pp. 21-36, St. Louis, May/June.

Schaller, H. and S. Junayed (2007): *The Credit Channel in a Small, Open Economy*, Working Paper, Carleton University, March.

Seater, J.J (2008): *The Demand for Currency Substitution*, E-conomics, The Open-Access, Open-Assessment E-journal, Vol. 2, pp. 1-30, November.

Sensier, M., D. van Dijk (2004): *Testing for Volatility Changes in US Macroeconomic Time Series*, The Review of Economics and Statistics, Vol. 86, pp. 833-839, August.

Shambaugh 2004, J.C. (2004): *The Effect of Fixed Exchange Rates on Monetary Policy*, The Quarterly Journal of Economics, Vol. 119, pp. 301-352, February.

Shuetrim, G. and C. Thompson (1999): *The Implications Of Uncertainty For Monetary Policy,* Research Discussion Paper 1999-10, Reserve Bank of Australia, November.

Simon, J. (2001): *The Decline In Australian Output Volatility*, Research Discussion Paper 2001-01, Reserve Bank of Australia, March.

Sims, C. A. (1992): *Interpreting the macroeconomic time series facts. The effects of monetary policy*, European Economic Review, Vol. 36, pp. 975-1000, June.

Sims, C.A. and T. Zha (2006): *Were There Regime Switches in U.S. Monetary Policy?*, The American Economic Review, Vol. 96, pp. 54-81, March.

Sousa, J.M. and A. Zaghini (2004): *Monetary policy shocks in the euro area and global liquidity spillovers*, ECB Working Paper No 309, European Central Bank, Frankfurt/Main, February.

Sousa, J.M. and A. Zaghini (2007): *Global Monetary Policy Shocks in the G5: A SVAR Approach*, Journal of International Financial Markets, Institutions and Money, Vol. 17, pp. 403-419, December.

Sousa, J.M. and A. Zaghini (2008): *Monetary policy shocks in the euro area and global liquidity spillovers*, International Journal of Finance and Economics, Vol. 13, pp. 205-218.

Stock, J.H. and M.W. Watson (1998): *Diffusion Indexes*, NBER Working Paper 6702, National Bureau of Economic Research, Cambridge, August.

Stock, J.H. and M.W. Watson (2002a): *Has The Business Cycle Changed And Why?*, NBER Working Paper 9127, National Bureau of Economic Research, Cambridge, September.

Stock, J.H. and M.W. Watson (2002b): *Macroeconomic Forecasting Using Diffusion Indexes*, Journal of Business and Economic Statistics, Vol. 20, pp. 147-162, April.

Stock, J.H. and M.W. Watson (2003): *Has the Business Cycle Changed? Evidence and Explanations*, Working Paper, prepared for the Federal Reserve Bank of Kansas City symposium "Monetary Policy and Uncertainty", September.

Stock, J.H. and M.W. Watson (2005a): *Implications Of Dynamic Factor Models For VAR Analysis*, NBER Working Paper 11467, National Bureau of Economic Research, Cambridge, July.

Stock, J.H. and M.W. Watson (2005b): *Understanding Changes in International Business Cycle Dynamics*, Journal of the European Economic Association, Vol. 3, pp. 968-1006, September.

Strahan, P. (2008): *Liquidity Production in 21st Century Banking*, NBER Working Paper 13798, National Bureau of Economic Research, Cambridge, February.

Svensson, L.E.O., and S. van Wijnbergen (1989): *Excess Capacity, Monopolistic Competition, And International Transmission of Monetary Disturbances*, The Economic Journal, Vol. 99, pp. 785-805.

Tanizaki, H. (2000): *Bias correction of OLSE in the regression model with lagged dependent variables*, Computational Statistics and Data Analysis, Vol. 34, pp. 495-511.

The Bank Credit Analyst (2007): *Booming Liquidity: Too much of a Good Thing*, Special Report, Montreal, 6 February.

Van Dijk, D., D.R. Osborn and M. Sensier (2002): *Changes in Variability of the Business Cycle in the G7 Countries*, Discussion Paper Series Number 016, Centre for Growth & Business Cycle Research, The University of Manchester, September.

VanHoose, D. (2004): *The New Open Economy Macroeconomics: A Critical Appraisal*, Open Economies Review, Vol. 15, pp. 193-215.

Vansteenkiste, I. and P. Hiebert (2009): *Do House Price Developments Spill Over Across Euro Area Countries? Evidence From A Global VAR*, ECB Working Paper No 1026, European Central Bank, Frankfurt/Main, March.

Walsh, C.E. (2004): *Implications of a Changing Economic Structure for the Strategy of Monetary Policy*, Working Paper No. 1023, Santa Cruz Center for International Economics, Santa Cruz, February.

Williams, J.C. (2006): *Robust Estimation and Monetary Policy with Unobserved Structural Change*, Economic Review, Federal Reserve Bank of San Francisco, San Francisco, pp. 1-16.

Woodford, M. (2007): *Globalization and Monetary Control*, NBER Working Paper 13329, National Bureau of Economic Research, Cambridge, August.

Woolridge, J.M. (2009): *Introductory Econometrics. A modern approach*, Mason, 4th edition.

APPENDIX

A.1 UNIT ROOT TESTS FOR DETRENDED EXCESS LIQUIDITIES

Log-first difference	ADF	PP	KPSS
US	-8.14***	-8.15***	0.15
EMU	-10.20***	-10.22***	0.84
Japan	-6.05***	-10.26***	0.17
UK	-8.54***	-9.19***	0.27
Canada	-8.38***	-8.50***	0.25
Linear time trend	ADF	PP	KPSS
US	-4.53***	-4.42***	0.03
EMU	-3.69*	-3.89***	0.04
Japan	-4.16***	-4.16***	0.02
UK	-4.89***	-5.53***	0.04
Canada	-2.21	-2.34	0.05
HP filter	ADF	PP	KPSS
US	-4.57***	-3.39**	0.03
EMU	-4.73***	-5.10***	0.02
Japan	-4.21***	-4.21***	0.03
UK	-5.06***	-5.84***	0.03
Canada	-4.37***	-3.91***	0.04

Note 1: ADF (Augmented Dickey-Fuller), PP (Phillips-Perron), KPSS (Kwiatkowski-Phillips-Schmidt-Shin)

Note 2: All tests based on standardized figures

Note 3: *** Indicates significance at 1% level, ** at 5% level, * at 10% level

Note 4: Null hypothesis of ADF and PP test assumes non-stationarity; null hypothesis of KPSS test assumes stationarity

A.2 UNIT ROOT TESTS FOR REDUCED-FORM RESIDUALS IN THE RECURSIVE G7 VAR MODELS

Residuals	US	EMU	Japan	UK	Canada
CP	-9.19***/-9.19***/0.03	-9.97***/-9.97***/0.03	-8.00***/-9.75***/0.03	-9.10***/-9.12***/0.03	-9.64***/-9.64***/0.04
YR	-9.67***/-9.70***/0.03	-9.37***/-9.40***/0.04	-9.50***/-9.50***/0.06	-11.5***/-11.47***/0.06	-9.80***/-9.79***/0.04
PI	-8.81***/-8.78***/0.03	-9.70***/-9.74***/0.04	-10.40***/-12.08***/0.07	-9.58***/-9.59***/0.04	-10.01***/-10.26***/0.04
M3	-9.34***/-9.34***/0.04	-10.22***/-11.07***/0.05	-5.13***/-10.25***/0.05	-9.21***/-9.31***/0.06	-9.08***/-9.10***/0.05
SR	-8.70***/-8.71***/0.03	-10.11***/-10.10***/0.03	-9.45***/-9.45***/0.03	-9.27***/-9.27***/0.06	-4.98***/-10.48***/0.04
ER	-11.32***/-14.47***/0.10	-9.76***/-9.75***/0.04	-9.87***/-9.96***/0.04	-9.10***/-9.10***/0.05	-8.67***/-9.39***/0.06

Note 1: ADF (Augmented Dickey-Fuller), PP (Phillips-Perron), KPSS (Kwiatkowski-Phillips-Schmidt-Shin)

Note 2: First figure in each cell refers to ADF test, the second one to PP test, the third one to KPSS test

Note 3: *** Indicates significance at 1% level, ** at 5% level, * at 10% level

Note 4: Null hypothesis of ADF and PP test assumes non-stationarity; null hypothesis of KPSS test assumes stationarity

A.3 MULTIVARIATE LM TESTS FOR SERIAL CORRELATION IN THE REDUCED-FORM RESIDUALS IN THE RECURSIVE G7 VAR MODELS

US VAR			EMU VAR		Japan VAR		UK VAR		Canada VAR	
Lags	LM-Stat	Prob	LM-Stat	Prob	LM-Stat	Prob	LM-Stat	Prob	LM-Stat	Prob
1	42.99	0.20	55.05	0.02	42.91	0.20	45.54	0.13	29.09	0.79
2	33.85	0.57	35.09	0.51	59.89	0.01	35.33	0.50	27.33	0.85
3	60.81	0.01	37.54	0.40	45.85	0.13	32.66	0.63	45.33	0.14
4	55.53	0.02	46.41	0.11	22.39	0.96	28.53	0.81	59.03	0.01
5	37.47	0.40	42.36	0.22	34.91	0.52	37.54	0.40	31.88	0.66
6	39.86	0.30	54.72	0.02	23.98	0.94	37.48	0.40	39.98	0.30
7	33.31	0.60	35.31	0.50	42.62	0.21	45.96	0.12	45.06	0.14
8	36.98	0.42	32.53	0.63	38.62	0.35	41.84	0.23	28.51	0.81
9	41.36	0.25	28.33	0.82	31.44	0.69	42.68	0.21	45.24	0.14
10	28.94	0.79	39.72	0.31	32.97	0.61	35.00	0.52	33.30	0.60
11	46.15	0.12	59.01	0.01	32.82	0.62	46.02	0.12	35.25	0.50
12	44.54	0.16	41.21	0.25	38.19	0.37	57.05	0.01	31.41	0.69

A.4 MULTIVARIATE WHITE TESTS FOR HETEROSKEDASTICITY IN THE REDUCED-FORM RESIDUALS IN THE RECURSIVE G7 VAR MODELS

	Chi-sq	df	Prob
US	1062.39	1050	0.39
EMU	686.55	546	0.00
Japan	647.71	546	0.00
UK	639.22	546	0.00
Canada	618.63	546	0.02

A.5 SINGLE-EQUATION LM ARCH TESTS FOR ARCH EFFECTS (4TH ORDER) IN THE RESIDUALS IN THE RECURSIVE G7 VAR MODELS

Residuals	US	EMU	Japan	UK	Canada
CP	0.59	0.27	0.23	0.15	1.12
YR	1.36	0.04	0.76	5.43***	5.38***
PI	0.11	0.38	0.13	0.14	0.48
M3	1.41	4.05***	2.42*	0.47	0.25
SR	0.42	1.08	9.81***	3.08**	0.38
ER	0.14	0.604	2.44*	0.74	3.25**

Note 1: F-statistic

Note 2: *** Indicates significance at 1% level, ** at 5% level, * at 10% level

A.6 MULTIVARIATE TESTS (JARQUE-BERA) FOR NORMALITY OF THE SYSTEM RESIDUALS IN THE RECURSIVE G7 VAR MODELS

US VAR			EMU VAR		Japan VAR		UK VAR		Canada VAR	
Residuals	Jarque-Bera	Prob	Jarque-Bera	Prob	Jarque-Bera	Prob	Jarque-Bera	Prob	Jarque-Bera	Prob
CP	6.37	0.04	4.44	0.11	3.43	0.18	3.18	0.20	3.11	0.21
YR	7.12	0.03	684.66	0.00	1.21	0.55	2.63	0.27	6.16	0.05
PI	4.39	0.11	2.98	0.23	1.60	0.45	47.98	0.00	8.69	0.01
M3	9.91	0.01	3.56	0.17	3.77	0.15	39.83	0.00	5.56	0.06
SR	6.42	0.04	1.41	0.49	78.69	0.00	1.93	0.38	7.37	0.03
ER	5.48	0.06	6.02	0.05	1.15	0.56	11.43	0.00	2.40	0.30
Joint	39.69	0.00	703.07	0.00	89.84	0.00	106.97	0.00	33.30	0.00

A.7 TESTING FOR OMITTED EXCESS LIQUIDITY SHOCKS IN RECURSIVE G7 VARS (COMMODITY PRICES ORDERED LAST, MONEY ORDERED AFTER THE SHORT-TERM INTEREST RATE)

	Additional excess liquidity shocks					
National VARs	Global	US	EMU	Japan	UK	Canada
US	2.40*	---	0.61/3.38**	1.11/1.13	1.61/0.60	2.79**/5.99***
EMU	3.93**	1.32/2.83**	---	1.68/1.89	1.61/2.29*	2.32*/1.60
Japan	0.14	0.45/0.31	3.38**/1.20	---	0.36/2.54*	0.18/0.75
UK	3.59**	2.92**/4.71***	0.91/4.93***	0.84/0.18	---	1.61/1.62
Canada	0.14	2.01/0.80	0.22/0.63	0.12/1.53	0.32/1.07	---

Note 1: F-statistics of heteroskedasticity-autocorrelation robust Wald tests (first figure based on autoregressive approach; second figure based on VAR)

Note 2: *** Indicates significance at 1% level, ** at 5% level, * at 10% level

A.8 MULTIVARIATE LM TEST FOR SERIAL CORRELATION, WHITE TEST FOR HETEROSKEDASTICITY, LM ARCH TEST AND JARQUE-BERA TEST IN EMU VARS

LM test for autocorrelation		
Lags	LM-Stat	Prob
1	60.48	0.16
2	56.97	0.20
3	56.97	0.20
4	52.81	0.33
5	55.66	0.24
6	74.64	0.01
7	46.04	0.59
8	51.23	0.39
9	46.71	0.57
10	52.71	0.33
11	86.06	0.00
12	51.35	0.38
White test for heteroskedasticity		
	Chi-sq	Prob
	975.43	0.00
LM ARCH test (4th order)		
Residuals	F-Stat	Prob
CP	0.66	0.62
GEL_exEMU	0.20	0.94
YR	0.21	0.93
PI	0.94	0.45
M3	1.75	0.15
SR	0.71	0.59
ER	0.39	0.81
Jarque-Bera test		
Residuals	Jarque-Bera*	Prob*
CP	6.11/5.46	0.05/0.07
GEL_exEMU	4.56/0.12	0.10/0.94
YR	410.55/430.85	0.00/0.00
PI	3.23/4.15	0.20/0.13
M3	4.74/2.04	0.09/0.36
SR	1.02/3.11	0.60/0.21
ER	6.93/4.72	0.03/0.09
Joint	437.14/450.44	0.00/0.00

Note: * First figure of Jarque-Bera test refers ro Cholesky VAR, second figure to SVAR

A.9 UNIT ROOT TESTS FOR REDUCED-FORM RESIDUALS IN THE EMU VAR MODEL

Residuals	ADF	PP	KPSS
CP	-9.57***	-9.58***	0.03
GEL_exEMU	-10.14***	-10.14***	0.04
YR	-9.56***	-9.58***	0.04
PI	-9.65***	-9.69***	0.04
M3	-10.49***	-12.11***	0.08
SR	-10.17***	-10.16***	0.03
ER	-9.68***	-9.68***	0.03

Note 1: ADF (Augmented Dickey-Fuller), PP (Phillips-Perron), KPSS (Kwiatkowski-Phillips-Schmidt-Shin)

Note 2: *** Indicates significance at 1% level, ** at 5% level, * at 10% level

Note 3: Null hypothesis of ADF and PP test assumes non-stationarity; null hypothesis of KPSS test assumes stationarity

A.10 IMPULSE RESPONSE ANALYSIS IN CHOLESKY VAR AND SVAR FOR THE EMU

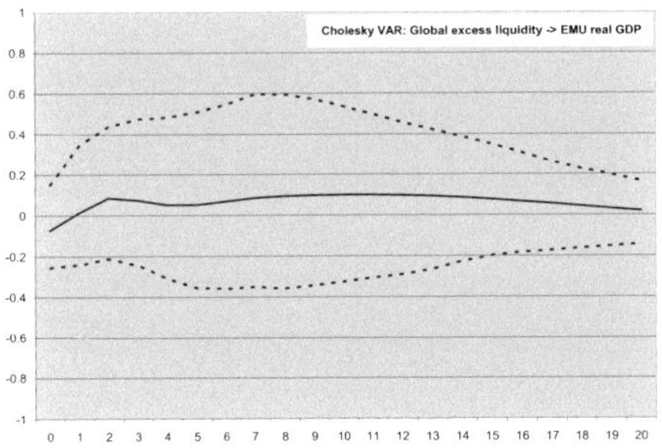

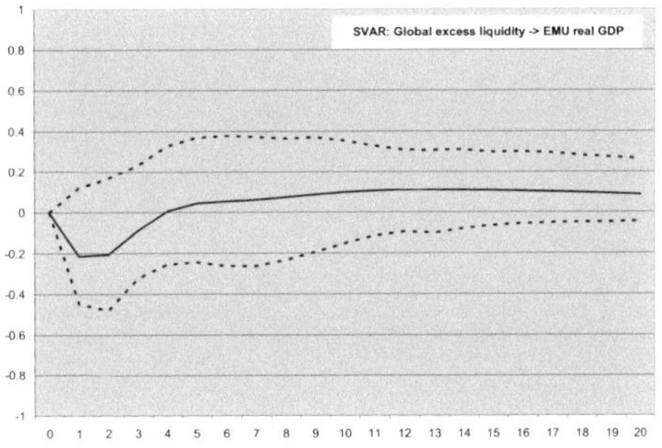

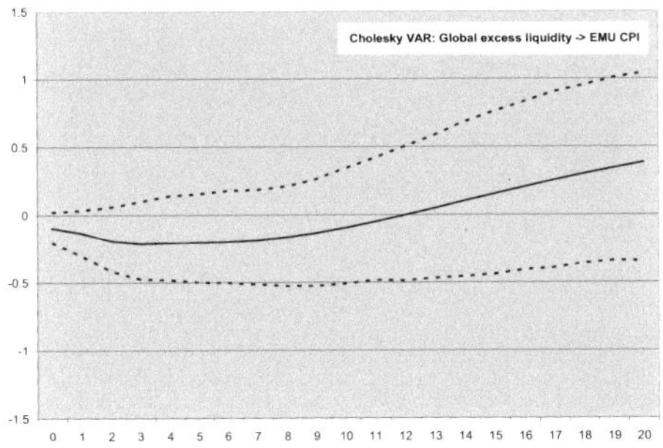

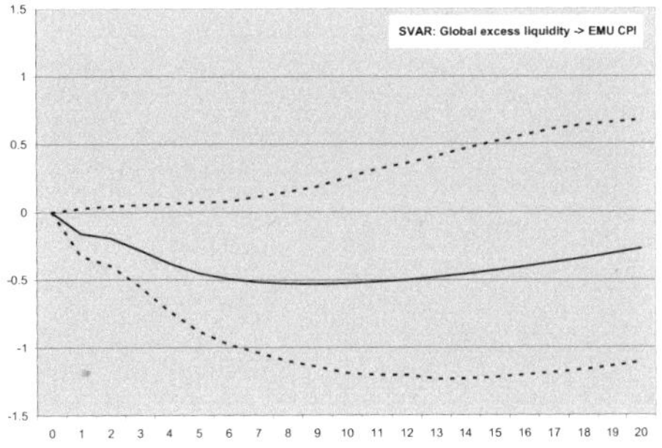

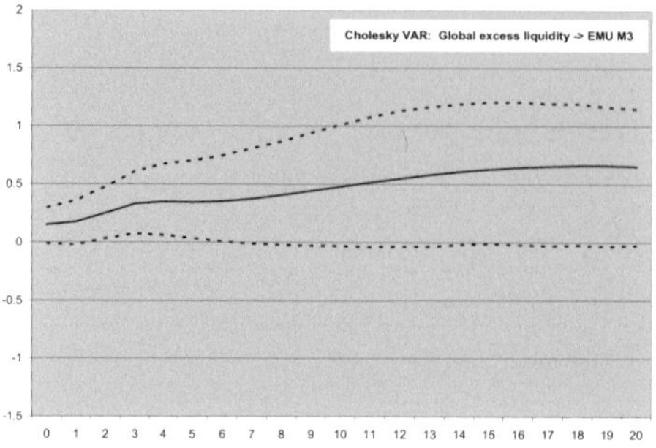
Cholesky VAR: Global excess liquidity -> EMU M3
2
1.5
1
0.5
0
-0.5
-1
-1.5
0 1 2 3 4 5 6 7 8 9 10 11 12 13 14 15 16 17 18 19 20

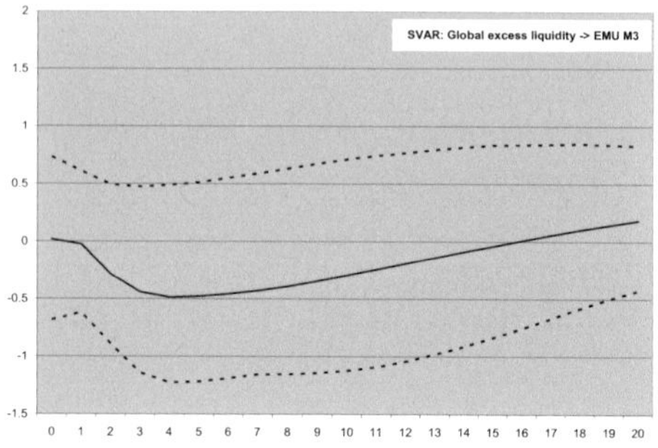
SVAR: Global excess liquidity -> EMU M3
2
1.5
1
0.5
0
-0.5
-1
-1.5
0 1 2 3 4 5 6 7 8 9 10 11 12 13 14 15 16 17 18 19 20

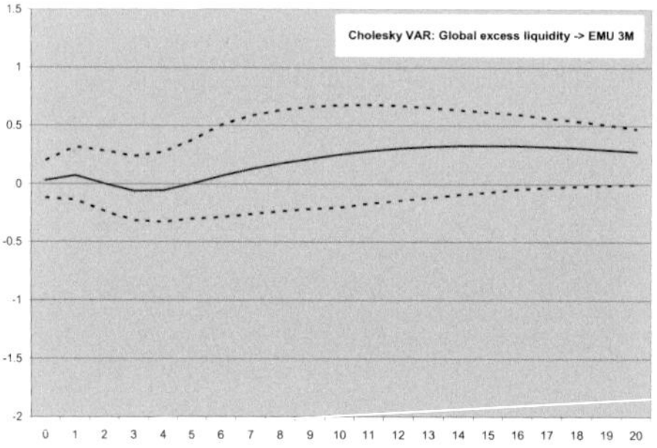
Cholesky VAR: Global excess liquidity -> EMU 3M
1.5
1
0.5
0
-0.5
-1
-1.5
-2
0 1 2 3 4 5 6 7 8 9 10 11 12 13 14 15 16 17 18 19 20

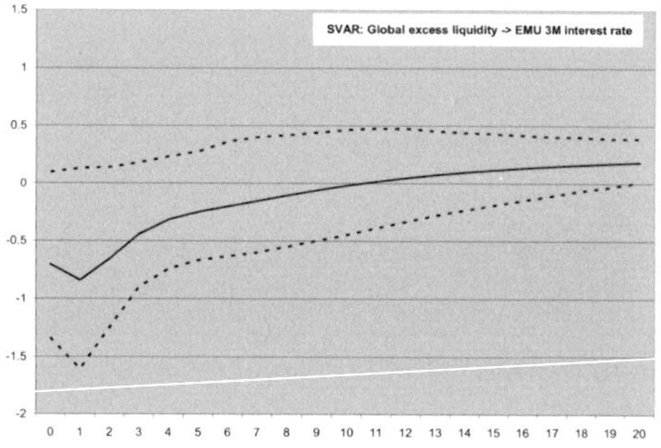
SVAR: Global excess liquidity -> EMU 3M interest rate
1.5
1
0.5
0
-0.5
-1
-1.5
-2
0 1 2 3 4 5 6 7 8 9 10 11 12 13 14 15 16 17 18 19 20

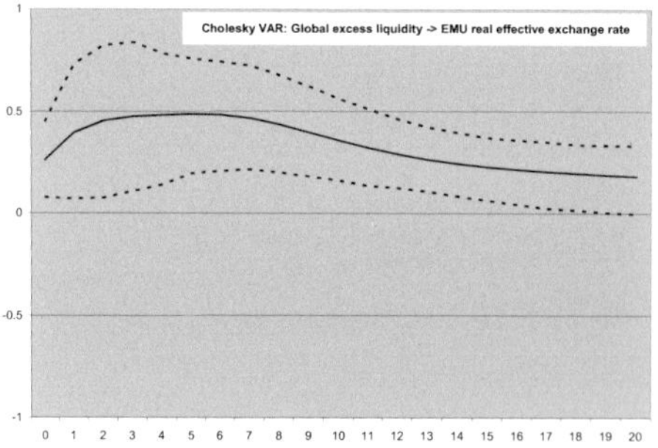
Cholesky VAR: Global excess liquidity -> EMU real effective exchange rate
1
0.5
0
-0.5
-1
0 1 2 3 4 5 6 7 8 9 10 11 12 13 14 15 16 17 18 19 20

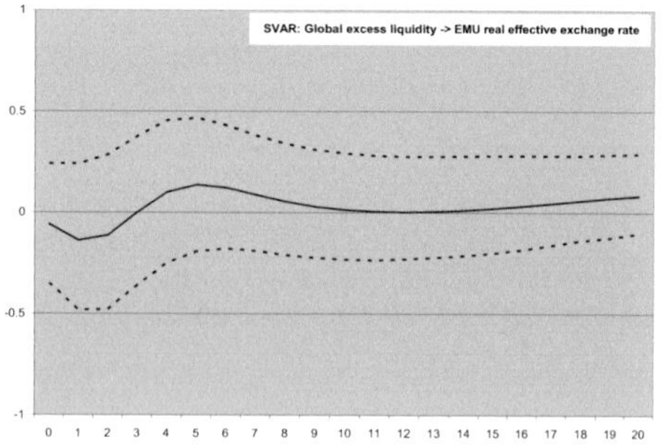
SVAR: Global excess liquidity -> EMU real effective exchange rate
1
0.5
0
-0.5
-1
0 1 2 3 4 5 6 7 8 9 10 11 12 13 14 15 16 17 18 19 20

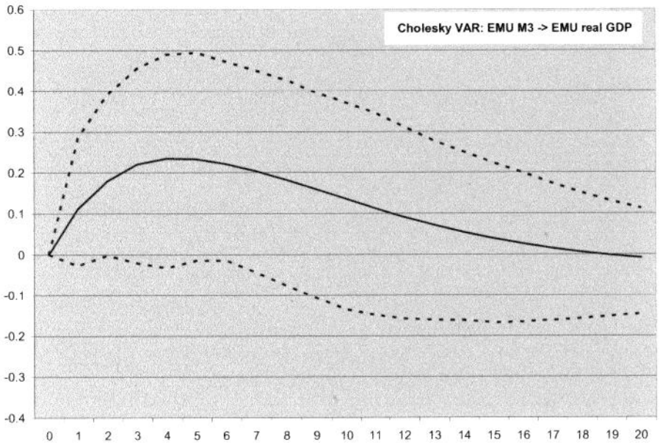
Cholesky VAR: EMU M3 -> EMU real GDP

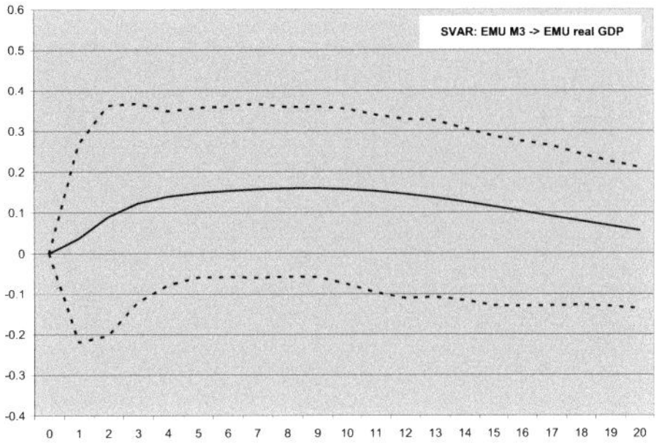
SVAR: EMU M3 -> EMU real GDP

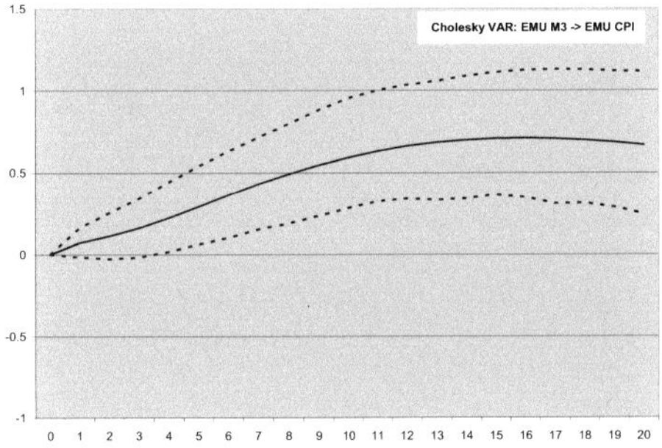
Cholesky VAR: EMU M3 -> EMU CPI

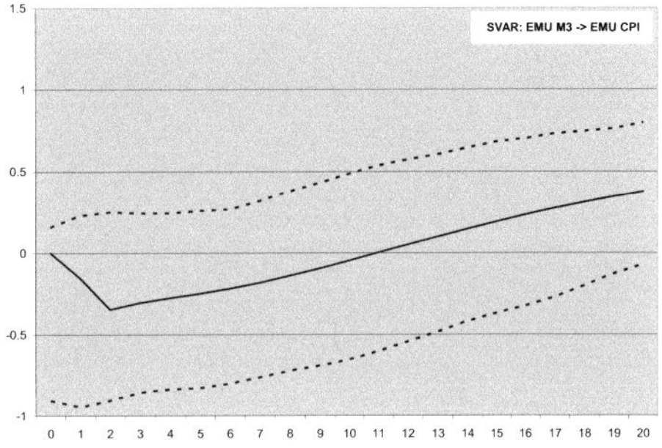
SVAR: EMU M3 -> EMU CPI

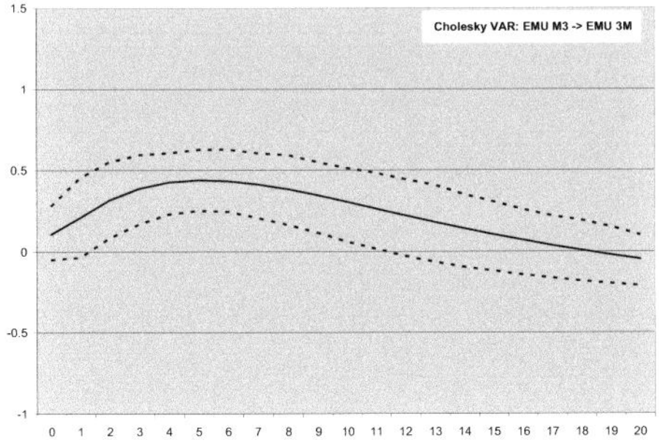
Cholesky VAR: EMU M3 -> EMU 3M

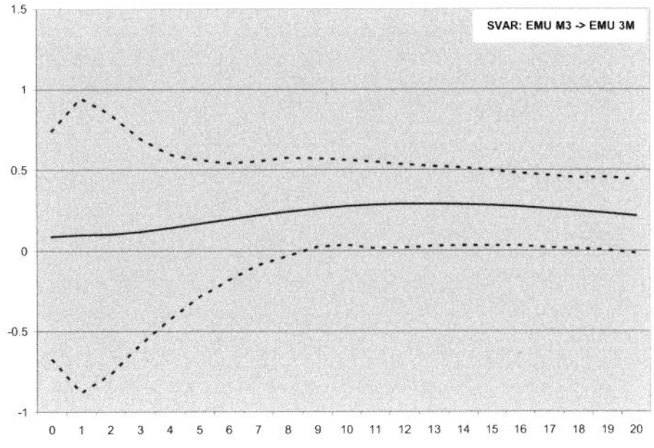
SVAR: EMU M3 -> EMU 3M

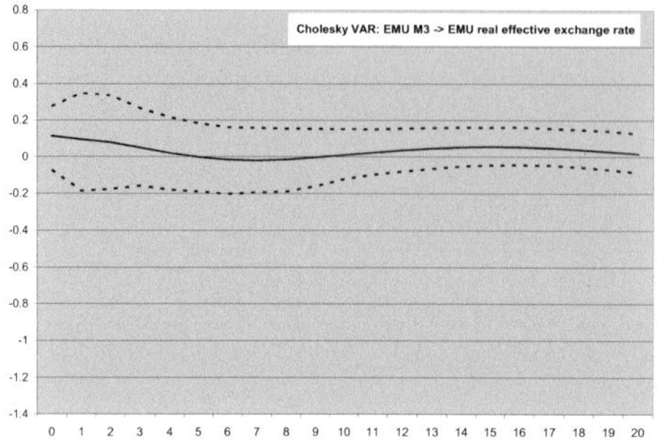
Cholesky VAR: EMU M3 -> EMU real effective exchange rate

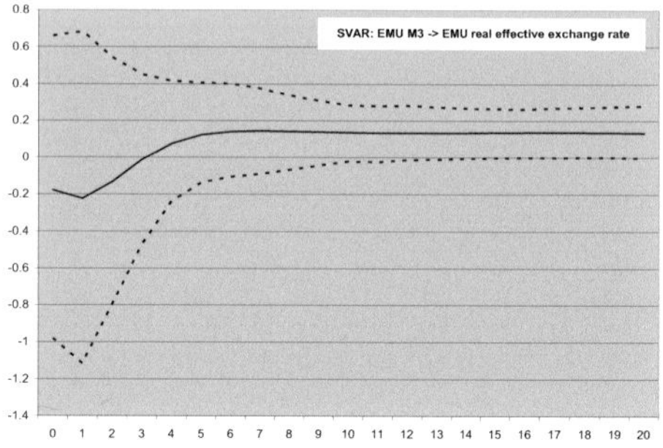
SVAR: EMU M3 -> EMU real effective exchange rate

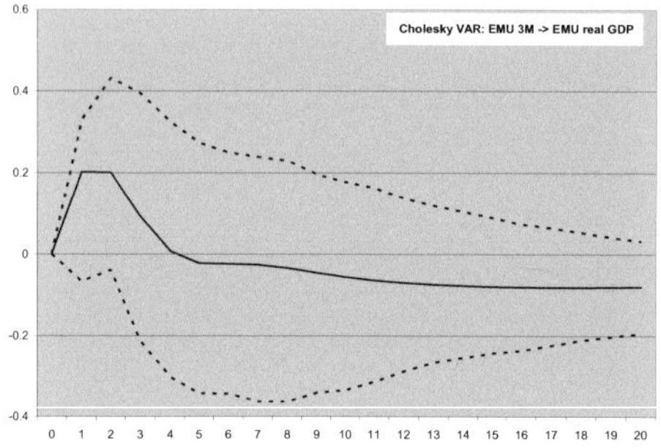
Cholesky VAR: EMU 3M -> EMU real GDP

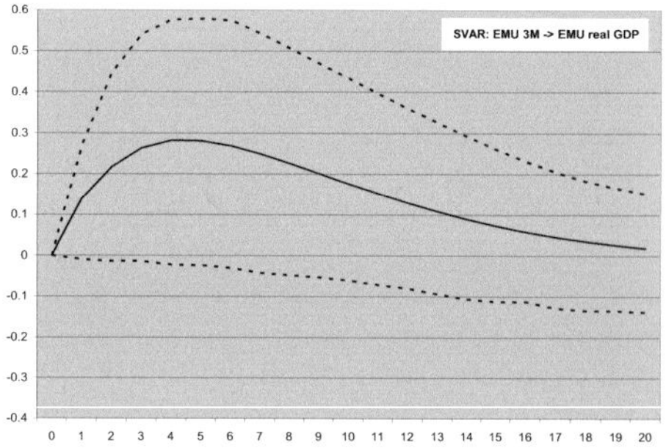
SVAR: EMU 3M -> EMU real GDP

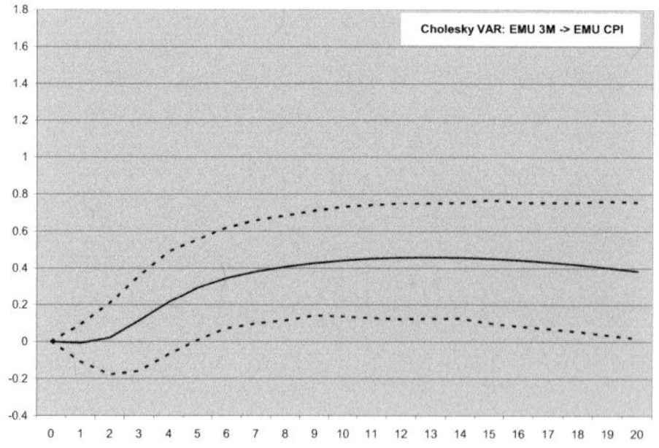
Cholesky VAR: EMU 3M -> EMU CPI

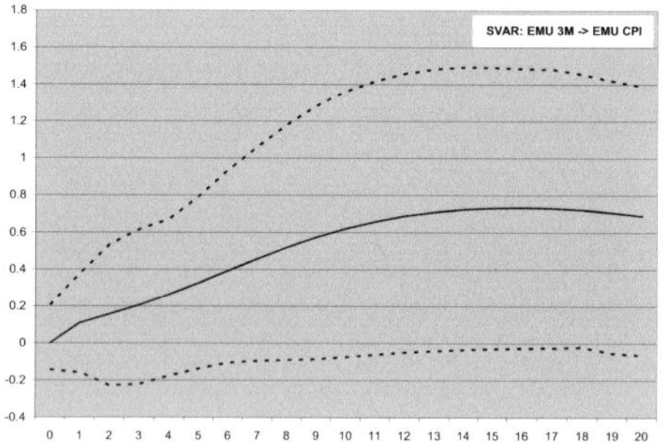
SVAR: EMU 3M -> EMU CPI

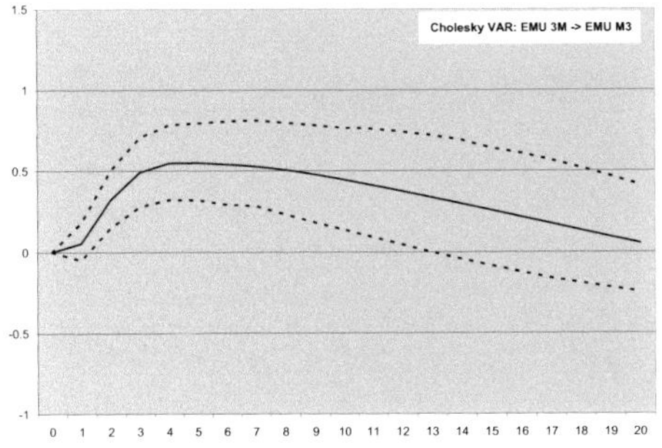
Cholesky VAR: EMU 3M -> EMU M3

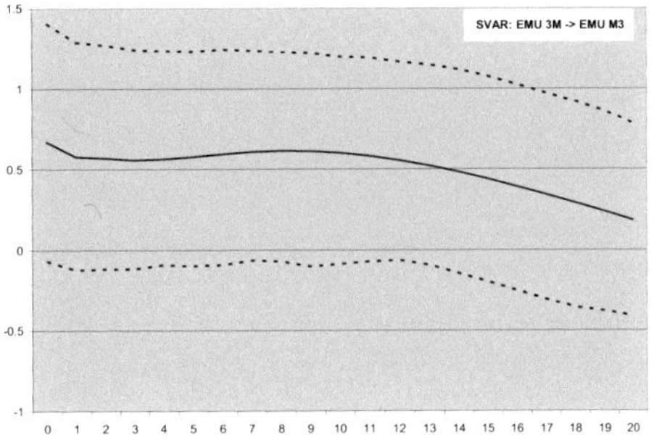
SVAR: EMU 3M -> EMU M3

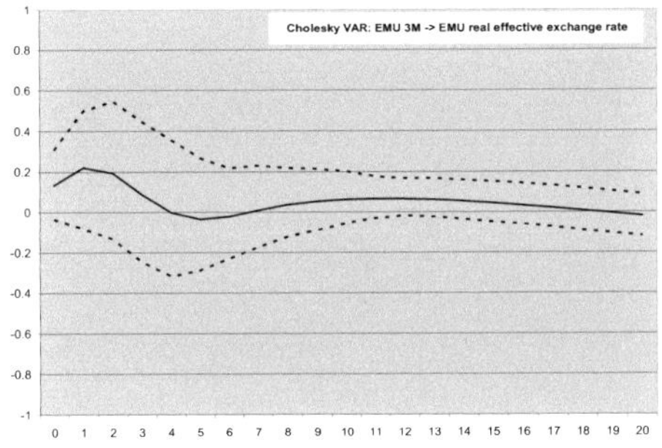
Cholesky VAR: EMU 3M -> EMU real effective exchange rate

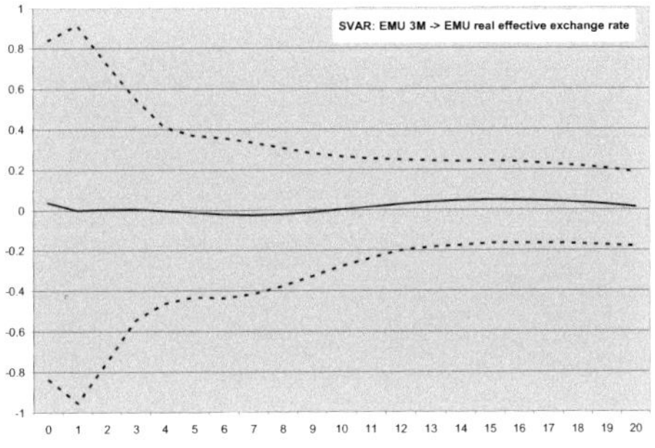
SVAR: EMU 3M -> EMU real effective exchange rate

A.11 ROBUSTNESS CHECK: IMPULSE RESPONSES FOR EMU CHOLESKY VAR

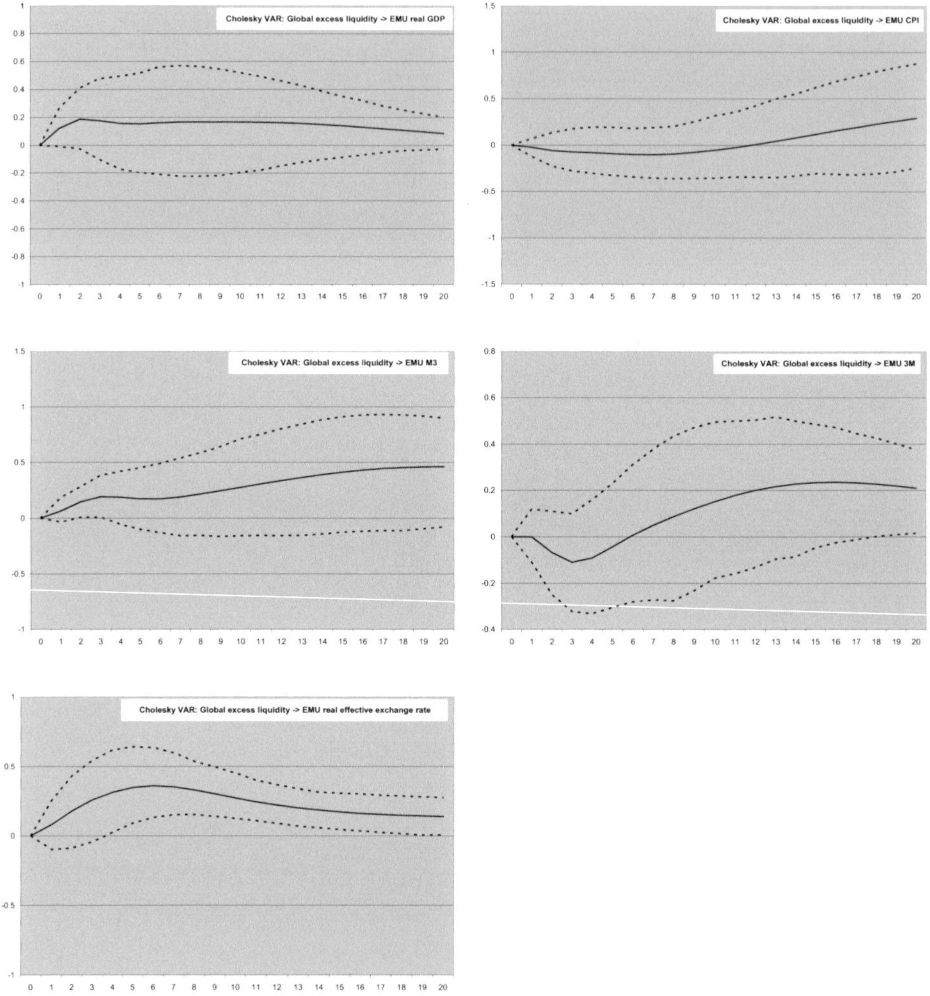

A.12 ROBUSTNESS CHECK: IMPULSE RESPONSES FOR EMU SVAR

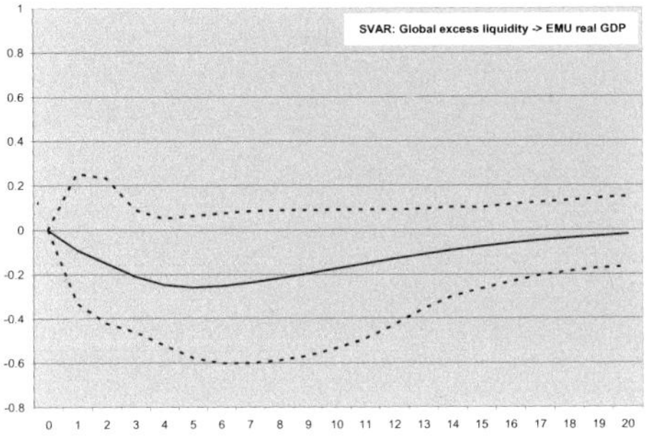

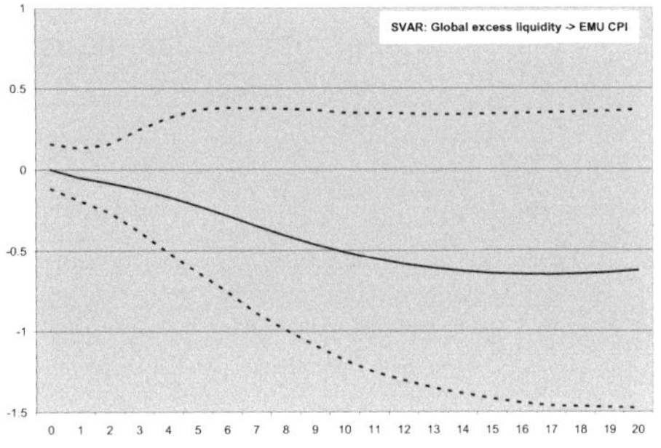

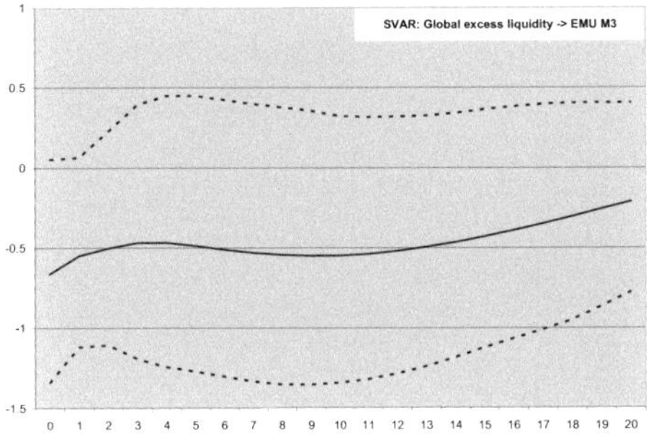

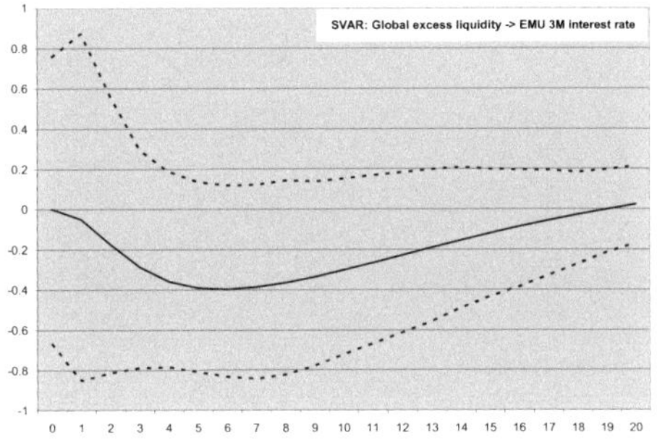

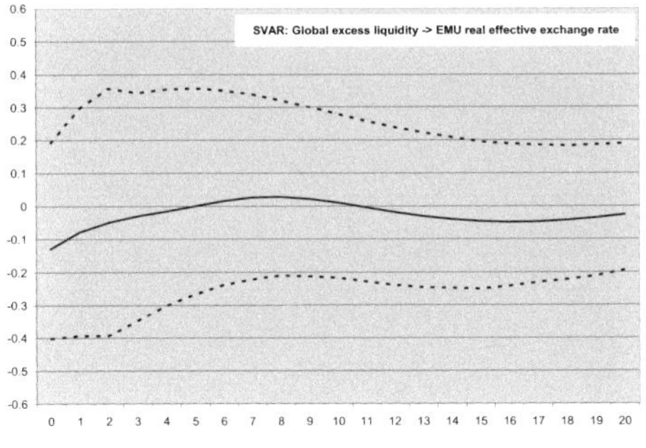

A.13 UNIT ROOT TESTS FOR REDUCED-FORM RESIDUALS IN THE SFAVAR MODEL (GLOBAL LEVEL)

Residuals	ADF	PP	KPSS
YR	-9.73***	-9.88***	0.05
PI	-10.50***	-10.52***	0.04
CP	-9.59***	-9.60***	0.03
HP	-10.09***	-10.26***	0.03
M	-10.02***	-10.03***	0.05
SR	-9.13***	-9.14***	0.03
SP	-9.54***	-9.54***	0.04

Note 1: ADF (Augmented Dickey-Fuller), PP (Phillips-Perron), KPSS (Kwiatkowski-Phillips-Schmidt-Shin)

Note 2: *** Indicates significance at 1% level, ** at 5% level, * at 10% level

Note 3: Null hypothesis of ADF and PP test assumes non-stationarity; null hypothesis of KPSS test assumes stationarity

A.14 MULTIVARIATE LM TEST FOR SERIAL CORRELATION, WHITE TEST FOR HETEROSKEDASTICITY AND JARQUE-BERA TEST IN FAVAR MODEL

LM test for autocorrelation		
Lags	LM-Stat	Prob
1	57.39	0.19
2	51.81	0.36
3	51.02	0.39
4	49.46	0.45
5	62.12	0.10
6	48.06	0.51
7	47.65	0.53
8	70.03	0.03
9	53.56	0.30
10	44.89	0.64
11	44.41	0.66
12	38.64	0.86
White test for heteroskedasticity		
	Chi-sq	Prob
	879.34	0.17
Jarque-Bera test		
Residuals	Jarque-Bera	Prob
CP	17.20	0.00
GEL_exEMU	3.20	0.20
YR	3.05	0.22
PI	0.44	0.80
M3	7.06	0.03
SR	3.71	0.16
ER	11.34	0.00
Joint	45.99	0.00

A.15 IMPULSE RESPONSES FOR BASELINE SFAVAR (GLOBAL LEVEL)

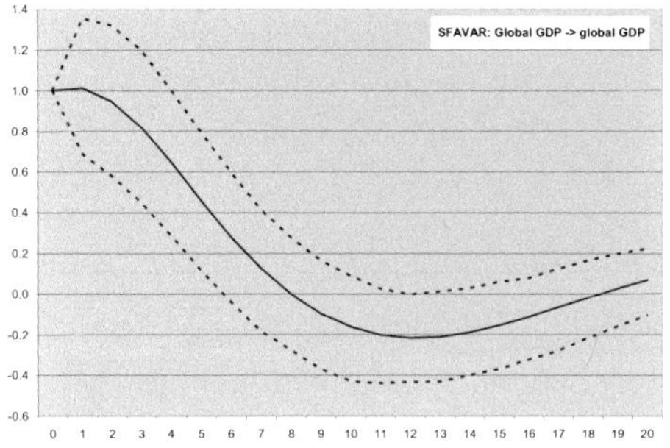

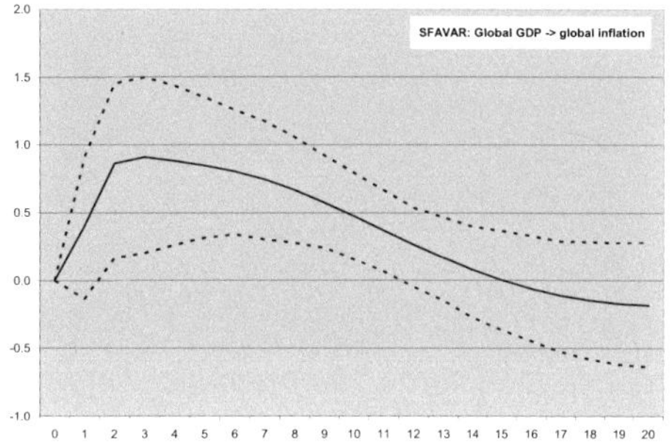

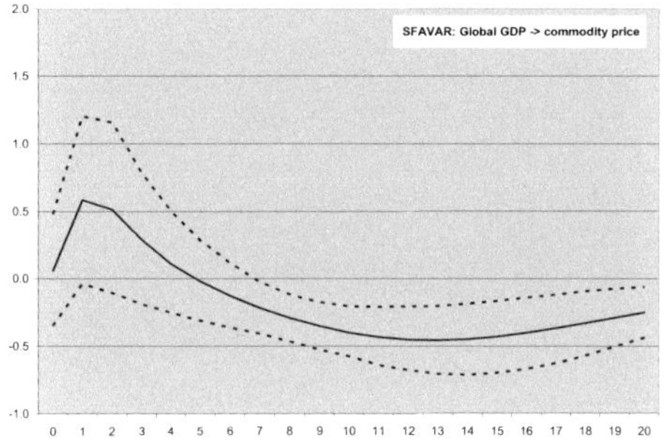

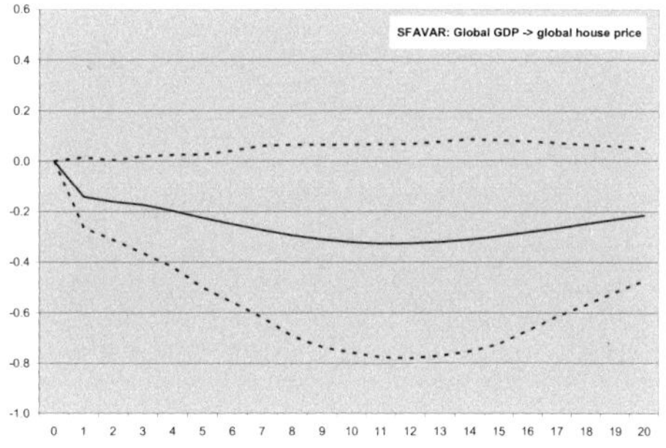

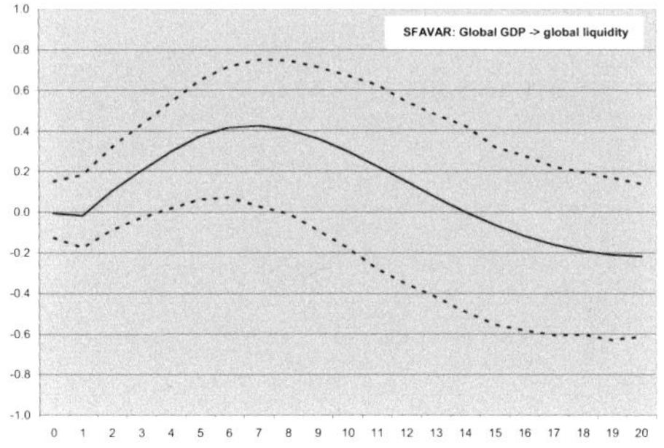

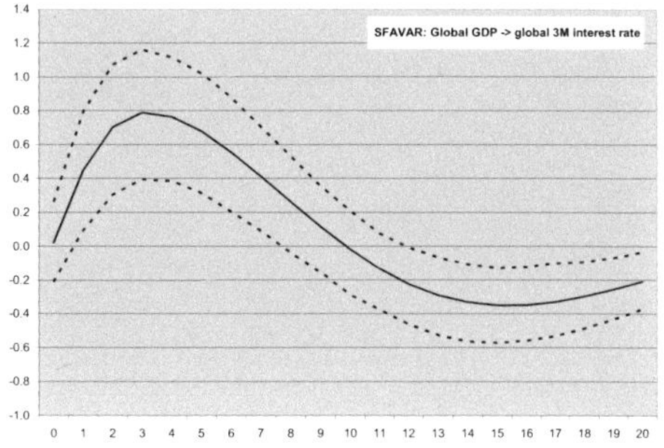

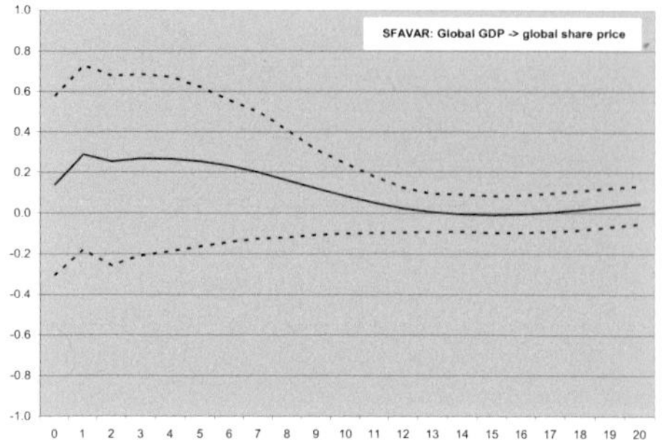
SFAVAR: Global GDP -> global share price

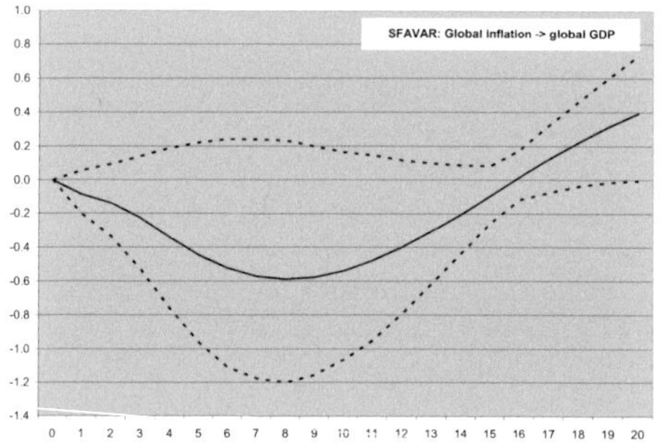
SFAVAR: Global inflation -> global GDP

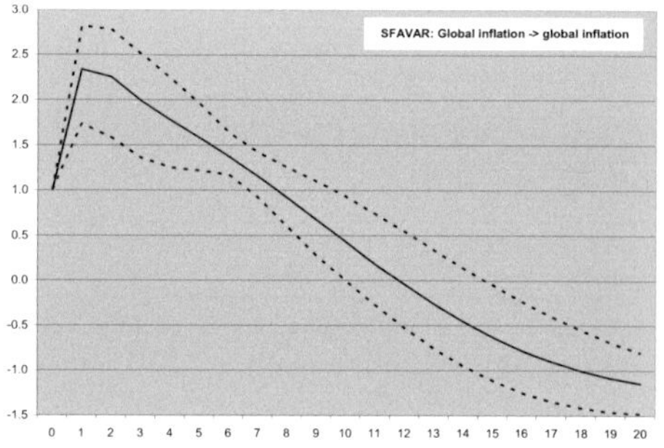
SFAVAR: Global inflation -> global inflation

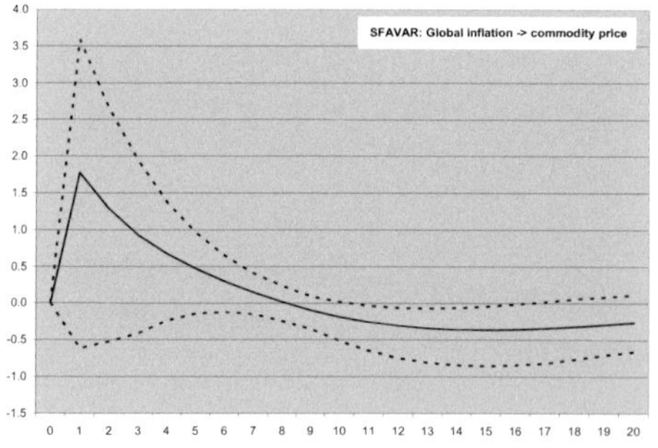
SFAVAR: Global inflation -> commodity price

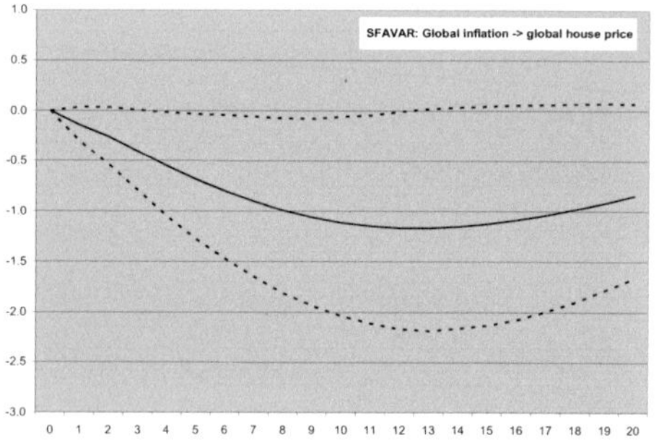
SFAVAR: Global inflation -> global house price

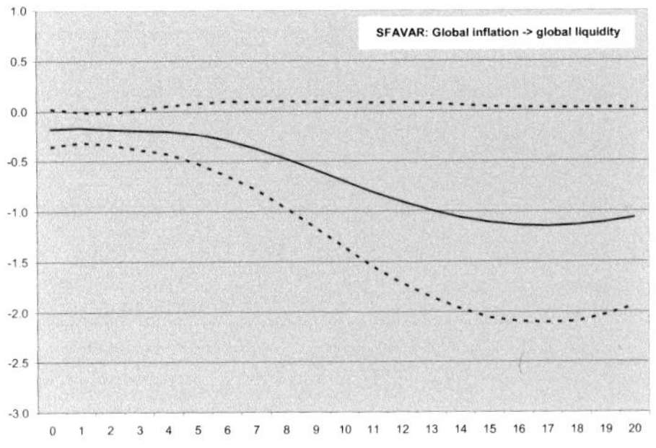
SFAVAR: Global inflation -> global liquidity

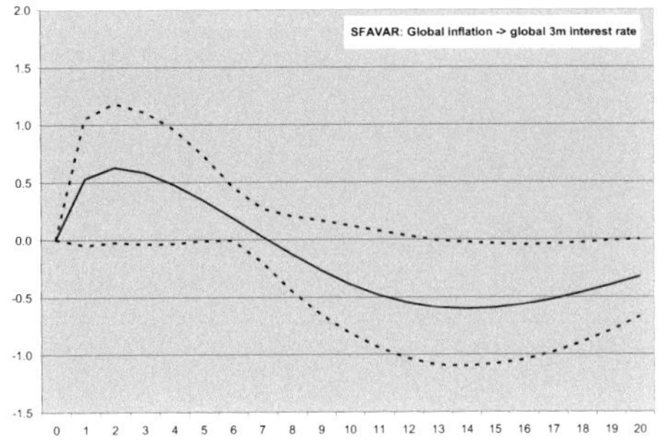
SFAVAR: Global inflation -> global 3m interest rate

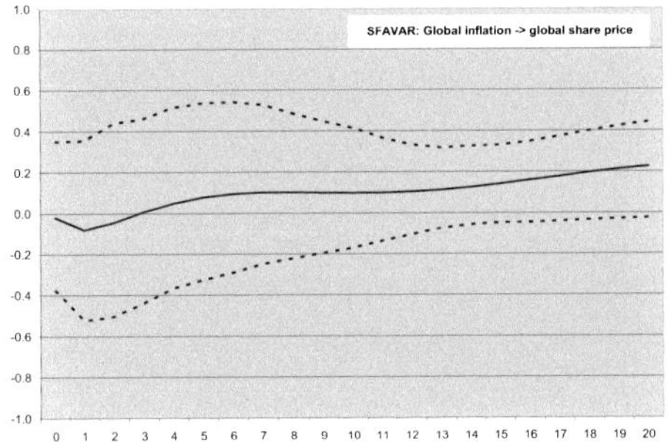
SFAVAR: Global inflation -> global share price

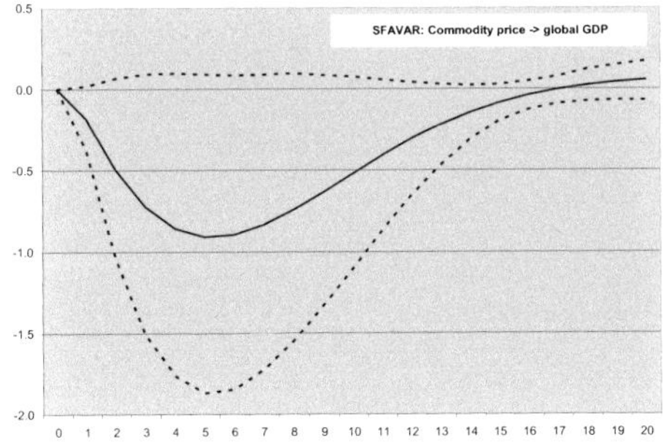
SFAVAR: Commodity price -> global GDP

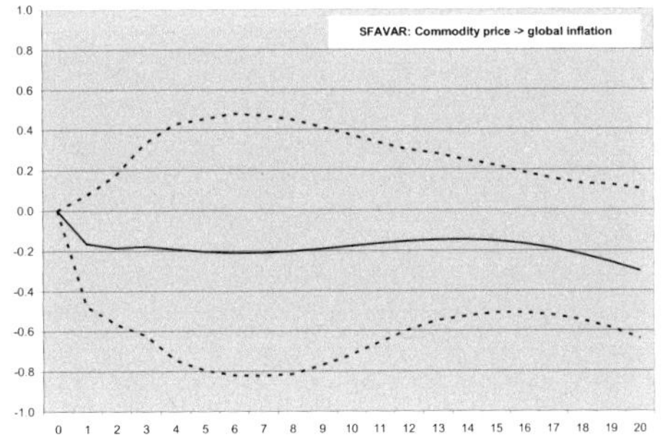
SFAVAR: Commodity price -> global inflation

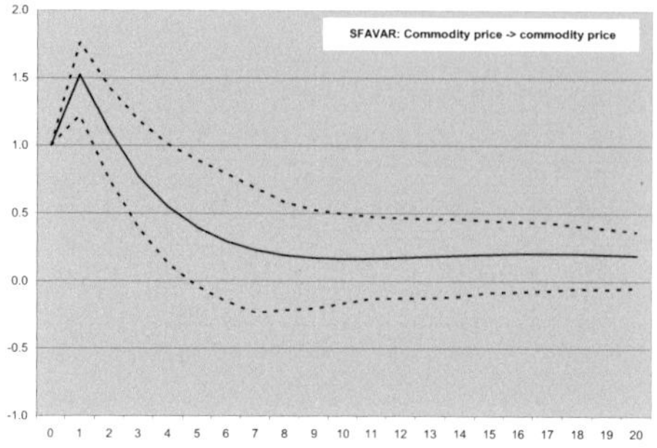
SFAVAR: Commodity price -> commodity price

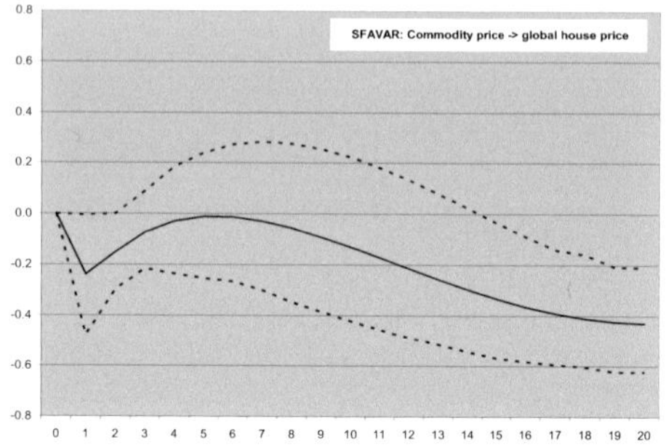
SFAVAR: Commodity price -> global house price

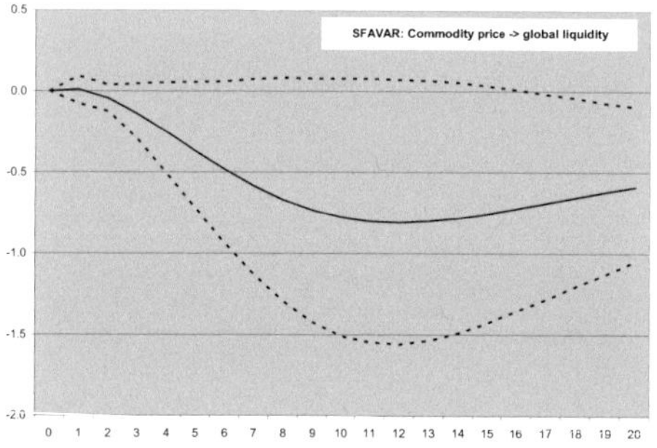
SFAVAR: Commodity price -> global liquidity

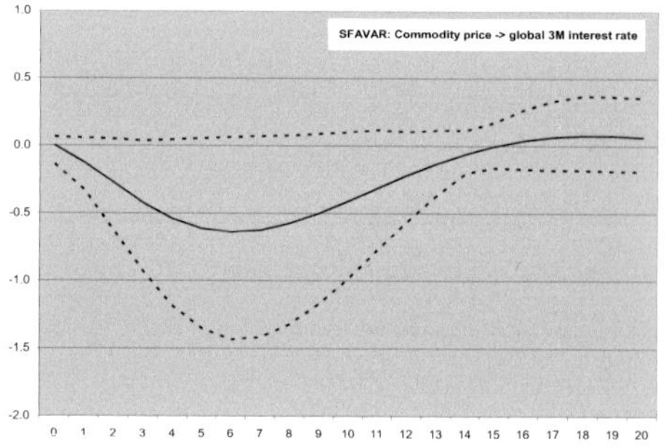
SFAVAR: Commodity price -> global 3M interest rate

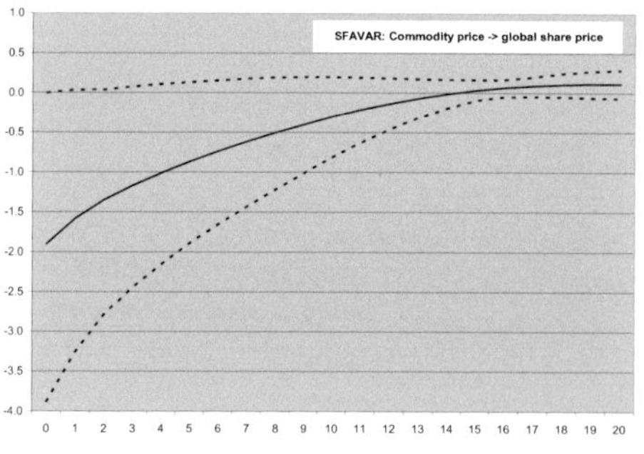
SFAVAR: Commodity price -> global share price

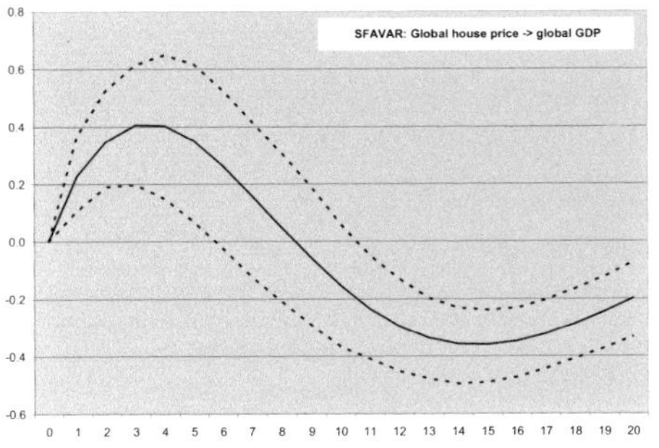
SFAVAR: Global house price -> global GDP

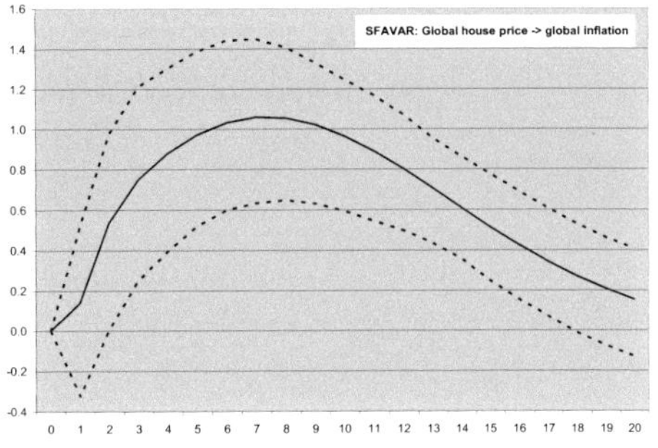
SFAVAR: Global house price -> global inflation

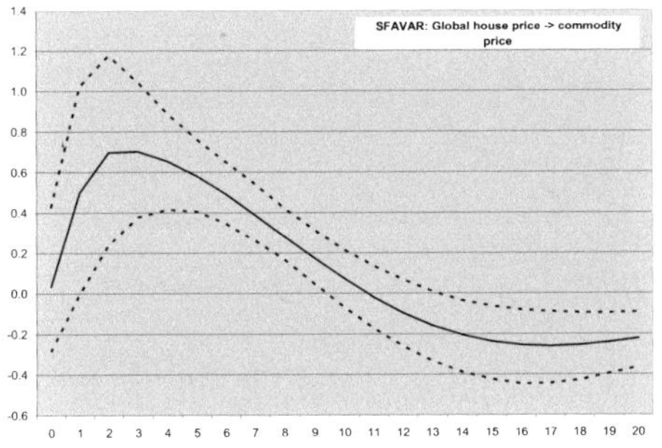
SFAVAR: Global house price -> commodity price

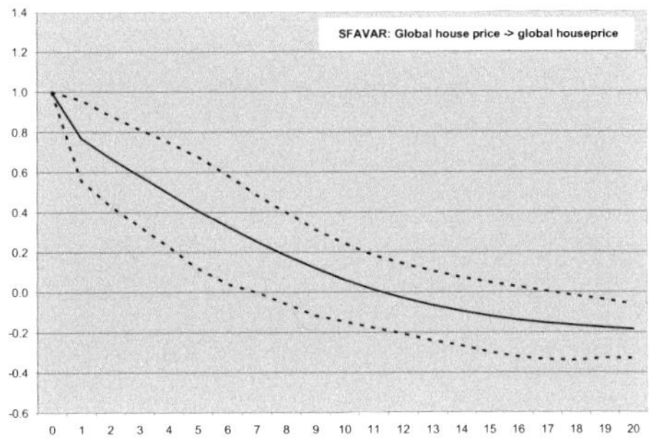
SFAVAR: Global house price -> global houseprice

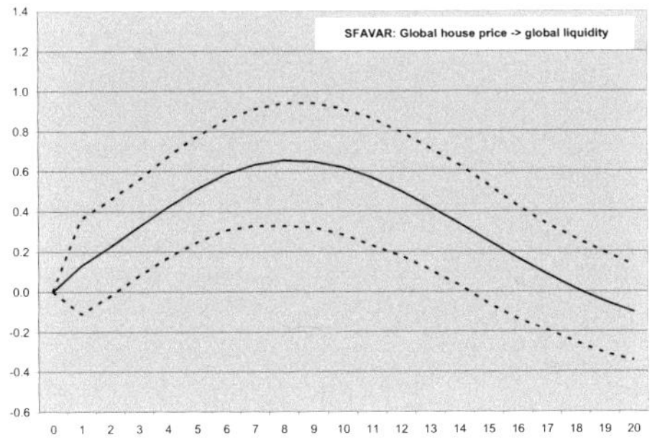
SFAVAR: Global house price -> global liquidity

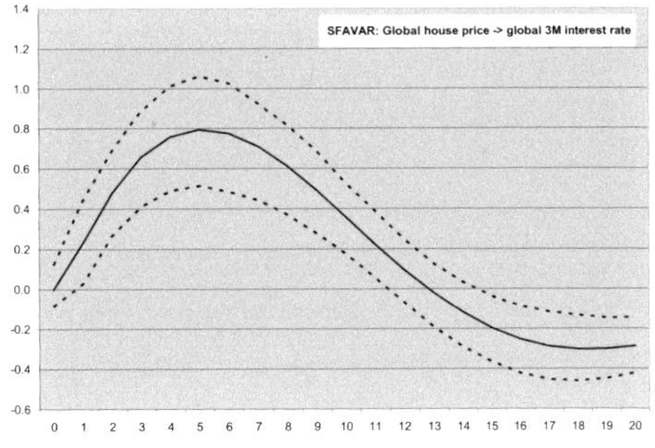
SFAVAR: Global house price -> global 3M interest rate

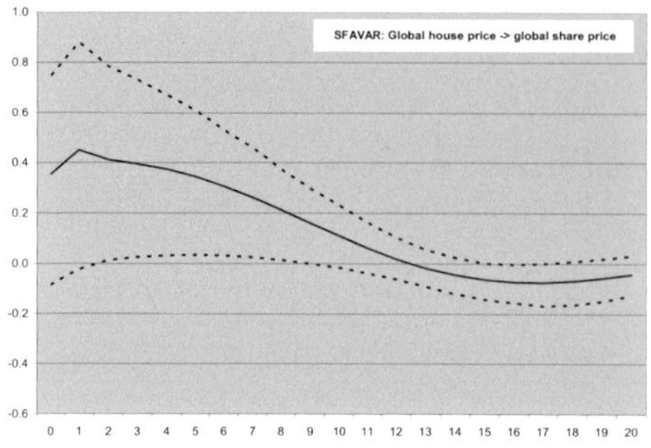
SFAVAR: Global house price -> global share price
1.0
0.8
0.6
0.4
0.2
0.0
-0.2
-0.4
-0.6
0 1 2 3 4 5 6 7 8 9 10 11 12 13 14 15 16 17 18 19 20

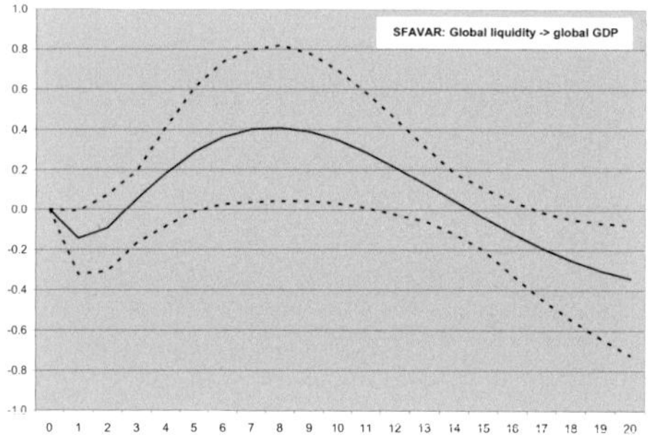
SFAVAR: Global liquidity -> global GDP
1.0
0.8
0.6
0.4
0.2
0.0
-0.2
-0.4
-0.6
-0.8
-1.0
0 1 2 3 4 5 6 7 8 9 10 11 12 13 14 15 16 17 18 19 20

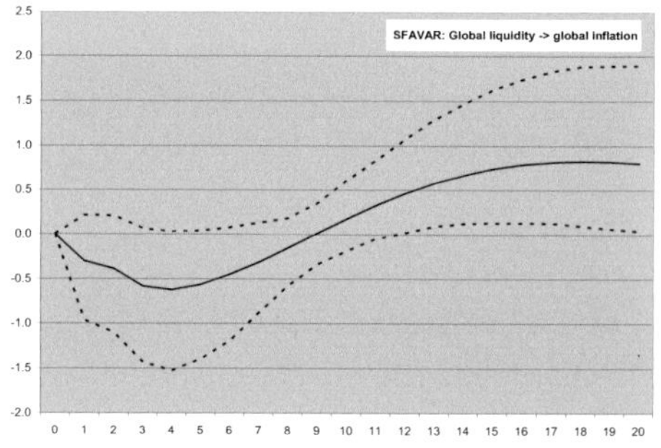
SFAVAR: Global liquidity -> global inflation
2.5
2.0
1.5
1.0
0.5
0.0
-0.5
-1.0
-1.5
-2.0
0 1 2 3 4 5 6 7 8 9 10 11 12 13 14 15 16 17 18 19 20

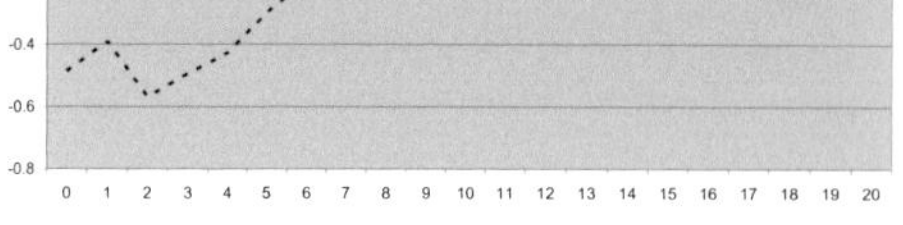
SFAVAR: Global liquidity -> commodity price
1.0
0.8
0.6
0.4
0.2
0.0
-0.2
-0.4
-0.6
-0.8
0 1 2 3 4 5 6 7 8 9 10 11 12 13 14 15 16 17 18 19 20

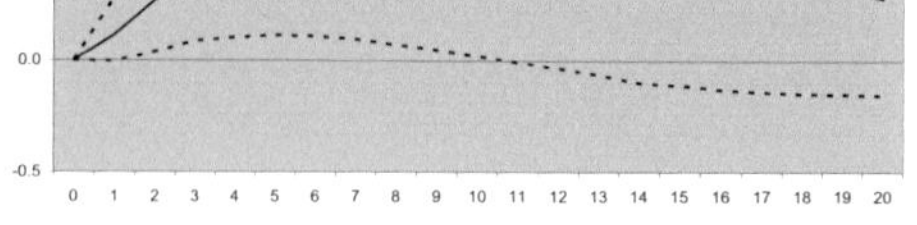
SFAVAR: Global liquidity -> global house price
2.0
1.5
1.0
0.5
0.0
-0.5
0 1 2 3 4 5 6 7 8 9 10 11 12 13 14 15 16 17 18 19 20

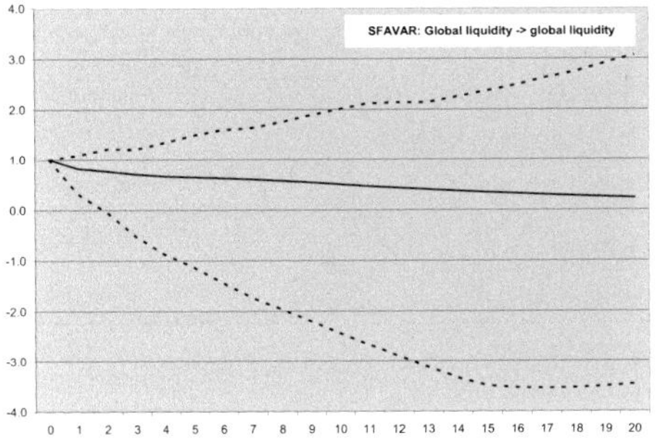
SFAVAR: Global liquidity -> global liquidity

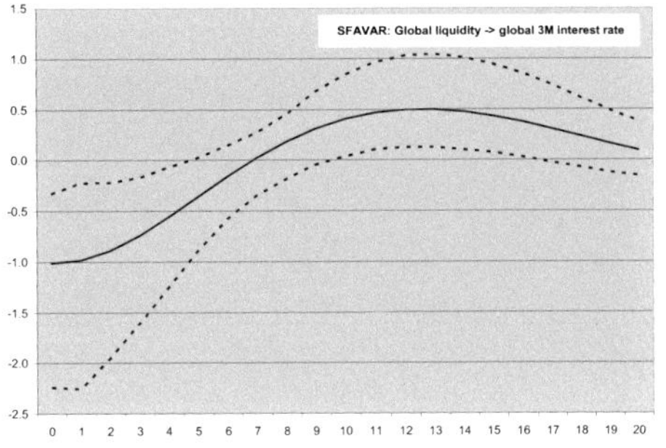
SFAVAR: Global liquidity -> global 3M interest rate

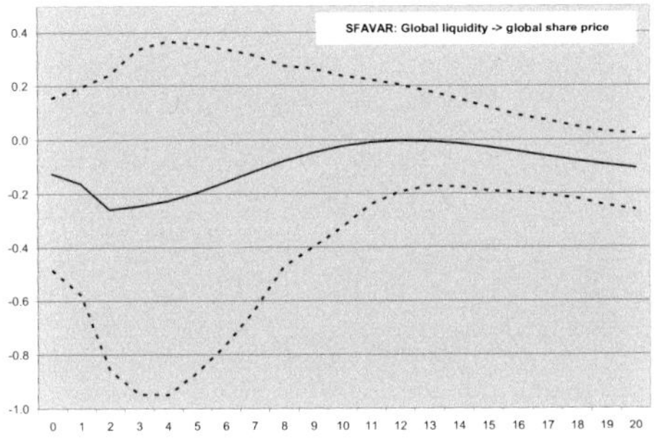
SFAVAR: Global liquidity -> global share price

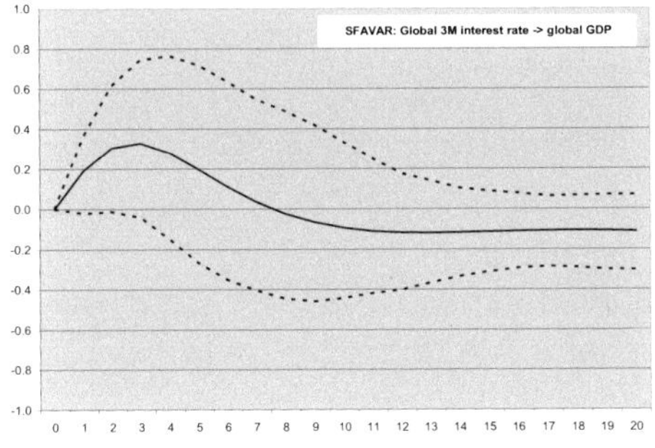
SFAVAR: Global 3M interest rate -> global GDP

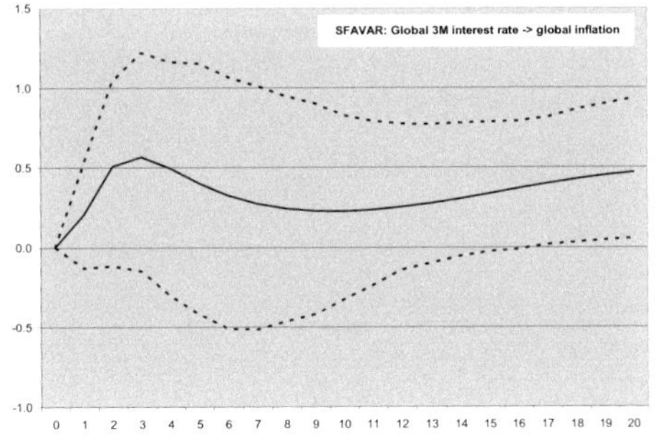
SFAVAR: Global 3M interest rate -> global inflation

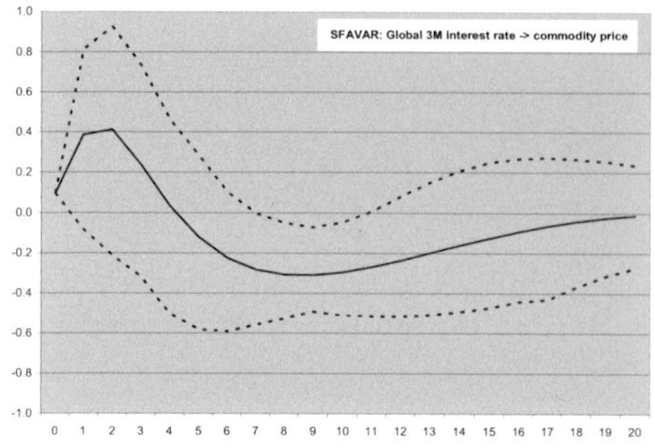
SFAVAR: Global 3M interest rate -> commodity price

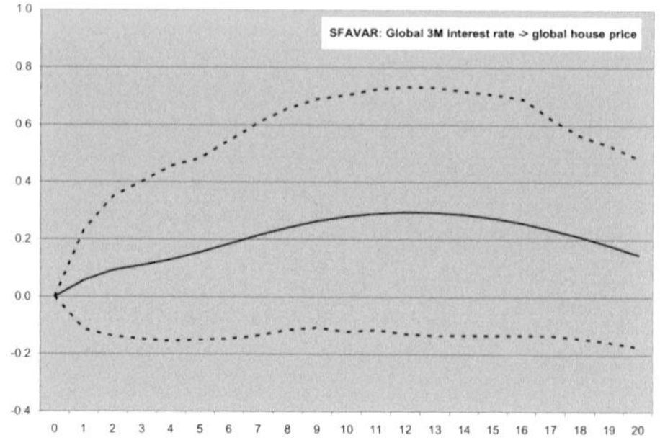
SFAVAR: Global 3M interest rate -> global house price

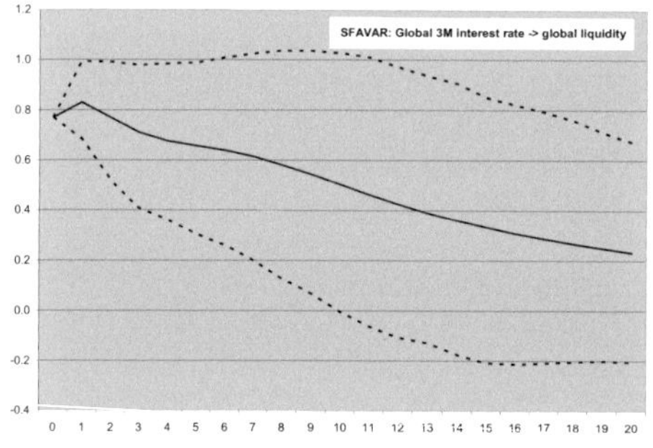
SFAVAR: Global 3M interest rate -> global liquidity

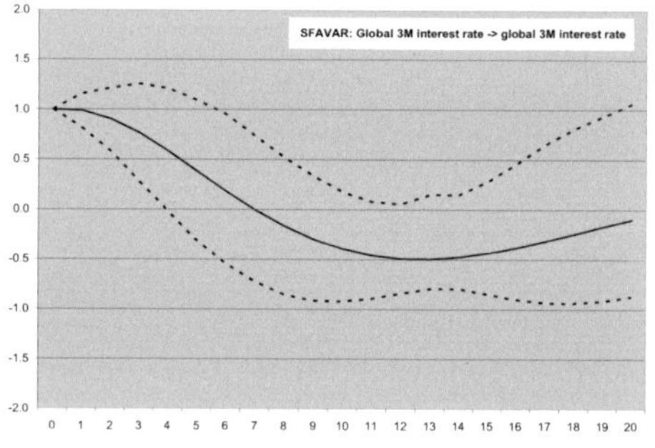
SFAVAR: Global 3M interest rate -> global 3M interest rate

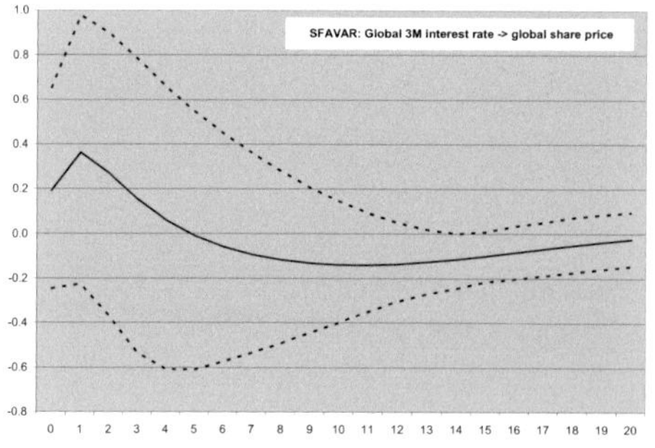
SFAVAR: Global 3M interest rate -> global share price

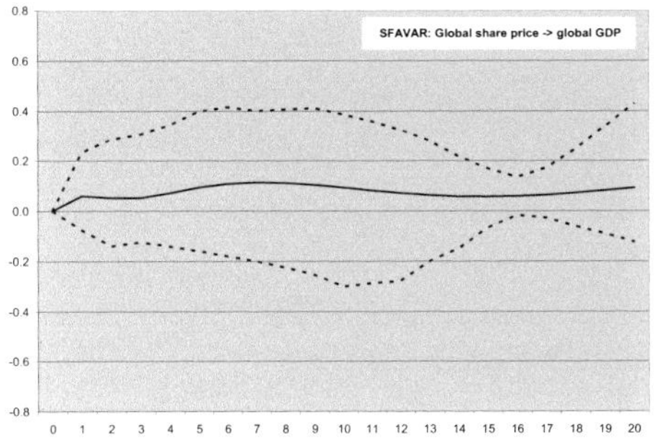
SFAVAR: Global share price -> global GDP
0.8
0.6
0.4
0.2
0.0
-0.2
-0.4
-0.6
-0.8
0 1 2 3 4 5 6 7 8 9 10 11 12 13 14 15 16 17 18 19 20

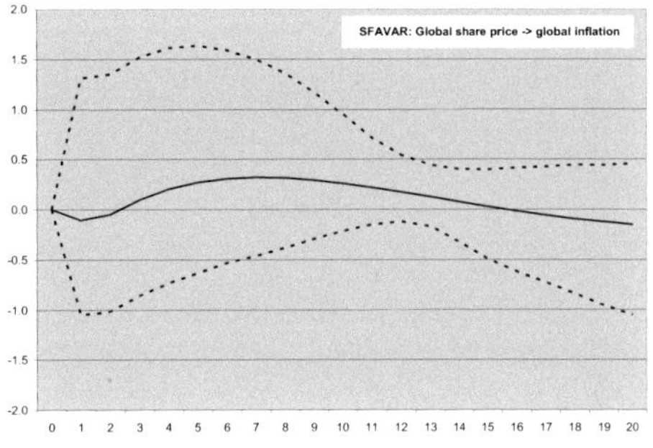
SFAVAR: Global share price -> global inflation
2.0
1.5
1.0
0.5
0.0
-0.5
-1.0
-1.5
-2.0
0 1 2 3 4 5 6 7 8 9 10 11 12 13 14 15 16 17 18 19 20

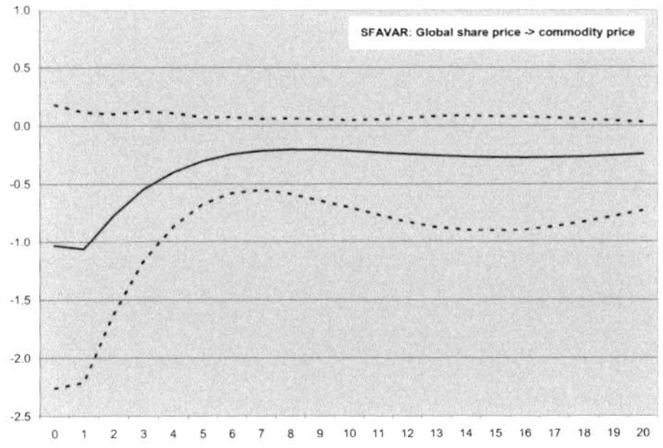
SFAVAR: Global share price -> commodity price
1.0
0.5
0.0
-0.5
-1.0
-1.5
-2.0
-2.5
0 1 2 3 4 5 6 7 8 9 10 11 12 13 14 15 16 17 18 19 20

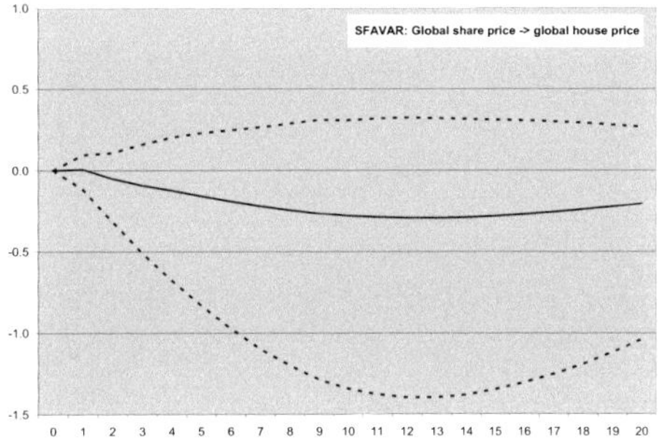
SFAVAR: Global share price -> global house price
1.0
0.5
0.0
-0.5
-1.0
-1.5
0 1 2 3 4 5 6 7 8 9 10 11 12 13 14 15 16 17 18 19 20

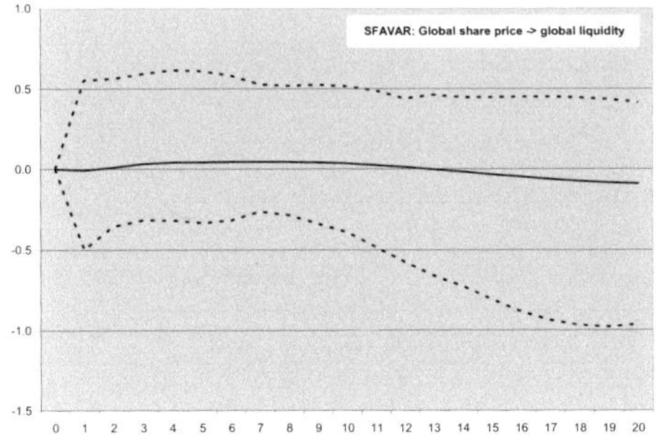
SFAVAR: Global share price -> global liquidity
1.0
0.5
0.0
-0.5
-1.0
-1.5
0 1 2 3 4 5 6 7 8 9 10 11 12 13 14 15 16 17 18 19 20

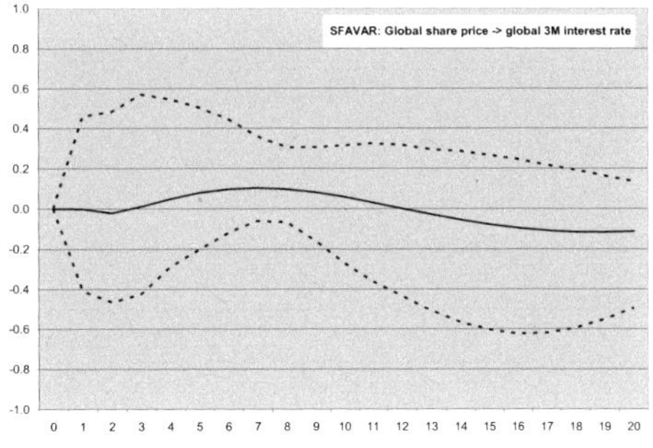
SFAVAR: Global share price -> global 3M interest rate
1.0
0.8
0.6
0.4
0.2
0.0
-0.2
-0.4
-0.6
-0.8
-1.0
0 1 2 3 4 5 6 7 8 9 10 11 12 13 14 15 16 17 18 19 20

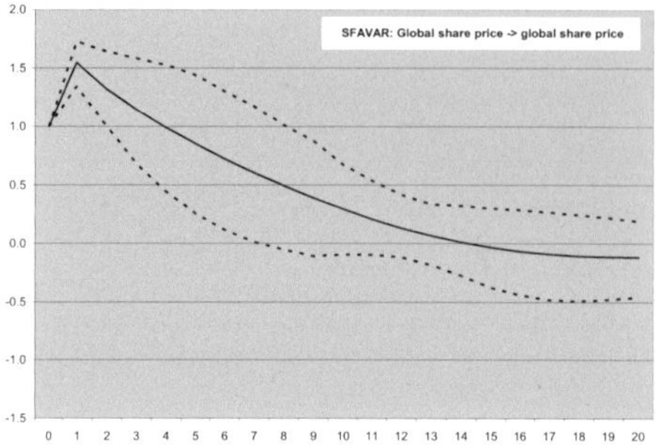

A.16 MULTIVARIATE LM TEST FOR SERIAL CORRELATION, WHITE TEST FOR HETEROSKEDASTICITY, LM ARCH TEST AND JARQUE-BERA TEST IN FAVAR MODEL (NATIONAL LEVEL)

US model			**EMU model**			**Japan model**		
LM test for autocorrelation			**LM test for autocorrelation**			**LM test for autocorrelation**		
Lags	LM-Stat	Prob	Lags	LM-Stat	Prob	Lags	LM-Stat	Prob
1	59.97	0.14	1	38.76	0.85	1	39.91	0.82
2	59.02	0.15	2	55.64	0.24	2	64.44	0.07
3	64.59	0.07	3	53.54	0.30	3	60.25	0.13
4	41.83	0.76	4	67.66	0.04	4	58.69	0.16
5	60.89	0.12	5	48.32	0.50	5	53.69	0.30
6	68.37	0.04	6	61.82	0.10	6	59.93	0.14
7	42.31	0.74	7	34.94	0.94	7	45.64	0.61
8	52.77	0.33	8	41.83	0.76	8	49.27	0.46
9	61.63	0.11	9	55.94	0.23	9	60.89	0.12
10	47.61	0.53	10	68.61	0.03	10	60.69	0.12
11	64.14	0.07	11	53.69	0.30	11	62.98	0.09
12	41.22	0.78	12	44.77	0.65	12	65.36	0.06
White test for heteroskedasticity			**White test for heteroskedasticity**			**White test for heteroskedasticity**		
	Chi-sq	Prob		Chi-sq	Prob		Chi-sq	Prob
	1702.58	0.09		1697.49	0.10		1713.83	0.06
LM ARCH test (4th order)			**LM ARCH test (4th order)**			**LM ARCH test (4th order)**		
Residuals	F-Stat	Prob	Residuals	F-Stat	Prob	Residuals	F-Stat	Prob
YR	3.08	0.02	YR	5.25	0.00	YR	0.92	0.00
PI	5.11	0.00	PI	8.40	0.00	PI	6.37	0.00
HP	5.55	0.00	HP	11.99	0.00	HP	34.44	0.00
M	3.86	0.00	M	5.50	0.00	M	2.19	0.08
SR	5.90	0.00	SR	6.64	0.00	SR	4.08	0.00
ER	0.80	0.53	ER	0.26	0.90	ER	0.77	0.55
SP	0.04	0.99	SP	0.11	0.98	SP	3.92	0.01
Jarque-Bera test			**Jarque-Bera test**			**Jarque-Bera test**		
Residuals	Jarque-Bera	Prob	Residuals	Jarque-Bera	Prob	Residuals	Jarque-Bera	Prob
YR	9.88	0.01	YR	22.27	0.00	YR	11.74	0.00
PI	10.54	0.01	PI	8.84	0.01	PI	12.72	0.00
HP	7.55	0.02	HP	1.68	0.43	HP	5.29	0.07
M	6.08	0.05	M	6.46	0.04	M	11.40	0.00
SR	8.07	0.02	SR	11.67	0.00	SR	10.60	0.01
ER	11.97	0.00	ER	7.00	0.03	ER	10.78	0.00
SP	10.16	0.01	SP	3.01	0.22	SP	6.65	0.04
Joint	64.26	0.00	Joint	60.93	0.00	Joint	69.18	0.00

UK model			Canada model		
LM test for autocorrelation			**LM test for autocorrelation**		
Lags	LM-Stat	Prob	Lags	LM-Stat	Prob
1	41.83	0.76	1	49.27	0.46
2	88.04	0.00	2	58.69	0.16
3	43.61	0.69	3	46.49	0.58
4	58.62	0.16	4	59.59	0.14
5	40.79	0.79	5	39.91	0.82
6	48.32	0.50	6	65.22	0.06
7	42.74	0.72	7	60.92	0.12
8	53.05	0.32	8	38.76	0.85
9	39.91	0.82	9	46.31	0.58
10	53.66	0.30	10	48.06	0.51
11	59.02	0.15	11	49.27	0.46
12	41.14	0.78	12	26.78	1.00
White test for heteroskedasticity			**White test for heteroskedasticity**		
	Chi-sq	Prob		Chi-sq	Prob
	1737.45	0.03		1649.04	0.33
LM ARCH test (4th order)			**LM ARCH test (4th order)**		
Residuals	F-Stat	Prob	Residuals	F-Stat	Prob
YR	1.29	0.28	YR	2.93	0.03
PI	6.29	0.00	PI	8.00	0.00
HP	5.41	0.00	HP	5.15	0.00
M	7.07	0.00	M	7.34	0.00
SR	2.70	0.04	SR	1.05	0.39
ER	2.74	0.03	ER	3.99	0.00
SP	0.22	0.93	SP	0.05	0.99
Jarque-Bera test			**Jarque-Bera test**		
Residuals	Jarque-Bera	Prob	Residuals	Jarque-Bera	Prob
YR	12.73	0.00	YR	1.37	0.50
PI	14.12	0.00	PI	8.35	0.02
HP	8.28	0.02	HP	5.64	0.06
M	5.79	0.06	M	6.50	0.04
SR	8.84	0.01	SR	7.05	0.03
ER	7.17	0.03	ER	6.19	0.05
SP	10.51	0.01	SP	5.24	0.07
Joint	67.43	0.00	Joint	40.34	0.00

A.17 IMPULSE RESPONSES FOR BASELINE SFAVAR (NATIONAL LEVEL)

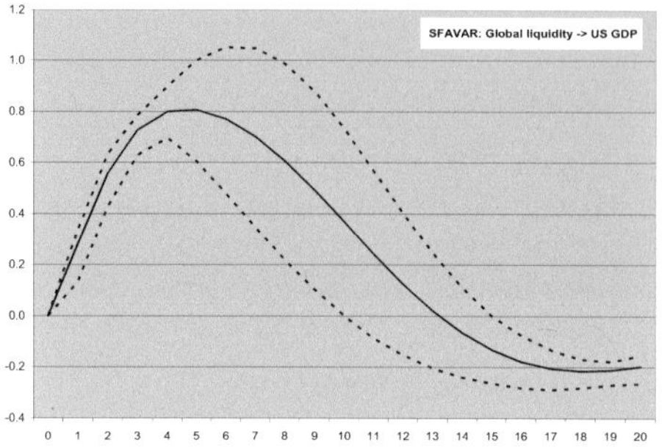

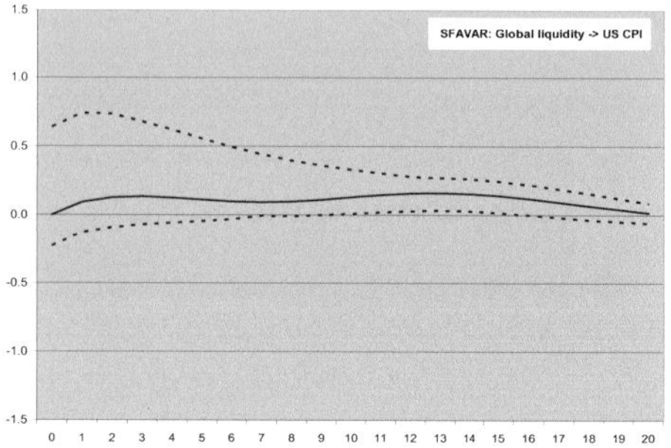

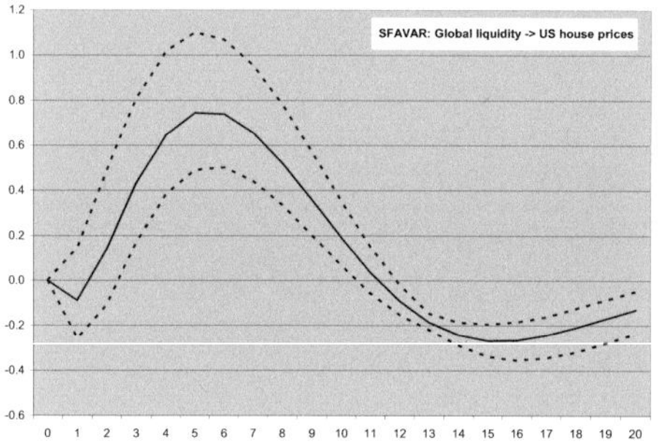

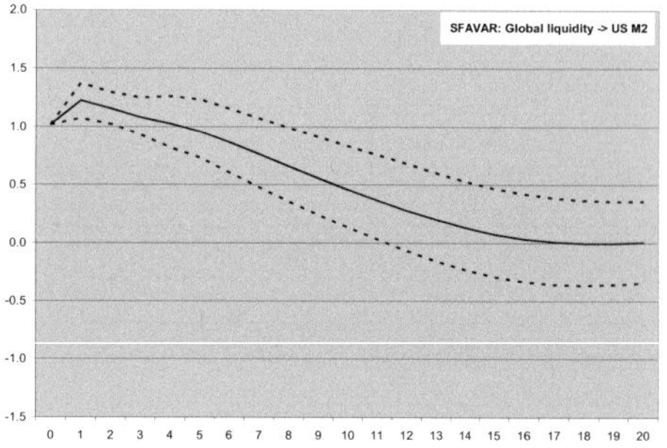

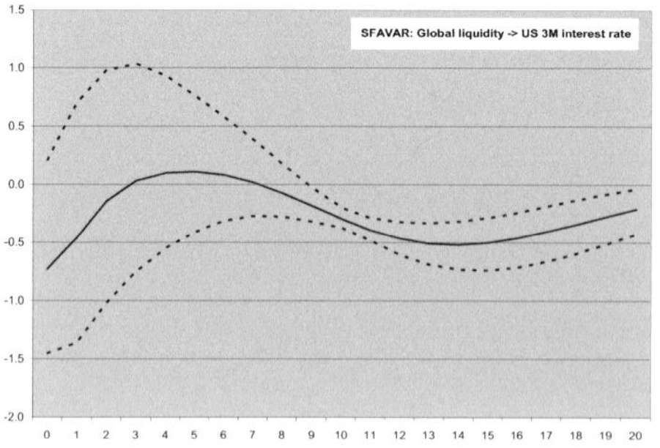

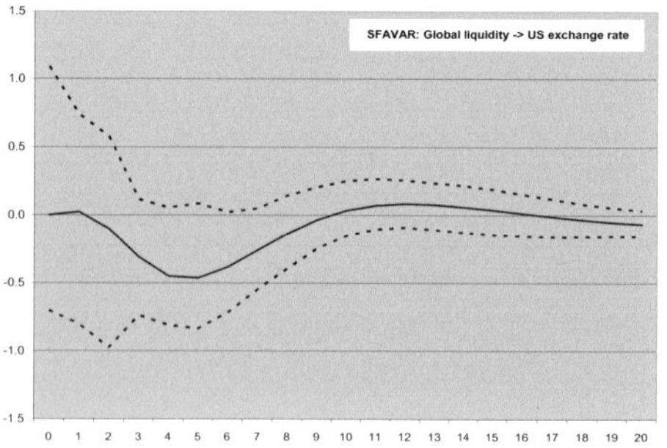

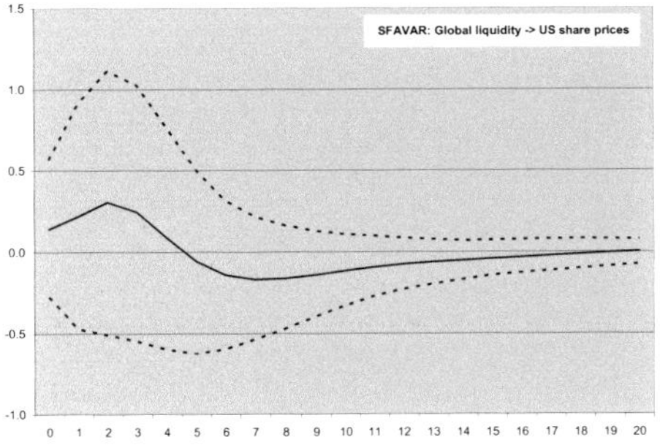
SFAVAR: Global liquidity -> US share prices
1.5
1.0
0.5
0.0
-0.5
-1.0
0 1 2 3 4 5 6 7 8 9 10 11 12 13 14 15 16 17 18 19 20

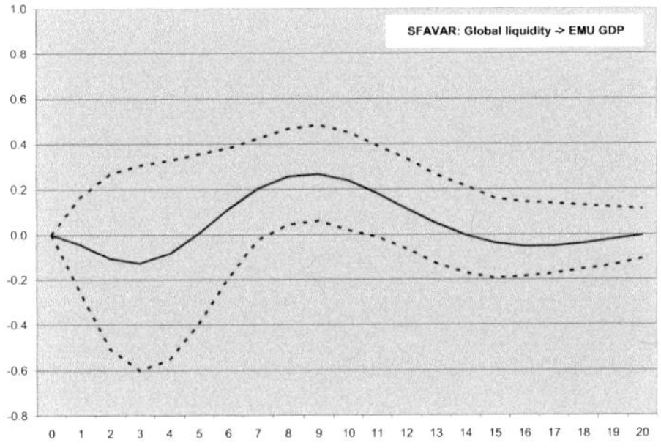
SFAVAR: Global liquidity -> EMU GDP
1.0
0.8
0.6
0.4
0.2
0.0
-0.2
-0.4
-0.6
-0.8
0 1 2 3 4 5 6 7 8 9 10 11 12 13 14 15 16 17 18 19 20

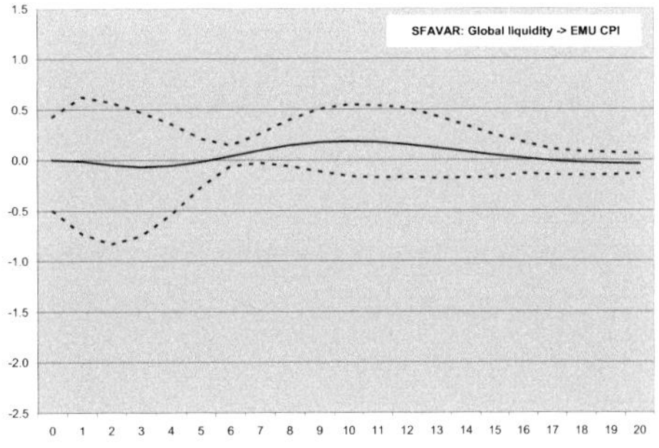
SFAVAR: Global liquidity -> EMU CPI
1.5
1.0
0.5
0.0
-0.5
-1.0
-1.5
-2.0
-2.5
0 1 2 3 4 5 6 7 8 9 10 11 12 13 14 15 16 17 18 19 20

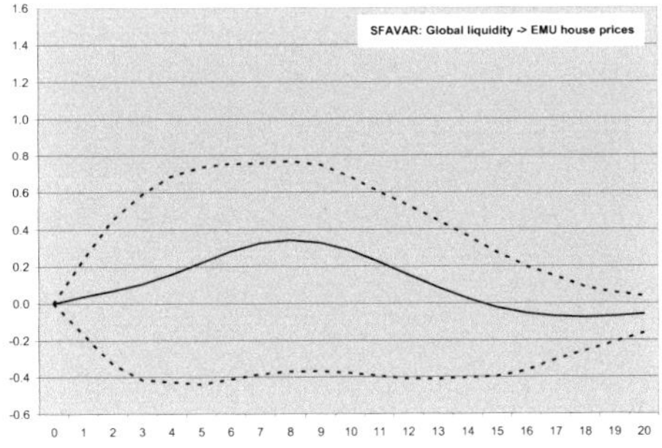
SFAVAR: Global liquidity -> EMU house prices
1.6
1.4
1.2
1.0
0.8
0.6
0.4
0.2
0.0
-0.2
-0.4
-0.6
0 1 2 3 4 5 6 7 8 9 10 11 12 13 14 15 16 17 18 19 20

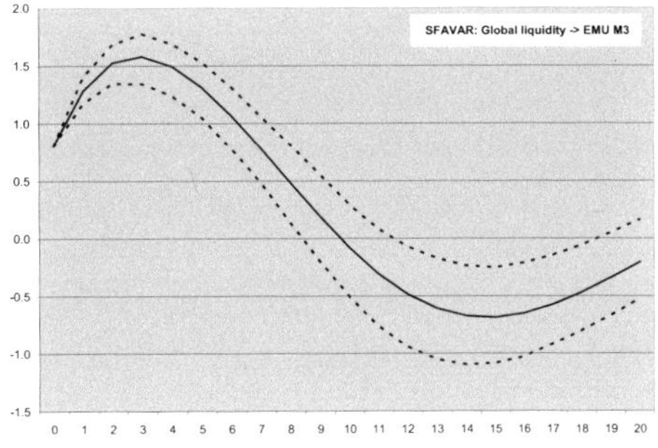
SFAVAR: Global liquidity -> EMU M3
2.0
1.5
1.0
0.5
0.0
-0.5
-1.0
-1.5
0 1 2 3 4 5 6 7 8 9 10 11 12 13 14 15 16 17 18 19 20

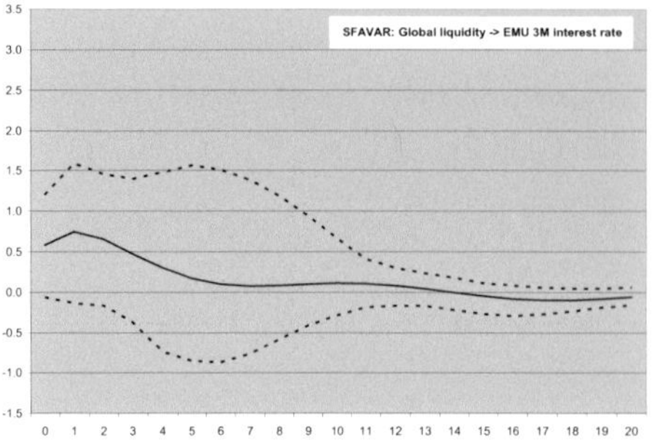
SFAVAR: Global liquidity -> EMU 3M interest rate

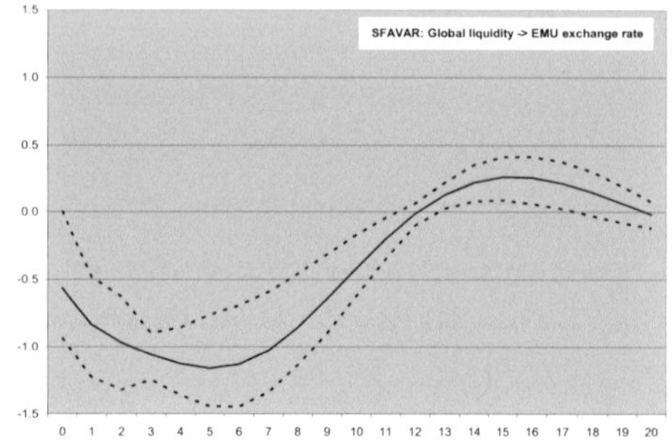
SFAVAR: Global liquidity -> EMU exchange rate

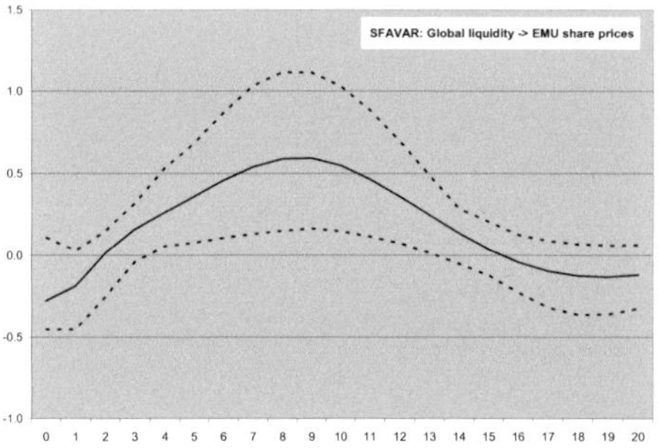
SFAVAR: Global liquidity -> EMU share prices

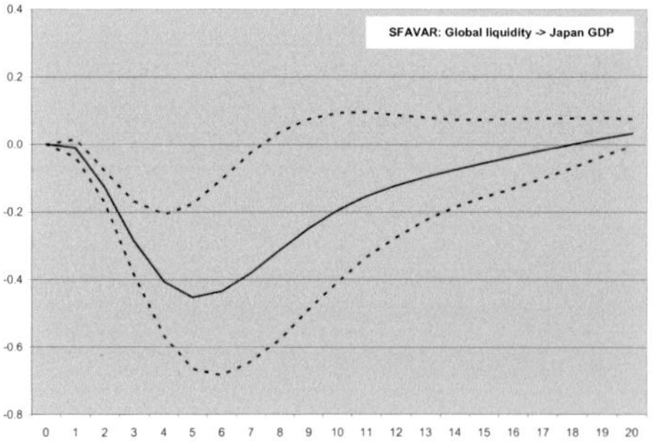
SFAVAR: Global liquidity -> Japan GDP

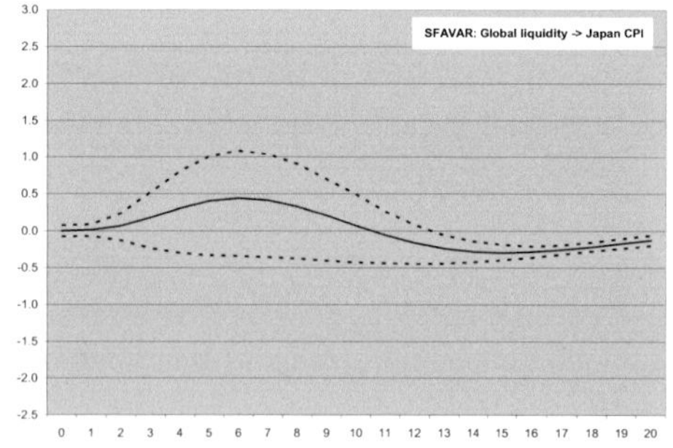
SFAVAR: Global liquidity -> Japan CPI

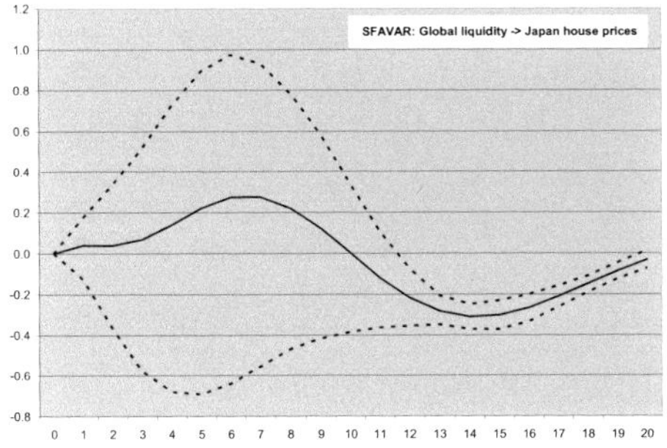
SFAVAR: Global liquidity -> Japan house prices

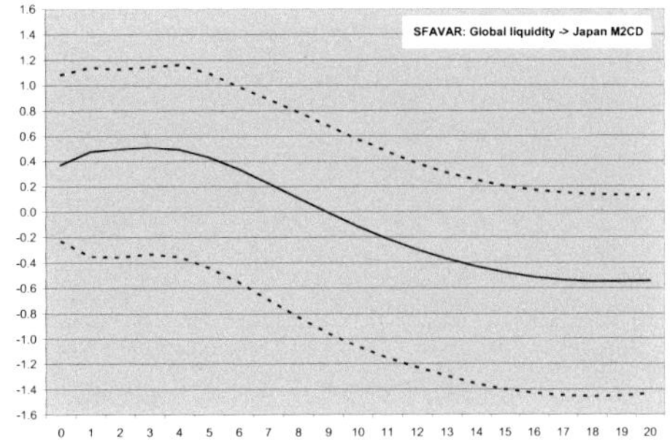
SFAVAR: Global liquidity -> Japan M2CD

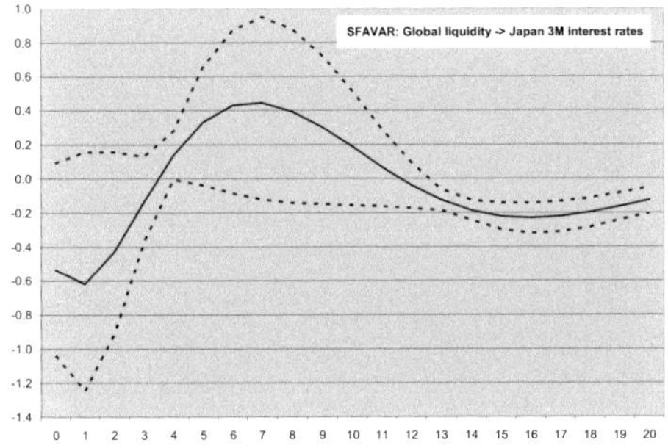
SFAVAR: Global liquidity -> Japan 3M interest rates

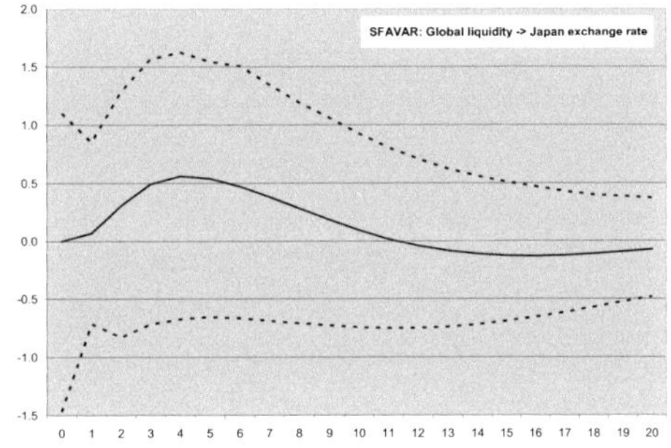
SFAVAR: Global liquidity -> Japan exchange rate

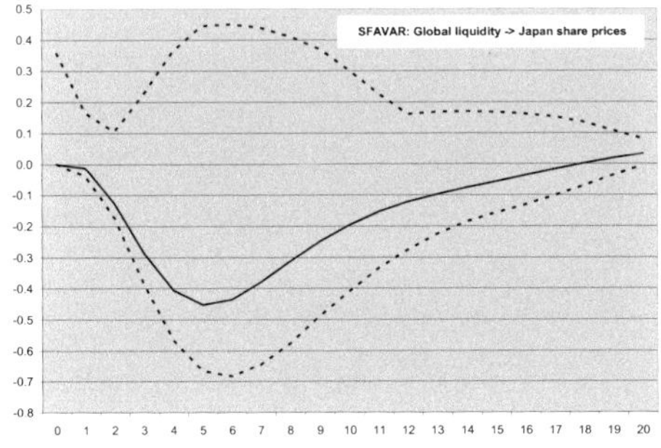
SFAVAR: Global liquidity -> Japan share prices

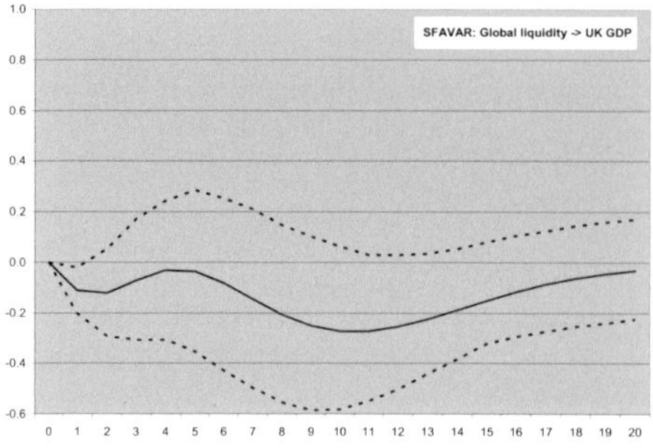
SFAVAR: Global liquidity -> UK GDP

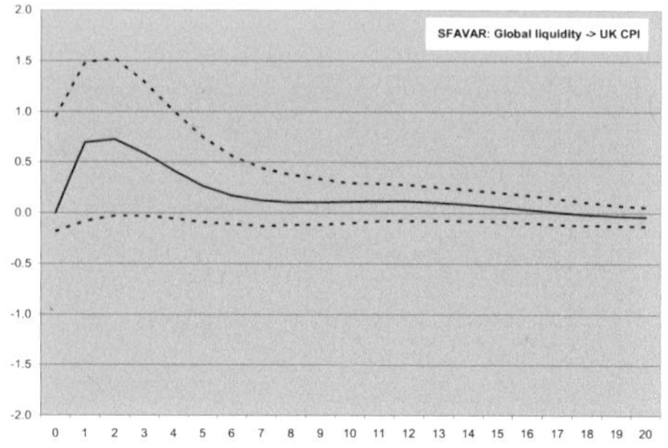
SFAVAR: Global liquidity -> UK CPI

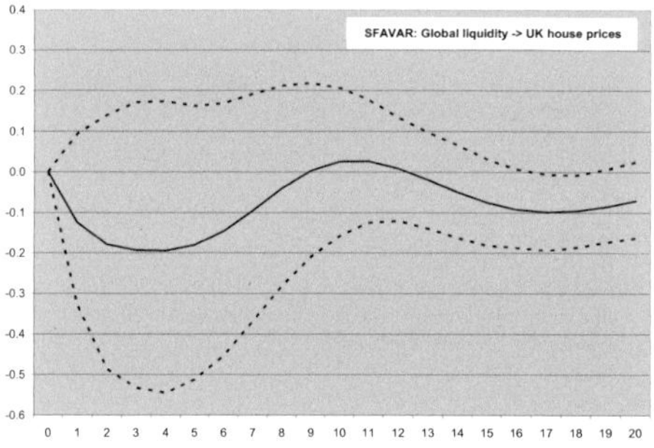
SFAVAR: Global liquidity -> UK house prices

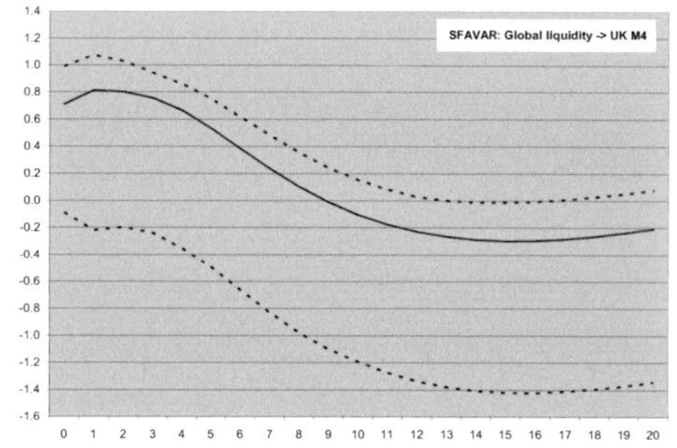
SFAVAR: Global liquidity -> UK M4

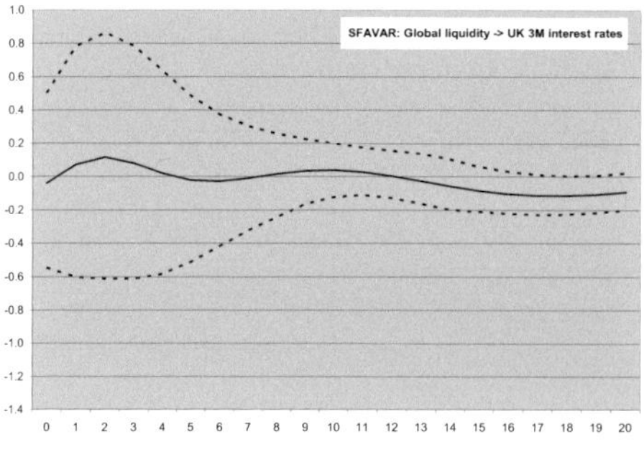
SFAVAR: Global liquidity -> UK 3M interest rates

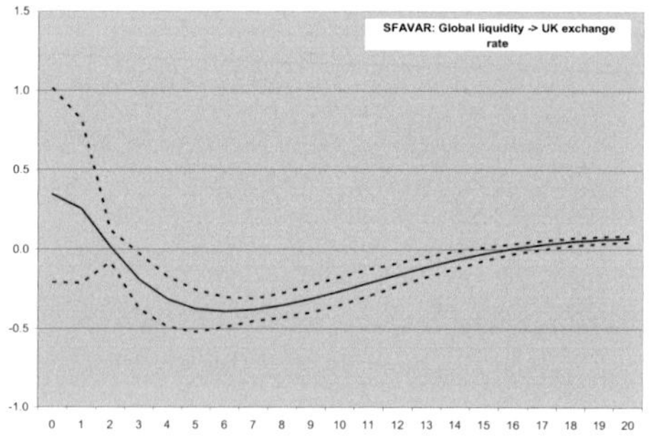
SFAVAR: Global liquidity -> UK exchange rate

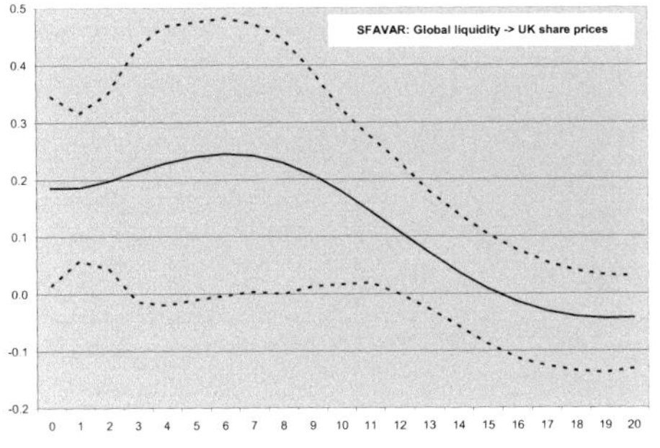
SFAVAR: Global liquidity -> UK share prices

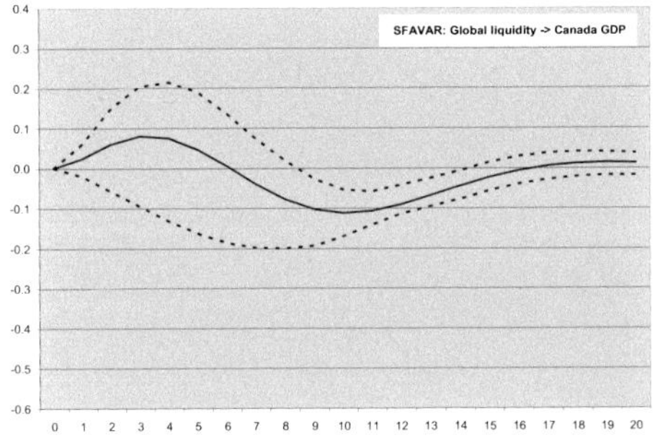
SFAVAR: Global liquidity -> Canada GDP

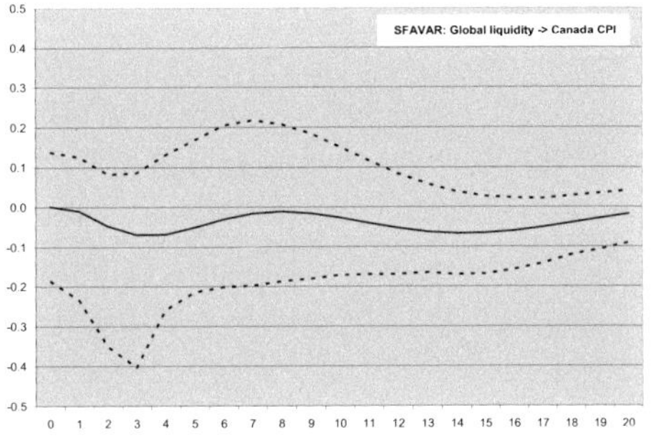
SFAVAR: Global liquidity -> Canada CPI

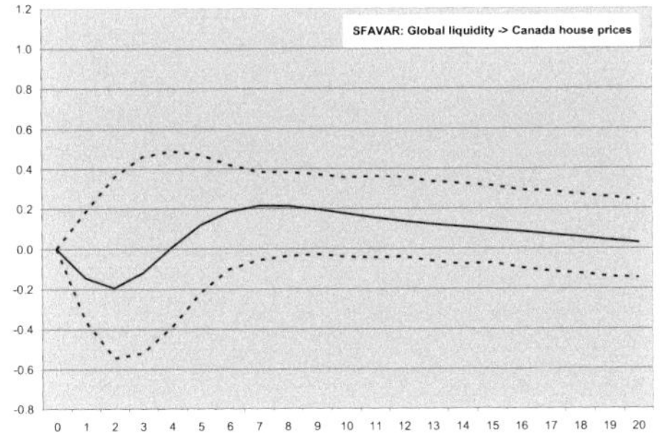
SFAVAR: Global liquidity -> Canada house prices

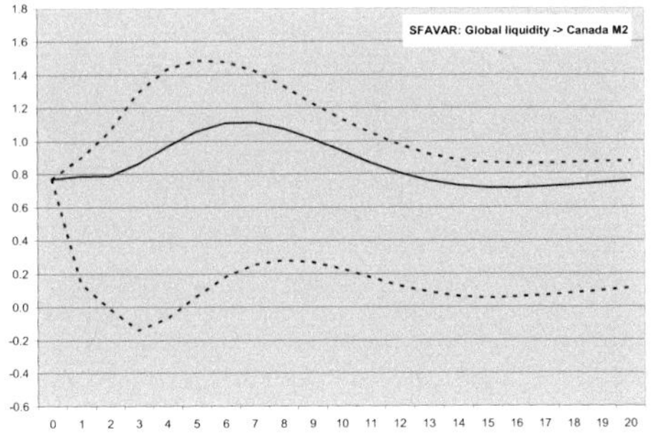
SFAVAR: Global liquidity -> Canada M2

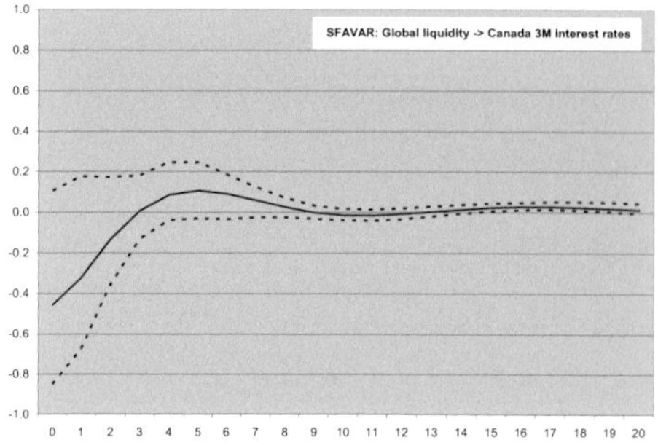
SFAVAR: Global liquidity -> Canada 3M interest rates

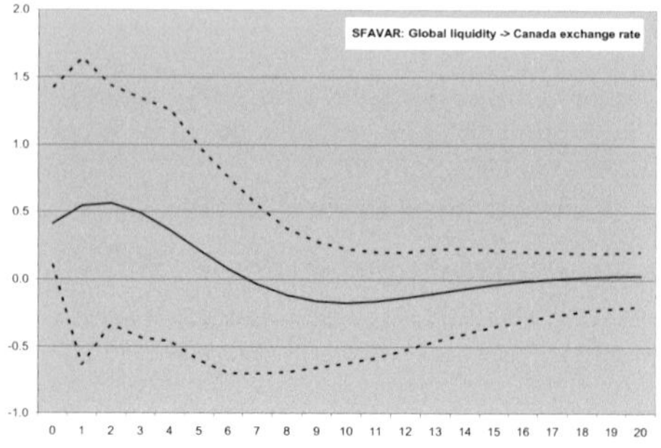
SFAVAR: Global liquidity -> Canada exchange rate

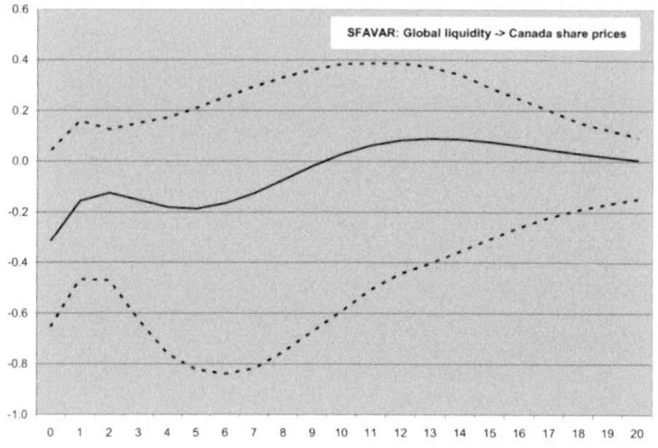
SFAVAR: Global liquidity -> Canada share prices

A.18 COMPARISON OF IMPULSE RESPONSES AFTER GLOBAL AND IDIOSYNCRATIC MONEY SHOCKS

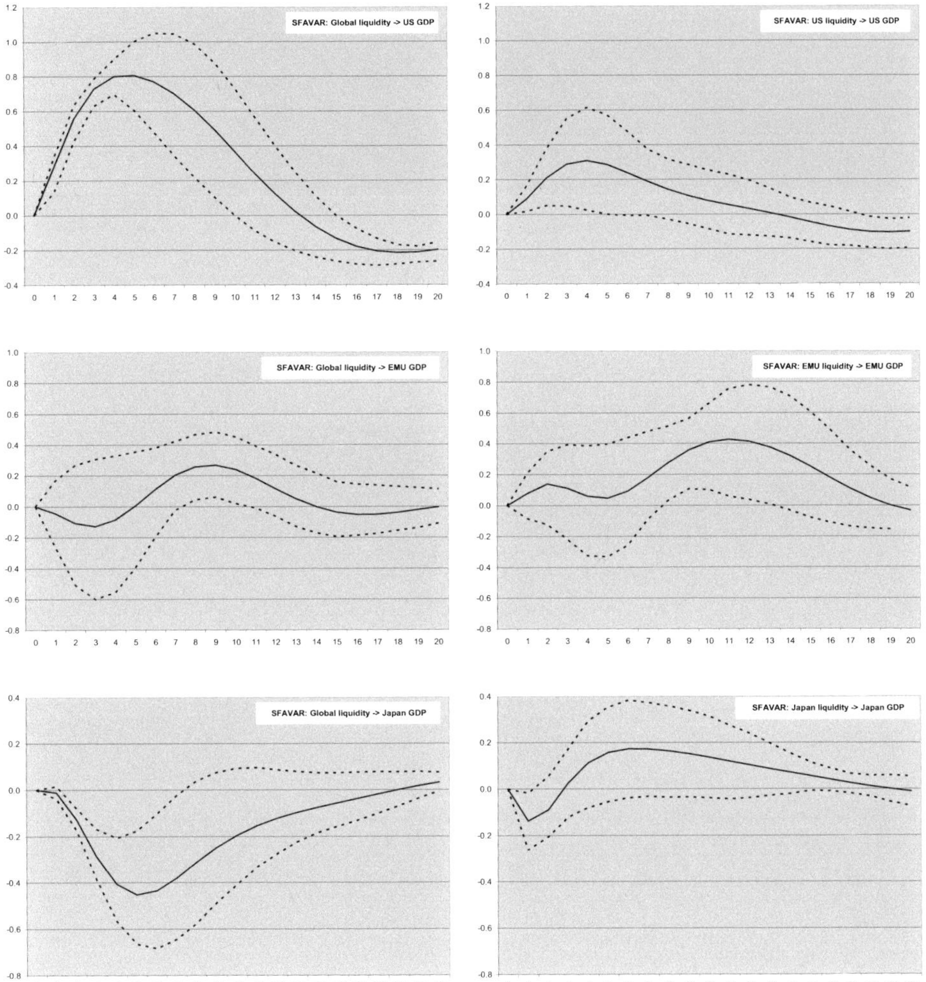

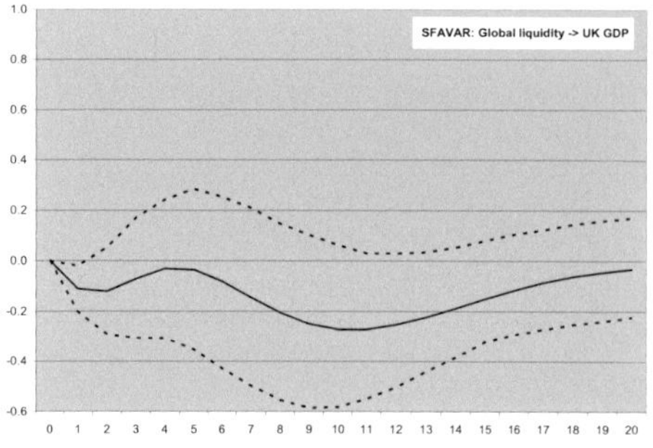
SFAVAR: Global liquidity -> UK GDP

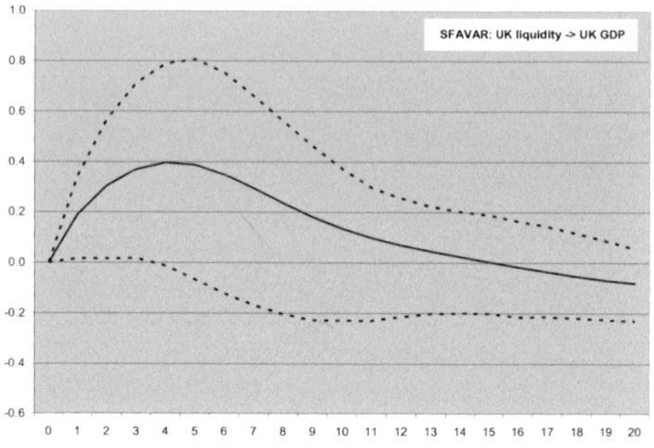
SFAVAR: UK liquidity -> UK GDP

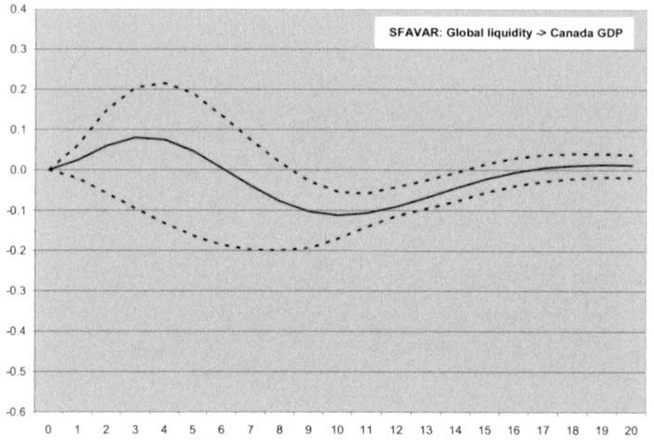
SFAVAR: Global liquidity -> Canada GDP

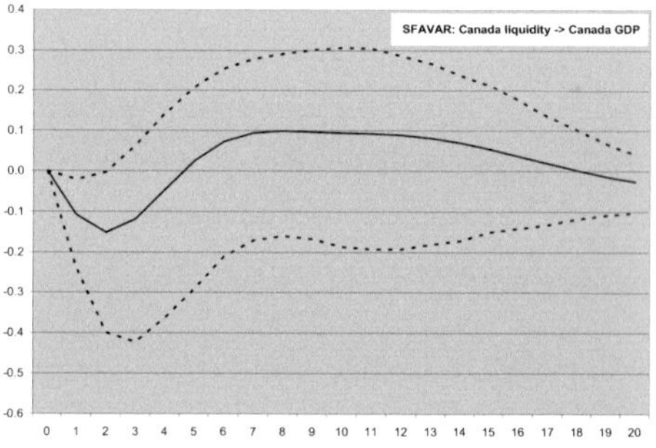
SFAVAR: Canada liquidity -> Canada GDP

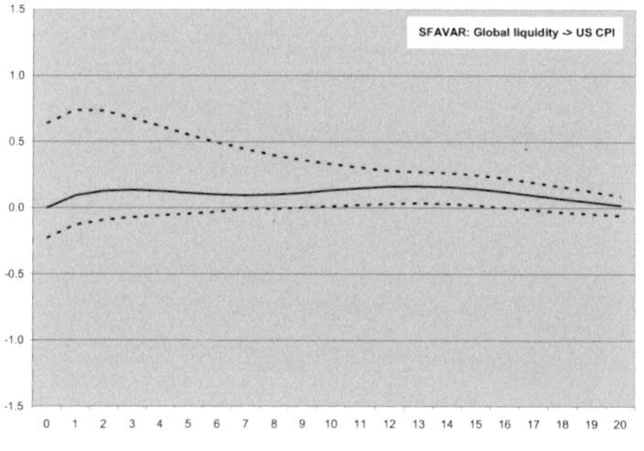
SFAVAR: Global liquidity -> US CPI

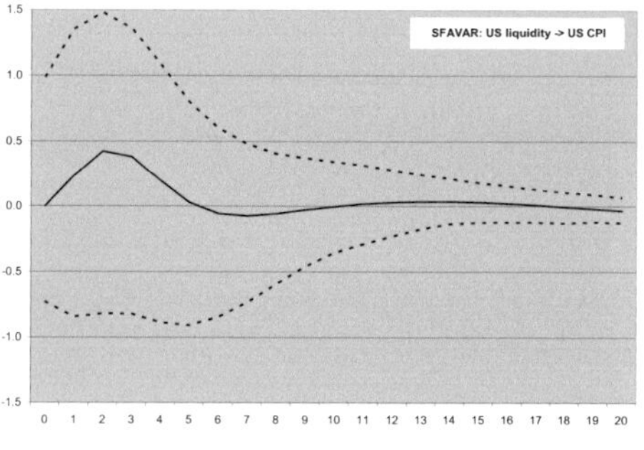
SFAVAR: US liquidity -> US CPI

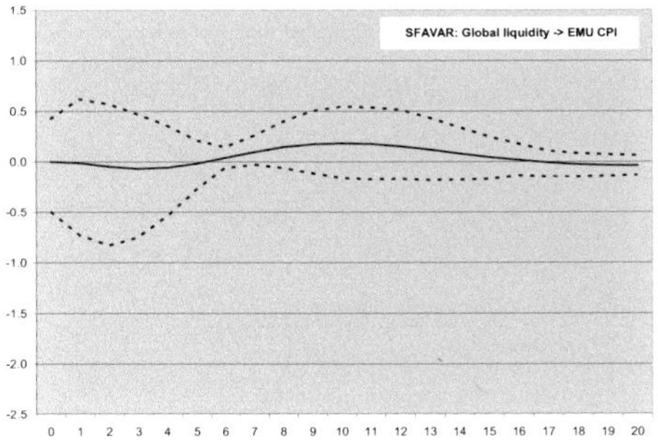
SFAVAR: Global liquidity -> EMU CPI

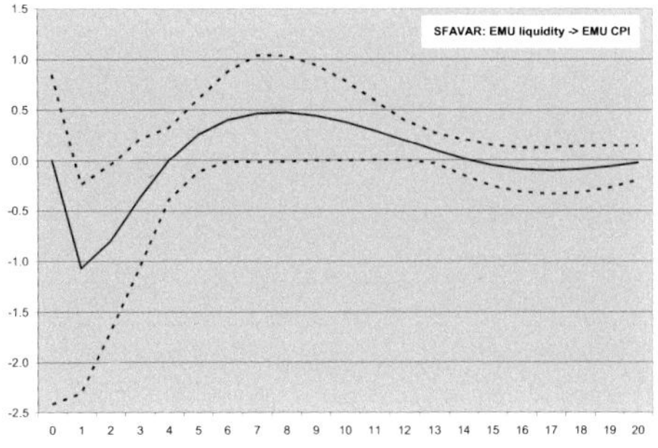
SFAVAR: EMU liquidity -> EMU CPI

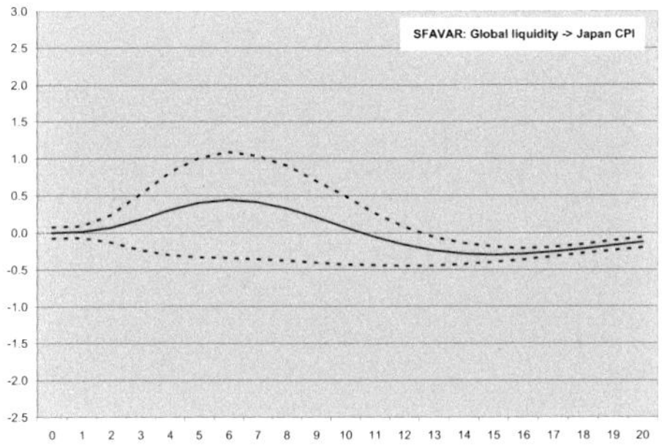
SFAVAR: Global liquidity -> Japan CPI

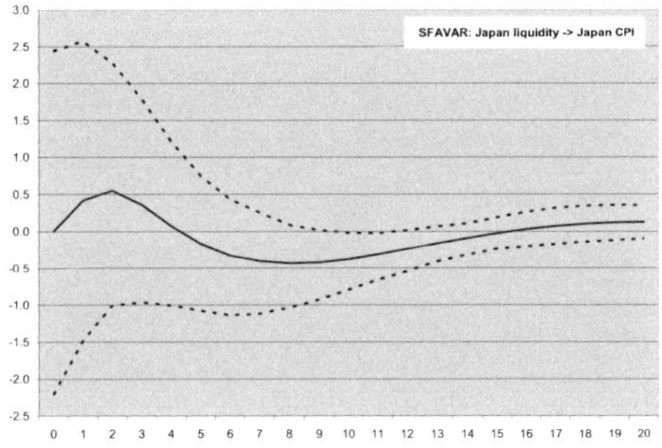
SFAVAR: Japan liquidity -> Japan CPI

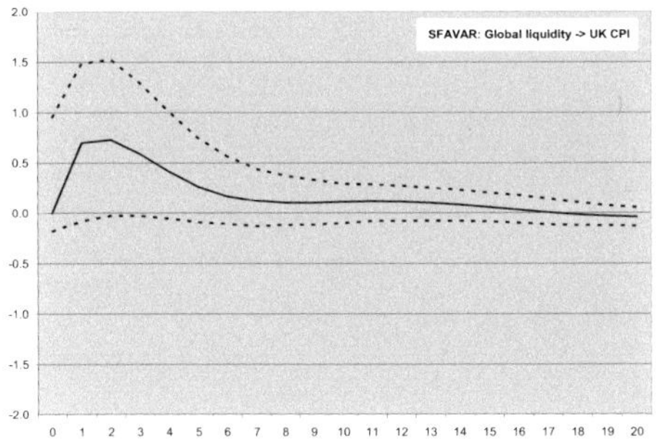
SFAVAR: Global liquidity -> UK CPI

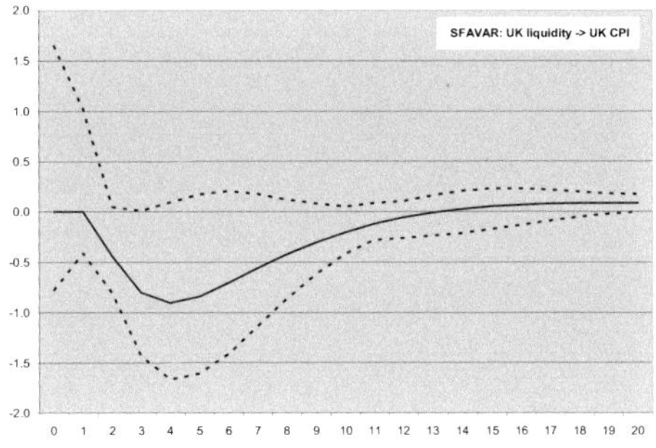
SFAVAR: UK liquidity -> UK CPI

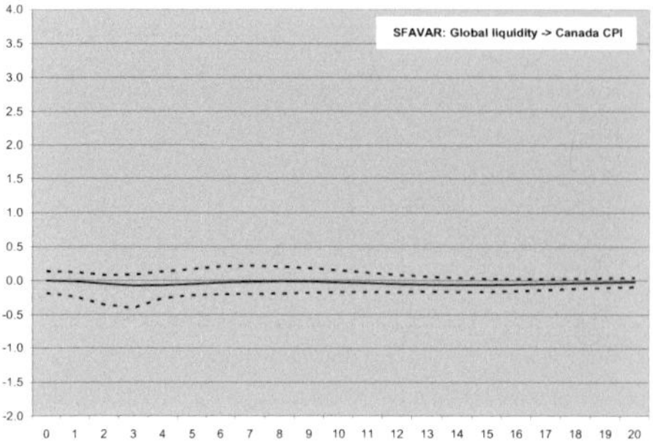
SFAVAR: Global liquidity -> Canada CPI

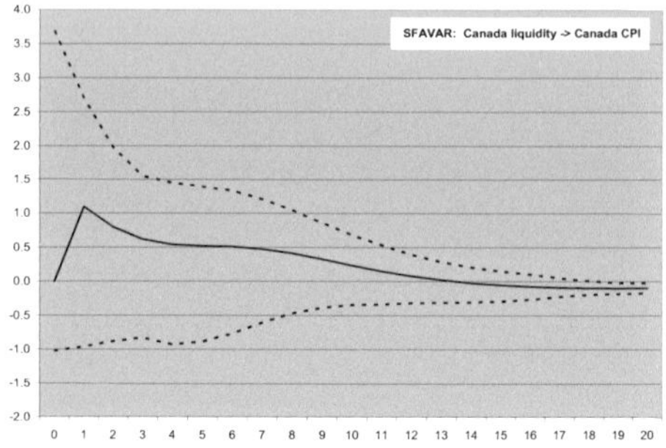
SFAVAR: Canada liquidity -> Canada CPI

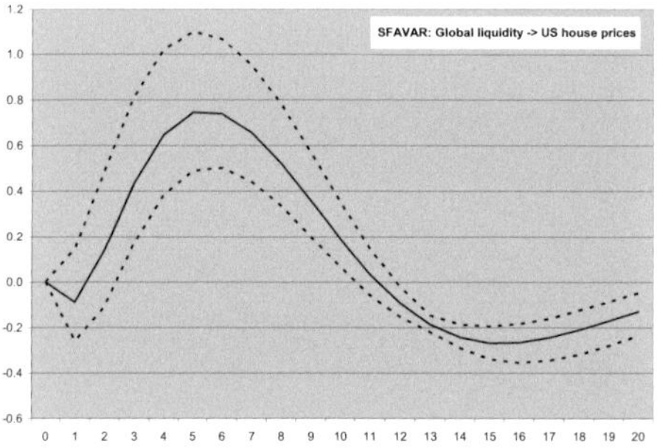
SFAVAR: Global liquidity -> US house prices

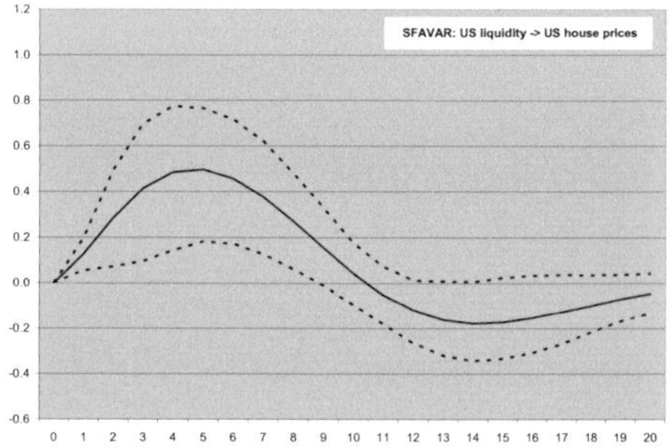
SFAVAR: US liquidity -> US house prices

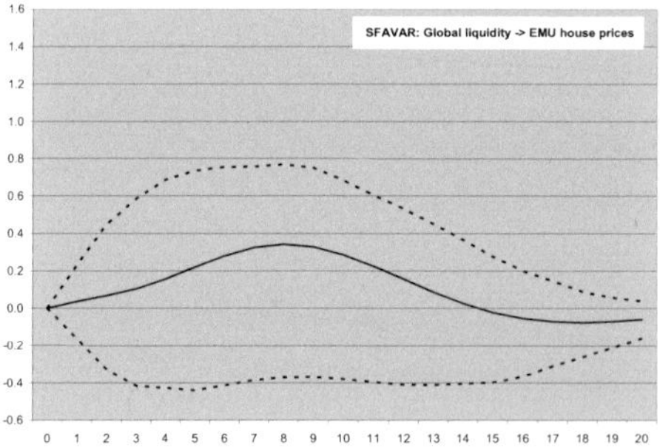
SFAVAR: Global liquidity -> EMU house prices

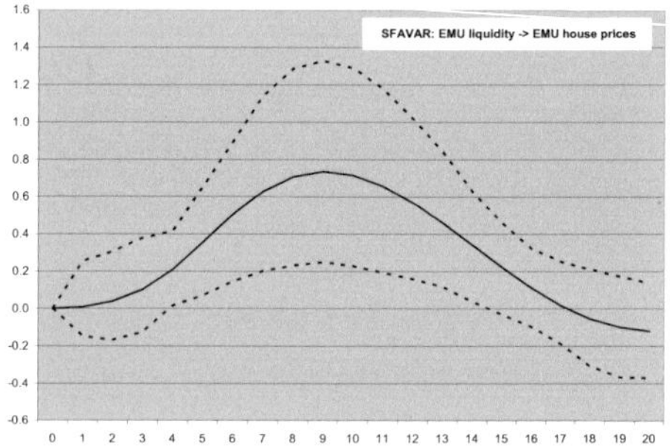
SFAVAR: EMU liquidity -> EMU house prices

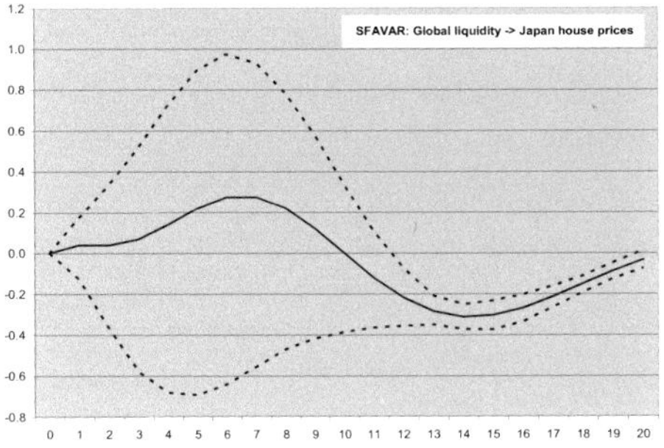
SFAVAR: Global liquidity -> Japan house prices

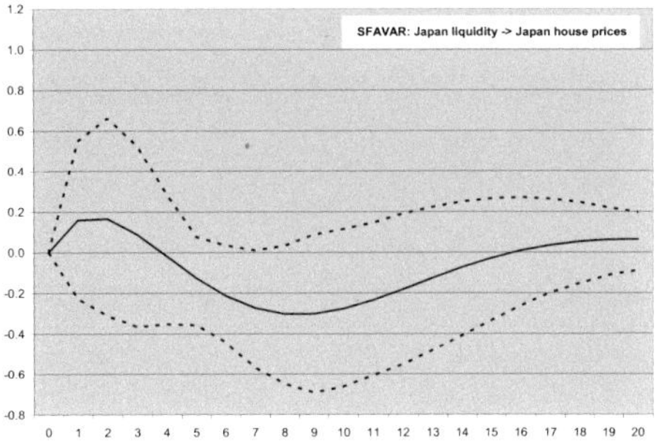
SFAVAR: Japan liquidity -> Japan house prices

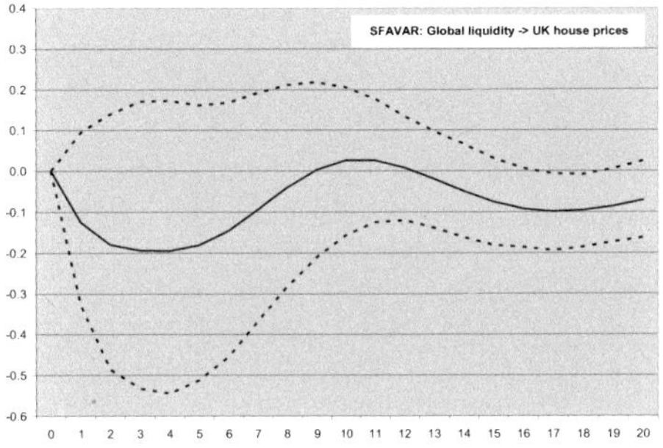
SFAVAR: Global liquidity -> UK house prices

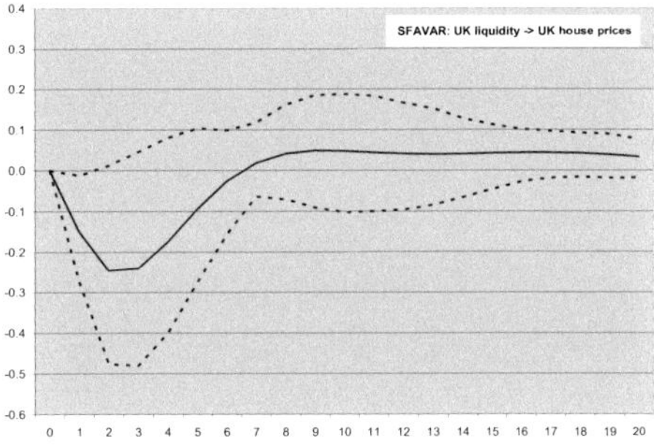
SFAVAR: UK liquidity -> UK house prices

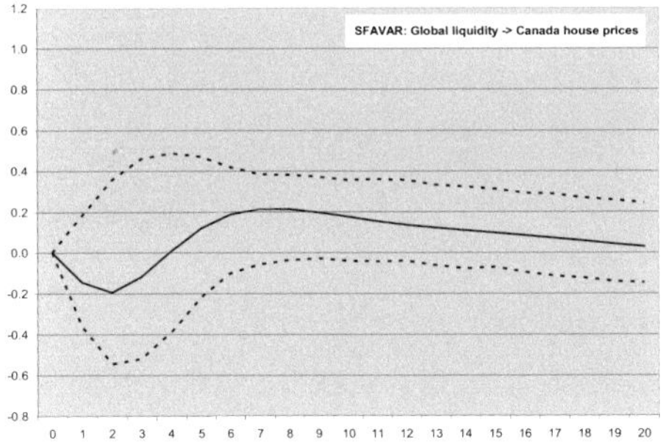
SFAVAR: Global liquidity -> Canada house prices

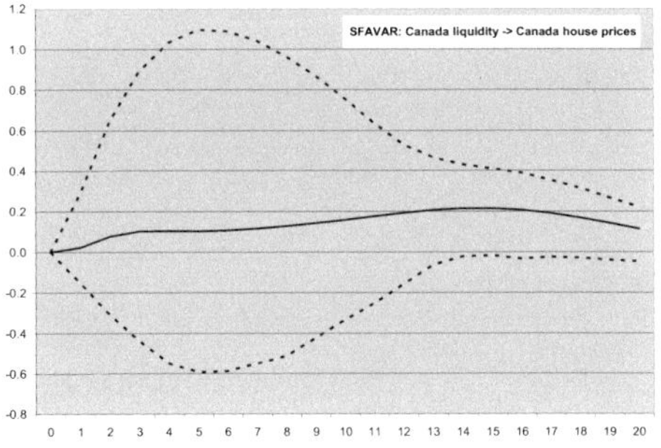
SFAVAR: Canada liquidity -> Canada house prices

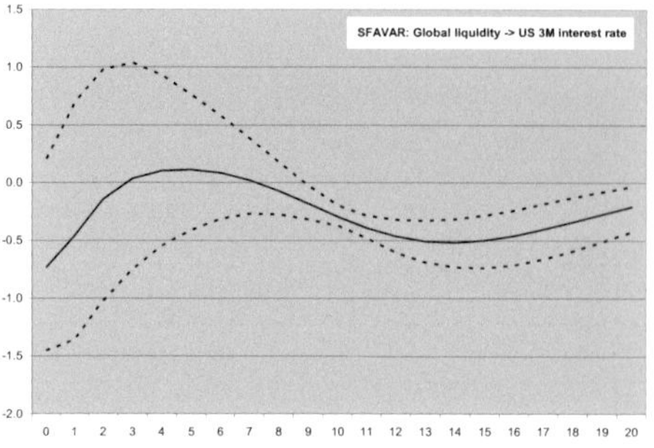
SFAVAR: Global liquidity -> US 3M interest rate

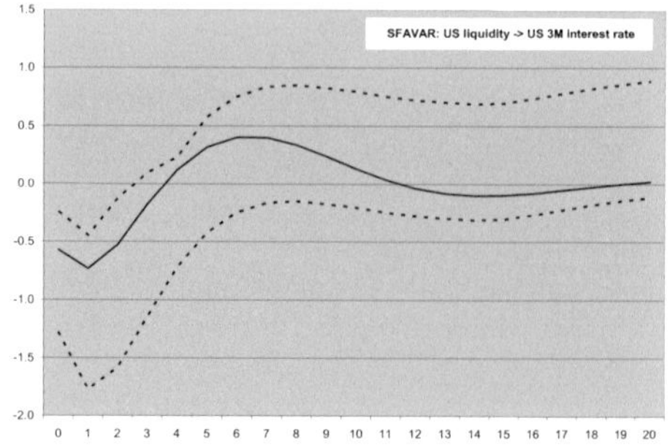
SFAVAR: US liquidity -> US 3M interest rate

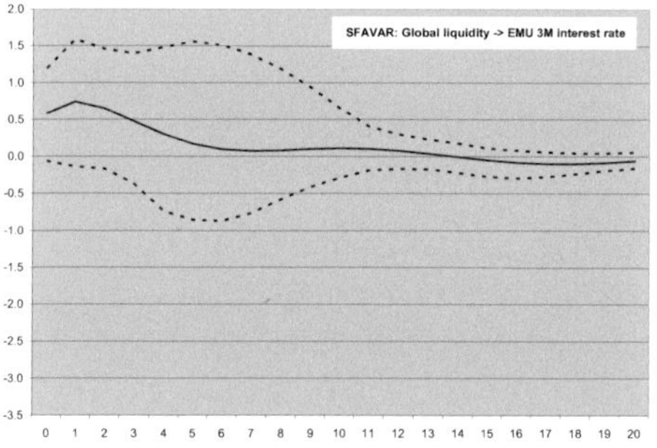
SFAVAR: Global liquidity -> EMU 3M interest rate

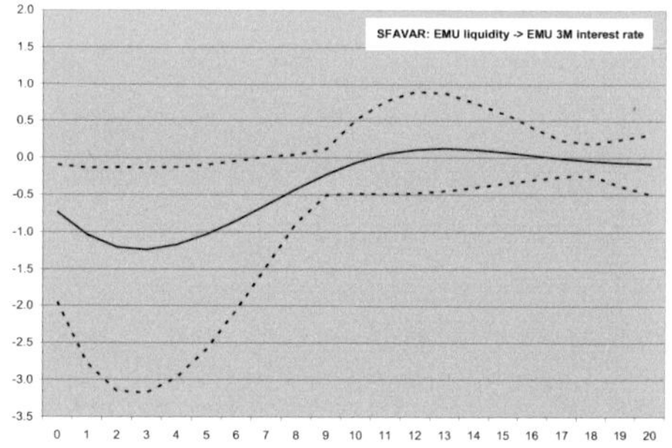
SFAVAR: EMU liquidity -> EMU 3M interest rate

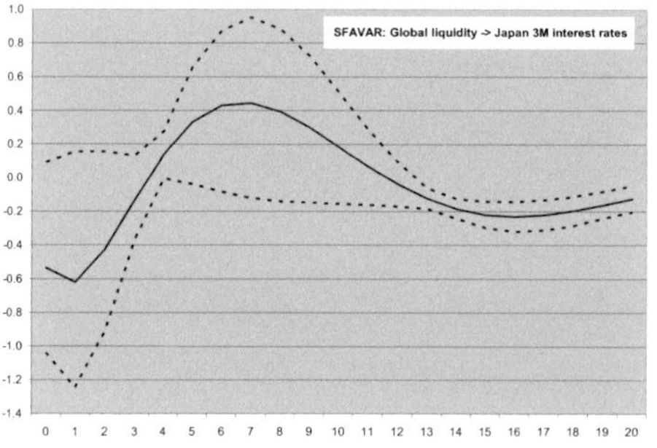
SFAVAR: Global liquidity -> Japan 3M interest rates

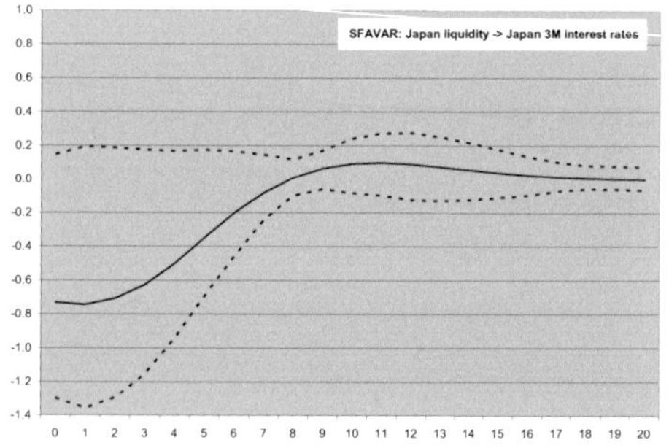
SFAVAR: Japan liquidity -> Japan 3M interest rates

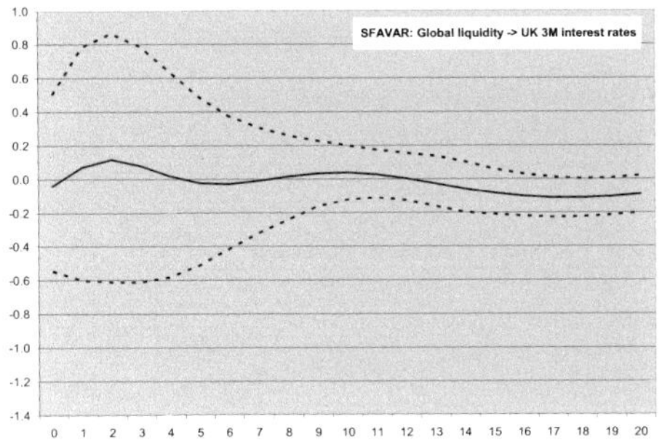
SFAVAR: Global liquidity -> UK 3M interest rates

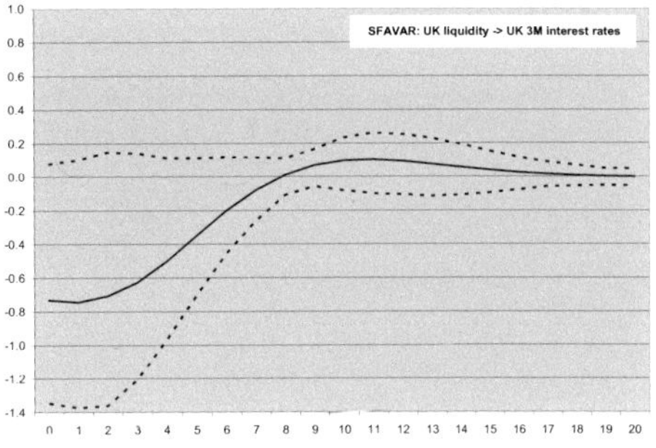
SFAVAR: UK liquidity -> UK 3M interest rates

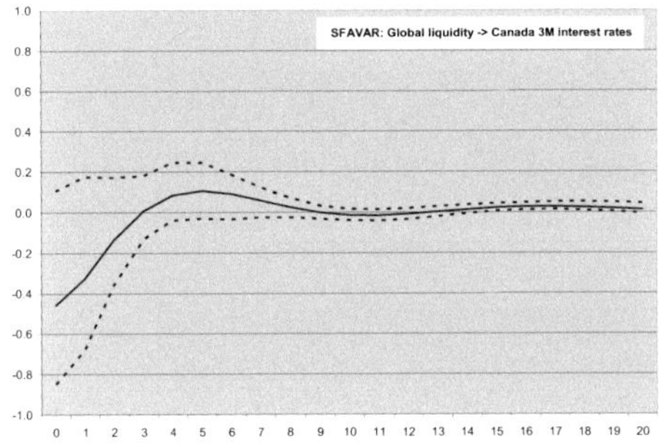
SFAVAR: Global liquidity -> Canada 3M interest rates

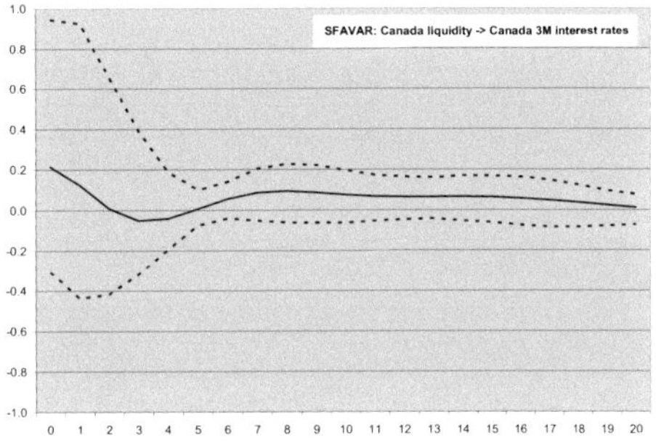
SFAVAR: Canada liquidity -> Canada 3M interest rates

A.19 Factor loadings of global labor productivity, global hours worked, global long-term interest rate and global credit

Labor productivity	PC1	PC2	PC3
US	0.429 (0.098)	-0.541 (0.087)	-0.072 (0.099)
EMU	0.151 (0.116)	0.391 (0.117)	0.769 (0.133)
Japan	-0.573 (0.087)	0.394 (0.084)	-0.149 (0.096)
UK	0.602 (0.073)	0.404 (0.096)	0.043 (0.104)
Canada	-0.320 (0.123)	-0.486 (0.089)	0.615 (0.176)
Hours worked	PC1	PC2	PC3
US	0.524 (0.095)	-0.400 (0.116)	0.319 (0.185)
EMU	0.281 (0.117)	0.683 (0.119)	-0.510 (0.138)
Japan	0.136 (0.114)	0.598 (0.092)	0.781 (0.101)
UK	0.558 (0.076)	-0.123 (0.153)	-0.085 (0.135)
Canada	0.563 (0.070)	0.010 (0.166)	-0.146 (0.108)
Long-term interest rate	PC1	PC2	PC3
US	0.462 (0.040)	-0.559 (0.123)	0.002 (0.163)
EMU	0.452 (0.039)	0.262 (0.145)	-0.474 (0.180)
Japan	0.410 (0.052)	0.388 (0.160)	0.812 (0.167)
UK	0.437 (0.034)	0.482 (0.163)	-0.336 (0.203)
Canada	0.473 (0.036)	-0.485 (0.167)	0.057 (0.194)
Credit	PC1	PC2	PC3
US	0.155 (0.096)	0.888 (0.038)	-0.064 (0.129)
EMU	0.502 (0.077)	-0.051 (0.095)	-0.326 (0.141)
Japan	0.464 (0.063)	-0.369 (0.115)	-0.436 (0.064)
UK	0.573 (0.056)	0.219 (0.137)	0.037 (0.130)
Canada	0.424 (0.069)	-0.154 (0.089)	0.836 (0.067)

Note: Standard errors in paranthesis using Newey-West

A.20 R-squared, in % (global labor productivity, global hours worked, global long-term interest rate and global credit)

Labor productivity	US	EMU	Japan	UK	Canada
PC1	24.0	3.0	42.9	47.3	13.4
US	---	0.0	3.8	0.1	0.0
Hours worked	US	EMU	Japan	UK	Canada
PC1	52.6	15.1	13.5	59.5	60.6
US	---	0.3	0.3	20.0	17.7
Long-term interest rate	US	EMU	Japan	UK	Canada
PC1	70.6	67.3	55.5	63.0	73.8
US	---	34.3	23.3	23.3	68.5
Credit	US	EMU	Japan	UK	Canada
PC1	4.2	43.8	37.4	56.8	31.2
US	---	0.4	0.3	4.8	0.0

A.21 UNIT ROOT TESTS FOR GLOBAL PRODUCTIVITY FACTOR AND GLOBAL HOURS WORKED FACTOR

	ADF	PP	KPSS
Global productivity (level)	1.74	2.15	0.27
Global productivity (log first difference)	-8.68***	-8.77***	0.23
Global hours worked (level)	-2.66*	-1.72	0.44
Global hours worked (log first difference)	-2.82*	-2.92**	0.12

Note 1: ADF (Augmented Dickey-Fuller), PP (Phillips-Perron), KPSS (Kwiatkowski-Phillips-Schmidt-Shin)

Note 2: *** Indicates significance at 1% level, ** at 5% level, * at 10% level

Note 3: Null hypothesis of ADF and PP test assumes non-stationarity; null hypothesis of KPSS test assumes stationarity

A.22 ROLLING REGRESSIONS FOR FACTOR LOADINGS (MONEY)

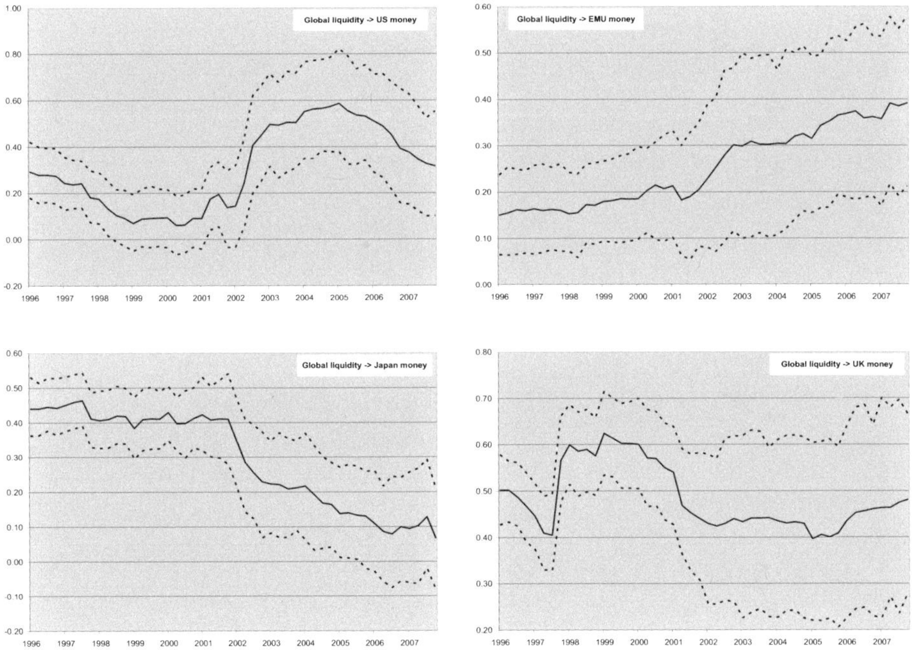

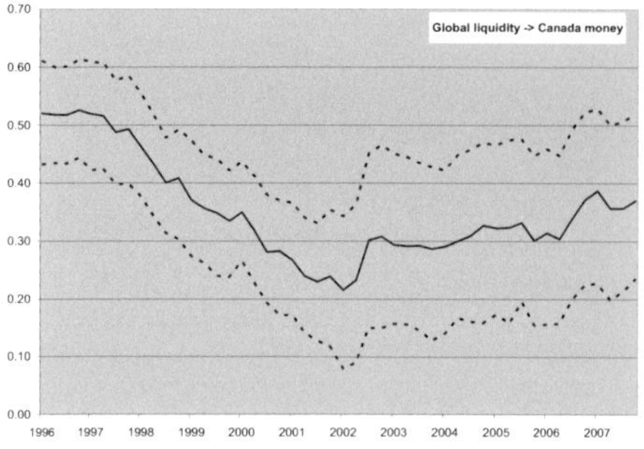

A.23 ROLLING REGRESSIONS FOR FACTOR LOADINGS (GDP)

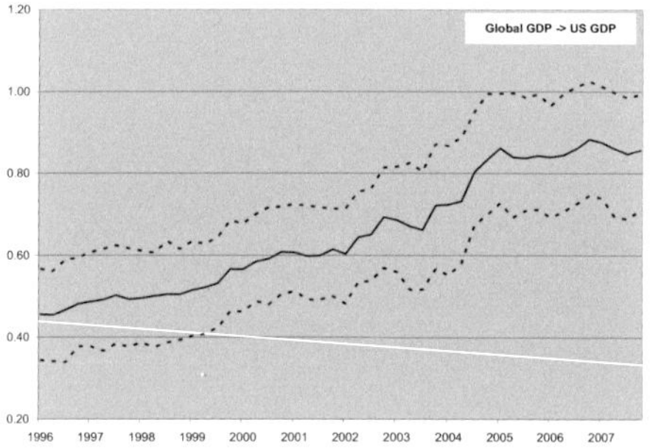

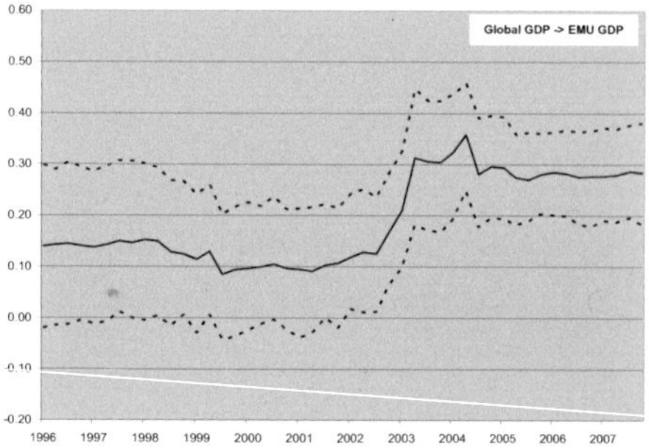

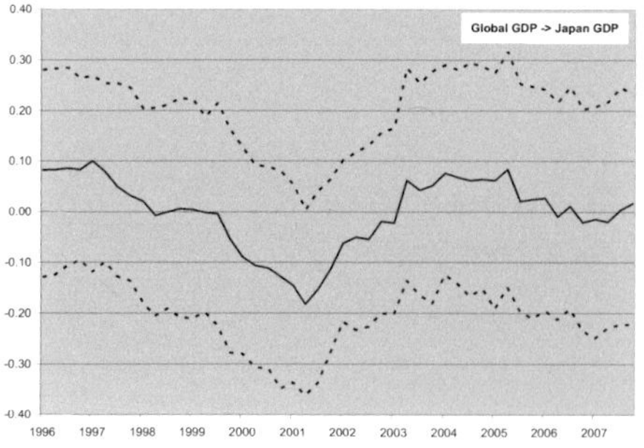

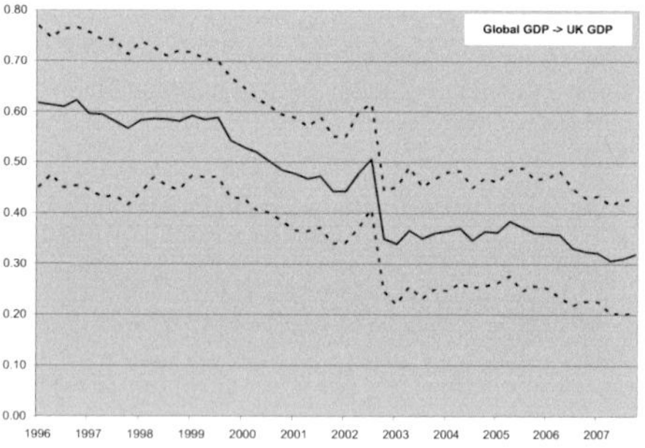

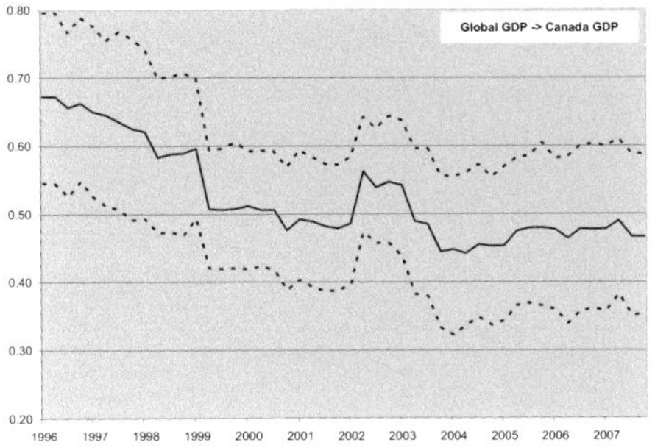

A.24 ROLLING REGRESSIONS FOR FACTOR LOADINGS (HOUSE PRICES)

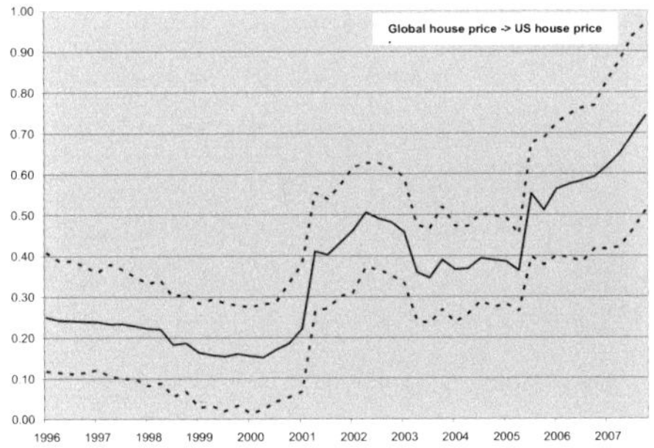

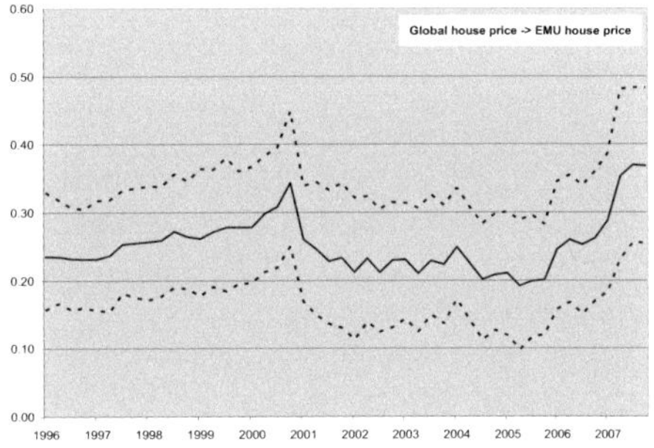

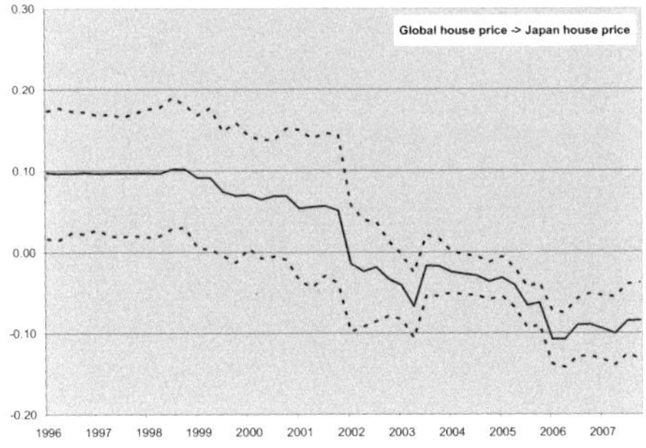

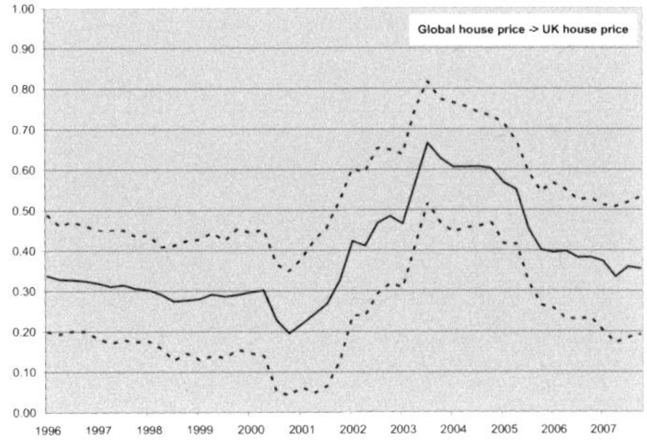

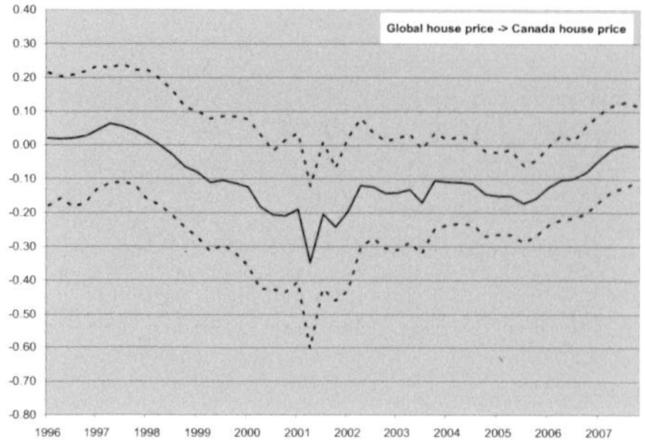

A.25 ROBUSTNESS TEST FOR SFAVAR (LEFT-HAND SIDE BASELINE SFAVAR, RIGHT-HAND SIDE NEWLY IDENTIFIED SFAVAR)

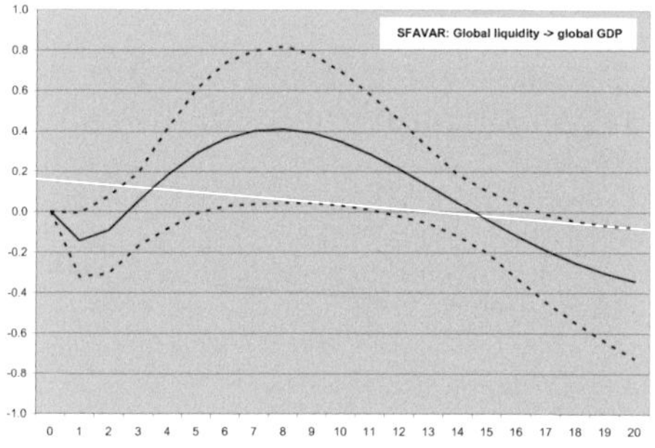

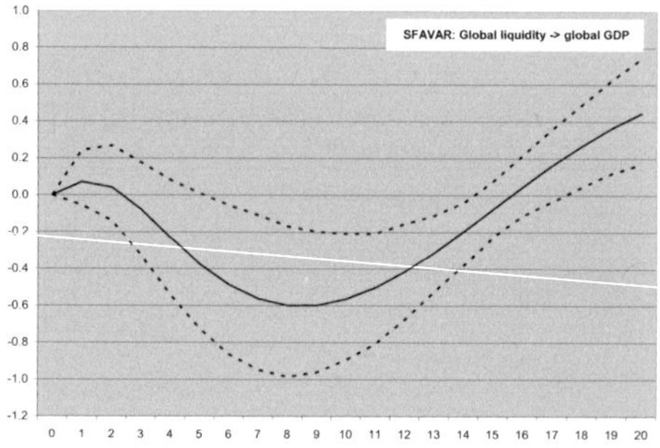

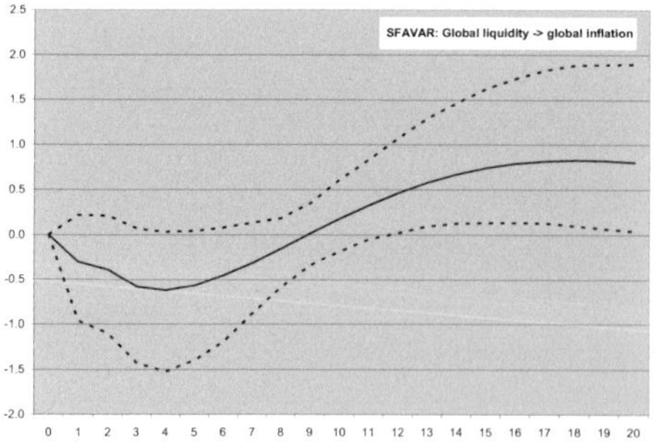

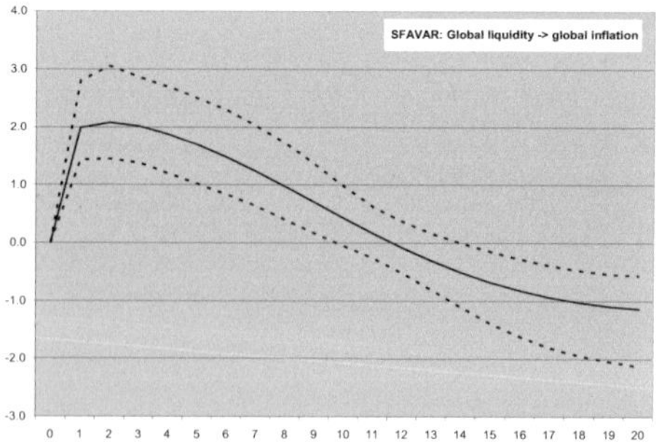

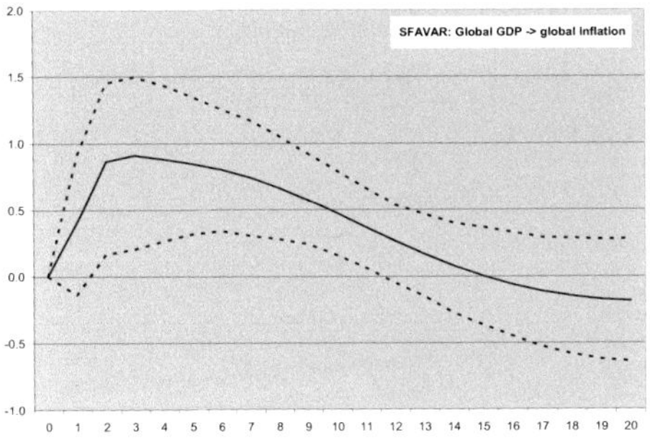
SFAVAR: Global GDP -> global inflation

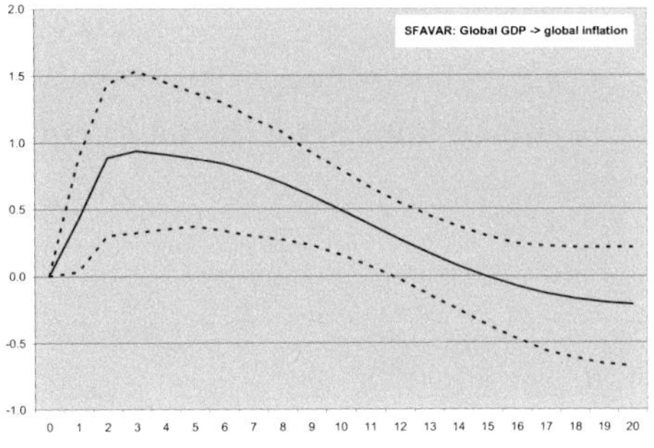
SFAVAR: Global GDP -> global inflation

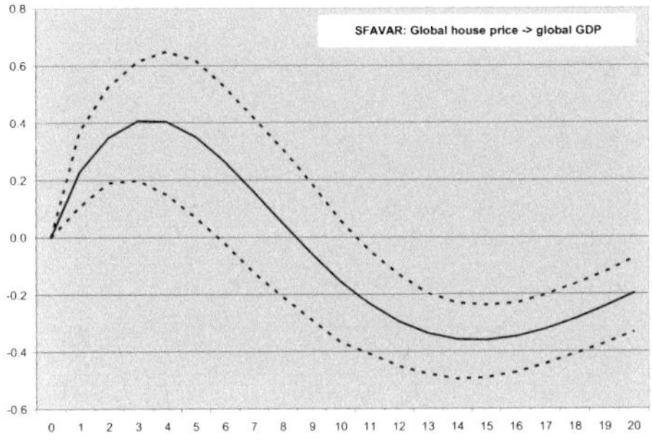
SFAVAR: Global house price -> global GDP

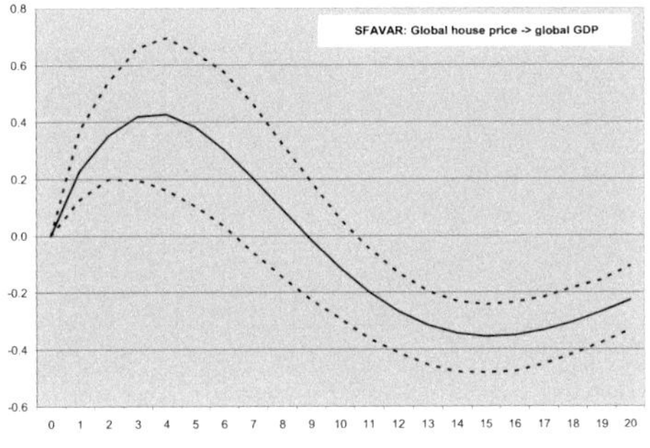
SFAVAR: Global house price -> global GDP

A.26 DATA SET

Format is as follows: series number; series mnemonic in EViews programs; data span, series description; original source and database provider.

	Mnemonic	--------- Monetary aggregates			
1	us_m2	1973:1-2007:4	US monetary aggregate M2	Federal Reserve Board	Feri
2	emu_m3	1973:1-2007:4	EMU monetary aggregate M3	OECD	Feri
3	japan_m2cd	1973:1-2007:4	Japan monetary aggregate M2 plus cash deposits	Bank of Japan	Feri
4	uk_m4	1973:1-2007:4	UK monetary aggregate M4	OECD	Feri
5	canada_m2	1973:1-2007:4	Canada monetary aggregate M2	Bank of Canada	Bloomberg

	Mnemonic	--------- GDP			
6	us_real_gdp	1973:1-2007:4	US real GDP	Bureau of Economic Analysis	Feri
7	us_nom_gdp	1973:1-2007:4	US nominal GDP	Bureau of Economic Analysis	Feri
8	emu_real_gdp	1973:1-2007:4	EMU real GDP	ECB, Eurostat	ECB, Feri
9	emu_nom_gdp	1973:1-2007:4	EMU nominal GDP	ECB, Eurostat	ECB, Feri
10	japan_real_gdp	1973:1-2007:4	Japan real GDP	Economic and Social Research Institute	Feri
11	japan_nom_gdp	1973:1-2007:4	Japan nominal GDP	Economic and Social Research Institute	Feri

12	uk_real_gdp	1973:1-2007:4	UK real GDP	Office for National Statistics	Feri
13	uk_nom_gdp	1973:1-2007:4	UK nominal GDP	Office for National Statistics	Feri
14	canada_real_gdp	1973:1-2007:4	Canada real GDP	Statistics Canada	Feri
15	canada_nom_gdp	1973:1-2007:4	Canada nominal GDP	Statistics Canada	Feri
	Mnemonic	**--------- Short-term interest rates**			
16	us_3m	1973:1-2007:4	Yield 3M US treasury bill	Federal Reserve Board	Feri
17	emu_3m	1973:1-2007:4	3M EMU interbank rate	ECB	ECB, Feri
18	japan_2m_3m	1973:1-2007:4	Yield 2M Japanese treasury bill until 1995, afterwards 3M interbank rate	Japanese Bankers Association, Bank of Japan	Bank of Japan, Feri
19	uk_3m	1973:1-2007:4	Yield 3M UK treasury bill	Bank of England	Feri
20	canada_m3	1973:1-2007:4	Yield 3M Canada treasury bill	Bank of Canada	Feri
	Mnemonic	**--------- Prices**			
21	us_cpi_sa	1973:1-2007:4	US consumer prices	Bureau of Labor Statistics	Feri
22	emu_cpi_sa	1973:1-2007:4	EMU consumer prices	ECB, Eurostat	ECB, Feri
23	japan_cpi_sa	1973:1-2007:4	Japan consumer prices	Japanese Statistics Bureau	Feri
24	uk_cpi_sa	1973:1-2007:4	UK consumer prices	Office for National Statistics	Feri
25	canada_cpi_sa	1973:1-2007:4	Canada consumer prices	Statistics Canada	Feri
26	us_gdp_defl	1973:1-2007:4	GDP deflator	Bureau of Economic Analysis	ECB, Feri

27	emu_gdp_defl	1973:1-2007:4	GDP deflator	ECB, Feri	ECB, Feri
28	japan_gdp_defl	1973:1-2007:4	GDP deflator	Economic and Social Research Institute	Feri
29	uk_gdp_defl	1973:1-2007:4	GDP deflator	Office for National Statistics	Feri
30	canada_gdp_defl	1973:1-2007:4	GDP deflator	Statistics Canada	Feri
31	us_imp_defl	1973:1-2007:4	Import prices	Bureau of Labor Statistics	Feri
32	emu_imp_defl	1973:1-2007:4	Import prices	ECB, Eurostat	ECB, Feri
33	japan_imp_defl	1973:1-2007:4	Import prices	Bank of Japan	Feri
34	uk_imp_defl	1973:1-2007:4	Import prices	IMF	Feri
35	canada_imp_defl	1973:1-2007:4	Import prices	Statistics Canada	Feri
36	us_ppi	1973:1-2007:4	Producer prices	Bureau of Labor Statistics	Feri
37	emu_ppi	1981:1-2007:4	Producer prices	Eurostat	Feri
38	japan_ppi	1973:1-2007:4	Producer prices	Bloomberg	Bloomberg
39	uk_ppi	1973:1-2007:4	Producer prices	OECD	Feri
40	canada_ppi	1973:1-2007:4	Producer prices	Statistics Canada	Feri
	Mnemonic	**--------- Exchange rates**			
41	us_exchange	1973:1-2007:4	US real effective exchange rate (CPI based)	OECD	Feri
42	emu_exchange	1973:1-2007:4	EMU real effective exchange rate (CPI based)	Feri	Feri
43	japan_exchange	1973:1-2007:4	Japan real effective exchange rate (CPI based)	OECD	Feri

44	uk_exchange	1973:1-2007:4	UK real effective exchange rate (CPI based)	OECD	Feri
45	canada_exchange	1973:1-2007:4	Canada real effective exchange rate (CPI based)	OECD	Feri
	Mnemonic	**--------- Share prices**			
46	us_share_msci	1973:1-2007:4	US MSCI share price index (local currency based)	Morgan Stanley Capital International	Feri
47	emu_share_msci	1973:1-2007:4	EMU MSCI share price index (local currency based)	Morgan Stanley Capital International	Feri
48	japan_share_msci	1973:1-2007:4	Japan MSCI share price index (local currency based)	Morgan Stanley Capital International	Feri
49	uk_share_msci	1973:1-2007:4	UK MSCI share price index (local currency based)	Morgan Stanley Capital International	Feri
50	canada_share_msci	1973:1-2007:4	Canada MSCI share price index (local currency based)	Morgan Stanley Capital International	Feri
	Mnemonic	**--------- House prices**			
51	us_prop	1973:1-2007:4	US house prices	National Association of Realtors	Datastream
52	emu_prop	1973:1-2007:4	EMU house prices	Gros, various national sources	Gros, Datastream, IMF
53	japan_prop	1973:1-2007:4	Japan house prices	Gros, Japan Real Estate Institute	Gros, Bloomberg

54	uk_prop	1973:1-2007:4	UK house prices	Nationwide Building Society	Bloomberg
55	canada_prop	1973:1-2007:4	Canada house prices	Gros, OECD	Gros, Datastream
	Mnemonic	**--------- Commodity prices**			
56	crb_future_usd	1973:1-2007:4	CRB commodity futures index	CRB	Feri
57	crb_future_eur	1973:1-2007:4	CRB commodity futures index on EUR basis	CRB, own calculations	Feri
58	crb_future_jpy	1973:1-2007:4	CRB commodity futures index on JPY basis	CRB, own calculations	Feri
59	crb_future_gbp	1973:1-2007:4	CRB commodity futures index on GBP basis	CRB, own calculations	Feri
60	crb_future_cad	1973:1-2007:4	CRB commodity futures index on CAD basis	CRB, own calculations	Feri
61	hwwi_usd	1973:1-2007:4	HWWI commodity price index	HWWI	Feri
62	hwwi_eur	1973:1-2007:4	HWWI commodity price index	HWWI, own calculations	Feri
63	hwwi_jpy	1973:1-2007:4	HWWI commodity price index	HWWI, own calculations	Feri
64	hwwi_gbp	1973:1-2007:4	HWWI commodity price index	HWWI, own calculations	Feri
65	hwwi_cad	1973:1-2007:4	HWWI commodity price index	HWWI, own calculations	Feri
	Mnemonic	**--------- Long-term interest rates**			
66	us_10y	1973:1-2007:4	10Y government bond yield	Federal Reserve Board	Feri

67	emu_10y	1973:1-2007:4	10Y government bond yield	Eurostat	Feri
68	japan_10y	1973:1-2007:4	Government bond yield average maturity	Bank of Japan	Feri
69	uk_10y	1973:1-2007:4	10Y government bond yield	OECD	Feri
70	canada_10y	1973:1-2007:4	10Y government bond yield	Bank of Canada	Feri
	Mnemonic	**--------- Credit aggregates**			
71	us_credit	1973:1-2007:4	Domestic credit	IMF	Feri
72	emu_credit	1973:1-2007:4	Domestic credit	IMF	Feri
73	japan_credit	1973:1-2007:4	Domestic credit	IMF	Feri
74	uk_credit	1973:1-2007:4	Domestic credit	IMF	Feri
75	canada_credit	1973:1-2007:4	Domestic credit	IMF	Feri
	Mnemonic	**--------- Hours worked**			
76	us_hours	1973:1-2007:4	Hours worked total economy	OECD, own calculations	Feri
77	emu_hours	1973:1-2007:4	Hours worked total economy	OECD, own calculations	Feri
78	japan_hours	1973:1-2007:4	Hours worked total economy	OECD, own calculations	Feri
79	uk_hours	1973:1-2007:4	Hours worked total economy	OECD, own calculations	Feri
80	canada_hours	1973:1-2007:4	Hours worked total economy	OECD, own calculations	Feri